Brute Meaning
Essays in Materialist Criticism
from Dickens to Hitchcock

LEGENDA

LEGENDA is the Modern Humanities Research Association's book imprint for new research in the Humanities. Founded in 1995 by Malcolm Bowie and others within the University of Oxford, Legenda has always been a collaborative publishing enterprise, directly governed by scholars. The Modern Humanities Research Association (MHRA) joined this collaboration in 1998, became half-owner in 2004, in partnership with Maney Publishing and then Routledge, and has since 2016 been sole owner. Titles range from medieval texts to contemporary cinema and form a widely comparative view of the modern humanities, including works on Arabic, Catalan, English, French, German, Greek, Italian, Portuguese, Russian, Spanish, and Yiddish literature. Editorial boards and committees of more than 60 leading academic specialists work in collaboration with bodies such as the Society for French Studies, the British Comparative Literature Association and the Association of Hispanists of Great Britain & Ireland.

The MHRA encourages and promotes advanced study and research in the field of the modern humanities, especially modern European languages and literature, including English, and also cinema. It aims to break down the barriers between scholars working in different disciplines and to maintain the unity of humanistic scholarship. The Association fulfils this purpose through the publication of journals, bibliographies, monographs, critical editions, and the MHRA Style Guide, and by making grants in support of research. Membership is open to all who work in the Humanities, whether independent or in a University post, and the participation of younger colleagues entering the field is especially welcomed.

ALSO PUBLISHED BY THE ASSOCIATION

Critical Texts
Tudor and Stuart Translations • *New Translations* • *European Translations*
MHRA Library of Medieval Welsh Literature

MHRA Bibliographies
Publications of the Modern Humanities Research Association

The Annual Bibliography of English Language & Literature
Austrian Studies
Modern Language Review
Portuguese Studies
The Slavonic and East European Review
Working Papers in the Humanities
The Yearbook of English Studies

www.mhra.org.uk
www.legendabooks.com

SELECTED ESSAYS

Each title in *Selected Essays* presents influential, but often scattered, papers by a major scholar in the Humanities. While these essays will, we hope, offer a model of scholarly writing, and chart the development of an important thinker in the field, the aim is not retrospective but to gather a coherent body of work as a tool for future research. Each volume contains a new introduction, framing the debate and reflecting on the methods used.

Selected Essays is curated by Professor Susan Harrow (University of Bristol).

APPEARING IN THIS SERIES

Managing Editor
Dr Graham Nelson, 41 Wellington Square, Oxford OX1 2JF, UK

www.legendabooks.com

Brute Meaning

*Essays in Materialist Criticism
from Dickens to Hitchcock*

DAVID TROTTER

LEGENDA

Selected Essays 9
Modern Humanities Research Association
2020

Published by Legenda
an imprint of the Modern Humanities Research Association
Salisbury House, Station Road, Cambridge CB1 2LA

ISBN 978-1-78188-919-0 (HB)
ISBN 978-1-78188-920-6 (PB)

First published 2020

Copy-Editor: Richard Correll

CONTENTS

LIST OF SOURCES

The essays reprinted here originally appeared as follows, and are reprinted with the kind permission of the publishers. Special thanks are due to the editor and publisher of *Critical Quarterly*, which has proved unfailingly hospitable to the kinds of approach they have sought to develop.

'The New Historicism and the Psychopathology of Everyday Modern Life', *Critical Quarterly*, 42.1 (2000), 36–58. Published by Wiley-Blackwell

'Household Clearances in Victorian Fiction', in David Trotter, *The Uses of Phobia: Essays on Literature and Film* (Oxford: Wiley-Blackwell, 2010), pp. 17–28

'Dickens's Idle Men', in *Dickens Refigured: Bodies, Desires and Other Histories*, ed. by John Schad (Manchester: Manchester University Press, 1996), pp. 200–17

'Dickens and Frith', in *William Powell Frith: Painting the Victorian Age*, ed. by Mark Bills and Vivien Knight (New Haven, CT, and London: Yale University Press in association with Guildhall Art Gallery, City of London, 2006), pp. 29–39

'Space, Movement, and Sexual Feeling in *Middlemarch*', in *Middlemarch in the Twenty-First Century*, ed. by Karen Chase (Oxford: Oxford University Press, 2006), pp. 37–63

'On the Nail: Functional Objects in Thomas Hardy's *The Woodlanders*', in *Literary Bric-à-Brac and the Victorians: From Commodities to Oddities*, ed. by Jonathon Shears and Jen Harrison (Farnham: Ashgate, 2013), pp. 115–27

'Gissing's Fry-Ups: Food and the Definition of Working-Class Culture in Britain in the 1880s', *New Comparison*, 24 (1997), 158–81. Published by the British Comparative Literature Association.

'Lesbians before Lesbianism: Sexual Identity in Early Twentieth-Century British Fiction', in *Borderlines: Genders and Identities in War and Peace, 1870–1930*, ed. by Billie Melman (London: Routledge, 1998), pp. 193–211

'Feminist Nausea', in David Trotter, *The Uses of Phobia: Essays on Literature and Film* (Oxford: Wiley-Blackwell, 2010), pp. 59–76

'Dis-Enablement: Subject and Method in the Modernist Short Story', *Critical Quarterly*, 52.2 (2010), 4–13. Published by Wiley-Blackwell

'Fascination and Nausea: Finding Out the Hard-Boiled Way', in *The Art of Detective Fiction*, ed. by Warren Chernaik, Martin Swales, and Robert Vilain (Basingstoke: Macmillan, 2000), pp. 21–35

'Fanon's Nausea', *Parallax*, 5.2 (1999), 32–50. Published by Taylor & Francis Limited

'The Space Beside: Lateral Exposition, Gender, and Urban Narrative Space in D. W. Griffith's Biograph Films', in *Cities in Transition: The Moving Image and the Modern Metropolis*, ed. by Andrew Webber and Emma Wilson (London and New York: Wallflower Press, 2008), pp. 40–55

'Come-Hither Looks: The Hollywood Vamp and the Function of Cinema', *Critical Quarterly*, 62.2 (2020). Published by Wiley-Blackwell

'Representing Connection: A Multimedia Approach to Colonial Film, 1918–1939', in *Empire and Film*, ed. by Lee Grieveson and Colin MacCabe (Basingstoke: Palgrave, 2011), pp. 151–66

'The Woman in the Plastic Mackintosh: Sexuality, Material Substance, and Narrative Space in 1930s Film'. Unpublished research paper, Department of Comparative Literature, Yale University, 12 April 2010

'Shakespeare in Tombstone: Stanley Cavell Goes West'. Unpublished conference paper: 'Acknowledging Cavell', University of Cambridge, 24–25 November 2006

'Hitchcock's Threshold Moments'. First published as 'Hiatus at 4 a.m.: What Scared Hitchcock?', *London Review of Books*, 4 June 2015, pp. 18–20

'Modernism and Empire: Reading *The Waste Land*', in *Futures for English*, ed. by Colin MacCabe (Manchester: Manchester University Press, 1988), pp. 143–53

'A Media Theory Approach to Representations of "Nervous Illness" in the Long Nineteenth Century', *Journal of Victorian Culture*, 24.2 (2019), 146–58. Published by Oxford University Press

'Posthuman? Animal Corpses, Aeroplanes, and Very High Frequencies in the Work of Valentine Ackland and Sylvia Townsend Warner', *Sylvia Townsend Warner Society Journal*, 2020.1 (2020). Published by UCL Press

LIST OF ILLUSTRATIONS

INTRODUCTION

There are worse things to have to do in professional life than select from pieces already written — the hard work done — and in most cases published. Some sort of look in the mirror is nonetheless required, and decisions have to be made. In making those decisions, I have been guided by the stated purpose of this Legenda series: to assemble a coherent body of work which might conceivably serve as a prompt to further research. The body of work presented here began to cohere in the late 1980s.

Back in the day, my regular beat was seventeenth- and early eighteenth-century literature in English: the poetry of Abraham Cowley, whose first-hand testimony to Civil War and Scientific Revolution seemed worthy of greater attention than it was then receiving, and of the reliably scandalous, witty Earl of Rochester; the adventurously mundane fiction of Daniel Defoe; and, in a less concentrated way, non-fiction forms such as spiritual autobiography, sermon, pamphlet, and scientific treatise which arose directly or indirectly out of the ferment of economic, social, and political modernization. During the 1980s, however, the focus of my research shifted decisively in a direction in which they had long been heading: towards nineteenth- and early twentieth-century literature in English (and French), sometimes with reference to the visual arts; and then, in the 1990s, towards the history of cinema. *Brute Meaning* has accordingly been organized into two main sections, one concerned with 'Fictional Embodiment' from Charles Dickens to Elizabeth Bowen, the other with 'Narrative Space in Cinema' from D. W. Griffith to Alfred Hitchcock. A shorter third and final section offers a snapshot of 'Materialist Criticism Then and Now' by juxtaposing an essay first published in 1988 with two dating from the last couple of years.

Abraham Cowley was in his own day a celebrated essayist as well as poet, and researching his mild-mannered contributions to the genre led me to its inventor, the unsurpassable Michel de Montaigne. In Montaigne's usage, to 'essay' — to attempt, or have a go — is also to 'assay': to test the composition of an ore or alloy. The topic he essayed and assayed for well over 1000 pages was himself, kidney stones and all. The essays which follow are altogether less personal in emphasis. They arise, for the most part, out of exactly the kind of scholarly debate that Montaigne, for all his vast learning, sought to avoid. But they aim nonetheless to preserve something of the spirit in which he pursued his more worldly enquiries. They, too, prefer to catch their topic from an unusual angle ('par quelque lustre inusité'). The protocols of scholarly debate discourage the bravado nurtured by the success of such an approach. 'Scattering broadcast a word here, a word there, out-of-the-way examples, or ones ripped from their contexts (échantillons dépris de leur pièce), with no plan and no promises, I am under no obligation to make a good job of it, nor to stick to the subject.' But those protocols need not altogether preclude Montaigne's ready acknowledgement of doubt and uncertainty. Ignorance, he wrote, had supplied his 'master-form (maîtresse forme)', the very structure of his thinking.[1]

So what, exactly, is being essayed, here? Hunches and hypotheses, primarily: questions, prompted by an encounter with written and filmed material, which look as though they might lead somewhere, possibly even to the illumination of that material from within. Why does Dickens's prose gain an extra bounce in its step whenever it encounters the spectacle of an idle man (his women do not appear to suffer from this affliction)? Why does Will Ladislaw, in George Eliot's *Middlemarch*, so often leap to his feet as though electrocuted while conversing with Dorothea? Why do the various iron nails described in Thomas Hardy's novels retain their functional status, whereas in Dickens's, or Walter Scott's, they would have had to have rusted, or fallen out of the wall, in order to become interesting? Why did Cairo — or, more precisely, images of pyramid and sphinx — feature so prominently in documentaries concerning tea grown in Ceylon (Sri Lanka) and drunk in Britain? Why do so many women in American, British, and French films of the 1930s prove inseparable from a plastic raincoat, even, or especially, when rain is the least of their problems? On other occasions, questions of a more general nature have been prompted by the oblique, diffuse, fleeting representation in word and image of a specific practice: philanthropic slum-visiting, say, or the spread of a rumour about chapatti-shaped tokens passing from village to village in India in 1857, or self-identification as a lesbian by means of appearance and costume in early twentieth-century Britain, or the come-hither looks dispensed by vamps stalking their victims in Manhattan in the 1920s.

The essay has the look of a form that wants to get to grips with material practice, with *stuff*, knowing that it need neither begin nor end in explanation. To 'assay' might once have meant to test by handling, or flavour; or to try on a set of clothes. Montaigne's great meditation on the human mind's boundless capacity for diversion from the thing in itself ('la chose en soi') defines the essay as a way not to be diverted. Philosophical argument, by contrast, sidesteps or runs alongside the matter at issue, merely 'grazing' its 'surface'.[2] Cutting into 'la chose en soi' from their unusual angle, his essays reveal it decisively for what it is. What they have said about it cannot be unsaid, even if there is always more to be found out. The practical lesson they teach is that the world's density is best assayed by as dense as possible a reflection upon it. Stuff attracts stuff. Nothing is more characteristic of

---

1   Michel de Montaigne, 'De Democritus et Heraclitus', in *Les Essais*, ed. by Jean Céard et al. (Paris: Livre de Poche, 2001), pp. 489–94 (p. 490); 'On Democritus and Heraclitus', in *The Complete Essays*, ed. and trans. by M. A. Screech (Harmondsworth: Penguin Books, 2003), pp. 337–40 (p. 338: translation emended).
2   Montaigne, 'De la Diversion', in *Essais*, pp. 1296–1312 (p. 1304); 'On Diversion', in *Complete Essays*, pp. 935–46 (p. 940).

the technique of *Les Essais* than the concluding paragraph stacked high — just as you are ready to concede that the point has been made — with yet further examples.

It is probably true to say that no theories have been harmed in the making of the stuff-obsessed pieces which follow. No theories have been advanced, certainly. But it is also true to say that experiments do not take place in a vacuum. The aim of this Introduction is to describe the various contexts — some of them involving the rise and fall of theories — in which the hunches and hypotheses I have harboured over the years gradually took shape. Considered as a brief history of the development of English Studies during that period, it would be as notable for what it omits as for what it includes. But it may nonetheless serve an indicative function of a kind. For some of the critical and theoretical initiatives it surveys have quite dramatically come back into favour during the last ten years or so. They are not recalled here out of nostalgia alone.

The flame that flickers in much of what I have written about literature and film was first lit when I read a translation of Maurice Merleau-Ponty's *Phénoménologie de la Perception* (1945) — unsystematically, in short, puzzled bursts — as an undergraduate studying English literature at the University of Cambridge in the early 1970s. 'Because we are in the world,' Merleau-Ponty declared in the Preface to the *Phenomenology*, 'we are *condemned to meaning*.'[3] The emphasis is in the original. 'Condamner', in French, can mean to condemn, but also to convict in a court of law or to damn. Merleau-Ponty seems to have nursed an almost personal grievance against the severity of the sentence thus passed by a combination of nature and nurture on the human species. His observation has stuck with me ever since, because it casts such a coolly uncomplimentary light on what we are constantly being told is the primary purpose of our existence on earth: the search for meaning. It turns out that we had no choice in the matter. Do we really need to spend quite so much time and effort in a quest for something we have been up to our necks in all along?

Literature and film are made of meaning. Their materials have been selected and shaped for a purpose. Pleasure and instruction flow from our ability at once to savour and to interpret their design. A zen resolve merely to absorb them, to float among rare signifiers, would itself be an interpretation. Merleau-Ponty appealed (and still appeals) to me because, having established that meaningfulness is no more and no less than our condition, he set out to distinguish between the different kinds of meaning available to us, and the different functions they might serve. He was a fan of Montaigne, who in dialogue with himself had addressed and sought answers from a being as 'opaque' as objects in the world around him, or the animals 'reposing in their nature (qui reposent dans la nature)'. Montaigne's achievement, Merleau-Ponty observed, was to imagine 'a book in which for once there would be expressed not only ideas but also the very life which they appear in and which modifies their meaning.'[4] The kinds of meaning which prove hard

---

3   Maurice Merleau-Ponty, *Phénoménologie de la Perception* (Paris: Gallimard, 1945), p. xiv; *The Phenomenology of Perception*, trans. by Colin Smith (London: Routledge & Kegan Paul, 1962), p. xix.
4   Merleau-Ponty, 'Lecture de Montaigne', in *Signes* (Paris: Gallimard, 1960), pp. 250–66 (p.

to distinguish from the life in which they appear remained his great theme, from *Phénoménologie de la Perception* all the way through to the late, unfinished *Le Visible et l'Invisible* (1964). According to him, the world's unity in our experience 'is "lived" as ready-made or already there,' before knowledge can even begin to grasp it by means of a specific act of identification or analysis.' In knowledge, chance, the 'very process' by means of which 'the hitherto meaningless takes on meaning,' finds itself transformed continually into rational explanation.[5] In a book which began to think about nineteenth-century art and fiction in roughly comparable terms, I argued that mess has often been understood as contingency's signature.[6] If there is a search undertaken by the essays gathered here, it is a search for the truly secular in literature and film: for the kind of meaning which makes a minimal claim to transcend its circumstance.

In 'L'Œil et l'esprit' (1961), the last work he saw into print, Merleau-Ponty turned to the art of painting for evidence of the richness of what the eye knows before the mind. Reprinted in book form in 1964, with the accompaniment of eloquent if not lavish illustration, this lengthy meditation on Cézanne, Klee, Rodin, and others did not seem like a work of philosophy at all. 'Scientific thinking,' Merleau-Ponty declared, 'a thinking which looks on from above, and thinks of the object-in-general, must return to the "there is" which underlies it: to the site, the soil of the sensible and opened world such as it is in our life and for our body.' Painting could show science the way back because, to a greater extent than any other art, it draws upon the 'fabric of brute meaning (sens brut)' which science, like most other forms of knowledge, would prefer to ignore. Brute meaning is raw, or crude, as in crude oil. *L'Œil et l'Esprit* proposed a phenomenology of brute meaning as an alternative to the new 'ideology of cybernetics', at that time gaining traction in the United States, according to which 'human creations are derived from a natural information process.'[7] I would not now endorse its critique of science in general, or of cybernetics. Chapter 21 in this collection is evidence that I have since found cybernetic theory a productive way to think about some of the most adventurous initiatives undertaken in British writing in the 1930s. What I needed, then, was the stimulus rather than the critique. The concept of 'sens brut' seemed to offer unique access to the kind of meaning which makes a minimal claim to transcend its circumstance. What is more, Merleau-Ponty appears to have seen in Cézanne, his exemplary phenomenologist, a faint resemblance to Michel de Montaigne. A brilliant account of 'Cézanne's Doubt', first published in 1945, opens with the painter, Montaigne-like, in the midst of his own avowed ignorance. 'He needed one hundred working sessions for a still life,' Merleau-Ponty remarked, 'one

252); 'Reading Montaigne', in *Signs*, trans. by Richard C. McCleary (Evanston, IL: Northwestern University Press, 1964), pp. 198–210 (p. 199).

5   Merleau-Ponty, *Phénoménologie*, pp. xii, 197; *Phenomenology*, pp. xvii, 169.

6   David Trotter, *Cooking with Mud: The Idea of Mess in Nineteenth-Century Art and Fiction* (Oxford: Oxford University Press, 2000).

7   Merleau-Ponty, *L'Œil et l'Esprit* (Paris: Gallimard, 1964), pp. 12–13; 'Eye and Mind', in *The Primacy of Perception*, trans. by James M. Edie (Evanston, IL: Northwestern University Press, 1964), pp. 159–90 (pp. 160–61).

hundred and fifty sittings for a portrait. What we call his work was, for him, only an essay, an approach to painting.'[8]

There were, of course, several other versions of existential phenomenology available: Martin Heidegger's star, in particular, waxed and waned cyclically during the final decades of the twentieth century. My preference was for the more acidic Jean-Paul Sartre, a temporary phenomenologist at best, but one who nonetheless found time to deliver memorable jeremiads concerning the essential sliminess or viscosity of the stuff of which the world is composed. *La Nausée* (1938) and *L'Être et le Néant* (1943) taught me how to get to grips with experiences (and representations of experience) which derive their meaning and value from an acknowledgement of contingency, which has neither meaning nor value.[9] Confronted by objects or by the animals 'reposing in their nature', Merleau-Ponty was to note in his essay on Montaigne, 'consciousness is hollow and avid. It is consciousness of all things because it is nothing; it grasps at all things and holds to none.'[10] For him, it was the body, in the first instance, which enabled consciousness to grasp all things while holding to none. Sartre, by contrast, revelled thrillingly in negation. He hymned hollowness and avidity. For him, consciousness comes alive in and through the revulsion induced in it by the world's ineradicable stickiness. Reviewing *L'Être et le Néant* in 1945, Merleau-Ponty objected to Sartre's insistence on an absolute 'antithesis' between the 'for-itself' (consciousness) and the 'in-itself' (the world).[11] Sartre's phenomenology always looked to me like a crypto-religion. But it did capture, uniquely, something of the *force* of negation. For Sartre, nausea, while undoubtedly a shock to the system, does not disable. Rather, it enables, or re-enables. It produces freedom: from the world, or perhaps just from a particular set of economic, social, and political circumstances. I began to investigate the figure of the *nauséaste*: someone, I imagined, at once disabled and re-enabled by stickiness. The specific kinds of stickiness addressed in these essays range from garrison-town brothels (Chapter 9) through decomposing meals in Zola, Maupassant, Chekhov, Gissing, and Joyce (Chapter 7) and decomposing corpses in hard-boiled detective fiction (Chapter 11) to the white child's astonished gaze at a black man in Frantz Fanon's *Black Skin, White Masks* (Chapter 12).

Merleau-Ponty's review of *L'Être et le Néant* amounted to a staunch defence of the book against Marxist critique. 'A living Marxism,' he concluded, 'should "save" and integrate existentialist research instead of stifling it.'[12] While Sartre re-tooled in the 1940s, swapping phenomenological for Marxist method, Merleau-Ponty clung — for a while, at least — to the prospect of integration. The primary source of his 'living Marxism' was Marx's early 'economic and philosophical manuscripts':

---

8   Merleau-Ponty, 'Le Doute de Cézanne', in *Sens et Non-Sens*, 3rd edn (Paris: Nagel, 1961), pp. 15–44 (p. 15); 'Cézanne's Doubt', in *Sense and Non-Sense*, trans. by Hubert L. Dreyfus and Patricia Allen Dreyfus ((Evanston, IL: Northwestern University Press, 1964), pp. 9–25 (p. 9).
9   Trotter, *Cooking with Mud*, pp. 15–16, 206–15.
10   Merleau-Ponty, 'Lecture de Montaigne', p. 252; 'Reading Montaigne', p. 199.
11   Merleau-Ponty, 'La Querelle de l'Existentialisme', in *Sens et Non-Sens*, pp. 123–43 (p. 125); 'The Battle over Existentialism', in *Sense and Non-Sense*, pp. 71–82 (p. 72).
12   Ibid., p. 143; p. 82.

a series of notes written in Paris between April and August 1844, but not published during his lifetime, which began to exert a considerable influence in the years after the end of the Second World War.[13] Marx, he thought, had understood that human identity resides not in consciousness, but in a 'relation to instruments and objects'. Merleau-Ponty was attracted to the 'economic and philosophical manuscripts' by their advocacy of a 'practical materialism': their understanding of the ways in which 'matter enters into human life as the support (point d'appui) and body of praxis.' Marxism could only ever be a philosophy not so much of subject and object as of their continually reconstituted relation; that is, of history.[14] That such an approach held a greater appeal for me than either the full-on, near-mystical phenomenology of *Le Visible et l'Invisible* or the gravitation towards Marx's later writings instigated by Louis Althusser had much to do with my increasing familiarity with the work of Raymond Williams.

Williams loomed large in the Faculty of English at Cambridge during the time I spent there as an undergraduate and graduate student. I was never taught by him (for one thing, I did not share his enthusiasm for drama). But I certainly felt his influence; all the more so during the 1980s, after I had left Cambridge, as my research and teaching interests shifted gradually towards one of his other major preoccupations: British literature and culture in the nineteenth and early twentieth centuries. Successive copies of his invaluable *The English Novel from Dickens to Lawrence* (1970) fell apart in my hands.[15] My subtitle carries a faint echo of that work.

By the 1980s, Williams's version of historical materialism had begun to play an active part in a broad reshaping of Marxist theory. *Marxism and Literature* (1977), methodical in its approach to the point of dourness, nonetheless captures something of the excitement of what felt to him like a 'time of radical change'. The position Williams had developed over a number of years, 'differs,' he wrote, 'at several key points, from what is most widely known as Marxist theory, and even from many of its variants. It is a position which can be briefly described as cultural materialism: a theory of the specificities of material cultural and literary production within historical materialism.' For Williams, in the 1970s, as for Merleau-Ponty in the 1940s, the job of the term 'material' was to stick as closely as possible to the terms 'practice' and 'history'. At a time when linguistics in its many resplendent guises had begun to install itself as a master-science, I warmed to his nose-to-the-ground attitude. 'Language, then,' he maintained,

> is not a medium: it is a constitutive element of material social practice. But if this is so, it is clearly also a special case. For it is at once a material practice and a process in which many complex activities, of a less manifestly material

13   The economic and philosophical manuscripts were first released by researchers in the Soviet Union in the early 1930s. T. B. Bottomore's translation into English was included in Erich Fromm, *Marx's Concept of Man* (New York: F. Ungar, 1961). See also Karl Marx, *Economic and Philosophical Manuscripts of 1844*, trans. by Dirk J. Struik (London: Lawrence and Wishart, 1969).
14   Merleau-Ponty, 'Marxisme et Philosophie', in *Sens et Non-Sens*, pp. 221–41 (pp. 230–31); 'Marxism and Philosophy', in *Sense and Non-Sense*, pp. 125–36 (p. 130).
15   Raymond Williams, *The English Novel from Dickens to Lawrence* (London: Chatto & Windus, 1970).

kind — from information to interaction, from representation to imagination, and from abstract thought to immediate emotion — are specifically realized.[16]

Evidence that I thought of *literary* language as at once the constitutive element of a material social practice and a special case is to be found in the earliest essay reprinted in this book, 'Modernism and Empire: Reading *The Waste Land*', from 1988 (Chapter 19). The essay does not aim simply to 'situate' Eliot's poem in or among debates about the regeneration of empire. Rather, it claims that the juxtaposition in 'A Game of Chess' of conversations which reveal the paralysis gripping a bourgeois marriage, on one hand, and the apparently reckless fertility of a chorus of working-class women, on the other, was determined by a thorough acquaintance with eugenics: the science of the regeneration of an imperial 'race' through population control. Eliot does not advocate empire. But his poem's form practices the 'new imperialism' of the first decades of the twentieth century.

Williams is not invoked directly in the essays on nineteenth-century fiction I have chosen to include in this selection, but his influence can be felt in their choice of author (Thomas Hardy, George Gissing) and of topic: fiction's grasp of the fracturing of the phenomenology of 'common' everyday experience — work, leisure, habitation, nourishment, disposal — by differences in class-perspective. When I came to write about film, I tried to approach that, too, less as a medium than as the constitutive element of a material social practice. Chapter 15, for example, examines the ways in which documentaries made about Ceylon (Sri Lanka) in the 1930s hesitate between the idea of empire as the occupation of territory and the idea of empire as connectivity.

A more rigorous exponent either of phenomenology or of historical materialism might well have found these two approaches harder to reconcile than I did. In 2000, Steven Connor and I co-edited an issue of *Critical Quarterly* which sought to investigate some such reconciliation under the heading of 'cultural phenomenology'. As far as I am aware, hardly anyone saluted the flag we jauntily ran up the pole. But the issue did at least provide the occasion for Stephen Clucas to demonstrate in detail that cultural phenomenology — had it ever come about — would have been able to draw on a rich tradition of philosophical and sociological enquiry into everyday experience in which Marxists and non-Marxists featured in roughly equal measure.[17] My own contribution to it, reprinted here as Chapter 1, explores the revulsion expressed by a doctor who had undertaken to supply evidence of the effects of extreme poverty to Edwin Chadwick's *Report on the Sanitary Condition of the Labouring Population of Great Britain* (1842). Such expressions were on the whole held to constitute either, under the influence of Sigmund Freud, a reaction-formation against desire for their object; or, under the influence of Michel Foucault, a 'discourse' of surveillance and discipline targeting the *Lumpenproletariat*. The slum doctor was by these accounts at once policeman and sex-tourist. I thought that the failure of the resulting scholarship fully to acknowledge the force of disgust's negations obscured its potential as the basis for social and political action: its

16   Williams, *Marxism and Literature* (Oxford: Oxford University Press, 1977), pp. 1, 5. 165.
17   Stephen Clucas, 'Cultural Phenomenology and the Everyday', *Critical Quarterly*, 42 (2000), 8–34.

existence, even, in some cases, as a material social practice. Still, the contributors to *Critical Quarterly* were not entirely alone in seeking to merge the cultural (broadly understood) with the phenomenological. In his introduction to a 2005 volume of essays on the topic of 'materiality', Daniel Miller identifies Pierre Bourdieu's *Outline of a Theory of Practice* (1977) as the work which first established the importance of material culture studies within anthropology. Bourdieu, Miller writes, had managed to combine 'Marx's emphasis on material practice' with Merleau-Ponty's 'insights into our fundamental "orientation" to the world'.[18]

By 2000, the steady insistence on the 'construction' both of subjective and of objective reality in and through 'language' or 'discourse' which had dominated the humanities and the social sciences since the 1970s — the so-called 'cultural turn' — was already coming under pressure from a variety of directions. A further 'affective' turn, gathering momentum during the 1990s, sought to reinstate the body in all its dimensions; while the yet more recent and in many ways complementary 'material turn' was soon to declare itself the remedy for errors committed in the 1970s. In 2003, the physicist and philosopher Karen Barad complained that feminist scholarship had to some degree lost the plot. 'Language matters,' Barad wrote. 'Discourse matters. Culture matters. There is an important sense in which the only thing that does not matter any more is matter.'[19]

The problem with the term 'affect' is that there would appear to be little in its ramifying theoretical uses to distinguish it on a consistent basis from 'feeling' or 'emotion'. Its virtue, from my point of view, is that it readily encompasses both active and passive implication, so that a person's capacity to affect can be understood as essential to their capacity to be affected, and vice versa. By the 1980s, at any rate, some such understanding had been incorporated into avant-garde philosophy, in France, in particular.[20] The work of the psychologist Sylvan Tomkins, widely influential since, was further to reinforce it. According to Tomkins, affect's relative autonomy renders it dynamic, and potentially productive. 'It is enjoyable to enjoy. It is exciting to be excited. It is terrifying to be terrorized and angering to be angered. Affect is self-validating with or without any further referent.'[21] It is disgusting, we might add, to be disgusted. Even the most apparently immobilizing of affective experiences can set events in motion. There is force, as Sartre had demonstrated, in negation. Recent affect theory does not appear to have shown a great deal of interest in his phenomenological moment.[22] As I explain in Chapter

---

18   Daniel Miller, 'Materiality: An Introduction', in *Materiality*, ed. by Daniel Miller (Durham, NC: Duke University Press, 2005), pp. 1–50 (p. 6).

19   Karen Barad, 'Posthumanist Performativity: Towards an Understanding of How Matter Comes to Matter', *Signs: Journal of Women in Culture and Society*, 28 (2003), 801–31 (p. 801).

20   Gilles Deleuze and Félix Guattari, *A Thousand Plateaus: Capitalism and Schizophrenia*, trans. by Brian Massumi (Minneapolis: University of Minnesota Press, 1987), pp. 256–57; and Deleuze, *Spinoza: Practical Philosophy*, trans. by Robert Hurley (San Francisco: City Lights, 1988), pp. 97–104.

21   Silvan Tomkins, *Affect, Imagery, Consciousness*, 4 vols (New York: Springer, 1962–92), III, 404. Tomkins's brief discussion of nausea and disgust occurs in *Affect, Imagery, Consciousness*, II, 148–54.

22   *The Affective Turn: Theorizing the Social*, ed. by Patricia Tincineto Clough and Jean Halley (Durham, NC: Duke University Press, 2010); *The Affect Theory Reader*, ed. by Melissa Gregg and Gregory J. Seigworth (Durham, NC: Duke University Press, 2010); Ruth Leys, *The Ascent of Affect:*

13, my own recourse to the theories of affect developed in Paris in the 1930s, by Sartre, Heidegger, Georges Bataille, Emmanuel Levinas, and others was in part an attempt to find in that intellectual ferment something other than an anticipation of the 'cultural turn' (of Foucault, Jacques Derrida, Julia Kristeva). The *nauséaste*, disgusted by disgust, no longer feels entirely at home in discourse.

The 'material turn' has not (yet) seen a return to Raymond Williams's emphasis on history and practice. In their introduction to a flagship volume of essays on the topic published in 2010, Diana Coole and Samantha Frost struck a different note, arguing that after decades of exclusive attention to language, discourse, and culture, it was time 'to reopen the issue of matter and once again to give material factors their due in shaping society and circumscribing human prospects.' The 'materiality' now at issue — namely, the 'excess, force, vitality, relationality, or difference that renders matter active, self-creative, productive, unpredictable' — does not sound very much like a social practice.[23] And yet the suspicion remains that historical materialism may have done rather more than is sometimes admitted to rescue matter from its erasure by language, discourse, and culture. Jason Edwards, writing in the same volume, observes that during the twentieth century a whole range of enquiries into the sociology of culture built on the relatively un-programmatic examination of the quotidian in the chapter on 'The Working Day' in *Das Kapital* in order to explore the routines and procedures of a leisure-based consumer capitalism.[24]

By contrast, phenomenology (minus the vomiting) is now back in vogue, either as a method in its own right, or as an influence on the various kinds of ecologically minded and object-oriented 'speculative realism' which have recently been put forward as a 'theory of everything'.[25] In her widely influential *Vibrant Matter: A Political Ecology of Things* (2010), Jane Bennett proposes to counter the 'hermeneutics of suspicion' promoted during the cultural turn of the 1970s by 'giving voice' to a 'vitality' intrinsic to matter itself which she terms 'thing-power'. *Vibrant Matter* opens in bravura fashion with Bennett contemplating the odds and ends heaped in a gutter in front of Sam's Bagels on Cold Spring Lane, in Baltimore: a black plastic work glove, a dense mat of oak pollen, a dead rat, a white plastic bottle cap, a smooth stick of wood. Her initial response is to note the ways in which these objects shimmer back and forth 'between debris and thing', between 'stuff to ignore, except insofar as it betokened human activity' and 'stuff that commanded attention in its own right, as existents in excess of their association with human meanings, habits, or projects'. It is by means of such shimmers, I would say, that brute meaning appears. For Bennett, however, there is a second 'moment' in store, an epiphany.

> In the second moment, stuff exhibited its thing-power: it issued a call, even
> if I did not quite understand what it was saying. At the very least, it provoked

Genealogy and Critique (Chicago, IL: University of Chicago Press, 2017).

23   Diana Coole and Samantha Frost, 'Introducing the New Materialisms', in *New Materialisms: Ontology, Agency, and Politics*, ed. by Diana Coole and Samantha Frost (Durham, NC: Duke University Press, 2010), pp. 1–43 (pp. 3, 9).

24   Jason Edwards, 'The Materialism of Historical Materialism', in *New Materialisms*, pp. 281–98.

25   Graham Harman, *Object-Oriented Ontology: A New Theory of Everything* (Harmondsworth: Penguin Books, 2018).

affects in me: I was repelled by the dead (or was it merely sleeping?) rat and dismayed by the litter, but I also felt something else: a nameless awareness of the impossible singularity of *that* rat, *that* configuration of pollen, *that* otherwise utterly banal, mass-produced plastic water-bottle cap.[26]

Bennett could almost be Roquentin, in *La Nausée*, contemplating existence as such as revealed by the formlessness of a tree-root; except that she does not mean, as Sartre does, to stay with or to enquire further into formlessness as such: the act of declassing and declassification, as Bataille might have put it, performed by disgust.[27] She chooses epiphany instead. 'But they *were* all there just as they were, and so I caught a glimpse of an energetic vitality inside each of these things, things that I generally conceived as inert.'[28] Coole and Frost observe that the new materialism is 'posthumanist' in the sense that it conceives of matter itself as lively, as 'exhibiting' agency.[29] Bennett maintains that a properly 'posthuman' vitalism should attempt a more radical 'displacement of the human subject' than existential phenomenology was ever able to accomplish; 'although Merleau-Ponty himself,' she concludes, 'seemed to be moving in this direction in his unfinished *The Visible and the Invisible*.'[30] It is symptomatic that the new materialism should find Merleau-Ponty most appealing when at his most mystical.

Some of the essays reprinted here resonate less with the new materialism than with critiques of it. Alfred López, for instance, argues that the new materialism's 'implicit aspirations to a unified theory (particularly in its nonhuman iteration) make its apparent reluctance to engage race and ethnicity especially problematic.' López supports his contention with a detailed analysis of Bennett's contemplation of the odds and ends in the gutter outside Sam's Bagels. In her narration of this scene, he maintains, 'the seemingly specific assemblage is carefully curated in a way that disconnects it from larger systems of wealth/poverty, safety/danger, whiteness/blackness — in short, systems of power — that would open it up to alternative gazes, alternative humanities.' Intriguingly, López goes on to propose that one way to advance the 'unfinished work' of acknowledging the agency of the many human beings Western metaphysics has re-inscribed as 'nonhuman' would be by way of 'Sartre's formulation of "indifference towards others" from *Being and Nothingness*, a term he does not unfold in racial terms but which finds a later postcolonial formulation in the work of Fanon and Stuart Hall.'[31] In Chapter 13 (first published as an essay in 1999), I return to Paris in the 1930s, and to Sartre in particular, in order also to arrive at Fanon and Hall. The chapter describes how the nausea provoked by stuff — by incidental messes — can open up the colonial encounter to 'alternative gazes, alternative humanities'.

26   Jane Bennett, *Vibrant Matter: A Political Ecology of Things* (Durham, NC: Duke University Press, 2010), p. 5.
27   'Formless', in *Encyclopaedia Acephalica*, ed. by Alexander Brotchie, trans. by Iain White (London, Atlas Press, 1995), pp. 51–52.
28   Bennett, *Vibrant Matter*, p. 5.
29   Coole and Frost, 'Introducing the New Materialisms', p. 7.
30   Bennett, *Vibrant Matter*, p. 30.
31   Alfred López, 'Contesting the Material Turn; or, the Persistence of Agency', *Cambridge Journal of Postcolonial Literary Enquiry*, 5 (2018), 371–86 (pp. 373, 377, 382).

It should be clear by now that while the essays reassembled here scratch at more or less the same set of itches, they do not do so in a systematic fashion. They remain of their time. Some arose out of the new perspectives provided on old topics by developments such as the emergence within German media studies of a theory of 'cultural techniques' (Chapter 20) or the impetus given to the idea of the 'posthuman' by Donna Haraway, Rosa Braidotti, Elizabeth Grosz, and others (Chapter 21). Posthumanism's assault on the claims made for the sovereignty of human consciousness has produced a variety of incisive commentaries on humankind's relation to its companion species and companion machines. In Chapter 31, I draw on some of these commentaries in order to establish the critical significance and value of the work which was the product of the unique creative partnership developed by Valentine Ackland and Sylvia Townsend Warner during the 1930s. More generally, investigations of brute meaning are bound to run counter to claims made for the sovereignty of human consciousness. It has not escaped me that, in English at least, 'brute' can mean animal-like, often with derogatory intent. Neither of the two thinkers who did most to inspire those investigations would have hesitated to draw comparisons between human and animal intelligence. There can be few more compelling statements of the need to reset humankind's relation to other species than the almost imperceptible shift of focus in the middle of Montaigne's magnificent essay on cruelty from the tortures inflicted on human beings 'for the fun of it' to those inflicted, with even less scruple, on animals.[32] Nor is it without consequence that Merleau-Ponty's 1947 essay on 'The Metaphysical in Man' should draw extensively on Wolfgang Koehler's research into the 'behavioural universe' of chimpanzees, which was to contribute substantially to the development during the twentieth century of cognitive ethology — the comparative, evolutionary, and ecological study of animal minds.[33]

Other essays in this collection remain resolutely occasional, shaped by the nature of the commission. It may be significant that the most occasional of all — one originating as a book review (Chapter 18), two as research papers (Chapters 16 and 17) — belong to the second part of the book, which concerns narrative space in cinema. I started to teach film alongside literature in the 1990s, and the research deriving from that new emphasis took some time to filter through into print.[34] That research responded only in the most indirect way to the methodological twists and turns I have thus far outlined. Indeed, these essays on film now have for me the feel of an exhilarating off-duty plunge into an unfamiliar medium.

It is not, of course, that the academic study of film has ever lacked for twists and turns. Film, summarily reconceived as a 'language', was the first medium to receive

32 Montaigne, 'De la Cruauté', in *Essais*, pp. 665–88 (pp. 683–84); 'On Cruelty', in *Complete Essays*, pp. 472–88 (pp. 484–85).
33 Merleau-Ponty, 'La Métaphysique dans l'Homme', in *Sens et Non-Sens*, pp. 145–72 (pp. 146–48); 'The Metaphysical in Man', in *Sense and Non-Sense*, pp. 83–98 (pp. 83–85). For a deft account of Merleau-Ponty's exposition of philosophies of nature in lecture courses delivered between 1956 and 1960, see Diana Coole, 'The Inertia of Matter and the Generativity of Flesh', in *New Materialisms*, ed. by Coole and Frost, pp. 92–115.
34 Trotter, *Cinema and Modernism* (Oxford: Blackwell, 2007).

the full brunt of the cultural turn.[35] To me, however, the 'actualities' produced by the Lumière brothers in the 1890s positively reek of brute meaning. Taken in long shot, almost invariably from a fixed camera, and lasting about fifty seconds, these actualities comprised all of whatever it was that took place in front of the camera, staged or unstaged, essential or inessential, during the fifty seconds. Workers pour out through a factory gate; a train arrives in a crowded station, and passengers alight; some courageous (or handsomely paid) pedestrians cross the Champs-Elysées during the rush-hour; fire-engines clamour down a city street; a small boat heads out to sea. The cameras used to shoot these scenes had no view-finder. They offered little instruction or guidance as to how and where to look. There is a sense of the image's repleteness. Even when empty, it is full to overflowing. All that happens is people going about their business. There may be story, or the basis for a story (the gates open, the gates close); but there is no plot, no causal relation between one event and another. To me, the repleteness of the images comprising these actualities has remained the basis of cinema's appeal as medium. In describing that repleteness, I drew heavily on the work of one of Stephen Clucas's proto-cultural phenomenologists, Siegfried Kracauer. A film cannot adequately account for the 'emotional and intellectual events' which are its subject, Kracauer wrote, unless it 'leads us through the thicket of material life from which they emerge and in which they are embedded.'[36]

In the years immediately before the outbreak of the First World War, cinema became, overwhelmingly, a narrative medium. As my teaching and research centred increasingly on narrative cinema, I began to explore the proposition that the cavernous sound stages of the studio era became a laboratory for experiments in narrative space which configure the relation between a building's interior and exterior in social (and even political) terms intelligible from our experience of the world outside the cinema. To be sure, these spaces no longer engender repleteness. They do not overflow with brute meaning. In the earliest film essay reprinted here, as Chapter 13, I identify the 'logic' informing the organization of narrative space in some of the more than 400 films D. W. Griffith made for the Biograph company between 1980 and 1913.[37] It was by at once exaggerating and defying that logic, I argue in Chapter 16, that brute meaning continued to make itself felt in some of the most important films made in the 1930s, in Britain, France, and America. These are the films in which the women wear the plastic mackintoshes.

Merleau-Ponty's insistence that painting draws more deeply than any other art upon the 'fabric of brute meaning' has nagged away at me throughout the framing of this Introduction. My topic, after all, is the kind of literature and the kind of cinema traditionally given over to the production of meaning of the cooked rather

35   Christian Metz, *Psychoanalysis and the Cinema: The Imaginary Signifier*, trans. by Celia Britton, Annwyl Williams, Ben Brewster, and Alfred Guzzetti (Basingstoke: Macmillan, 1982).

36   Siegfried Kracauer, *Theory of Film: The Redemption of Physical Reality* (Princeton, NJ: Princeton University Press, 1997), pp. 46–48.

37   That essay subsequently became the basis for a broader examination of mise-en-scène in interwar cinema, in *Literature in the First Media Age: Britain between the Wars* (Cambridge, MA: Harvard University Press, 2013), pp. 181–95.

than the raw variety. So it may be that what unites the essays collected here is a bias: a preference for one rhetorical technique over another; in particular, for description over narrative, and metonymy over metaphor. This bias does not arise out of a stupid dislike either of narrative or of metaphor. It is, rather, a critical tool designed to draw attention to the things literature and film do when narrative hesitates, momentarily, or metaphor fails to appear. Description and metonymy bring out the brute in meaning. Each constitutes an approach to formlessness, a levelling down, an act of declassing and declassification. Both situate human experience in social material practice, in messy companionship with other species and with machines.

'Narrate or Describe?' Georg Lukács asked, in an essay of 1936 which charts the novel's sorry decline into Naturalism, from Scott and Balzac to Flaubert, Zola, and beyond. 'Narration establishes proportions,' Lukács maintained, 'description merely levels.'[38] I have tried to reconceive such levelling as a kind of *informe*: as an act of declassing and declassification which approaches the limits of representation in order to deliver an intermittent account of (brute) meanings that do not derive from proportion. It is largely by means of description, I argue in several of the essays which constitute Part I of this book, that fiction grasps the fracturing along class, gender, and racial lines of the phenomenology of 'common' everyday experience.

Metonymy has always been, and still remains, a less fashionable trope than metaphor, rarely examined in its own right. It was hoisted into prominence, as metaphor's sparring partner, by Roman Jakobson, and thereafter installed as a structural paradigm in a wide variety of semiological enquiries. Metaphor works by analogy, Jakobson explained, while metonymy maps relations of contiguity.[39] Metonymy, the dictionaries tell us, substitutes the name of an attribute or adjunct for that of the thing meant. The problem with the Jakobsonian account is that no one was ever able to define contiguity. Unlike analogy, contiguity is a happening, rather than a logical relation. The best definition of metonymy I know, by the classicist Sebastian Matzner, confronts that problem head on. According to Matzner, the contiguity operative in metonymy is lexical, and pragmatic. Metonymy involves an exchange of terms within the same lexical field: that is, within a set of words defined by their semantic proximity and their joint occurrence in ordinary usage.[40] To take a familiar example, in describing the contents of a domestic interior, the writer could be thought to describe at the same time the person or persons customarily inhabiting that room. Metaphor, by contrast, substitutes a term from one semantic field for a term from another. It is the interaction between semantic fields which generates metaphor's decisive rhetorical and poetic force, thus ensuring its widespread identification with literature's entire scope and value.[41] Metonymy

38   Georg Lukács, 'Narrate or Describe?', in *Writer and Critic and Other Essays*, ed. and trans. by Arthur Kahn (London: Merlin Press, 1970), pp. 110–48 (pp. 127–28, 131).
39   Roman Jakobson, 'The Metaphoric and Metonymic Poles', in *Metaphor and Metonymy in Comparison and Contrast*, ed. by René Dirven and Ralf Pörings (Berlin: Mouton de Gruyter, 2003), pp. 41–48. First published in 1956.
40   Sebastian Matzner, *Rethinking Metonymy: Literary Theory and Poetic Practice from Pindar to Jakobson* (Oxford: Oxford University Press, 2016), pp. 49–53.
41   My campaign against the fetishization of metaphor began a long time ago with an investigation

is more mundane. There may even be some virtue in the concept's fuzziness: the sense that the relation it could be thought to configure happens 'out there' in an imagined world, rather than by means of a juggling of lexical items.

The act of description and the figure of metonymy both pose a simple but not unintelligent question. Is it more pleasurable, and more enlightening, in the end, to look at one thing and see another in its place; or to see the 'look' of the relation between that thing and the thing that stands next to it? It was, I think, a question Maurice Merleau-Ponty was asking in the 1940s, in those long-forgotten attempts to reconcile existential phenomenology with Marxism. The great thing about film, Merleau-Ponty thought, was that it presented consciousness 'thrown into the world, subject to the gaze of others and learning from them what it is.' Existential phenomenology, he went on, 'is largely an expression of surprise at this inherence of the self in the world and in others, a description of this paradox and permeation, and an attempt to make us *see* the bond between subject and world, between subject and others, rather than to *explain* it as the classical philosophies did by resorting to absolute spirit.'[42] The essays assembled here, some of them written a very long time ago, still feel to me like an expression of surprise.

---

of the teaching of poetry in schools: *The Making of the Reader: Language and Subjectivity in Modern American, English, and Irish Poetry* (London: Macmillan, 1984), pp. 242–50.
42   Merleau-Ponty, 'Le Cinéma et la Nouvelle Psychologie', in *Sens et Non-Sens*, pp. 85–106 (pp. 104–05); 'The Film and the New Psychology', in *Sense and Non-Sense*, pp. 48–59 (p. 58).

PART I

Fictional Embodiment

CHAPTER 1

The New Historicism and the Psychopathology of Everyday Modern Life

The histories of sensory experience produced during and partly as a result of the New Historicism's recent irresistible rise to methodological supremacy might be thought of as the supplement which reveals a lack. Justly celebrated studies like Alain Corbin's *The Foul and the Fragrant* (1982) and Peter Stallybrass and Allon White's *The Politics and Poetics of Transgression* (1986) deploy a model of subjectivity not at all incompatible with that which informs the grand New Historical survey of modern disciplining and punishing.[1] We learn from these studies, and others like them, that the sights and smells of the nineteenth-century metropolis gave rise in the bourgeois subject to a mixture of fascination and disgust which at times of social and political crisis sharpened into panic. And yet the very richness of the material brought to light by historians of sensory experience makes one wonder about the validity of some of the categories they have used to analyse it. Did fascination always and everywhere infiltrate the disgust provoked in the solid citizen by the prostitute and the overflowing sewer? Should we always and everywhere discern an anxiety about social and political unrest 'behind' the sanitary reformer's anxiety about poisonous miasmas? It is questions like this, questions which bear directly on the model of subjectivity deployed by the New Historicism, that I want to address here, with the help of material drawn from a variety of sources.

Esther Lyon's Point of View

I begin with some domestic odours: the smell of old clothes, the smell of tallow, the smell of cooking. The odours are described in George Eliot's *Felix Holt, the Radical*

---

1   Alain Corbin, *The Foul and the Fragrant: Odour and the French Social Imagination* (London: Picador, 1994); Peter Stallybrass and Allon White, *The Politics and Poetics of Transgression* (London: Methuen, 1986). Also of note is Hans J. Rindisbacher, *The Smell of Books: A Cultural-Historical Study of Olfactory Perception in Literature* (Ann Arbor: University of Michigan Press, 1992). Rindisbacher's main focus is on nineteenth-century French and German realism; he describes the New Historicism as the 'line of thinking' in which his study finds its appropriate place (p. 23). All three studies have a common point of reference in the work of Norbert Elias, *The Civilizing Process*, trans. by E. Jephcott, 2 vols (New York: Pantheon, 1978–82).

(1866), and I begin with them partly because they mattered to Eliot, in interesting ways, and partly because they do not feature at all in Catherine Gallagher's fine account of the novel's contexts, in the final chapter of *The Industrial Reformation of English Fiction* (1985). But the history it clarifies, unlike the novel which prompted the clarification, is oddly odourless: a history of secrets rather than of secretions.

In 1861, a painting in a London gallery provoked a sharp disagreement between two visitors. The visitors were George Eliot and the writer and political economist Harriet Martineau. The painting depicted a stork killing a toad. Martineau attacked it on the grounds both of coarseness and of amorality. Eliot defended it, on the grounds that art shows the world as it is, rather than as it ought to be.[2]

Gallagher uses this encounter in a London gallery to characterize the doctrine of literary realism which shaped Eliot's early fiction. Martineau's faith in Providential design decreed that the uninspiring habits of the stork were remarkable only to the extent that they made Providential design manifest; for her, facts had no meaning at all unless they could be shown to derive from and to exhibit general principles or values. Eliot, by contrast, thought that nothing short of the patient accumulation of evidence of every kind would make manifest whatever inscrutable design there might be in nature. For her, facts were continuous with values: the way to get from one to the other was, in Gallagher's words, 'by the process of inclusion, equalization, and acceptance, by the slow-moving narrative method we now call metonymic realism'.[3] The writer's job was to accumulate facts. The meaning and value of any principle which in due course emerged from the accumulation of facts would depend on its fidelity to the observable social world. Gallagher compares this doctrine of literary realism to the liberal theory of political representation developed in the 1820s by James Mill. Mill's best possible Parliament, like Eliot's best possible novel, would be a detailed proportional rendering of British society. In his view, the meaning and value of Parliamentary representation depended on the closeness of the fit between a representative and the social world (the specific constituency) he represented.[4] Both the political and the literary doctrine assume an unbroken continuity between facts and general principles. Gallagher goes on to propose, however, that the novels Eliot published in the 1860s 'manifest a deep scepticism about the principles of mere aggregation in literature as well as politics'. One source of this scepticism was the critique of liberal theories developed by John Stuart Mill, in 'On Representative Government' (1861), and Matthew Arnold, in *Culture and Anarchy* (1869). Mill sought to ensure the disproportionate representation of 'instructed minds' by giving plural votes to those who could demonstrate 'mental superiority'. 'His proposed Parliament would not correspond

2   R. K. Webb, *Harriet Martineau: A Radical Victorian* (London: Heinemann, 1960), p. 39. The staunchness with which Eliot held her ground has led one critic to associate her preference for unheroic subject matter with that of Gustave Courbet, most combative of contemporary Realists: Murray Roston, 'George Eliot and the Horizons of Expectation', in *Victorian Contexts: Literature and the Visual Arts* (New York: New York University Press, 1996), pp. 114–29.

3   Catherine Gallagher, *The Industrial Reformation of English Fiction: Social Discourse and Narrative Form, 1832–1867* (Chicago, IL: University of Chicago Press, 1985), p. 221.

4   Ibid., pp. 222–23.

to any empirical social reality,' Gallagher explains, 'but would, rather, directly express, by distorting what is, that which ought to be.' Parliament would thus represent value *to* the people.[5] Arnold's theory of culture gave a sharper definition to the disinterestedness Mill required from those who represent value to the people. Culture, Arnold maintained, is what enables a man or woman to set aside personal and class interests, and develop that 'best self' whose steady and diligent exercise will promote social harmony.[6] The best self, needless to say, was not a principle which could be derived from the accumulation of facts about individual anxieties and desires. Like Mill's theory of government, Arnold's theory of culture rested on a radical discontinuity between facts and principles. Eliot, who followed the work of both men closely, found in their revision of liberal doctrines of government a political role for the writer, and thus a reason to revise her own doctrine of literary realism. Gallagher compares Eliot's later work to the novels of Gustave Flaubert, Thomas Hardy, and Henry James in its readiness to separate fact from value. Like John Stuart Mill's ideal Parliament, these proto-Modernist works represent value (the value of art) *to* an audience mired in personal and class interests.[7]

Gallagher links Eliot to Mill and Arnold most astutely, drawing in particular on passages in 'The Natural History of German Life' (1856). Like Mill and Arnold, Eliot began in the 1860s to insist on a radical discontinuity between values and facts. Gallagher regards *Felix Holt* as the novel in which Eliot's increasingly Arnoldian politics finally overcame her allegiance to a cumulative or metonymic realism. Her argument turns on the characterization of Felix Holt; or, rather, on the near impossibility of characterizing a protagonist whose utter indifference to marks of personal and social distinction altogether disqualifies him from descriptive realism of *any* kind. How does one describe someone who has no self at all apart from his best self?

Felix's indifference becomes an object of analysis in Chapter 5, when he visits Mr Lyon, the dissenting minister. Throughout the visit, he remains indifferent both to social facts (such as household smells) and to social signs (such as the aspiration encoded in the use of candles made of wax rather than tallow). Mr Lyon does not. He is defined for us by the anxiety with which he points out to Felix that the wax-candle is not an 'undue luxury', but a result of the loathing his daughter feels for the smell of tallow.[8] It is Felix's indifference to social signs which makes him the embodiment of Arnoldian disinterestedness; he refuses a job which would oblige him to wear a high cravat and straps, and thus set him apart from his fellow-workers (*FH* 144). And yet such superficial marks of distinction, which Felix is too cultured to notice, are, as Gallagher points out, all that everyone else, including the narrator and the reader, has to go on.[9] We know Mr Lyon by his momentary alarm about

5   Ibid., pp. 224–33.
6   Matthew Arnold, *Culture and Anarchy*, ed. by J. Dover Wilson (Cambridge: Cambridge University Press, 1969), p. 95.
7   Gallagher, *Industrial Reformation*, p. 266.
8   George Eliot, *Felix Holt, the Radical*, ed. by Peter Coveney (Harmondsworth: Penguin Books, 1972), pp. 139–40. Henceforth *FH*.
9   Gallagher, *Industrial Reformation*, p. 238.

the wax-light. Felix would rather not exist than have his opinions about the smell of tallow or the prestige of wax count for anything. He asks to be known by a different criterion altogether; he belongs to a different world, to a different novel. Thus, when Esther Lyon suggests that there is a good way and a bad way to be refined, Felix condemns refinement out of hand (53). Gallagher's political reading of the novel demonstrates convincingly why its protagonist is as he is. But there is, I think, another point of view embedded in it: Esther Lyon's point of view.

Esther, we might suppose, pays too much attention, or at least more attention than a cultured person should pay, both to social signs (indications of status) and to social facts (the smell of tallow). She is, Gallagher observes, 'predefined as a user of conventional codes'.[10] Her distaste for the ostentatiously fashionable is itself a fashion-statement. For the point of her subtle bonnets is not that they should render modishness obsolete, but that they should extinguish the brazen variety sported by her rivals. 'A real fine-lady does not wear clothes that flare in people's eyes, or use importunate scents, or make a noise as she moves,' Esther tells Felix: 'she is something refined, and graceful, and charming, and never obtrusive.' To Felix, however, mere refinement and unobtrusiveness cannot be supposed to constitute authenticity: one sort of 'fine ladyism' is as good, or as bad, as another (FH 153). Indeed, Felix's true authentic culture explicitly defines itself against Esther's false culture, a combination of subtle bonnets and subtle poems: he is appalled to learn that she has been reading Byron (150–51).

However, the indiscriminate vehemence of Felix's 'strong denunciatory and pedagogic intention' (FH 150) towards Esther, his rudeness about absolutely everything she says and does, prompts a certain scepticism. One might wonder, for example, whether an aversion to tallow is a 'failure' of the same order as caring about bonnets. Felix undoubtedly thinks so; from his point of view, which is the point of view of the Arnoldian best self, mere contingencies of social fact and social sign have neither meaning nor value. The novel, I shall suggest, gives us reason to disagree. For it is remarkably precise about Esther's aversions. Some, such as her objection to the squinting George Whitfield, seem petty enough, and duly fall victim to Felix's scorn (154). Others invite a more complicated response. Thus, Esther feels genuine affection for her father.

> But his old clothes had a smoky odour, and she did not like to walk with him, because, when people spoke to him in the street, it was his wont, instead of remarking on the weather and passing on, to pour forth in an absent manner some reflections that were occupying his mind about the traces of the divine government, or about a peculiar incident narrated in the life of the eminent Mr Richard Baxter. (161)

Esther's reluctance to walk with Mr Lyon is attributed, with mild disapproval, to a 'horror of appearing ridiculous' (161). Of her dislike for the smoky odour of his old clothes, nothing further is said. Felix, of course, cares as little about smoky odours as he does about appearing ridiculous (it is all contingency). But the contrast between the silence maintained about the first of these aversions and the swift

10   Ibid., p. 246.

and comprehensive exegesis of the second gives pause for thought. It allows us to acknowledge that a dislike for the smoky odour of old clothes is not self-evidently frivolous: that it bears on the facts of co-existence and cohabitation rather than on a fantasy about status.

That Eliot knew the difference is made plain in Chapter 27, when Esther sufficiently overcomes her anxiety about status to walk out for the first time with Felix. The chapter opens on a mundane note, with Esther 'left alone in the parlour amidst the lingering odours of the early dinner, not easily got rid of in that small house'. On this occasion, the narrator immediately intervenes to point out that such 'vulgar details', easily overlooked by rich people who live in large houses, have made or broken many a humble life (FH 358). Esther, who hates the smell of cooking, endures it, now, because she thinks Felix may call. She learns to live with her own disgust, and by living with her own disgust learns to love Felix. She learns not to mind his patched boots and lack of cravat. Endurance of an unpleasant social fact (the smell of cooking) has prepared her, more effectively than any amount of denunciatory and pedagogic intention, to endure an unpleasant social sign (Felix's shabbiness). 'Esther was a little amazed at what she had come to' (360).

Esther's amazement occurs during a stroll along the river which rather alarmingly reinstates Felix's best self. 'When Felix had asked her to walk, he had seemed so kind, so alive to what might be her feelings, that she had thought herself nearer to him than she had ever been before; but since they had come out, he had appeared to forget all that' (FH 364). Felix's sublime disinterestedness, his forgetting all that, is the source of his superiority, as both Esther and the narrator fervently acknowledge; it expresses true meaning and value to mere women (and mere readers) mired in superficiality. And yet, unlike Felix, we have witnessed Esther's endurance of her own disgust. We do not 'forget all that' as easily as he appears to have done. Eliot wrote the scene fluently, making few alterations to the manuscript; she felt both sides of the exchange between Esther and Felix with equal intensity. So, I think, should we.

Fear, Anxiety, and Sanitary Reform

I shall have more to say later about the significance of Esther Lyon's aversion to domestic odours. But I want to turn now to another narrative whose ideological implications have recently become the focus of enquiry: Edwin Chadwick's *Report on the Sanitary Condition of the Labouring Population of Great Britain* (1842).[11] If Henry Mayhew's *London Labour and the London Poor*, with its huge cast of characters, its 'many and curious narratives', and its resemblance to oral history, suited the 1960s, when historians spoke of structures of feeling, of worlds turned (or not turned) upside down, then Chadwick's lugubrious compilation suits the 1990s, when historians speak of surveillance and discipline.[12] The New Historicism has

---

11   Edwin Chadwick, *Report on the Sanitary Condition of the Labouring Population of Great Britain*, ed. by M. W. Flinn (Edinburgh: Edinburgh University Press, 1965).
12   Henry Mayhew, *London Labour and the London Poor*, ed. by Victor Neuberg (Harmondsworth: Penguin Books, 1985), p. 163.

identified Chadwick as the czar of normalization: the man whose 'strategic genius' put in place the elements of a modern disciplinary regime.[13]

Joseph Childers describes the following passage, from observations made by a Dr J. F. Handley, as 'characteristic' of the *Report*'s emphasis on discipline and surveillance.[14]

> When the small-pox was prevalent in this district, I attended a man, woman, and five children, all lying ill with the confluent species of that disorder, in one bed-room, and having only two beds amongst them. The walls of the cottage were black, the sheets were black, and the patients themselves were blacker still; two of the children were absolutely sticking together. I have relished many a biscuit and glass of wine in Mr Grainger's dissecting-room when ten dead bodies were lying on the tables under dissection, but was entirely deprived of appetite during my attendance upon these cases. The smell on entering the apartments was exceedingly nauseous, and the room would not admit of free ventilation.[15]

Almost as striking as the passage itself is the commentator's reluctance to comment on it. What we have here, what the New Historicism cannot quite bring itself to notice, is a richly perverse banquet of the senses; or, rather, like masque and anti-masque, a banquet (in Mr Grainger's dissecting-room) and an anti-banquet (in the slum-cottage). In the dissecting-room, appetite flourishes under the protection of a gaze which engenders precise observation from a distance. Anatomy, a science predicated on sight, had of course long been the cynosure of a (modern) desire for knowledge.[16] Immunized twice over, by scientific enquiry, and by spectatorship, Handley is able to relish his biscuit and his glass of wine to the full. In the slum-cottage, however, objects no longer present themselves as discrete entities disposed, like the dissecting-room's ten dead bodies, within a coherent visual field. Everywhere, figure lapses into ground. The blackness of the walls cannot be distinguished from the blackness of the sheets, which cannot be distinguished from the blackness of the patients. The children stick together, presenting themselves less to the knowing eye than to the fantasized touch. Confluence is the note not only of the species of smallpox which has struck this family down, but of the scene itself, of the anti-banquet. As the sense of sight loses its way, baffled by confluence, the sense of smell takes over. The nauseating stench kills appetite. For Handley, the scene in the slum-cottage really does take the biscuit.

13   The most recent biography, by Anthony Brundage, is entitled *England's 'Prussian Minister': Edwin Chadwick and the Politics of Government Growth, 1832–1854* (University Park: Pennsylvania State University Press, 1988). Philip Corrigan and Derek Sayer emphasize Chadwick's 'strategic genius', in *The Great Arch: English State Formation as Cultural Revolution* (Oxford: Blackwell, 1985), p. 127. See also, Peter Logan, *Nerves and Narratives: A Cultural History of Hysteria in Nineteenth-Century British Prose* (Berkeley: University of California Press, 1997), p. 161.

14   Joseph Childers, *Novel Possibilities: Fiction and the Formation of Early Victorian Culture* (Philadelphia: University of Pennsylvania Press, 1995), p. 86.

15   Chadwick, *Report*, p. 316.

16   Jonathan Sawday, *The Body Emblazoned: Dissection and the Human Body* (London: Routledge, 1995); Lawrence Rothfield, *Vital Signs: Medical Realism in Nineteenth-Century Fiction* (Princeton, NJ: Princeton University Press, 1992).

The emphasis on confluence reminds me of *Bleak House*, the book D. A. Miller places at the centre of a tradition of narratives whose main function was to discipline their readers.[17] Think, for example, of the 'sallow prisoner' who makes a brief appearance in its opening chapter, and whose only function in the novel is to be described as in 'a state of conglomeration about accounts of which it is not pretended that he had ever any knowledge'.[18] Confluence, conglomeration: in novel and report alike, such flowing or gathering together baffles the panoptic gaze. The fog and the mud, in the opening chapter of *Bleak House*, are not, as Miller maintains, 'symbols' of power's ability to pervade and saturate: they pervade and saturate after their own distinct fashions; they belong to the novel's phenomenology of stickiness.[19] Krook combusts, on a 'fine steaming night' when there is a 'queer kind of flavour' in the air, which may or may not derive from the chops grilling at the Sol's Arms (*BH* 499–500), in the name of that phenomenology. Krook combusts so that Dickens may describe the soot on Mr Guppy's arm, which 'smears, like black fat' (505). Krook combusts so that Dickens may describe the 'stagnant, sickening oil, with some natural repulsion in it,' which oozes down the wall to lie 'in a little thick nauseous pool' on the floor (509). Miller's belief that the nature of a disciplinary system shapes the nature of any resistance it may encounter obliges him to regard this combustion as the necessary outcome of the law's pervasiveness. 'It is as though apocalyptic suddenness were the only conceivable way to put an end to Chancery's meanderings, violent spontaneity the only means to abridge its elaborate procedures.' [20] However, Krook's death, sudden in the event, is remarkably long-drawn-out in the discovery. It takes the best part of a chapter before Guppy and Jobling trace the uneasiness which so afflicts them back to its horrific source in Krook's smouldering remains (511). In that time, in the reading of those pages, the black grease they cannot help but touch whenever they move exemplifies nothing apart from itself. Continuous with the fog and mud of Chapter 1, and with the many other conglomerations described at length in the intervening chapters, it is the world's residue, not Chancery's.

The black confluence in a slum-cottage, the little thick nauseous pool: these representations solicit a new approach. They require, to begin with, I think, an analysis of the meanings and values which have been attributed to sensory perception, and of the moral, social, and political uses to which it has been put. I am indebted at this point to Steven Connor's exploratory work on the relation between the structures of identity and the structure of the sensorium.[21] Connor argues that

17   D. A. Miller, *The Novel and the Police* (Berkeley: University of California Press, 1988), pp. 58–106.

18   *Bleak House*, ed. by Norman Page (Harmondsworth: Penguin Books, 1971), p. 51. Henceforth *BH*.

19   Miller, *The Novel and the Police*, p. 60. There would be worse places to start, if one wished to develop a phenomenology of Dickensian stickiness, than the pages Gaston Bachelard devotes to the 'valorisation' of mud in *La Terre et les rêveries de la volonté* (Paris: Librairie José Corti, 1948), pp. 105–33.

20   Miller, *The Novel and the Police*, p. 62.

21   Steven Connor, 'The Modern Auditory I', in *Rewriting the Self: Histories from the Renaissance to the Present*, ed. by Roy Porter (London: Routledge, 1997), pp. 203–23; and 'Feel the Noise: Excess, Affect and the Acoustic', in *Emotion in Postmodernism*, ed. by Gerhard Hoffmann and Alfred Hornung

modernity should be understood not in terms of the subordination of the proximity senses, as typified by the ear, to the hegemony of the eye, but in terms of a fraught and continually renewed argument between the powers of ear and eye. His aim is to flesh out, with the help of literary and psychoanalytic descriptions, an 'auditory I', a 'self imaged not as a point, but as a membrane; not as a picture, but as a channel through which voices, noises and musics travel'.[22]

It seems doubtful that there ever was, or ever could be, an olfactory I. Even so, useful points of comparison can be established between the vicissitudes of hearing, as Connor describes them, and the vicissitudes of smell, which are my concern here. Connor points out that sound, unlike sight, has often been understood as a disintegrative principle. We can only see one thing at a time, but it is possible to hear several sounds simultaneously. Sound often carries menace unless and until we trace it back to and locate it in a specific source, or visualize its origin.[23] Similarly, the bad smells which so afflicted sanitary inspectors like Handley were threatening because they were sourceless and composite, a queer kind of flavour in the air. Noise, Connor observes, especially loud noise, is always agonistic: it involves the maximum at once of arousal and of passivity. Thus, 'noise creates communities of listening sealed by the revulsion and offence of others'.[24] Similarly, the stench of the slum engendered in the sanitary inspector both arousal and passivity. What was the slum if not a community of odour sealed by the revulsion and offence of others?

However, there is at least one important difference between hearing and smell. Smell ranks low, as William Miller has observed, indeed lowest of all, in the hierarchy of senses. That there are bad sounds need not diminish the glory of hearing. That there are delightful fragrances has done little to elevate smell: traditionally, the best odour is not a good odour, but no odour at all.[25] The sense of smell remained, in the representations which are my concern here, an overwhelmingly disintegrative and agonistic principle. To grasp the meanings and values attributed to it, we must be able to think the pure negativity of the nausea it provokes.

The sense of smell has two defining qualities which may help to explain why it featured so consistently as a disintegrative and agonistic principle in the literature of sanitary reform. One has to do with the way in which smells are conceptualized, the other with the way in which we remember them. In the first place, smells are hard to define. 'Even though the human sense of smell can distinguish hundreds of thousands of smells and in this regard is comparable to sight or hearing,' Dan Sperber observes, 'in none of the world's languages does there seem to be a classification of smells comparable, for example, to colour classification.' There is no taxonomy of smells, no 'semantic field'. When we designate smells, we do so in terms either of their causes (the smell of incense, the smell of excrement) or of their effects (a heady perfume, an appetising smell). In the domain of colour,

(Heidelberg: Universitätsverlag Carl Winter, 1997), pp. 147–62.

22   Connor, 'Auditory I', p. 207.

23   Ibid., p. 213.

24   Connor, 'Feel the Noise', p. 156.

25   William Miller, The Anatomy of Disgust (Cambridge, MA: Harvard University Press, 1997), p. 75.

designations become lexicalized (the term 'rose' can be used without bringing the flower to mind); in the domain of smell, 'metonymy remains active and infallibly evokes cause or effect'.[26] Whereas the tactile possesses its own rich and versatile idiom (oozy, squishy, gummy, mucky, dank, and so on), the odorous does not. 'Routine tactile sensation spurs language to inventiveness,' Miller points out, 'while the olfactory and gustatory reduce us to saying little more than yum or yuck.'[27] It is often routine tactile sensation which spurs Dickens to inventiveness in *Bleak House*. When, in passing, he compares a gas-lamp seen through fog to the sun seen by husbandman and ploughboy from the 'spongey fields' (*BH* 49), the detail's precision rapidly supplements and clarifies our sense that this is a world in which everyone and everything will stick fast. Indeed, the very richness and versatility of the account somewhat offset its pessimism. Similarly, Dr Handley's description of the slum-cottage becomes almost Dickensian in tone when it notes the two children 'absolutely sticking together'. Thus, the phenomenology of tactile sensation both appals and stimulates at the same time. By contrast, it is the *lack* of an appropriate semantic field which renders the mere allusion to a bad smell in narrative so profoundly unsettling. What would a phenomenology of odour be a phenomenology *of*? Meaning itself falters.

There are two ways, Sperber argues, in which we can retrieve memorized information: by deliberate recall, without external stimulus; and by recognition (in the presence of some 'new' fact, we remember that we already possess it). Some kinds of information are easier to recognize than to recall: we recognize many faces, but recall only a few. Smells are in this respect an extreme case: we recognize them easily, but find them almost impossible to recall. We recall the scent of a rose only by recalling (by re-visualizing) the flower; and yet we can recognize at a distance of years a scent we have only scented once, and know immediately that we have scented it before.[28] Every time the sanitary inspector enters a slum-cottage, he recognizes its utterly distinctive odour; but he will never be able to recall that odour without external stimulus (he will never be able to re-present it in his written report). A bad smell's other profoundly unsettling quality is that it always comes back from outside, from elsewhere, from beyond the limits of conscious recollection.

The rhetorical function of the shift of emphasis, in Handley's account, from sight and touch to smell, is to insist upon negativity. How can we grasp that insistence? The New Historicism's preoccupation with modernity's dominant visual regimes has produced some brilliant analyses of the moment at which those regimes falter: the moment, for example, at which the philanthropist or the colonial administrator finds his gaze turned back against him in menace, in mimicry. However, there is a problem with this form of analysis. The problem lies in the model of affect which

---

26   Dan Sperber, *Rethinking Symbolism*, trans. by Alice L. Morton (Cambridge: Cambridge University Press, 1975), pp. 115–16.
27   Miller, *Anatomy of Disgust*, p. 67.
28   Sperber, *Rethinking Symbolism*, pp. 116–17. Psychological research has demonstrated that the association between a smell and its verbal description tends to be weak. See Miller, *Anatomy of Disgust*, pp. 67–68; and Rindisbacher, *Smell of Books*, pp. 10–20.

the New Historicism more or less uniformly incorporates, whether its object is attitudes to the slum, or orientalism, or homosexual panic. That model is a Freudian model. Freud's insistence that the psyche is incurably split, and that ambivalence informs feeling through and through, has proved enormously productive in cultural theory. But it obscures the negativity of a feeling like disgust. According to Freud, disgust is a reaction-formation against an interest in and desire for its object; in particular, disgust defends the psyche against a shameful acknowledgement of anal eroticism.[29] It is this faith in the ambivalence of disgust which underpins the New Historicism's account of the nineteenth-century metropolis or the nineteenth-century Orient as a locus of mingled fascination and loathing. Stallybrass and White declare, influentially, that 'disgust always bears the imprint of desire'.[30] According to Peter Logan, the literature of sanitary reform endlessly reproduces, in its exposure of filth and decay, 'a fascination with repugnance'.[31]

I do not deny that desire may exist in a dialectical relation to loathing. However, if we are to understand disgust as a disintegrative and agonistic principle, we must be able to isolate, within the dialectic, its negating or antithetical moment. At this point in my argument, I want to make a knight's move, a move beyond psychoanalysis (beyond ambivalence) into phenomenology. A distinction I have found useful in thinking about Esther Lyon, and about Dr Handley in the slum-cottage, is the distinction Martin Heidegger develops in *Being and Time* between feeling and mood. One of Heidegger's terms for mood is *Befindlichkeit*: not 'state of mind', as it is sometimes translated, but something like 'how one finds oneself'.[32] 'How are you doing?' we say: that is an enquiry after *Befindlichkeit*. My subject is Dr Handley's *Befindlichkeit*; or, rather, the *Befindlichkeit* he seeks to induce, by such measures as the shift of emphasis from sight and touch to smell, in his readers.

Feelings are directed at specific entities, at people or things: a mood is directed at (or in a sense directed from) the world. Heidegger's favourite moods are of course boredom and *Angst* (anxiety, dread). We might think of the first chapter of *Bleak House* when he observes that profound boredom, 'drifting here and there in the abysses of our existence like a muffling fog, removes all things and all human beings and oneself along with them into a remarkable indifference'.[33] Anxiety, too, dissolves or cancels out the identities of subject and object alike. Heidegger distinguishes between fear, which is a feeling, and anxiety, which is a mood. Both are responses to threat: but whereas fear is a response to something specific *in* the world (a gun, an animal, a gesture), anxiety has no object, and is all the more

---

29   Sigmund Freud, letter to Wilhelm Fliess, 14 November 1897, in *The Complete Letters of Sigmund Freud to Wilhelm Fliess, 1887–1904*, ed. by Jeffrey M. Masson (Cambridge, MA: Harvard University Press, 1985), p. 280; *Three Essays on Sexuality*, in *The Standard Edition of the Complete Psychological Works*, ed. by James Strachey et al., 24 vols (London: Hogarth Press, 1966–74), I, 160–62, 177–78; *Civilization and Its Discontents* (1930), *Standard Edition*, XXI, 99–100.
30   Stallybrass and White, *Politics and Poetics of Transgression*, p. 191.
31   Logan, *Nerves and Narratives*, p. 164.
32   Martin Heidegger, *Being and Time*, trans. by John Macquarrie and Edward Robinson (Oxford: Blackwell, 1962), pp. 172–79, 388–96.
33   Heidegger, 'What Is Metaphysics?', in *Basic Writings*, rev. edn, ed. by David Farrell Krell (London: Routledge, 1993), pp. 93–110 (p. 99).

oppressive for that. You can run away from an animal or a gun, and respond to a gesture, but you cannot do anything about the world as such, about being-in-the-world as such. Anxiety confronts *Dasein* with the determining yet contingent fact of its own worldly existence.[34]

For Heidegger, at his most Kierkegaardian, anxiety is oppressive, but also a disclosure, a form of understanding. I want, for my own purposes, to halt his analysis at the moment before it finds in anxiety's oppressiveness a form of understanding: at the moment when it recognizes anxiety as a wholly disintegrative and agonistic principle. *Befindlichkeit*, Heidegger remarks, 'makes manifest "how one is"'. 'In anxiety,' he adds, 'one feels "*uncanny*" (In der Angst ist einem "*unheimlich*").'[35] Freud's interest in the *unheimlich*, by contrast, centred on the term's semantic density. For him, the uncanny was that kind of terrifying experience which 'leads back to what is known of old and long familiar'. 'Thus *heimlich* is a word the meaning of which develops in the direction of ambivalence, until it finally coincides with its opposite, *unheimlich*. *Unheimlich* is in some way or other a sub-species of *heimlich*.'[36] Heidegger's interest in the *unheimlich* was grammatical rather than semantic. It was an interest, not in ambiguity and ambivalence, but in the way in which language encodes a relation between subject and object, self and world.

> In anxiety, we say, 'one feels ill at ease ("es ist einem unheimlich").' What is 'it' that makes 'one' feel ill at ease? We cannot say what it is before which one feels ill at ease. As a whole it is so for one. All things and we ourselves sink into indifference [...] At bottom therefore it is not as though 'you' or 'I' feel ill at ease; rather, it is this way for some 'one'.

Heidegger wants to know not what uncanniness is, but what it does to the person who experiences it. He wants to know about the 'one' it manufactures out of a 'you' or an 'I'. This grammatical enquiry allows him to grasp the uncanny as a disintegrative and agonistic principle rather than as ambivalence. 'With the fundamental mood of anxiety,' he concludes, 'we have arrived at that occurrence in human existence in which the nothing is revealed and from which it must be interrogated.'[37]

Heidegger's grammatical enquiry maps onto that taking of position which so absorbs Dr Handley in the slum-cottage. When a threat emerges, Heidegger says, anxiety, unlike fear, 'does not "see" any definite "here" or "yonder"' from which the threat might be thought to come. That which threatens us in anxiety, he goes on, is 'already "there", and yet nowhere; it is so close that it is oppressive and stifles one's breath, and yet it is nowhere'.[38] Dr Handley, in the slum-cottage, or recalling the slum-cottage, suffers anxiety rather than terror. It is not, exactly, that there is nothing to be afraid of: smallpox is a contagious disease. But he does not represent himself as afraid. He represents himself as anxious and nauseated. In the cottage, he

34   Heidegger, *Being and Time*, pp. 228–35.
35   Ibid., p. 233.
36   Freud, 'The Uncanny', *Standard Edition*, XVII, 220, 226.
37   Heidegger, *Basic Writings*, p. 101.
38   Heidegger, *Being and Time*, p. 231.

can no longer see any definite here or yonder: people and things no longer appear to him as discrete entities disposed within a coherent visual field. The confluence stifles his breath: he knows it as the stench on which he gags. He knows, we might speculate, not the imminence, but the inevitability, of his own death.

The literature of sanitary reform, taken as a whole, relentlessly converts fear into anxiety. According to the zymotic theory of disease then prevalent, a bad smell was itself something to be afraid of, a specific threat: and yet in their reports the sanitary inspectors rarely identify the bad smells which so afflicted them in medical terms, as contagious matter.[39] Those smells are there, not for diagnostic purposes, but for the anxiety they have already provoked in the inspector (in 'one'), and for the anxiety they may yet provoke in the reader. So pervasive was this conversion of fear into anxiety and nausea that it provoked a counter-movement, in novels and reports alike: the conversion of anxiety back into fear, back into a specific threat against which steps could be taken. Esther Summerson's disfigurement by smallpox, in *Bleak House*, serves little purpose: it is no test of other peoples' feelings about her, since those feelings have never been based on appearance. But it does demonstrate that the world's stench can take the concrete and devastating form of a disease communicated from one identifiable person to another: there is something to be afraid of. It is with such conversions, of fear into anxiety, and, I shall argue, of anxiety into fear, that historical explanation can begin.

Fear has hitherto loomed larger than anxiety in New Historicist accounts of the politics and poetics of sanitary reform. Mary Poovey, for example, argues that the emphasis in Chadwick's *Report* on exteriors rather than interiors constitutes a further elaboration of the domestic ideology which the rising middle class had claimed as its own.[40] Domesticity was, in eighteenth- and nineteenth-century Britain, one of the most important means by which middle-class men represented and asserted their social superiority over both the spendthrift earl and the promiscuous and improvident factory-hand. A clean and orderly family life, with its concomitant separation of spheres, became the norm against which exponents of middle-class hegemony measured the pathologies only too apparent in the behaviour of aristocrat and proletarian alike. What Chadwick did in his *Report*, Poovey argues, was to figure domesticity's opposite in consistently powerful terms: some of its 'most graphic and emotionally charged descriptions' are those of working-class men who do not reside in anything remotely resembling a middle-class home.[41] The Parisian

---

39 For zymotic theory, see Christopher Hamlin, 'Providence and Putrefaction: Victorian Sanitarians and the Natural Theology of Health and Disease', *Victorian Studies*, 28 (1985), 381–411. Corbin notes that in France in the middle years of the nineteenth century, a new emphasis on the repulsive smell of the proletariat appears in accounts by doctors and visitors to the poor. 'Hitherto, doctors had seemed impervious to disgust; only fear of infection appeared to motivate precautions': *The Foul and the Fragrant*, p. 150. He does not develop the distinction between disgust and fear of infection.

40 Mary Poovey, *Making a Social Body: British Cultural Formation, 1830–1864* (Chicago, IL: University of Chicago Press, 1995), pp. 117, 121. Poovey acknowledges a debt to the most influential account of the normalization of domesticity: Leonore Davidoff and Catherine Hall, *Family Fortunes: Men and Women of the English Middle Class, 1780–1850* (Chicago, IL: University of Chicago Press, 1987).

41 Ibid., p. 121.

chiffoniers, or scavengers, for example, are described as 'outcasts from other classes of workmen' who 'sleep amidst their collections of refuse' and remain idle during the day. These men, Chadwick reports, 'rose in revolt' when the authorities had the streets swept during an outbreak of cholera. Their British counterparts were the 'bone-pickers' who scavenged for scraps of meat in gutters and dung-heaps. 'Often hardly human in appearance,' one witness recalls, 'they had neither human tastes nor sympathies, nor even human sensations, for they revelled in the filth which is grateful to dogs, and other lower animals, and which to our apprehension is redolent only of nausea and abomination.'[42]

But why was scavenging such an urgent issue? Poovey finds a political motive. According to her, the *Report* mobilized domestic ideology in support of an explicit denunciation of social *and* political pathologies. The 'precise historical referent' for the figuring of the scavengers was Chartism. It was in 1838, she observes, as Chadwick was laying the foundations of sanitary reform, that William Lovett and Francis Place published the People's Charter. In February 1839, the Convention of the Industrial Classes was held in London. On 6 May, a petition bearing 1,200,000 signatures in support of the Charter was presented to Parliament, and the leaders of the Convention threatened a general strike. Riots broke out in July, and again in September. Despite rigorous suppression, Chartism 'had proved by 1842 that working men could and would organize in favour of political enfranchisement'. It was these activities, Poovey concludes, which prompted Chadwick's emphasis on the savagery of the bone-pickers.[43]

There are some problems with this account. Chadwick and Francis Place were in touch throughout the 1830s. On 21 June 1829, Place warmly congratulated Chadwick on an article about poverty in the *London Review*. When Chadwick became Secretary to the Poor Law Commissioners, Place approached him more than once on behalf of friends seeking jobs, or information. On 21 April 1835, he urged Chadwick to enforce the new workhouse regime rigorously. The correspondence continued into and beyond the period of Place's involvement in Chartism.[44] These letters are significant because they articulate, in their forms of address, in the mutual understanding they assume, a professional relationship. Chadwick, no friend to Chartism, was a friend of Chartists. No doubt he disapproved of Place's views, moderate though they were. But it is inconceivable that he would have associated him with bone-pickers.

Furthermore, if anyone was responsible for introducing domestic ideology into the bitter industrial disputes of the 1830s and 1840s, it was the Chartists themselves. Working-class radicals had construed the social world in terms of gender since at least the 1820s.[45] Recent studies have shown that the twin ideals of female

---

42   Chadwick, *Report*, pp. 163–65.
43   Poovey, *Making*, pp. 126–27.
44   Francis Place, letters of 21 June 1829, 26 August 1834, 21 April 1835, and 21 October 1836 to Edwin Chadwick, in the Chadwick Collection of the Library of University College London: Chadwick MSS, 1587. The Collection includes eight letters from Place to Chadwick, 1829–41.
45   Catherine Hall, 'The Tale of Samuel and Jemima: Gender and Working-Class Culture in Early-Nineteenth-Century England', in *White, Male and Middle-Class: Explorations in Feminism and History*

domesticity and male breadwinning 'developed out of and were in harmony with values which originated in pre-industrial artisanal workshop culture'.[46] The separation of spheres was not a middle-class conspiracy. It remained axiomatic in working-class radicalism in the 1830s and 1840s.

My point is not that Chartism posed no threat, in Chadwick's mind, but that the threat it did pose was less than absolute. That threat has to be understood as an element in the complex of fears and anxieties which animated professional relationships among the sanitary reformers in the late 1840s. A remarkable letter written on 1 February 1847 by Dr Lyon Playfair, one of Chadwick's main collaborators, takes us as close to the centre of that complex (as close to sanitary reform's primal trauma) as we are ever likely to get. The letter itself denounces in vigorous terms the 'abominable system of cesspools'. Its remarkable postscript, however, turns unceremoniously from the cesspools to the men whose job it is to empty them. 'Our nightmen are a brutal set of men & fortunate will it be for the public if we can get rid of them.' Playfair goes on to describe the evacuation of a cesspool in which matter had been allowed to accumulate for five years.

> During the process of emptying, I saw one of the nightmen actually take up in his hand a quantity of the night soil & swallow it 'to see how it tasted'. After I left, I understand, in fact I have it in evidence under the signature of the nightman himself, one of the nightmen rubbed the nightsoil into his eyes, 'to see if it acted in the same way on the eyes as common night soil'. Could the chiffoniers of Paris classed among the 'classes dangereuses' equal these nightmen in their bestial habits?[47]

The postscript, which deliberately revives the 1842 *Report*'s allusion to the Parisian *chiffoniers*, clearly has implications for the debate about the politics and poetics of sanitary reform. It might be taken to confirm Poovey's hypothesis that anxiety about nightmen and nightsoil was determined in the last instance by a fear of social and political unrest, a fear of revolution. Or it might be taken to confirm my hypothesis that the sanitary reformers sometimes sought to control anxiety by converting it back into fear. The point of the comparison, I think, is not to make the nightmen seem even more dangerous than they actually are, by associating them with a politicized *Lumpenproletariat*, but, on the contrary, to humanize them, to find in their otherwise incomprehensible bestiality a feeling about material existence, and so about mortality: something, in short, for everyone to be afraid of. The comparison with the chiffoniers is then Playfair's way of not seeing, or rather of not smelling, his own inevitable death in these nightsoiled zombies.

(London: Polity Press, 1988), pp. 124–50.

46   Sonya O. Rose, *Limited Livelihoods: Gender and Class in Nineteenth-Century England* (London: Routledge, 1992), p. 141. See also W. Seccombe, 'Patriarchy Stabilized: The Construction of the Male Breadwinner Wage Norm in Nineteenth-Century Britain', *Social History*, 11 (1986), 53–76. In 1835, Place himself argued that men should refuse to work alongside women in mills and factories: Rose, *Limited Livelihoods*, p. 147.

47   Lyon Playfair, letter of 1 February 1847 to Edwin Chadwick, Chadwick MSS, 1588.

The Acknowledgement of Anxiety

I want to return, in conclusion, to Esther Lyon's *Befindlichkeit*, to the domestic odours. The issue here, for historical explanation, is not so much the nausea the odours provoke in her as its acknowledgement. Eliot wants us to acknowledge the force of her nausea: its justice. The odours do of course have an origin in particular objects or activities. But the condition of simultaneous arousal and passivity they induce in Esther would not be cured merely by the removal of those objects and activities: other objects, other activities would soon take their place. The cure lies, as Eliot knew, in public acknowledgement of the condition. And it so happens that an acknowledgement of anxiety and nausea was taking shape, as Eliot wrote, within a specific institutional context: that of the Divorce Court.

Before 1857, divorce law in England provided only for separation (divorce *a mensa et thoro*). Absolute divorce (*a vinculo matrimonii*) was restricted to those wealthy enough to finance a private Act of Parliament. The Divorce Court created by the Matrimonial Causes Act of 1857 made absolute divorce accessible to all, at least in theory, but maintained the double standard, by allowing a husband relief for his wife's adultery, but requiring a wife to prove adultery compounded by an offence such as cruelty, desertion, incest, or bigamy. However, the old divorce from bed and board, renamed 'judicial separation', was available to husbands and wives on grounds of cruelty alone. No further changes were made to the law until 1923, when the double standard was abolished; grounds other than adultery were first admitted in 1937. Slow to change, limited in application, and reproducing rigid inequalities of class and gender, divorce law has been taken to represent the underlying conservatism of the Victorian reforming impulse.[48] No wonder feminists campaigned against it.[49]

However, recent research has demonstrated that judicial conservatism masked 'an evolution in decision-making which was of central importance for women seeking relief from intolerable marriages'.[50] What evolved, after 1857, was the understanding of legal cruelty. According to the view authoritatively expressed by Sir William Scott (later Lord Stowell) in *Evans* v. *Evans* (1790), and still in force seventy years later, 'Mere austerity of temper, petulance of manners, rudeness of language, a want of civil attention and accommodation, even occasional sallies of passion, if they do not threaten bodily harm, do not amount to legal cruelty: they are high moral offences in the marriage state undoubtedly, not innocent surely in any state

---

48   Roderick Phillips, *Putting Asunder: A History of Divorce in Western Society* (Cambridge: Cambridge University Press, 1988), pp. 412–22; Mary Lyndon Shanley, '"One Must Ride Behind": Married Women's Rights and the Divorce Act of 1857', *Victorian Studies*, 25 (1982), 355–76.
49   Lucy Bland, 'The Married Woman, the "New Woman" and the Feminist: Sexual Politics of the 1890s', in *Equal or Different: Women's Politics, 1800–1914*, ed. by Jane Rendall (Oxford: Blackwell, 1987), pp. 141–64; David Rubinstein, *Before the Suffragettes: Women's Emancipation in the 1890s* (Hassocks: Harvester Press, 1986), Chapter 4; Mary Lyndon Shanley, *Feminism, Marriage and the Law in Victorian England* (London: I. B. Tauris, 1989).
50   A. James Hammerton, 'Victorian Marriage and the Law of Matrimonial Cruelty', *Victorian Studies*, 33 (1990), 269–92 (p. 272). See also J. M. Biggs, *The Concept of Matrimonial Cruelty* (London: Athlone Press, 1962).

of life, but still they are not that cruelty against which the law can relieve'. The only cruelty against which the law *could* relieve was 'bodily hurt', or a 'reasonable apprehension' of bodily hurt.[51] Thus, in *Chesnutt* v. *Chesnutt* (1854), a husband's habitual drunkenness and obscene and blasphemous language were not recognized as legal cruelty because, however disgusting such conduct might be, it did not amount to 'bodily ill treatment, or threats of the same'. Similarly, the Judge in *Tomkins* v. *Tomkins* (1858) pointed out that the Court had never yet been 'driven off' the ground established by Stowell in *Evans* v. *Evans*. 'There must [...] be bodily hurt — not trifling or temporary pain; or a reasonable apprehension of bodily hurt.'[52]

Some forms of conduct trod a narrow line between physical and mental abuse. In *Waddell* v. *Waddell* (1862), a wife petitioned for divorce on grounds of adultery compounded by cruelty. The cruelty involved, among other things, throwing cold water at her, and spitting in her face. Spitting does not cause injury, but there is none the less an edge of violence to it; it puts hatred into physical effect, it provokes a revulsion which is both physical and moral. The Judge who did not discern legal cruelty in Mr Chesnutt's drunkenness and obscenity had previously, in *Saunders* v. *Saunders* (1847), equated spitting in someone's face with the threat of physical violence. Recalling this equation, the Judge in *Waddell* v. *Waddell* concluded that so gross a 'personal insult' would be insufferable even in 'the lowest grades of life'. 'How much more criminal, how much more painful to the feelings of the injured wife when such an offence takes place between those who have been accustomed to the decencies of society, and have been educated to entertain a high regard for them.'[53]

These meditations reveal a shift of emphasis from the nature of offending acts to their effects on the victim.[54] The Judge in *Waddell* v. *Waddell* put himself in the place of a middle-class wife whose upbringing and expectations would almost certainly have led her to regard spitting at someone as an unpardonable outrage. The definition of legal cruelty had widened, by this time, to include severe mental suffering: a state of mind which could only be assessed in relation to a person's temperament and social status. Thus, in *Milner* v. *Milner* (1861), a wife was granted a divorce on the grounds of adultery compounded by 'the grossest and most abominable cruelty'.

> In April, 1858, whilst they were staying in the house of a friend in London, the petitioner insisted upon accompanying the respondent against his will on a certain occasion when he was leaving the house. They went together in an omnibus to the City, and upon getting out she followed him to Fenchurch Street, when he turned round and said she should go no further, and taking her by the shoulders and making use of the most filthy language, he pushed her against the wall, and thrust his umbrella against her person. The blow inflicted no pain, but in consequence of his conduct a man passing by at the

51   161 *English Reports* (henceforth *ER*), pp. 467–68.
52   164 *ER*, pp. 115, 679.
53   163 *ER*, pp. 1135–36; 164 *ER*, p. 1125.
54   Hammerton, *Cruelty and Companionship: Conflict in Nineteenth-Century Married Life* (London: Routledge, 1992), p. 126.

time took her for a prostitute, and seized hold of her leg. She being indignant
at this treatment, released herself from her husband's grasp, and returned to the
friend's house. She lived with him for a month afterwards, and then left him.

The pain here is not in the blow, but in the meaning attached to it. That a
respectable woman should be taken for a whore, as a result of her husband's actions,
was enough to constitute severe mental suffering. 'A man who has insulted his wife
by treating her in the street like a common prostitute is guilty of at least as great an
indignity as if he had spat in her face.'[55]

In the 1860s, while Eliot drew attention to the 'vulgar details' which have made or
broken many a humble life, the Divorce Court began to acknowledge not only the
fear in which a violent husband might put his wife by his violence, but the anxiety
and nausea he might provoke in her by his conduct and attitudes. Elizabeth and
George Boynton married on 25 July 1849. From the start, he was easily provoked
to violence. In October 1850, after a quarrel in a shop in Brussels, he dragged her
back to their hotel, and assaulted her in the lobby. When they returned from abroad,
in 1852, and settled in Yorkshire, he began to see other women. They separated
in April 1858. If Elizabeth Boynton could prove the adultery and the physical
violence, she had ample grounds for divorce. Significantly, her petition of 20 August
1858 supplements the charge of physical violence with a charge of non-physical
violence. The charge is that George Boynton, a devotee of the turf, 'introduced
your Petitioner to and compelled her to sit at table with a low person, apparently
a trainer, whose conduct and language were so disgusting as to excite the wonder
of your Petitioner's servants at the indignity put upon her by her said husband, in
so compelling your Petitioner to associate and sit at table with such a person.'[56] In
theory, such indignities carried less weight than a slap or kick, indeed no weight at
all. But Elizabeth Boynton's petition was by no means alone in placing a great deal
of emphasis upon them. The idea of indignity, the idea that a respectable woman
should be made to sit at table with a low person, was perhaps easier to grasp, or had
begun to be thought more shocking, than the idea of a physical injury whose traces
had long since disappeared. At any rate, petitioners tended to elaborate at greater
length on disgusting than on violent conduct. Like Dr Handley, they converted fear
into anxiety and nausea.

Kelly v. *Kelly* (1869) was, as James Hammerton has shown, 'a turning-point in
the law of matrimonial cruelty, since it established clearly that non-violent cruelty
might justify a decree, and departed from the earlier strict requirement of physical
violence.'[57] Frances Kelly petitioned for a judicial separation from her husband,
Rev. James Kelly, Anglican vicar of St George's, in Liverpool, on the grounds of
cruelty. The Kellys were married in 1841, and had one surviving son. Towards the
end of 1867, after a dispute about money, James Kelly became convinced that his
wife was plotting against him, and instituted, in the Judge's words, 'a deliberate

---

55   164 *ER*, p. 1508.
56   P. R. O. divorce files, *Boynton* v. *Boynton* (1860), J77/2/B27. When quoting at length from
petitions or related material in these files, I have where appropriate added punctuation.
57   Hammerton, *Cruelty and Companionship*, p. 94.

system of conduct towards his wife with the view of bending her to his authority.'
'He commenced opening her letters, and calling her a vile traitor and apostate.
He told her that no modest woman would associate with her more than with a
prostitute.' For several months, he had little or no communication with his wife,
except to rebuke and reproach her. In May 1868, Frances fell ill. She visited relatives
in Wales and Ireland. In October, she returned home, and was once again subjected
to her husband's 'system of conduct'. She was 'entirely deposed' from her 'natural
position' as mistress of her husband's household. Again, James watched her every
movement, but rarely spoke to her. 'On these occasions he appears to have occupied
the short time they were together in, what he called, putting her sin before her, in
strong, coarse, and abusive terms, applying to her the same epithets and language
as would be applicable to a woman who had been guilty of adultery.' Treated like
a child or a lunatic, even though she was over sixty, Frances again fell ill. Granting
a separation, the Judge declared that James Kelly 'had suffered his mind to become
filled and mastered by notions utterly extravagant, both as to the authority of a
husband, and the legitimate means of enforcing it'.[58] Kelly's conduct became a
touchstone for definitions of matrimonial cruelty.

Of particular interest for the current enquiry is the fact that the Divorce Court
had begun to take into account not only the mental suffering inflicted by violations
of social status, but also the mental suffering inflicted by the contingencies of
co-existence and co-habitation. Cornelius Green, a thirty-four-year-old widower,
son of a gentleman, married Emily, a builder's daughter, on 6 May 1896. His
gentlemanliness soon wore thin. On 11 August 1896, Emily filed for divorce, citing
his 'many acts of cruelty'. The Court required her, as it frequently did, to supply
'further and better particulars' of the acts of cruelty. By far the most vivid of the
particulars she supplied a month later are those which concern, not the appalling
physical violence Cornelius subjected her to, but the messes he made in their house.
'He emptied the contents of the Teapot on the Dining Room table. He fried steak
in [the] Kitchen, and then brought the pan into the dining room and emptied all the
fat and grease into the dining room fireplace, and cut up Cucumber and onions on
the table, and used abusive language to the said Emily Green.' On another occasion,
he pushed her about, kicked her, and spat in the face. 'He emptied the saucepan of
soup and bones on [the] floor of [the] Kitchen and then trod it about the house.'[59]
The case did not come to court, so we will never know what the learned Judge
would have made of these messes. It is significant, all the same, that Emily Green
made so much of them.

One does not want to exaggerate the effect of accusations of non-violent abuse.
On 25 January 1893, Clifford John Cory, a colliery proprietor, married Jane Anne,
daughter of an army officer. She left him two months later to the day, and on 23
May 1894 sued for a judicial separation, citing cruelty, unkindness, and coarse
language. According to her, Clifford had intercepted letters to and from her mother,
and showed them to other people. In the presence of members of his own family,

58   2 *Law Reports (Probate and Divorce)*, pp. 32–37.
59   *Green* v. *Green* (1896): J77/593/18122.

he announced that he had been 'bustled' into marriage with 'indecent haste'; this sentiment notwithstanding, he also proved inordinately jealous, accusing her, in the presence of her mother and her maid, of unchastity before marriage. She, too, was asked to provide further and better particulars of the cruelty. She said that he come naked into her room, and come into her room while she was in the bath. Furthermore, he 'insisted on addressing coarse and unrefined remarks to the Petitioner in regard to his own previous experience of ladies, and as to girls sitting out with men in dark corners of ball rooms, and asking the Petitioner whether men had ever put their hands up her petticoat.'[60] These accusations appear to have had little or no effect, probably because they did not demonstrate a threat to health. The petition was dismissed on 21 June 1895. Again, though, it is surely significant that Jane Anne Cory thought it worth her while to insist upon her husband's personal habits: his coarse remarks, his coming naked into her room. She did not fear him. She loathed him. And she had reason to believe that the Court would acknowledge her loathing.

By the 1890s, petitions for divorce had long since incorporated the kind of personal habit which so damages Rufus Lyon in his daughter's eyes. When Graham Smith sued for divorce on the grounds of his wife's adultery, in April 1882, she accused him in return of 'scurrilous and filthy language', and of smoking in her presence shortly after her recovery from the breakdown his language had driven her to. Furthermore, on a later occasion, when they were returning from Ascot in their carriage, 'the Petitioner used very abusive and foul language to the Respondent in the presence of his niece and young lady visitor.'[61] The Court recognized anxiety rather than fear in Anne Smith's response: it recognized a *Befindlichkeit* for which the only remedy was legal separation. Commenting in May 1891, in the aftermath of the celebrated Clitheroe case, where the verdict again went with the wife, Eliza Lynn Linton complained that marriage had become a 'voluntary union during pleasure', and that women were now free to leave their husbands on a mere caprice: an aversion to tobacco, perhaps, or incompatible tastes in music.[62]

What the Divorce Court records reveal is that Esther Lyon's unwillingness to overlook her father's dirt and stench had, in the aftermath of *Kelly* v. *Kelly*, received a measure of public acknowledgement. By the 1890s, perhaps, Felix Holt would not have been able to dismiss her revulsion as mere fastidiousness. It seems to me that the acknowledgement of the meaning and value of anxiety and nausea, whether by the London Divorce Court or by the readers of nineteenth-century novels and sanitary reports, solicits a fuller and more versatile account of the psychopathology of everyday modern life than we have yet been given.

---

60   *Cory* v. *Cory* (1895): J77/537/16393.
61   *Smith* v. *Smith* (1882): J77/275/8081.
62   Eliza Lynn Linton, 'The Judicial Shock to Marriage', *Nineteenth Century*, 29 (1891), 691–700: quoted by Shanley, *Feminism, Marriage, and the Law*, p. 182.

CHAPTER 2

Household Clearances in Victorian Fiction

The deathbed apart, there are few more scenes more profoundly disturbing in nineteenth-century fiction than household clearance, or the process of 'selling up': the identification of domestic material goods for sale at auction, either *in situ*, or elsewhere. Of course, we should not be surprised at this, if the Victorians took the idea of home anything like as seriously as they made out. How could such a violation or wilful sacrifice of domesticity *not* prove as profoundly disturbing to those who witnessed it as to its victims? How could it not constitute a traumatic event? But I want to argue that scenes of household clearance in nineteenth-century fiction possess a density and an edge which at once falls short of and exceeds any shock they might have administered to the sensibilities of the house-proud. Such scenes expose to critical view an aspect of existence generally understood, then as now, not to benefit from too much direct illumination: mortality. Illuminate it, however, they most certainly do. Far from extinguishing fiction's will to represent in trauma, the dismay and loathing provoked by the scene of household clearance renew its vigour.

Some Household Clearances

Chapter 17 of W. M. Thackeray's *Vanity Fair* (1847–48) describes the sale by auction of the possessions of John Sedley, a City of London merchant who has gone bankrupt. The chapter begins with Thackeray, in Bunyanesque mood, contemplating the moral to be drawn from the advertisements for sale by auction which at that time covered the back page of *The Times*. Here is an example, from *The Times* of 10 March 1847 (the part of the novel containing Chapter 17 appeared in *Punch* in May 1847).

Bedford row.

MESSRS. DEBENHAM and STORR will SELL by AUCTION, upon the Premises, 11, Chapel-street, Bedford row. Tomorrow, March 11. at 12. by order of the Executors of the late Miss Burrows, all the capital HOUSEHOLD FURNITURE, a handsome rosewood drawing room suite in blue damask, comprising chairs, sofa, card, loo, and occasional tables, what-nots, and

Davenport, Brussels carpets, or-moulu suspending lamp, noble chimney and pier glasses, two superior Spanish mahogany pedestal sideboards, (one of them with plate-glass door and back,) a set of mahogany extending dining tables, an eight-feet Spanish mahogany winged wardrobe, handsome toilet and wash stands with marble top, four-post and French bedsteads, and suitable bedding, numerous kitchen requisites, cut glass, china, &c. may be viewed on the day previous to and on the morning of sale, when catalogues may be obtained upon the premises; of Mr. Handisyde, 55. Lamb's Conduit-street; and of Messrs. Debenham and Storr, auctioneers and valuers, King-street, Covent-garden.[1]

All that remains of Miss Burrows is the faint trace of the meaning these objects might once vividly have held for her; and the auctioneer's insinuating prose (a *handsome* rosewood drawing-room suite, two *superior* Spanish mahogany pedestal sideboards) does its level best to rub that out. Even so, who, Thackeray asks, witnessing 'this sordid part of the obsequies of a departed friend', could fail to feel 'some sympathies and regrets'?[2]

Still, pathos, or moral enquiry, was by no means all he was after. The melancholic rumination on advertisements gives way to a much spikier account of the goings-on in a house which could be any house whose owner has died recently, or lost a lot of money, including the Sedley mansion in Russell Square:

How changed the house is, though! The front is patched over with bills, setting forth the particulars of the furniture in staring capitals. They have hung a shred of carpet out of an upstairs window — a half-dozen of porters are lounging on the dirty steps — the hall swarms with dingy guests of oriental countenance, who thrust printed cards into your hand and offer to bid. Old women and amateurs have invaded the upper apartments, pinching the bed-curtains, poking into the feathers, shampooing the mattresses, and clapping the wardrobe drawers to and fro. (*VF* 201)

There is a new energy in the writing, here. Something has stirred within Thackeray's elegiac tone, so that he now finds it hard to distinguish between dismay at all the pinching and poking and racial hatred. The dingy guests of oriental countenance *swarming* in the hall seem by their actions to justify a measure of social and cultural pest-control. Two years after this instalment of the novel was published, Thackeray's friend Lady Blessington had to sell up, ignominiously. He could not resist taking a look.

I have just come away from a dismal sight — Gore House full of Snobs looking at the furniture — foul Jews, odious bombazeen women who drove up in mysterious flies wh. they had hired, the wretches, to be fine as to come in state to a fashionable lounge — Brutes keeping their hats on in the kind old drawing-rooms — I longed to knock some of 'em off: and say Sir be civil in a lady's room.[3]

---

1   'Sales by Auction', *The Times*, 10 March 1847, p. 12.
2   W. M. Thackeray, *Vanity Fair: A Novel without a Hero*, ed. by John Sutherland (Oxford: Oxford University Press, 1983), p. 200. Henceforth *VF*.
3   Thackeray, *Letters and Private Papers*, ed. by Gordon N. Ray, 4 vols (Cambridge, MA: Harvard University Press, 1945–46), I, 532.

The contempt, sharpened by personal allegiance, is now all-embracing. Indeed, it barely stops short of fury. What, exactly, has provoked it? The contempt hesitates, as such feelings often do, between absorption in existence as such and a compensatory symbolic adjustment to or complaint about the unfairness of it all. Both kinds of feeling merit description as phobia. One is a compulsive and compelling disquiet, the other an ideology. Critically, they need to be kept apart.

In the novel, if not the letter, Thackeray's account of what happens when a person's worldly goods are prepared for auction is unrelentingly particular. This is a household turned inside out for inspection, laid bare in its material being; indeed, understood as matter. And it is hard not to sense, at the same time as the fierce moral indignation, a certain relish. Thackeray may not like the invasive bargain-hunters, who pinch bed-curtains, poke pillows, prod ('shampoo') mattresses, and clap wardrobe drawers to and fro; but he likes describing their penetration into the very substance of objects customarily rendered to all intents and purposes invisible by habitual use. He enjoys as a writer the brutality he deplores as a moralist. Whatever may have motivated it, the description seems utterly unforgiving. It is hard to see how there could be any redemption for those who pinch and prod, or keep their hats on in kind old drawing-rooms. Indeed, so intense is the feeling produced in him by the spectacle that Thackeray, in the novel at any rate, draws back a little from it. For the resumption of the narrative, in a lengthy account of the sale of the Sedley family's possessions, cherished and uncherished, does at least hold out the hope that something may yet be saved from the wreckage. Chapter 17 of *Vanity Fair* is entitled: 'How Captain Dobbin Bought a Piano'. The piano Captain Dobbin buys is Amelia Sedley's; he will restore it to her, without advantage to himself, as soon as he gets the chance (*VF* 221–23). We could even say that narrative itself, by resuming at all, by advancing purposefully, and so demonstrating that purpose is conceivable, in literature if not always in life, has got the novel out of the hole into which too bleak a description had dug it.

Some Theories

How might we explain what is revealed in and through scenes of household clearance? It would seem to be a topic tailor-made for object studies, or 'thing-theory'. In such scenes, objects predominate. But I am not convinced that thing-theory can help us, here. What troubles me about that mode of enquiry is its ineradicable preoccupation with subjectivity.

Object studies could be said to take its bearings from Max Weber's claim, in an essay of 1916, that 'culture' will come when people in general have learnt how to address themselves to the simple inanimate things of life: a pot, a cup, a piece of calico, a chair. To address yourself to the simple things of life, Weber goes on, is at once to appreciate them and to see them with a 'penetrating' eye; in seeing them, we see ourselves. 'What first reads like the effort to accept things in their physical quiddity,' Bill Brown has observed of Weber's thesis, 'becomes the effort to penetrate them, to see through them, and to find [...] within an object [...] the subject.' For Brown, it would seem, the subject is all there is to find 'within' objects. The texts he discusses in his study of the 'object matter' of American literature are texts which 'ask why and how we use objects to make meaning, to make or re-make ourselves, to organize our anxieties and affections, to sublimate our fears and shape our fantasies.'[4]

Object studies, thus conceived, has both an historical and a phenomenological or psychoanalytic dimension. Among the theorists Brown has in mind as discoverers of the subject in objects are Heidegger, Lacan, and Bachelard. Peter Schwenger, in his book about melancholy and physical objects in literature and painting, adds Sartre, Blanchot, and Baudrillard to the list. Schwenger's topic is the distinctive feeling generated in and by the subject's perception of an object. 'This perception, always falling short of full possession, gives rise to a melancholy that is felt by the subject and is ultimately *for* the subject.' Failing to grasp the object fully, even as we perceive it, we fail to grasp ourselves as fully perceiving subjects. The subject's 'embodiedness in the world' will never achieve even that 'degree of focus' which perception grants the object. Out of that failure, Schwenger concludes, arises the melancholy which has proved the stimulus to so much still-life art and literature, as well as to the activities of collecting, classification, and connoisseurship.[5]

Thackeray, contemplating the back page of *The Times*, with its serried catalogues of objects in limbo, grows melancholic. But at the moment when he begins to imagine a particular household turned inside out by the prospect of auction, his mood alters. What arouses him, now, what engages him, are the consequences of a ferocious pinching and poking. The attention he devotes to the pinching and poking is as little melancholic as the activity itself. We could say that he has held melancholy back, for Dobbin's subsequent purchase of the piano. Melancholy belongs to narrative. The description of household clearance yields some other feeling altogether.

In contrast to phenomenological or psychoanalytic approaches, historicism emphasizes the reader's attribution of social and political meaning to objects the literary text invites her or him at once to look at (by describing them in detail) and to overlook (by doing no more than describe them). Elaine Freedgood has recently argued that many of these objects, although inconsequential in the text's 'rhetorical hierarchy', turn out to have been 'highly consequential in the world in which the text was produced'. Her primary example is the 'old mahogany' furniture which Jane Eyre installs in Moor House, the home of the Rivers siblings, who have taken her in after her departure from Thornfield. Understood in historical context, Freedgood claims, the mahogany tells a story of 'imperial domination' strikingly at odds with the novel's 'manifest narrative', from which empire is expunged by Bertha Mason's suicide.[6] Jane Eyre's furniture, then, which the novel's 'manifest

4   Bill Brown, *The Sense of Things: The Object Matter of American Literature* (Chicago, IL: Chicago University press, 2004), pp. 12, 4.

5   Peter Schwenger, *The Tears of Things: Melancholy and Physical Objects* (Minneapolis: University of Minnesota Press, 2006), pp. 2–3.

6   Elaine Freedgood, *The Ideas in Things: Fugitive Meaning in the Victorian Novel* (Chicago, IL: University of Chicago Press, 2006), pp. 2–3.

narrative' at once looks at and overlooks, had a hidden social and political meaning. But for whom? What subject, melancholy or otherwise, what set of anxieties about empire, is to be found 'within' the old mahogany? To that question, which her own argument continually raises, Freedgood has no real answer. It is a shame, perhaps, that Miss Burrows, proud possessor of 'two superior Spanish mahogany pedestal sideboards (one of them with plate-glass door and back)' and an 'eight-feet Spanish mahogany winged wardrobe', did not quite live long enough to read *Jane Eyre*. Thackeray, a connoisseur of the back page of *The Times*, could easily have incorporated such specification, and with it a hint of social and political meaning, into the account he gave of household clearance in *Vanity Fair*. He chose instead to think about mattresses and wardrobes in general, and what might happen to them when inspected vigorously. No more than melancholy do the histories of deforestation and slavery appear to be the point of the account. His compulsive and compelling disquiet enquires into existence as such, rather than in the meaning and value attributed to it, for better or for worse.

Genre as Context

Freedgood is right, I think, to conceive of a 'rhetorical hierarchy' which in large measure determines what the reader can or cannot make out of the objects a novel at once looks at and overlooks. But rather than use a historical knowledge of the production of an object or substance in order to unsettle the hierarchy which has (in theory) hitherto obscured its significance, we should investigate the history of the formation of that hierarchy: that is, the history of the development of the novel as a genre. Under what generic conditions have objects appeared as objects in the literary text? And did that appearance, at its most complete, depend upon a fundamental re-ordering of the elements of fiction?

'Narrate or Describe?' Georg Lukács asked, in an essay of 1936 which charts the novel's sorry decline into Naturalism, from Scott and Balzac to Flaubert, Zola, and beyond. Lukács understood that decline as a re-ordering of the elements of fiction, to the point where description predominated over narrative. Revising this account slightly, we could say that Naturalist doctrine encouraged a particular kind of description, of a more or less de-populated environment, of objects without (or so it might seem) a subject. A predominance of description of that kind could be thought to affect adversely the novel's capacity to articulate meaning and value. 'Narration establishes proportions,' Lukács observed, 'description merely levels.'[7] It fails to sort the significant from the insignificant. Where there is proportion, one person understood in relation to another, person and environment conceived as foreground and background, as in Scott and Balzac, there can be meaning. And where there is meaning, there can be value (moral, social, political). I want to retain Lukács's distinction, even though the tendency among theorists now is to insist that description, too, narrates.[8]

7   Georg Lukács, 'Narrate or Describe?', in *Writer and Critic and Other Essays*, ed. and trans. by Arthur Kahn (London: Merlin Press, 1970), pp. 110–48 (pp. 127–28, 131).

8   Mieke Bal, 'Over-writing as Un-writing: Descriptions, World-Making, and Novelistic Time',

Lukács, as we have seen, located the fall into description somewhere between Balzac and Flaubert. But Henry James was surely not the first, and has not been the last, to marvel at Balzac's 'mighty passion for *things*'. For Balzac, James wrote, 'mise-en-scène' mattered as much as 'event'.[9] Mise-en-scène, or description, was the mode in which objects without a subject began to appear, on a grand scale, in the literary text. It is not that there are no things in eighteenth-century fiction. It is rather that the things there are there lack physical or sensuous texture.[10] They are not described in the sort of detail which would enable them to emerge as objects (relatively speaking) without a subject.

In eighteenth-century fiction, objects emerge as objects in and through the temporary suspension of narrative. Narrative's failure to establish proportion, for whatever reason, creates an opportunity for a performance of levelling. Heroes and heroines who have been brought low by misfortune or miscalculation, who are at an impasse, about whom there is for the moment nothing further to say, often find themselves in the company of objects whose existence does not depend on whether or not they have attracted that young person's attention. As the protagonists sink, so the novel sinks with them, from narrative to description. And those objects — described in detail, with full regard for physical, sensuous texture — are, more often than not, objects in a state of disrepair or decay: they have themselves been levelled. Defoe's Robinson Crusoe, contemplating the shipwreck which he alone has survived, remarks that the only sign he ever saw of his dead comrades was 'three of their Hats, one Cap, and two Shoes that were not Fellows'.[11] Not a great deal of sensuous texture there, perhaps: but Crusoe has observed the shoes closely enough to know that they are not fellows. Richardson's Clarissa Harlowe, after escaping from the brothel in which she had been raped, ends up in a bailiff's house, under arrest for debt, in surroundings so sordid that Belford cannot resist describing them to Lovelace in almost sumptuous detail.[12]

Protagonists brought low in this fashion would have to include Fanny Price, in *Mansfield Park* (1814), whose lengthy visit to her family in Portsmouth, in Chapter 46, forces her to acknowledge that her life has reached an impasse. Fanny feels the loss of Mansfield Park's moral and physical comforts acutely; she expects to hear at any moment that Edmund Bertram, the man she loves, has engaged himself to Mary Crawford; while Henry Crawford, a man she does not love, courts her assiduously. Austen renders this impasse by ceasing to tell us what is going on in her

in *The Novel*, ed. by Franco Moretti, 2 vols (Princeton, NJ: Princeton University Press, 2006), I, 571–610.

9   Henry James, 'Honoré de Balzac', in *Literary Criticism: French Writers, Other European Writers, The Prefaces to the New York Edition*, ed. by Leon Edel and Mark Wilson (New York: Library of America, 1984), pp. 31–68 (pp. 49–50). Emphasis in original.

10   Cynthia Wall, 'The Rhetoric of Description and the Spaces of Things', in *Eighteenth-Century Genre and Culture: Serious Reflections on Occasional Forms*, ed. by Dennis Todd and Cynthia Wall (Newark: University of Delaware Press, 2001), pp. 261–79.

11   Daniel Defoe, *Robinson Crusoe*, ed. by J. Donald Crowley (Oxford: Oxford University Press, 1983), p. 46.

12   Samuel Richardson, *Clarissa, or the History of a Young Lady*, ed. by Angus Ross (Harmondsworth: Penguin Books, 1985), pp. 1064–65.

head, and instead showing us what she sees: the 'stains and dirt' brought forward by the 'sickly glare' of sunlight through the parlour window.

> She sat in a blaze of oppressive heat, in a cloud of moving dust, and her eyes could only wander from the walls, marked by her father's head, to the table cut and notched by her brothers, where stood the tea-board never thoroughly cleaned, the cups and saucers wiped in streaks, the milk a mixture of motes floating in thin blue, and the bread and butter growing every minute more greasy than even Rebecca's hands had first produced it. Her father read his newspaper, and her mother lamented over the ragged carpet as usual, while the tea was in preparation, and wished Rebecca would mend it; and Fanny was first roused by his calling out to her, after humphing and considering over a particular paragraph: 'What's the name of your great cousins in town, Fan?'[13]

What 'brings forward' stains and dirt that might otherwise have slept on unnoticed is the frustration of narrative desire: of Fanny's desire for Edmund, of the reader's desire for crystallizing event. There is melancholy, here, to be sure, as Fanny's eyes 'wander' from one stain to another. But it is not a melancholy provoked by the stains themselves, which are too much the outcome of other people's habitual actions, and other people's habitual feelings about those actions, for Fanny to find herself in them. Fanny's eyes level down to matter or stuff already levelled down to the point where there is no proportion in it any longer. The hiatus is soon at end. Austen, feeling, perhaps, on her own part, and on our part, that narrative desire has been frustrated for long enough, supplies an event. The butter is not a moment greasier before Mr Price broadcasts the news of Henry Crawford's elopement with Maria Rushworth. Edmund is free again! Fanny will be able to resume immediately the 'active indispensable employment' she craves.

These examples from Defoe, Richardson, and Austen make me want to insist on the negative function of a certain kind of description: the description, itself a levelling down, of objects levelled down to matter or stuff. Such descriptions are a description of the world as it will be like when we are no longer here to see it (when for us there is no longer any narrative desire to be frustrated). They oblige us to conceive the indifference of a subject to objects which are already indifferent to it. They are prospective, and therefore not melancholic. The prospect almost excludes meaning and value altogether. That almost exclusion defines the nature and scope of nausea's critique.

Commodity Fetishism

With Balzac, James said, the book fills up with things. But what kinds of things? There are, to be sure, descriptions in the nineteenth-century novel after Balzac of the equivalent of pairs of shoes that don't match, where the not matching is the point, and streaky cups and saucers, where the streakiness is the point. But there are also descriptions, by the yard, of arrays of objects whose significance is not in

---

13   Jane Austen, *Mansfield Park*, ed. by Kathryn Sutherland (Harmondsworth: Penguin Books, 1996), pp. 362–63.

doubt: for example, of objects which stand forth primarily in and through their potential exchange-value. The social and cultural transformation which above all made new work for description was the establishment in nineteenth-century life and literature of the commodity as the object par excellence. Novels began to fill up with commodities.

The objects described in detail in eighteenth- and early nineteenth-century novels are often objects laid low by accident or neglect. A commodity, by contrast, is an object raised in and through its preparedness for exchange — its abstraction from the sensuous human activity of which it is the product — to the status of an idea. Marx's chapter on commodity-fetishism in *Das Kapital* defines commodification as a form of transcendence, so that the common household table stands not only with its feet on the ground, but, in relation to all other commodities, 'on its head,' evolving out of its wooden brain 'grotesque ideas'.[14] Studies of nineteenth-century commodity culture have taught us that the commodity 'steps forth as commodity,' in Marx's phrase, in shop-window, exhibition hall, and novel alike, by reason of its self-transcendence. According to Thomas Richards, it was the Great Exhibition of 1851 which demonstrated 'once and for all that the capitalist system had not only created a dominant form of exchange but was also in the process of creating a dominant form of representation to go along with it.'[15] Commodification turned things into signs. Object studies has on the whole sought to distance itself, in its concern for the objectness of objects, from such accounts of the 'culture of consumption'.[16] But we may need to return to them if we are to understand the objectness of the objects on view in a household clearance, objects, I shall argue, at once newly consumable and already beyond consumption.

Andrew Miller has argued that *Vanity Fair* imagines more thoroughly than any other Victorian novel the 'fetishistic reduction of the material environment to commodities, to a world simultaneously brilliant and tedious, in which value is produced without reference either to the needs or to the hopelessly utopian desires of characters.' According to Miller, Thackeray's main interest lay in the stimulus provided by the display of private possessions at public auction to the recirculation not only of wealth but of 'significance'. Jos Sedley's 'significance' certainly suffers some recirculation when a portrait of him on an elephant is put up for sale, and eventually knocked down for half a guinea, amid much ribaldry, to Rawdon and Becky Crawley. There is a reduction, here, from one kind of significance to another, from cherished possession to mere commodity. In theory, it is possible to restore value and meaning to objects thus reduced by means of moral action. Some young stockbrokers buy back 'one dozen well-manufactured spoons and forks at per oz., and one dozen dessert ditto ditto' on Mrs Sedley's behalf; while Captain Dobbin, hopelessly in love with Amelia Sedley, fiancée of his best friend and fellow-officer George Osborne, bids, as we have seen, for her piano. As Miller points out, objects

14   Karl Marx, *Capital*, trans. by Ben Fowkes, 3 vols (Harmondsworth: Penguin Books, 1976), I, 163–64.
15   Thomas Richards, *The Commodity Culture of Victorian England: Advertising and Spectacle, 1851–1914* (Stanford, CA: Stanford University press, 1990), p. 3.
16   For example, Brown, *Sense of Things*, p. 13.

can gain a 'lonely meaning' for Thackeray's characters through 'an allegorical process in which they seem to prefigure a distant realm of satisfaction'. However, such 'libidinal' transcendence of an object's commodity-status rarely proves anything other than a delusion.[17] When Amelia learns, many years later, that it was Dobbin who bought the piano on her behalf, not George Osborne, as she had always supposed, it at once ceases to have any value for her (*VF* 758–59).

I am not sure that 'libidinal' quite covers the nature and extent of Mrs Tulliver's emotional investment in her silver tea-pot, in George Eliot's *The Mill on the Floss* (1860), but there is a kind of loneliness to that, too, which the novel explores during an extended account of the consequences of Mr Tulliver's bankruptcy. The Tullivers will have to sell up, and a chapter entitled 'Mrs Tulliver's Teraphim, or Household Gods' shows her seated in the store-room inspecting her 'laid-up treasures'. Eliot pokes gentle fun at Mrs Tulliver's abiding anxiety that the silver tea-pot will end up in the local inn, 'being scratched, and set before the travellers and folks — and my letters on it — see here — E. D. — and everybody see 'em'.[18] But there is a serious concern, too, with the potential loss of the history sedimented in personal possessions, a history which can easily come to mean either too little or too much. The title of the chapter refers to Judges 18. 14–20, in which armed men forcibly remove 'household gods', the ephod and the teraphim, from the house of their possessor. In this case, the moral action required to restore meaning and value will indeed prove biblical in scope. However, a necessary emphasis on the auction as a system for the recirculation of wealth and significance should not be allowed to obscure the intensity of the interest shown by writers like Thackeray and Eliot in what precedes it: in the curious condition of abandonment which afflicts a household awaiting clearance.

We have already witnessed Thackeray's distress, in life and in literature, at such dismal sights. Eliot, concerned though she is above all to explore the moral implications of being sold up, or having the bailiff in the house, none the less takes trouble to register the nauseous sensation it induces. The first thing Tom and Maggie Tulliver notice when they return home on the fateful day is an overpowering smell of tobacco. 'There was a coarse, dingy man, of whose face Tom had some vague recollection, sitting in his father's chair, smoking, with a jug and glass beside him.'[19] Dismal sights can usually be held at distance: an odour is already inside us by the time we notice it. Thackeray and Eliot were not alone in thinking that such physical revulsions mattered.

There is a vivid instance in Charles Reade's *Hard Cash* (1863).[20] Despite his novel's title, Reade was not interested primarily in the recirculation of value and

17   Andrew Miller, *Novels behind Glass: Commodity Culture and Victorian Narrative* (Cambridge: Cambridge University Press, 1995), pp. 9, 21, 202, 205–06, 35.
18   George Eliot, *The Mill on the Floss*, ed. by A. S. Byatt (Harmondsworth: Penguin Books, 1979), pp. 281, 294.
19   Ibid., p. 280.
20   Other instances well worth investigating would include Anthony Trollope, *Framley Parsonage*, ed. by P. D. Edwards (Oxford: Oxford University Press, 1980), p. 527; and Gustave Flaubert, *Madame Bovary* (Paris: Gallimard, 1972), p. 377.

meaning, any more than he was in melancholy, or the social and political history of objects. What interested him was rawness, or stuff: the matter in material culture.

> Jane Hardie had found Albion Villa in the miserable state that precedes an auction; the house raw, its contents higgledy-piggledy. The stair carpets, and drawing-room carpets, were up, and in rolls in the dining-room; the bulk of the furniture was there too; the auction was to be in that room. The hall was clogged with great packages, and littered with small, all awaiting the railway carts; and Edward, dusty and deliquescent, was cording, strapping, and nailing them at the gallop, in his shirt sleeves.[21]

Albion Villa and its inhabitants have been brought down low, into a 'miserable state'. The misery inhibits narrative. That failure becomes the opportunity for description: for a description of objects without (or so it might seem) a subject. Reade finds a suitably down-to-earth term for this misery. The *OED* defines 'higgledy-piggledly' as a vocal gesture, the word conforming to the thing described: 'whether founded on *pig*, with some reference to the disorderly and utterly irregular fashion in which a herd of these animals huddle together, is uncertain, though examples show that such an association has often been present to persons using it.' Even the chief human being on the scene, dusty and deliquescent, appears to have been reduced to matter.

Scenes of household clearance imagine the object's double reduction: from household god to commodity; from commodity to matter, or stuff. The first reduction deprives objects of their past, of that surplus of meaning and value they have acquired since their purchase: of everything but their exchange value in the here and now. It can, of course, be quite brutal, as in the case of Mrs Tulliver's silver tea-pot. But the transaction at issue does no more (or no worse) than replace the meaning and value a commodity has had for one person by the meaning and value it will sooner or later have for another. It thus remains possible to see how, under favourable circumstances, or as a result of charitable intervention, its original meaning and value might be restored to it. In *Vanity Fair*, the young stockbrokers buy back Mrs Sedley's spoons for her. In Elizabeth Gaskell's *Cranford* (1853), some 'friends in need' step in to spare Miss Matty, who has been ruined by the crash of the Town and County Bank, from recourse to the auctioneer.[22]

As often as not, however, in the scene of household clearance, a second reduction accompanies, and violently exacerbates, the first. This second reduction, enforced by the ruthless scepticism of the bargain-hunters who thumb curtains, prod mattresses, and clap wardrobe drawers to and fro, deprives the objects awaiting disposal not only of their past, but of their future as well. It demonstrates that these still radiant commodities have, beyond a certain point, no future at all. The thumbing and prodding threatens to expose them as the waste-matter they will before very long become. The reduction from commodity to waste-matter which household clearance distinctively fosters is not just the assault of one system of value and meaning on another. It is an assault on the very possibility of systems of

21   Charles Reade, *Hard Cash*, new edn (London: Chatto and Windus, n.d.), p. 306.
22   Elizabeth Gaskell, *Cranford*, ed. by Elizabeth Porges Watson and Charlotte Mitchell (Oxford: Oxford University Press, 1998), ch. 14.

value and meaning. Since this is literature, it is likely that the assault will have been mounted, ultimately, on behalf of meaning and value, or in the name of critique. That is what the world looks like when you stop having ideas about it, such scenes announce; and, furthermore, it is no bad thing to be reminded, on occasion, of its nakedness. One of literature's great assets is its ability *almost* to squeeze the meaning and value out of existence. To grasp the significance of that achievement, we will need more than the new ways of thinking about objects that thing-theory has to offer. We will need a way to think about objects *as they cease to be objects*.

I have proposed a generic context, because it may well be that a shift in the relation between narrative and description in the nineteenth-century novel recreated in modern terms the always useful illusion of a direct insight into the stuff of existence, into what happens when meaning and value appear to come to an end. To demonstrate as much would require a far more systematic account than I have been able to offer here of how and why narrative abruptly gives way to description, in the texts at issue. I would like to conclude, however, by suggesting that in the nineteenth-century as in the eighteenth-century novel, the stuff of existence gets laid bare at precisely the moment when the pressure to generate meaning and value is (for a variety of reasons) at its most intense; and nowhere more so than in novels which concern the moral and sentimental education of a young man of indeterminate origins. The topic of such novels is nothing less than the emergence and gradual self-definition during the nineteenth century of a professional or non-capitalist middle class.[23] At especially low points in their as yet none-too-brilliant careers, these young men find themselves after one fashion or another unable altogether to avoid the dismal sight of a household clearance. It happens to Pip, in Dickens's *Great Expectations* (1861); to Will Ladislaw, in Eliot's *Middlemarch* (1870–71), and to Jude, in Hardy's *Jude the Obscure* (1895).[24] All three feel thoroughly sick.

These episodes, in texts by writers as diverse as Dickens, Eliot, and Hardy, can surely be taken to indicate both the pervasiveness and the intrinsic interest of the scene or trope of household clearance. Indeed, they give that scene or trope an additional twist. In each case, the household whose clearance the young men witness is not their own, evidently, since a household is something they can still only aspire to. The event — or, rather, the levelling description it brings about — draws attention to the very specific problem of identity which afflicts those whose capital is symbolic through and through: those who only have their own integrity to sell, rather than muscle, or the contents of a bank account. For aspirants to professional status, at that particular moment in history, the dialectic of necessary illusion and necessary disillusionment which constitutes *Bildung*, or moral and sentimental

23   A topic I discuss at greater length in *Paranoid Modernism: Literary Experiment, Psychosis, and the Professionalization of English Society* (Oxford: Oxford University Press, 2001), ch. 3. The classic account is Harold Perkin, *The Origins of Modern English Society, 1780–1880* (London: Routledge & Kegan Paul, 1969).
24   Charles Dickens, *Great Expectations*, ed. by Charlotte Mitchell and David Trotter (Harmondsworth: Penguin Books, 1996), pp. 473–74; Eliot, *Middlemarch*, ed. by David Carroll and Felicia Bonaparte (Oxford: Oxford University Press, 1997), p. 574; Thomas Hardy, *Jude the Obscure*, ed. by Patricia Ingham (Oxford: Oxford University Press, 1985), p. 72.

education, must have appeared thoroughly perplexing. Nausea is vigorously at ontological work in these levelling descriptions of the spectacle of clearance. Its persistence suggests that disillusionment is necessary in *Bildung*, rather than merely the result of avoidable error. Whether that makes the whole experience less painful than it might be to a Mrs Tulliver, or more so, is of course open to debate.

CHAPTER 3

Dickens's Idle Men

The opening chapter of *American Notes* (1842) describes the two stages of Dickens's embarkation n the steam-packet *Britannia*, 'twelve hundred tons burden per register, bound for Halifax and Boston, and carrying Her Majesty's mails.' The first stage begins in sharp disillusionment, as a preliminary inspection exposes the inadequacy of the ship's facilities, and concludes, after a survey of a stewardess's 'merry eyes' and some convincing nautical bustle, with spirits partially recovered, and a return to solid ground for the night. The second stage begins with the final journey out to the packet, and a revival of Dickens's writerly interest in his fellow-passengers. The ship attracts murmurs of admiration.

> Even the lazy gentleman with his hat on one side and his hands in his pockets, who has dispensed so much consolation by inquiring with a yawn of another gentleman whether he is 'going across' — as if it were a ferry — even he condescends to look that way, and nods his head, as if to say 'No mistake about *that*'.

The lazy gentleman has made the passage thirteen times before, and soon acquires the status of a veteran, an expert, an oracle. He remains utterly unperturbed by the 'bewildering tumult' of departure.

> In the midst of all this, the lazy gentleman, who seems to have no luggage of any kind — not so much as a friend, even — lounges up and down the hurricane-deck, coolly puffing a cigar; and, as this unconcerned demeanour again exalts him in the opinion of those who have leisure to observe his proceedings, every time he looks up at the masts, or down at the decks, they look there too, as wondering whether he sees anything wrong anywhere, and hoping that, in case he should, he will have the goodness to mention it.[1]

One person who clearly does have the leisure to observe these proceedings, and to admire the unconcerned demeanour they reveal, is the author himself. The lazy gentleman establishes, through sheer laziness, a position that the observer, encumbered not only by luggage and friends, but by the duties of observation, would dearly like to occupy. Dickens, I will suggest, occasionally found the leisure in his fiction to reflect upon displays of unconcern: moments worth commenting on because they are, like the one in the opening chapter of *American Notes*, wonderfully poised and inventive.

1   Charles Dickens, *American Notes*, ed. by John S. Whitley and Arnold Goldman (Harmondsworth: Penguin Books, 1972), pp. 53, 58–60.

There can be no doubt about the lazy gentleman's dedication to laziness. Dickens encounters him once more on the voyage out when, miserably sea-sick, he stumbles up on deck in the middle of a storm.

> Even in that incapable state, however, I recognised the lazy gentleman standing before me: nautically clad in a suit of shaggy blue, with an oilskin hat. But I was too imbecile, although I knew it to be he, to separate him from his dress; and tried to call him, I remember, *Pilot*. After another interval of total unconsciousness, I found he had gone.[2]

One might hallucinate a function for this layabout by addressing him as 'pilot'. But he is not to be defined in that way. He has no function, either in life, as far as one can tell, or in the narrative. His departure from the tale, during an 'interval of total unconsciousness', is as abrupt as his entrance into it. He never reappears. Dickens accords him an epithet, but not a name, not a part to play.

This chapter is about the imaginative appeal of unconcern, of vacancy, of lack of purpose. I will try to demonstrate, first, that there is a connection between the idler's neglect of purposeful activity and his narrative inconsequence; and, secondly, that it is the narrative inconsequence which frees Dickens to write with a particular and extraordinary command. When he contemplates his lazy gentlemen, he grows as lazy as they are, as unencumbered by duties. I do not claim any great significance for them. Indeed, their appeal lies in their marginality.

Descriptions

In Dickens's fiction, the lazy gentlemen constitute a technique for the description of city life. In this respect, they perhaps have something in common with the *flâneurs*, those dandyish observers of the urban crowd who supposedly made the nineteenth-century arcades their own, and whose self-display and inquisitive detachment have been seen as symptomatic of the formation of recognizably modern attitudes to the city.[3] John Rignall has argued convincingly that in nineteenth-century realist fiction the *flâneur*'s remote yet curious gaze 'duplicates that of the novelist himself, who confidently assigns meaning to details of physical appearance, dress, and milieu, and reads the visible exterior as a clue to the truth or life behind it.' However, the novelist's self-mirroring is not necessarily uncritical: the *flâneur*'s frequent inability to make sense of what he sees, the perplexity into which his observations so often appear to plunge him, might be taken to mark the limit of realist technique.[4] Rignall's thesis illuminates the part played by strolling spectators in *Bleak House* (1852–53) and other novels. But the lazy gentlemen I wish to draw attention to differ from these spectators in two respects: first, their gaze does not so much duplicate that of the novelist as offer an enticing alternative to it; secondly, they make no effort to make sense of what they see, and therefore cannot be said either to succeed or to fail as interpreters.

2   Ibid., p. 65.
3   See *The Flâneur*, ed. by Keith Tester (London: Routledge, 1994).
4   John Rignall, *Realist Fiction and the Strolling Spectator* (London: Routledge, 1992), p. 2.

In Chapter 32 of *Nicholas Nickleby* (1832–33), Nicholas and Smike arrive in London by stagecoach. The spectacle which greets them exemplifies the baffling heterogeneity of city life.

> Streams of people apparently without end poured on and on, jostling each other in the crowd and hurrying forward, scarcely seeming to notice the riches that surrounded them on every side; while vehicles of all shapes and makes, mingled up together in one moving mass like running water, lent their ceaseless roar to swell the noise and tumult.

The noise and tumult happen *to* Nicholas and Smike, on the stage-coach roof, but not *for* them. They do not respond to it, and it does not reveal or provoke anything in them. Who, then, is it for? Dickens uses an impersonal construction ('it was curious to observe') to define the point of view from which the tumult is observed. The spectacle activates a generalized curiosity which might be thought to include Nicholas and Smike, but which does not belong to them. Half a page later, Dickens delivers a moralizing exegesis of it which is pretty clearly outside their current preoccupations. 'Life and death went hand in hand; wealth and poverty stood side by side; repletion and starvation laid them down together.'[5]

Dickens understood that he could not depend on his characters to convey what he himself knew about London. In *Oliver Twist* (1837–39), Oliver and Sikes, *en route* from Bethnal Green to Chertsey, pass through Smithfield Market, 'from which latter place arose a tumult of discordant sounds that filled Oliver Twist with amazement': there follows a description of tumult so resourceful that it evidently cannot be attributed to the dumbfounded child protagonist. Which would be fine, except that Dickens did usually feel obliged to attribute such descriptions to someone. The pseudo-biblical cadence of the passage I have quoted from *Nicholas Nickleby* ('repletion and starvation laid them down together') shows him invoking the wisdom of ages as a perspective on modern urban experience — and thus perhaps missing its specificity. What he needed was a point of view confined neither to the particular nor to the general.

Chapter 37 of *Nicholas Nickleby* introduces both the hero and the reader to the counting-house run by the Cheeryble brothers, situated in a pleasant backwater in the City.

> It is a quiet, little-frequented, retired spot, favourable to melancholy and contemplation, and appointments of long-waiting; and up and down its every side the Appointed saunters idly the hour together, wakening the echoes with the monotonous sound of his footsteps on the smooth worn stones, and counting first the windows and then the very bricks of the tall silent houses that hem him round about. (*NN* 553)

There is a new feeling here, about London: one of melancholy, perhaps, but a melancholy which does not incapacitate. The Appointed is kept waiting, and the wait subjects him to some monotonous pacing and calculating. But a man who 'saunters idly' is not a man whom the delay of business has reduced to anxiety or

---

5   Dickens, *Nicholas Nickleby*, ed. by Michael Slater (Harmondsworth: Penguin Books, 1978), pp. 488–89. Henceforth *NN*.

anger. He has that much in common with the lazy gentleman of *American Notes*. Idle sauntering is perhaps what he does best; and doing that best is an activity which reveals aspects of city life barely perceptible to those whose appointments are strenuously kept. It is an activity, we might note, which steadfastly refuses to become a point of view (a position from which meaning can be grasped or ascribed). Whereas the *flâneur* reads the city like a book, ceaselessly decoding manner and behaviour, Dickens's lazy gentlemen count bricks or stare into space.

This absolute failure to produce meaning dissociates the lazy gentlemen both from the wisdom of ages and from the novel's characters, whose narrative destinies require of them some measure of intentionality. The Appointed has no name. He plays no part in events. His disappearance, like his appearance, is abrupt and unmotivated. He constitutes a degree zero of narrative as well as of hermeneutic momentum. And yet he does make something happen. He makes possible a rhetorical event, in the ensuing description of the square. 'It is so quiet that you can almost hear the ticking of your own watch when you stop to cool in its refreshing atmosphere' (*NN* 553). Dickens steps outside the novel, for a moment, outside the preoccupations of his characters, in order to reveal an aspect of urban experience; and yet he does not feel the need to invoke a panoramic or generalizing perspective. The silence in which you listen for the sound of your own watch reproduces the hermeneutic degree zero of the silence in which the Appointed counts bricks; and it creates a further narrative degree zero, a bubble of inconsequence. For a moment, Dickens occupies the position marked out by an unnamed idler. The idler may or may not be refreshed by the square's atmosphere; the author certainly is, by this temporary suspension of narratorial responsibilities.

There is some reason to think that those responsibilities might have been weighing heavily on the author's shoulders. When Nicholas returns to London, in Chapter 32, it is in response to an urgent message from Newman Noggs. Not finding Newman at home, he wanders the streets, as he often does when anxious, and eventually turns into an expensive hotel for a pint of wine and a biscuit. There he overhears two dissolute men-about-town, Sir Mulberry Hawk and Lord Verisopht, discussing his sister Kate in salacious terms. *Nicholas Nickleby* is a novel about class, about the proper definition of gentility; and this stage-managed coincidence serves the purpose of introducing Nicholas at first hand to a gentility defined by status and appearance rather than by conduct. When he returns to London in Chapter 32, he returns to an allegorized city where rakes transparently abuse class privilege in pursuit of virtuous maidens. He will shortly encounter a gentility defined by conduct in the shape of the self-made and unsparingly charitable Cheeryble brothers. Chapter 37, which begins with the Appointed counting bricks, ends with a transparent display of Cheeryble-ness, as the brothers throw a party for their faithful old retainer, Tim Linkinwater. The inconsequence of the former event offers Dickens blissful if momentary relief from the gathering momentum of his own allegory. Unlike the *flâneurs*, Dickens's lazy gentlemen do not appear to be dandies; their function is to see, not to be seen. And yet they are men of leisure, or at least men unperturbed by the delay of business. It may be that their idleness, like that of the *flâneurs*, only in a more radical fashion, constitutes an implicit reproach to narratives which endorse strenuous self-making.

The tendency of criticism has been to tuck these loose ends back into the allegorical weave. A famous essay by Dorothy Van Ghent proposes that the view from the roof of Todgers's boarding-house, in *Martin Chuzzlewit* (1843–44), a view attributed to an unnamed — and not notably purposeful — observer, should be understood as characteristic of 'the Dickens world'. 'The prospect from Todgers's,' Van Ghent argues,

> Is one in which categorical determinations of the significance of objects — as of the chimney pots, the blank upper window, or the dyer's cloth — have broken down, and the observer on Todgers's roof is seized with suicidal nausea at the momentary vision of a world in which significance has been replaced by naked and aggressive existence.[6]

While there is undoubtedly some truth in this account, it may insist too much on the scene's centrality, and on the extreme nature of the breakdown it portrays.

Todgers's features prominently enough in the action of the novel. The Pecksniffs board there, and are visited there by Jonas Chuzzlewit, among others. Yet none of the main characters ever makes it as far as the roof. Whatever happens on the roof happens incidentally, by way of distraction from the gathering pace of events; events in which the unnamed observer plays no part at all. Indeed, the scene which unfolds would seem to be removed from action of any kind, or indeed representativeness of any kind, by the interest it manifestly takes in the mechanics of perception. 'After the first glance, there were slight features in the midst of this crowd of objects, which sprung out from the mass without any reason, as it were, and took hold of the attention whether the spectator would or no.'[7] The interlude on the roof allows Dickens to explore, as Edmund Husserl and Maurice Merleau-Ponty were later to do, the phenomenology of perception: to grasp the way in which the world appears to us by bracketing off conscious acts of mind (willing, judging, expecting, and so on).[8]

'The man who was mending a pen at an upper window over the way, became of paramount importance in the scene, and made a blank in it, ridiculously disproportionate in its extent, when he retired' (*MC* 188). The disproportion of the effect indicates that perception is never unmediated: that the mind makes sense of the world by processing sensory data in the context provided by data stored in the memory. The gap left by the pen-mender's retirement from the window is a gap left not so much *in* what is perceived as *between* what is seen and what is remembered: a gap created, one might say, in the mind's grasp of experience, in the illusion of stability it seeks to create. The rupture of that illusion might well

6   Dorothy Van Ghent, 'The Dickens World: The View from Todgers's', *Sewanee Review*, 58 (1950), 419–38 (p. 426).
7   Dickens, *Martin Chuzzlewit*, ed. by P. N. Furbank (Harmondsworth: Penguin Books, 1968), p. 188. Henceforth *MC*.
8   Edmund Husserl, *Cartesian Meditations*, trans. by Dorion Cairns (The Hague: Martinus Nijhoff, 1977); Maurice Merleau-Ponty, *The Phenomenology of Perception*, trans. by Colin Smith (London: Routledge & Kegan Paul, 1962).

be thought to provoke unease. But it is scarcely a moral or social unease. Dickens's phenomenology of perception scrupulously avoids, as yet, any gesture at 'naked and aggressive existence'. By exceeding the preoccupations of the novel's characters without recourse to a panoramic or generalizing perspective, by delineating a roof which is neither place of rendezvous nor panopticon, it makes for him a moment of blissful unconcern.

From this point on, however, the scene becomes increasingly self-conscious, and it is this self-consciousness, I would argue, which has been mistaken for a protest against naked and aggressive existence.

> The gambols of a piece of cloth upon the dyer's pole had far more interest for the moment than all the changing motion of the crowd. Yet even while the looker-on felt angry with himself for this, and wondered how it was, the tumult swelled into a roar; the hosts of objects seemed to thicken and expand a hundredfold; and after gazing round him quite scared, he turned into Todgers's again, much more rapidly than he came out; and ten to one he told M. Todgers afterwards that if he hadn't done so, he would certainly have come into the street by the shortest cut: that is to say, head-foremost. (*MC* 188–89)

This looker-on, unlike those I have discussed so far, is not entirely immune to narrative. He even extrudes a micro-narrative of his own, a story of panic and hasty descent, of 'suicidal nausea'. But we should note that the panic is to some extent self-induced. The looker-on feels guilty for allowing himself to find greater interest in the gambols of a piece of cloth (and in the appearance and disappearance of a man mending a pen) than in the changing motion of the crowd. He feels guilty because he has taken a holiday from the exegetic responsibilities of the strolling spectator. It is only *after* his guilt has become manifest that his failure to make sense of what he sees begins to unsettle him, and he feels sick. At this point, he enters a story, a story about the modern city, about naked and aggressive existence. While I would concede that the story he then recounts to M. Todgers is a disturbing one, I think that its significance lies less in the vision it conveys than in the speed with which it is hashed up. To my mind, the looker-on's belated guilt is also the novelist's. Dickens recoils from the pleasures of unmotivated observation into a micro-narrative whose hysteria betrays its origin. Another moment on the roof and he might have *become* Merleau-Ponty.

Inspectors

In Chapter 4 of *Nicholas Nickleby*, we encounter a variant of the 'lazy gentleman' trope. Nicholas and his uncle seek out Mr Wackford Squeers at the Saracen's Head Inn, Snow Hill. Dickens identifies the inn's yard as a site at once outside and inside the novel.

> When you walk up this yard, you will see the booking-office on your left, and the tower of Saint Sepulchre's church darting abruptly up into the sky on your right, and a gallery of bedrooms on both sides. Just before you, you will observe a long window with the words 'coffee-room' legibly painted above it; and looking out of that window, you would have seen in addition, if you had gone at the right time, Mr Wackford Squeers with his hands in his pockets. (*NN* 90)

On this occasion, the phantom observer is neither named nor designated by epithet. But he or she is like the lazy gentleman and the Appointed in conspicuously have no business, at a moment when the main characters are preoccupied with business; and in having no further part to play in the tale.

Chapter 4 opens in more abstract fashion, identifying the Saracen's Head not by the appearance it might present to an observer but by its proximity to nearby landmarks: Newgate, Smithfield Market, the 'squalid tottering houses' of Snow Hill. These landmarks are defined institutionally, through the positions they occupy in a social and economic system: 'at the very core of London, in the heart of its business and animation' (*NN* 89). We can sense, as Dickens lengthens his historical stride in the paragraphs which describe them, something of the threat they posed, in his mind, to the very possibility of business and animation. What emerges here is an institutional apprehension of the city which the later novels were to extend and refine considerably. The stroller in the yard thus obtrudes her or his laziness not only against Nicholas's embryonic career, but also against an institutional apprehension of the city, and indeed against the very idea that novels might have a strenuous diagnostic function.

Social commentary had always been an important feature of Dickens's novels. In the early 1940s, however, the emphasis altered from attacks on relatively isolated abuses like Poor Law reform or the Yorkshire schools to a general mapping of social and economic malaise. Dickens began to believe that they way to ensure the wealth of the nation was to ensure its health. One of his closest friends was his brother-in-law, Henry Austin, an engineer who had become involved in the politics of public health while working on the construction of the Blackwall Railway in East London. In 1842, Edwin Chadwick asked Austin to present a copy of his recent *Report on the Sanitary Condition of the Labouring Population of Great Britain* to Dickens. Dickens was at first suspicious of Chadwick, holding him responsible for the tyrannies of the 1834 Poor Law Amendment Act. But he soon relented. Throughout the 1840s he worked closely with Austin to promote sanitary reform, collaborating on articles and speeches. In 1848, Austin became Secretary to the General Board of Health. K. J. Fielding and A. W. Brice, who have examined this collaboration in detail, conclude that Dickens 'not only had access to the most important central authority on public health, on the sanitary problems brought by the great cities, and on measures to be taken against the dreaded visitation of cholera, but [...] was also enlisted as an ally and received help with his own writing in return.'[9] In the preface to the 1849 edition of *Martin Chuzzlewit*, he claimed that he had taken 'every possible opportunity' to expose in his novels the 'want of sanitary improvements' in the dwellings of the poor (*MC* 40).

The sanitary reformers argued that bad housing and bad drainage caused disease. Organic matter accumulated in cesspools and blocked drains putrefies and gives off a foul miasma, a 'disease-mist' or noxious gas; anyone inhaling the miasma sickens. Chadwick's solution was to pump water through a comprehensive system of glazed

---

9   K. J. Fielding and A. W. Brice, '*Bleak House* and the Graveyard', in *Dickens the Craftsman*, ed. by Robert B. Partlow (Carbondale: University of Illinois Press, 1970), pp. 115–39 (p. 128); and 'Dickens and the Tooting Disaster', *Victorian Studies*, 12 (1968), 227–44.

sewers, and so sweep away any deposits of solid matter before they could putrefy. He believed that 'continuous circulation' should be the fundamental principle of sanitary reform. In cities as in bodies, the primary cause of malfunction was blockage. Clear the blockage, and you restore the organism to health.

Sanitary reform was conceived as part of an ambitious programme of economic, social, and moral discipline. In *The Health of Nations*, a posthumous epitome and review of Chadwick's work published in 1887, the various essays on wealth and population are supplemented by others on every imaginable aspect of social and moral policing. Few things were beneath his notice. The last essay he wrote urges the issue of tricycles to the Metropolitan Police, for reasons of fitness as well as efficiency. Another draws attention to the disciplinary effects of Dickens's novels on an apprentice who, since he preferred reading to working, was invited to read aloud.

> The idle apprentice read from *Pickwick*, and soon the laughter became epidemic, with such an improvement in the rapidity of the work that the master appointed Tom to be reader in general, with the best success.

Chadwick reported the experiment to Dickens, assigning to Tom 'the function, economically, of a fifer or drummer to animate, regulate, and quicken the march of production'.[10]

The credence Dickens gave to the metaphor of circulation produced in his later novels an almost obsessive recurrence to examples of blockage such as Newgate prison, Smithfield Market, and the Snow Hill slum. The sticky, foul-smelling deposits lodged in attic-rooms and burial-grounds find analogies in financial irregularity and administrative incompetence, in repressed feeling and the 'perpetual stoppage' of fashionable society.[11] The writing clots and exfoliates at such junctures as Dickens contemplates the effects of obstruction.[12] In a world mapped by metaphor there is as little room for an idle observer as there is for an idle apprentice. The early novels had, however, already created a place for a different kind of observer, a man (uniformly) with a keen and in some cases officially sanctioned appetite for meaning.

Consider, for example, the description of the Three Cripples, in *Oliver Twist* (1837–39), an inn notable for the moral 'repulsiveness' of its patrons.

> Cunning, ferocity, and drunkenness in all its stages, were there, in their strongest aspects; and women: some with the last lingering tinge of their early freshness almost fading as you looked: others with every mark and stamp of their sex utterly beaten out, and presenting but one loathsome blank of profligacy and crime; some mere girls, others but young women, and none past the prime of life; formed the darkest and saddest portion of this dreary picture.[13]

10   Edwin Chadwick, *The Health of Nations*, ed. by Benjamin Ward Richardson, 2 vols (London: Longmans, 1887), I, 354–55.

11   Dickens, *Bleak House*, ed. by Nicola Bradbury (Harmondsworth: Penguin Books, 1996), p. 211. Henceforth *BH*.

12   See David Trotter, *Circulation: Defoe, Dickens and the Economies of the Novel* (London: Macmillan, 1988).

13   Dickens, *Oliver Twist*, ed. by Peter Fairclough (Harmondsworth: Penguin Books, 1985), p. 237. Henceforth *OT*.

The distended syntax of this sentence reveals a desire at once to draw a general 'picture', from the moralist's position of relative detachment, and to savour novelistically its pungent detail: to narrow the focus first to the women present, and then to those women who most vividly display, for the benefit of an observer whose position is distinctly if faintly marked, the very process of corruption ('almost fading as you looked'). The excitement of observation, of simply being there, in such spectacularly low company, has to be reframed ('this dreary picture') even as the sentence advances so as to include a justifying alertness to social symbolism.

This alertness comes into play again as the novel reaches its climax, in Chapter 50, with the pursuit of Sikes to Jacob's Island, in Southwark, a neighbourhood which must rank as 'the filthiest, the strangest, the most extraordinary of the many localities that are hidden in London, wholly unknown, even by name, to the great mass of its inhabitants.' A neighbourhood so strange, so wholly unknown, is not susceptible to casual description. It requires a map, a plan of action. 'To reach this place, the visitor has to penetrate through a maze of close, narrow, and muddy streets.' It is through the eyes of the intrepid visitor that we see Jacob's Island.

> Jostling with unemployed labourers of the lowest class, ballast-heavers, coal-whippers, brazen women, ragged children, and the raff and refuse of the river, he makes his way with difficulty along, assailed by offensive sights and smells from the narrow alleys which branch off on the right and left, and deafened by the clash of ponderous wagons that bear great piles of merchandise from the stacks of warehouses that rise from every corner. (*OT* 442)

The emphasis on class differences ('unemployed labourers of the lowest class', 'raff and refuse of the river') serves to separate out and identify the visitor, even before we have registered the difficulties and dangers he faces on his journey. This is no idle observer. The only possible explanation for his presence among such offensive sights and smells is official business. He belongs, or might well belong, to the growing band of Chadwickian reformers. The next two paragraphs record the evidence such a man might want to examine: 'every repulsive lineament of poverty, every loathsome indication of filth, rot, and garbage' (443). In these lineaments and indications is the meaning the reformer seeks.

Passages such as this develop a position for the figure prepared institutionally and rhetorically by the social reform movement. Reports such as James Kay's *The Moral and Physical Condition of the Working Classes Employed in the Cotton Manufacture in Manchester* (1832) had already imagined the cholera doctor as an urban explorer.

> He whose duty it is to follow the steps of this messenger of death must descend to the abodes of poverty, must frequent the close alleys, the crowded courts, the overpeopled habitations of wretchedness, where pauperism and disease congregate round the source of social discontent and political disorder in the centre of our large towns, and behold with alarm, in the hot-bed of pestilence, ills that fester in secret, at the very heart of society.[14]

Dickens was not blind to the authority and the dramatic potential of the narrative

---

14   James Kay (later Kay-Shuttleworth), *The Moral and Physical Condition of the Working Classes Employed in the Cotton Manufacture in Manchester* (London: James Ridgway, 1832), p. 8.

position marked out by the reports of reformers like Kay. Where an implicitly purposeful 'visitor' or 'stranger' ventures in the early novels, an explicitly purposeful doctor or engineer will venture thereafter. *Dombey and Son* (1848) contrasts the magistrate's abstract denunciation of the poor with the reformer's empirical knowledge: 'follow the good clergyman or doctor, who, with his life imperilled at every breath he draws, goes down into their dens, lying within the echoes of our carriage wheels and daily tread upon the pavement stones.'[15] In *Bleak House*, we follow Allan Woodcourt into just such dens. It was through the eyes of men like Woodcourt that Dickens increasingly chose to view urban experience.

Enigma and its Antidotes

One kind of blockage which worried and excited Dickens was any obstruction of the flow of information upon which the business of the world depended. The metaphor of circulation which had given both shape and savour to his imagining of social process turned excessive or malevolent secrecy into an object of compelling horror. Think, for example, of the lawyer Tulkinghorn in *Bleak House* (1853), a 'silent repository' of 'family confidences' who hoards information as others hoard money (*BH* 58). Tulkinghorn's calling is, as Lady Dedlock points out, 'the acquisition of secrets, and the holding possession of such powers as they give him, with no sharer or opponent in it' (567). The criminality of his conduct needs (and receives) no explanation, because miserliness represented to Dickens the worst kind of 'perpetual stoppage'. In the later novels, the secretive secrete. Like a tumour, they extract matter from the bloodstream of society; and the matter they have extracted stagnates and festers in its hiding places. *Bleak House* abounds in characters dedicated to the acquisition of secrets which they hope to exploit for personal gain.

Such blockages could be cleared only by a new type of specialist: Nadgett, in *Martin Chuzzlewit*; Inspector Bucket, in *Bleak House*; and Pancks, in *Little Dorrit* (1855–57). These men do not merely resolve the particular mysteries which at once bind together and isolate the main protagonists. They enact the resolution of mystery itself. They cleanse and disinfect a landscape fouled by secretiveness. In this respect, they might be said to constitute a counter-type to the lazy gentlemen of the earlier novels. They are neither lazy nor gentlemen. Strenuously purposeful, tenacious to a fault, they do not merely scan a scene, as a stroller would, but devour it instantly, extract its essence, and then move on.

Dickens slyly compares type and counter-type by allowing his detectives to masquerade, on occasion, as idlers. Mr Nadgett, who makes enquiries on behalf of the Anglo-Bengalee Disinterested Loan and Life Assurance Company, is always keeping appointments in the City, 'and the other man never seemed to come'. He sits for hours in business coffee-houses, occasionally drying a damp handkerchief before the fire, and 'still looking for the man who never appeared' (*MC* 517). Even when in hot pursuit of a suspect, Inspector Bucket still manages to seem at a

---

15   Dickens, *Dombey and Son*, ed. by Peter Fairclough (Harmondsworth: Penguin Books, 1970), p. 737.

loose end. He 'pervades' houses and 'strolls about an infinity of streets: to outward appearance rather languishing for want of an object' (*BH* 768). No wonder lazy gentlemen are something of a rarity in the later novels: their very *modus operandi* has been requisitioned for official purposes.

It is those official purposes which now expose and render the city. Inspector Bucket, in search of Jo the crossing-sweeper, dives into a street 'reeking' with such smells that his companion, Snagsby, who has lived in London all his life, can scarcely believe his senses (*BH* 364). His pursuit of Lady Dedlock takes him and Esther Summerson down the 'narrowest and worst streets' in the capital (858). The very extremity of the pollution requires an informed and committed presence: a detective, a sanitary inspector. But Dickens could not quite bring himself to relinquish altogether the pleasures of vacancy. Indeed, he occasionally revived them, in the later novels, by temporarily de-commissioning a minor character: by releasing her or him, for a spell, from any obligations to the narrative.

The solicitor's clerk William Guppy, in *Bleak House*, belongs to a group of virulently malign petty-bourgeois blackmailers which also includes the Smallweeds, the Chadbands, and Mrs Snagsby. The resentment and acquisitive fury of this group brings down the Dedlocks. Chadband expresses their philosophy when he flaunts their hoarded knowledge in front of Sir Leicester. 'Air we in possession of a sinful secret, and doe we require corn, and wine, and oil — or, what is much the same thing, money, for the keeping thereof? Probably so, my friends' (*BH* 789). Guppy's inquisitiveness about Esther Summerson is a milder, if potentially harmful, version of this malevolence. But in Chapter 20 Dickens releases him for a blissful moment from his social climbing.

Much of the novel's action takes place during a hot summer when the law courts are in recess and the clerks at Kenge and Carboy have little to do but swelter and chafe. 'Mr Guppy has been lolling out of the window all morning, after trying all the stools in succession and finding none of them easy, and after several times putting his head into the iron safe with a notion of cooling it' (*BH* 327). While lolling out of the window, 'surveying', as the Appointed had done in *Nicholas Nickleby*, 'the intolerable bricks and mortar' (328), he spots his friend Tony Jobling. The moment of vacancy generates a virtuoso comic interlude as Guppy and Jobling repair, with Guppy's colleague Bart Smallweed, to a chophouse known as the Slap-Bang.

During this interlude, Bart Smallweed, otherwise barely perceptible, comes stupendously alive. In the office, he is Guppy's pale and obsequious shadow. But the Slap-Bang enables him to deploy to brilliant effect his profound knowledge of life in general, and waitresses in particular. He supervises the ordering of an epic meal. Towards the end of the meal, Guppy resumes his narrative function, thus distinguishing himself from his deputy, who has none. He proposes that Jobling should rent a room above Krook's rag and bottle shop, with a view to acquiring some of the old man's secrets. Smallweed, who later turns out to be Krook's nephew, shows no interest in the project. While Guppy and Jobling hurry off to interview Krook, he stays behind in slap-bang heaven, reading the papers, the very antithesis of purposeful activity. *The Times* is so large in proportion to himself that when he holds it up to run his eye over the columns he 'seems to have retired for the night, and to have disappeared under the bedclothes' (*BH* 337). Bart is to some extent dissociated from the utterly repellent Smallweed clan (342–47), and he escapes the punishment meted out to them. He is not present when the older Smallweeds and the Chadbands invade Chesney Wold to blackmail Sir Leicester Dedlock, and are defeated by the guileful Inspector Bucket (785–91). Nor is he present when Guppy, accompanied by Jobling, renews his suit to Esther Summerson, and is suavely dismissed by Jarndyce (915–20). Bart Smallweed is a connoisseur of vacancy, and as such exempted from the possessive hermeneutic fury which sours Guppy and Jobling, corrodes the rest of the Smallweed clan, and kills Tulkinghorn.

Harmlessness

I want by way of conclusion to examine briefly two issues connected with Dickens's lazy gentlemen: the company they keep, and the ground they occupy. For although they are marginal figures, their influence is, to a limited extent, contagious. They disseminate laziness. And this laziness, although scarcely commendable in the moral and political terms proposed by the novels, does no harm.

In *Nicholas Nickleby*, the Appointed is not the only person hanging around in the City square where the Cheeryble brothers have their headquarters. 'The ticket-porter leans idly against the post at the corner, comfortably warm, but not hot, although the day is broiling. His white apron flaps languidly in the air, his head gradually droops upon his breast' (*NN* 553). London ticket-porters were licensed to carry messages and run errands, but in Dickens's novels they seem strangely untroubled by anything in the nature of business. 'A crop of grass would grow in the chinks of the stone pavement outside Lincoln's Inn Hall,' we learn in *Bleak House*, 'but that the ticket-porters, who have nothing to do beyond sitting in the shade there, with their white aprons over their heads to keep the flies off, grub it up and eat it thoughtfully' (*BH* 313). These benign ruminants are a reproach to the obsessiveness of law-court and counting-house.

Dickens rarely missed an opportunity to introduce small groups of loafers. Each group constitutes a miniature utopia of unconcern: utopias created, in some cases, in the teeth of a prevailing concern which motivates not only the main participants in the scene, but the novel itself. For example, the members of the crowd assembled outside the magistrate's house where Pickwick and his entourage have been taken, in Chapter 25 of *The Pickwick Papers* (1836–37), and so incensed by the lack of information, that they express their feelings by 'kicking at the gate and ringing the bell, for an hour or two afterwards.'[16] They might almost be the novel's impatient readers. But the pursuit of meaning does not drive everyone in the crowd to the same frenzied activity. Three or four 'fortunate individuals', having found a grating in the gate which 'commanded a view of nothing', stare through it with 'indefatigable perseverance' (*PP* 422). Their perseverance is, I think, a reproach to curiosity: they know perfectly well that nothing will come of a view of nothing.

16   Dickens, *The Posthumous Papers of the Pickwick Club*, ed. by Robert L. Patten (Harmondsworth: Penguin Books, 1972), p. 421.

In *Great Expectations* (1860–61), Pip spends the night before his first visit to Miss Havisham in Pumblechook's house in the nearby market town. It is the only time he does so, and his stay serves little purpose except to afford us a glimpse of Pumblechook's shop, and of the high street.

> The same opportunity served me for noticing that Mr Pumblechook appeared to conduct his business by looking across the street at the saddler, who appeared to transact *his* business by keeping his eye on the coach-maker, who appeared to get on in life by putting his hands in his pockets and contemplating the baker, who in his turn folded his arms and stared at the grocer, who stood at his door and yawned at the chemist.[17]

The chamber of commerce appears to have reconstituted itself as a chamber of idleness: these ruminants are the middle-class version of the herbivorous ticket-porters. But the scene also contains another group of loafers. The only tradesman in the high street who does any work at all is the watch-maker, 'always poring over a little desk with a magnifying glass at his eye, and always inspected by a group of smock-frocks poring over him through the glass of his shop-window' (*GE* 84). The smock-frocks point back down virtually the whole length of Dickens's career to the scene outside the magistrate's house in *The Pickwick Papers*. They have a view of something, to be sure, but it might just as well be nothing, for all they are likely to make of it: a vacancy captured immaculately by the repetition of 'poring' and 'glass'. Again, I think, the novel glimpses utopia as it hesitates for a moment in the approach to Satis House, where Miss Havisham has hidden herself away, and the relentless pursuit of meaning that will be inaugurated there.

To return to *Pickwick*, the three or four fortunate individuals who gaze at nothing do so with the unwavering perseverance of people who 'flatten their noses against the front windows of a chemist's shop, when a drunken man, who has been run over by a dog-cart in the street, is undergoing a surgical inspection inside' (*PP* 422). There, as in *Great Expectations*, the microscopic inspection which repairs the damaged fabric of man or mechanism seems to require as its complement a macroscopic inspection which, applied through the lens of grating or window, produces absolutely nothing at all. Dickens wanted both of these benevolences. The former he was able to embody in a figure like Allan Woodcourt, in *Bleak House*; his acknowledgement of the latter proved irregular, but rather more vivid.

There is also a connection, although admittedly a more distant one, between the lazy gentlemen and the spaces they inhabit. Dickens warmed to the portrayal of one kind of space in particular: a reality which, had he been alive today, he might have conceived as virtual. I am thinking, for example, of Dick Swiveller's apartments, in *The Old Curiosity Shop* (1841), a 'single chamber' which 'was always mentioned in the plural number'.

> In its disengaged times, the tobacconist had announced it in his window as 'apartments' for a single gentleman, and Mr Swiveller, following up the hint, never failed to speak of it as his rooms, his lodgings, or his chambers, conveying

17   Dickens, *Great Expectations*, ed. by Charlotte Mitchell and David Trotter (Harmondsworth: Penguin Books, 1996), p. 84.

to his hearers a notion of indefinite space, and leaving their imaginations to wander through long suites of lofty halls, at pleasure.[18]

The fiction is sustained by an ingenious piece of furniture which doubles as bookcase and bedstead: its bedstead function being firmly suppressed during the day, its bookcase function at night. Another obvious example of virtual reality is Wemmick's 'castle' in Walworth, in *Great Expectations*. In this case, the fiction is sustained by a painted gun-emplacement and a moat. 'It was worth any money to see Wemmick waving a salute to me from the other side of the moat,' Pip remarks, 'when we might have shaken hands across it with the greatest ease' (*GE* 312). The garden contains a bower which is about twelve yards from the back door, but approached 'by such ingenious twists of path that it took quite a long time to get at' (229–30). The important aspect of these illusory spaces, for my purpose, is the essential innocence of the illusions they foster. Dick Swiveller's bookcase-bedstead is a subtle indication that, however callow and self-absorbed he may be, he will turn out alright in the end; while Wemmick's castle harbours his integrity and kindliness, as well as his aged father. Similarly, the sinister but essentially benevolent Nadgett, in *Martin Chuzzlewit*, constitutes a one-man virtual reality. He spends much of his time sending letters which never arrive anywhere, 'for he would put them into a secret place in his coat, and deliver them to himself weeks afterwards, very much to his own surprise, quite yellow' (*MC* 517).

Some of this innocence rubs off on the lazy gentlemen. In the opening chapter of *American Notes*, Dickens's spirits are restored by a stewardess who, producing sheets and table-cloths from the entrails of sofas, demonstrates that his cabin is not quite as small as he had at first thought. Each nook and corner, each article of furniture, is something other than what it pretends to be: 'a mere trap and deception and place of secret stowage'. The traps and deceptions revealed by the stewardess's preparations are as well-meaning as her 'piously fraudulent' account of safe January voyages. The cabin is rendered harmless by its exposure as virtual reality: 'by this time it had expanded into something quite bulky, and almost boasted a bay-window to view the sea from' (*AN* 56–57). Thus fortified, Dickens is able to relish, on his return to the ship, the lazy gentleman's equally benevolent laziness.

My faith in the harmlessness of the view from Todgers's roof, in *Martin Chuzzlewit*, is strengthened by the establishment's position at the centre of a kind of benevolent maze. 'Nobody had ever found Todgers's on a verbal direction, though given within a minute's walk of it.' Here is another array of harmless traps and deceptions.

> A kind of resigned distraction came over the stranger as he trod these devious mazes, and, giving himself up for lost, went in and out and round about and quietly turned back again when he came to a dead wall or was stopped by an iron railing, and felt that the means of escape might possibly present themselves in their own good time, but that to anticipate them was hopeless. (*MC* 185)

This observer, like the Appointed, seems to have business in the area; but he, too,

---

18 Dickens, *The Old Curiosity Shop*, ed. by Angus Easson (Harmondsworth: Penguin Books, 1972), p. 101.

does not seem terribly concerned about his failure to carry it out. Similarly, people who have been invited to dine at Todgers's, and fail to find it even though they have for some considerable time its chimney-pots in view, return home 'with a gentle melancholy on their spirits, tranquil and uncomplaining' (185). The harmlessness of the maze underwrites the harmlessness (the bliss) of not getting where you're going to, of not fulfilling your commitments. The looker-on on Todgers's roof seems at least to have found the place; but I cannot believe that he, any more than the fortunate individuals who gaze perseveringly through gratings and shop-windows, or chew grass in city squares, will come to any harm — or do any harm.

CHAPTER 4

Dickens and Frith

Dickens liked painters. In fact, he liked them rather more than he liked his fellow writers. Among the eminent artists he kept company with, both in the interminable round of banquets and excursions which made up the social life of the Victorian celebrity, and by regular correspondence, were David Wilkie, William Clarkson Stanfield, Edwin Landseer, Frank Stone, Augustus Egg, Daniel Maclise, and W. P. Frith. The illustrators of the novels (Landseer and Maclise, but also Marcus Stone, George Cattermole, and Luke Fildes) were assimilated swiftly into the Dickens circle.[1] Writers, although by no means left out, do not seem to have loomed quite so large as a species. Dickens's friendships with painters were long-lasting and deeply felt. Should the occasion arise, he could usually be relied upon for an affectionate obituary. *Little Dorrit* (1855), one of his most ambitious novels, was dedicated to Stanfield.

In November 1842, Dickens, who had seen Frith's picture of an exultant Dolly Varden, the pert lower-middle-class heroine of *Barnaby Rudge* (1841), commissioned two companion pieces: Dolly Varden, again, this time 'tripping through the woods, and looking back saucily at her lover', and Kate Nickleby, from *Nicholas Nickleby* (1839). When the pictures were ready, Dickens came round to inspect them. Dickens, of whom Frith stood in considerable awe, turned out to be a pale young man with long hair, a white hat, and a heavy stick. The young man extended his hand 'with a frank cordiality, and a friendly clasp, that never relaxed till the day of his untimely death.' The following Sunday Dickens brought his wife, the party arriving in a carriage with a bright steel bar, of uncertain social and technological function, across the front. The friendly clasp was still active in 1859, when Dickens sat for his portrait to Frith. His expression then was, Frith thought, that of a man who had 'reached the topmost rung of a very high ladder and was perfectly aware of his position.'[2] Dickens, for his part, noted that the portrait was 'a little too much (to my thinking) as if my next-door neighbour were my deadly foe, uninsured, and I had just received tidings of his home being afire.'[3] The friendship proved durable.

1   For an informative brief account of who was in and who was out, see Philip Collins, 'The Dickens Circle', in *Oxford Reader's Companion to Dickens*, ed. by Paul Schlicke (Oxford: Oxford University Press, 1999), pp. 176–79.
2   W. P. Frith, *My Autobiography and Reminiscences*, 3 vols (London: Richard Bentley and Son, 1887–88), I, 101–06, 307–17.
3   Charles Dickens, *Letters*, ed. by Madeline House, Graham Storey, and Kathleen Tillotson, 12 vols (Oxford: Clarendon Press, 1965–2002), IX, 71. Letter of 31 May 1859 to Mrs Richard Watson.

Frith recalled a visit to Dickens's house at Gad's Hill, in Kent, in July 1868.[4] Frith's memoirs provide plentiful evidence of the consistent pleasure Dickens took in the company of artists. But how much pleasure did he take in the company of art?

It is probably not too much of an exaggeration to say that Dickens liked artists more than he liked art; more, at any rate, than he liked contemporary art. To be sure, he took an interest in the visual arts, both classical and contemporary. There is plenty of evidence of that interest in essays, reviews, speeches, and letters.[5] He regularly attended Royal Academy exhibitions, and wrote at some length to his friend John Forster about the paintings on display at the Paris International Exhibition of 1855.[6] Where contemporary painting was concerned, however, Dickens's taste had been formed at a relatively early age by his acquaintance with Sir David Wilkie, whose vivid genre scenes he admired intensely: prints from two of the most characteristic of them, *Rent Day* (1809) and *Reading the Will* (1820), hung in the entrance hall of his house in Devonshire Place.[7] The contemporary art Dickens most admired was literary and historical genre painting. The work by Frith he singled out at the 1855 Paris Exhibition was *Mr Honeywood Introduces the Bailiffs to Miss Richland as his Friends*, from Oliver Goldsmith's comedy of 1768: a costume-piece entirely lacking the scope and vitality of the previous year's *Margate Sands*.[8] Wilkie's name heads the list of the Royal Academicians whose achievement had been dishonoured, in his view, by the inclusion of Millais's *Christ in the House of His Parents* in the Royal Academy Exhibition of 1850.[9]

The note of Dickens's commentary on art, classical or contemporary, was one of defensive facetiousness. Any departure from what he thought of as truth to nature, or truth to an idea generally understood, received the stigma of instant derision. Millais's Pre-Raphaelite carpenter's shop got short shrift.

> In the foreground of that carpenter's shop is a hideous, wry-necked, blubbering, red-headed boy, in a bed-gown; who appears to have received a poke in the hand from the stick of another boy with whom he has been playing in an adjacent gutter, and to be holding it up for the contemplation of a kneeling woman, so horrible in her ugliness, that (supposing it were possible for any human creature to exist for a moment with that dislocated throat) she would stand out from the rest of the company as a Monster, in the vilest cabaret in France, or the lowest gin-shop in England.

And so on. What most offended Dickens about the painting was its departure from the orthodox idea of the essential nobility of Christ's sacrifice of himself in and through his life on earth. 'Wherever it is possible to express ugliness of feature, limb, or attitude, you have it expressed.'[10] Millais's realism, Dickens evidently thought, would have had Wilkie spinning in his grave.

4   Frith, *My Autobiography*, III, 232.
5   Richard Lettis, 'Dickens and Art', *Dickens Studies Annual*, 14 (1985), 93–146.
6   *Letters*, VII, 742–44. Letter of 11–12 November 1855 to John Forster.
7   Leonee Ormond, 'Dickens and Painting: Contemporary Art', *Dickensian*, 80 (1984), 3–25 (pp. 3–6).
8   Dickens, *Letters*, VII, 743.
9   Dickens, 'Old Lamps for New Ones', first published in *Household Words*, 15 June 1850; *Dickens' Journalism*, ed. by Michael Slater, 4 vols (London: Phoenix, 1996), II, 242–48 (p. 244).
10   Dickens, 'Old Lamps', p. 245.

And yet, for all his evident alarm, Dickens did not want to be seen as a dyed-in-the-wool reactionary. The title he chose for his review was 'Old Lamps for New Ones'. He maintained that the Pre-Raphaelites had by their insistence on ugliness undone the 'revolution in Art' brought about by Raphael in the fifteenth century. It was they who were the reactionaries, he thought, because they balked at the intensity of Raphael's devotion to 'what was most sublime and lovely in the expression of the human face divine'. Indeed, so anxious was Dickens to avoid any imputation of conservatism that he concluded by imagining what would happen if contemporary science were to follow the example of contemporary art. A Pre-Newtonian Brotherhood might be founded, to revoke the laws of gravity; or a Pre-Galileo Brotherhood, to arrange for the earth not to circle around the sun. In literature, perhaps, a Pre-Chaucer Brotherhood would restore the ancient English style of spelling, and weed out from the libraries the works of such dangerous innovators as William Shakespeare.[11] The jokes are laboured, and their labour tells a story. Dickens was profoundly ambivalent about change. Ambivalence about change is, I would suggest, the proper ground for a comparison between Dickens and Frith. Both wanted to be modern, with an urgency which everywhere shapes their work; neither quite knew how to be.

Frith made no effort to disguise his ambivalence.

> One of the greatest difficulties besetting me has always been the choice of subject. My inclination being strongly towards the illustration of modern life, I had read the works of Dickens in the hope of finding material for the exercise of any talent I might possess; but at that time the ugliness of modern dress frightened me, and it was not till the publication of *Barnaby Rudge*, and the delightful Dolly Varden was presented to us, that I felt my opportunity had come, with the cherry-coloured mantle and the hat and pink ribbons.

The cherry-coloured mantle and the hat and pink ribbons were evidently the aspect of modern life Frith found it easiest to come to terms with. Dickens, too, it seems. According to Frith, his response to the Dolly Varden and Kate Nickleby was 'All I can say is, they are exactly what I meant, and I am very much obliged to you for painting them for me.'[12] The compliment should not be thought idle, because fidelity to the original conception mattered a great deal to Dickens. In this case, he put his money where his mouth was, paying Frith £40 for the two pictures.

Barnaby Rudge enabled Frith to modernize himself because it was itself both an old lamp and new one, at once historical and contemporary in reference. The novel begins on a blustery March evening in 1775, at the Maypole Inn, at Chigwell, in Essex, where the landlord John Willet and his cronies rehearse the story of the murder of Reuben Haredale at the Warren twenty-two years before. Reuben's brother Geoffrey had been the prime suspect, but nothing could be proved against him. A steward, Rudge, was later found stabbed in the vicinity. His son Barnaby, born the day after the murder, has grown up a simpleton. Geoffrey Haredale's niece Emma has fallen in love with Edward, the son of the haughty Sir John Chester,

11   Ibid., pp. 244, 247–48.
12   Frith, *My Autobiography*, I, 101–02, 104.

but the fathers conspire to thwart the match. A second romance, between Willet's son Joe and Dolly, daughter of the London locksmith Gabriel Varden, is also going nowhere fast, in part because Dolly is a world-class coquette, and Joe too modest and straightforward (i.e. dim) to call her bluff. Joe enlists in the army, and Dolly becomes Emma's paid companion. She is persecuted by Hugh, the Maypole's brutish ostler, and by Varden's apprentice, Sim Tappertit, a fizzing human cocktail of vanity, resentment, and ambition.

At the end of Chapter 32, after Joe's departure abroad, and Edward's banishment from his father's home, the story breaks off; to resume, in Chapter 33, with the outbreak of the 'No Popery!' riots provoked by Lord George Gordon, leader of the Protestant Association. For a week in June 1780, the London mob took over the city, in what seemed to many a fundamental challenge to the existing social and political order. These momentous events absorb, amplify, and eventually resolve the domestic melodrama which is the subject of the novel's first thirty-two chapters. The reviewers were quick to spot disparities of scale and intensity between its preoccupation with murder mystery, on one hand, and the pillaging of a capital city, on the other. However, the novel is consistent in its focus on rebellion. From the very outset, the sons (Edward Chester, Joe Willet) seem minded to rise up against the fathers; and with good reason, since the fathers persist in treating them as though they were children. Dickens is clearly on their side. Once the rising up has become general, he allows its anarchic energy to infuse and shape some of the most vivid descriptions of public violence ever written. He was not on the side of the rioters. But he knew that such violence was a topic made for him. The topic, furthermore, was topical. In the summer and autumn of 1839, violence provoked by the militant Chartist campaign for universal manhood suffrage had brought the Gordon Riots of the 1780s back into the news again.[13]

There was, however, another way in which *Barnaby Rudge*, while remaining historical, had brought itself up to date; through the topicality not of riots, but of a cherry-coloured mantle and pink ribbons. For Dolly Varden had been on the point of freeing herself from the narrative which contained her long before Frith rode to the rescue. In Chapter 19, the Varden family travels down to Chigwell, so that Dolly may visit Emma Haredale at the Warren, to deliver a message from Edward Chester. Their departure from town appears to drive Dickens to distraction.

> As to Dolly, there she was again, the very pink and pattern of good looks, in a smart little cherry-coloured mantle, with a hood of the same drawn over her head, and upon the top of that hood, a little straw hat trimmed with cherry-coloured ribbons, and worn the merest trifle on one side — just enough in short to make it the wickedest and most provoking head-dress that ever malicious milliner devised.[14]

Who, exactly, is in danger of being provoked by this display? In theory Sim Tappertit, who holds the horse's head. But it is hard not to feel that the author

---

13   Thomas J. Rice, 'The Politics of *Barnaby Rudge*', in *The Changing World of Charles Dickens*, ed. by Robert Giddings (London: Vision Press, 1983), pp. 51–74.
14   Dickens, *Barnaby Rudge*, ed. by Clive Hurst (Oxford: Oxford University Press, 2003), p. 161. Henceforth *BR*.

regards himself as the main victim of the milliner's malice. A few pages on, in the chapter's final paragraph, he admits as much. The Vardens safely stowed in the Maypole, Dolly sets off across the fields to discharge her mission at the Warren; 'and this deponent hath been informed and verily believes, that you might have seen many less pleasant objects than the cherry-coloured mantle and ribbons, as they went fluttering along the green meadows in the bright light of the day, like giddy things as they were' (*BR* 164). Dickens has in effect created a point of view, which is that not of any of the characters, but rather of a phantom 'deponent', or witness, from which alone Dolly can be seen truly, and truly appreciated. From that point of view, the mantle and ribbons thoroughly obscure the mission at the Warren.

Dickens has not done with Dolly yet. She is the most unashamedly sexual of his pretty young heroines; and yet he can only imagine her eroticism fully in and through the threat of rape. He arranges for her to walk back from the Warren along a path through a wood, where she is intercepted by the Maypole's ostler, Hugh, a 'handsome satyr' (*BR* 171) whose sexual ferocity at once intensifies the deponent's appreciation of her, and retrospectively guarantees its innocence. Worse is to come. During the Gordon Riots, Emma Haredale and Dolly Varden are kidnapped by Hugh and Sim Tappertit, who compete strenuously with each other for Dolly's favours. Dolly in distress is a Dolly ripe for something a little warmer than appreciation.

> When, forgetful for a moment of herself, as she was now, she fell on her knees beside her friend, and bent over her, and laid her cheek to hers, and put her arms about her, what mortal eyes could have avoided wandering to the delicate bodice, the streaming hair, the neglected dress, the perfect abandonment and unconsciousness of the blooming little beauty? (475)

Not Dickens's, evidently.

Dickens's 'lip-smacking authorial commentary' on the blooming little beauty might well make us feel uneasy.[15] But there is a further element to it, which complicates the otherwise mildly pornographic picture. Dolly's three suitors, Hugh, Joe Willet, and Sim Tappertit, all take part in the uprising of youth against age. Two of them, furthermore, Joe and Sim, are defined as much by social as by sexual desire. Both are petty-bourgeois aspirants. One aspires nobly, the other ignobly. For both, Dolly represents a social as well as a sexual prize. She is of the same class as them. So marriage to her would not count as elevation. But it would validate their claim to status, because her proven taste exemplifies her ability and her willingness to make something of herself. The millinery matters, in short. Dolly's eroticism constitutes her as an object, of the deponent's gaze; but also as a subject, as someone who spends in order to accumulate. Her sexual forwardness is a social vanguardism. Dickens ogles her because he is on her side. He wills her to be modern.

So strenuous is his advocacy that he creates for her a fourth hapless admirer, in the shape of a young coachmaker whom she had met at a party, and who 'had given her to understand, when he handed her into the chair at parting, that it was his fixed resolve to neglect his business from that time, and die slowly for the love

15   Michael Slater, *Dickens and Women* (London: J. M. Dent, 1983), p. 248.

of her' (*BR* 155). When the Vardens leave for Chigwell, the coachmaker is to be found on the pavement outside their house, 'looking so genteel that nobody would have believed he had ever had anything to do with a coach but riding in it, and bowing like any nobleman' (161). The coachmaker's sole function in the narrative is to serve momentarily, as Dolly is setting out on her great adventure, as the figure of social aspiration. His mournful loitering frames the emergence of her sexuality as a social event. When Joe Willet says a stoical farewell to Dolly in Chapter 31, the coachmaker is invoked as someone who under those circumstances 'would have been dissolved in tears, and would have knelt down, and called himself names, and clasped his hands, and beat his breast, and tugged wildly at his cravat, and done all kinds of poetry' (255). He receives one further mention, towards the end of the novel, as a young man who 'had turned out, years ago, to be a special donkey' (578). That is the thanks you get for acting as a signpost on the road to prosperity. The significant social change *Barnaby Rudge* foreshadows is the rise not of working-class militancy, but of a sexualized consumerism.

Hablot K. Browne, who illustrated the episode of Dolly's visit to the Warren under Dickens's supervision, chose to show her admiring herself in a mirror while Emma Haredale reads Edward Chester's letter, and then on the path through the wood, shrinking terrified from Hugh, and the coarseness in his admiring look. These images tell a moral tale, of narcissism and its consequences. Frith, by contrast, caught her at a moment of radiant, and rather strikingly amoral, ascendancy (**Fig. 4.1**). After leaving Emma, Dolly had been intercepted on her way out of the Warren by the forbidding Mr Haredale. The encounter discomposes her.

> The first thing to be done, of course, when she came to herself and considered what a flurry she had been in, was to cry afresh; and the next thing, when she reflected how well she had got over it, was to laugh heartily. The tears once banished gave place to the smiles, and at last Dolly laughed so much that she was fain to lean against a tree, and give vent to her exultation. (*BR* 169)

Frith captures that first flush of exultation. His Dolly stands out, or stands forward, from her ground: partly through the intensity of the cherry and pink of her mantle, stockings, and ribbon in contrast to the greys, greens, and yellowy-browns of the murky forest path; and partly through the extravagant curve which leaning against a tree has imparted to her body. Relatively little has been left to the imagination, with regard either to the female form, or to the commodities which enhance it. The thrust of Dolly's hip has placed the standard equipment of 'heart-rending shoes' and 'cruel little muff', as well as the bracelet just given her by Emma Haredale, firmly in the shop window. Her level gaze might be thought to single out and even to confront any lip-smacking deponents among the audience.

If we are to take the measure of this image, we need to find out from the novel why Dolly is laughing. When Mr Haredale intercepted her, her first thought had been that he meant to punish her for carrying messages between Emma and Edward Chester. In fact, he offers her a job: the 'office' of companion to his niece (*BR* 168). As Emma's companion, she will attain a social and economic status, not to mention an elegance of milieu, ordinarily far beyond the reach of a locksmith's daughter.

FIG. 4.1. William Powell Frith, *Dolly Varden* (1842).
Oil on canvas. Victoria and Albert Museum, London.

The role will enable the novel itself to take her seriously: to have her kidnapped at the same time as Emma, and thus given the chance to redeem herself from narcissism by her conduct in adversity. She is laughing, as she leans against the tree, because she has come good. Her sudden social ascendancy takes the form, in this image, of an eroticism of which she is both subject and object. Frith's achievement was to have captured not just Dolly, but Dickens's own allegiance to Dolly, an allegiance he felt deeply, and could never express directly.

The cherry-coloured mantle and the pink hat-ribbon mattered, in short. When John Ruskin grumpily recalled *Barnaby Rudge*, thirty years after its publication, it was as an 'entirely profitless and monstrous story' mixed up with a 'certain quantity of ordinary operatic pastoral stuff, about a pretty Dolly in ribands, a lover with a wooden leg, and an heroic locksmith.'[16] Dolly's ribbons, it would seem, are by no means the least among the novel's offences. Ruskin cared passionately about ribbons. In fact, he loathed them with a rare bitterness. In a remarkable passage in *The Seven Lamps of Architecture* (1849), he compared the beauty of seaweed, which 'has a marked strength, structure, elasticity, gradation of substance,' with the drabness of a ribbon:

> It has no structure: it is a succession of cut threads all alike; it has no skeleton, no make, no form, no size, no will of its own. You cut it and crush it into what you will. It has no strength, no languor. It cannot fall into a single graceful form. It cannot wave, in the true sense, but only flutter: it cannot bend, in the true sense, but only turn and be wrinkled. It is a vile thing; it spoils all that is near its wretched film of an existence.

In Ruskin's view, ribbon was a 'vile thing' because it lacked the organic form which gave even the humblest of natural substances a distinctive structure, a 'will of its own'. The same objection could of course be raised against more or less any of the products of the proliferating commodity culture which had begun to transform British society in its own image. In *The Seven Lamps of Architecture*, Ruskin raised it with characteristic vigour against the new suburban housing-estates around London: 'those gloomy rows of formalised minuteness, alike without difference and without fellowship, as solitary as similar.'[17] Ribbon, Ruskin thought, had the mechanically produced uniformity of all modern substances. It failed to be unlike.

What connects these esoteric speculations to Dolly Varden is the anxiety informing them. To Ruskin, the suburban houses were not just an eyesore. Their existence bore witness to a 'great and spreading spirit of popular discontent'. They were the product of a time 'when every man's aim is to be in some more elevated sphere than his natural one, and every man's past life is his habitual scorn.'[18] By this account, to elevate oneself was to exchange natural difference for a mechanically produced sameness. John Stuart Mill was later to worry that the supposedly all-inclusive social order in prospect in Britain from the 1850s onwards would

---

16   John Ruskin, 'Notes on the Present State of Engraving' (1872), in *Works*, ed. by E. T. Cook and Alexander Wedderburn, 39 vols (London: Longmans, Green, 1907), XXII, 467.
17   Ruskin, *The Seven Lamps of Architecture*, in *Works*, VIII, 148–49, 226.
18   Ibid., p. 226.

extinguish 'variety of situations'.[19] Among the instruments of that extinguishing sameness, the ribbon appears to have received as much attention as the suburban house, and not from Ruskin alone. In Thackeray's *Vanity Fair* (1847–48), set during the conclusion of the Napoleonic wars, the decrepit and debauched Sir Pitt Crawley causes a scandal by conspicuously enjoying the company (and no doubt the sexual favours) of the butler's daughter, Miss Horrocks, an 'individual in ribbons'. 'The rise and progress of those Ribbons had been marked with dismay by the county and family. The Ribbons opened an account at the Mudbury Branch Savings Bank; the Ribbons drove to church, monopolizing the pony-chaise, which was for the use of the servants at the Hall. The domestics were dismissed at her pleasure.'[20] Miss Horrocks's reign comes to an end when Sir Pitt collapses, and the dignitaries summoned to his aid catch her in the act of ransacking the study. Dolly Varden's favourite adornment, fluttering like 'giddy things' along green meadows in the bright light of day, had become the gold-digger's emblem.

Dickens, I have argued, had mixed feelings about giddiness. The novels he wrote at this time took an unrelentingly punitive attitude towards petty-bourgeois chancers whose ambition was, in Ruskin's words, to attain 'some more elevated sphere' than their 'natural' one: for example, Uriah Heep, in *David Copperfield* (1849–50), or Mr Guppy, in *Bleak House* (1852–53). But these variously loathsome or hapless social climbers, distant descendants of the coachmaker in *Barnaby Rudge*, are all men. Aspiration in women was a somewhat different matter. Unlike Thackeray, Dickens found that easy enough to accommodate, especially if there was a hint of millinery about it. In an essay published in the *Examiner* in 1848, he wrote admiringly of John Leech's readiness to incorporate 'beautiful faces or agreeable forms' into his sketches of fashionable young people.

> In Mr Punch's *Almanack* for the new year, there is one illustration by Mr Leech representing certain delicate creatures with bewitching countenances, encased in several varieties of that amazing garment, the ladies' paletot. Formerly these fair creatures would have been made as ugly and ungainly as possible, and there the point would have been lost, and the spectator, with a laugh at the absurdity of the whole group, would not have cared one farthing how such uncouth creatures disguised themselves, or how ridiculous they became.[21]

Dickens badly wants to think that these fair and delicate creatures will redeem themselves from their paletots, as Dolly Varden had redeemed herself from her ribbons. So much so, in fact, that he entirely overlooks Leech's decision to equip two of them with cigarettes. *Punch* readers would have considered women ostentatiously smoking in public, if not uncouth, exactly, then unfeminine.

Frith understood, and painted, the profound affinity Dickens felt with social aspiration at its most unapologetic. Joe Willet is as much the aspirant, in *Barnaby*

19   John Stuart Mill, *On Liberty and Other Essays*, ed. by John Gray (Oxford: Oxford University Press, 1991), p. 81.
20   W. M. Thackeray, *Vanity Fair: A Novel without a Hero*, ed. by John Sutherland (Oxford: Oxford University Press, 1983), p. 502.
21   Dickens, review of John Leech, *The Rising Generation: A Series of Twelve Drawings on Stone*, in *The Examiner*, 30 December 1848; *Dickens's Journalism*, II, 142–47 (p. 144).

Rudge, as Sim Tappertit or the hapless coachmaker. Autobiographical David Copperfield is as much the aspirant as Uriah Heep, his repulsive *alter ego*. Dickens, however, did make a habit of apologizing for social aspiration. Sim and Uriah are part of that apology. Indeed, it is notable that in *Barnaby Rudge* both aspirants, good and bad, take a beating for their temerity: Joe loses an arm in the wars; Sim's legs (his chief asset) are crushed, and he becomes a bootblack. Dickens made great literature both out of his affinity with social aspiration and out of his long apology for it.

Frith seems to have been less inclined to apologize. The affinity he felt for shameless social aspiration is plain enough in the genre paintings of the 1850s and 1860s. By his own account, he took it upon himself to stiffen Dickens's resolve in that respect. He was upset to discover that when Dickens delivered Sam Weller's humorous observations in public, he tended to lower his voice to the tones of someone 'rather ashamed of what he was saying, and afraid of being reproved for the freedom of his utterances.' He most likely regarded the young bootblack's sharp tongue as evidence of a desire to improve himself. 'Sam is self-possessed, quick, and never-failing in his illustrations and rejoinders, even to the point of impudence.' He told Dickens as much, and claims that the world's best-known writer thereafter amended his incarnation on stage of one of his best-known characters accordingly.[22]

Dolly Varden herself had the last laugh.[23] When Dickens died, in June 1870, the paintings and prints sent for auction included Frith's view of Dolly Varden tripping through the woods, and looking back saucily at her lover. According to a contemporary report, 'the enthusiasm culminated when the Dolly Varden was put up, and found vent in rounds of applause. The charming "mist of coquettishness" environing this dainty figure, its beauty, its tripping, lightsome step, the innocent playfulness of the fair young face, took the room by storm.'[24] And not just the room. By 1870, the costume of the 1770s had undergone something of a revival. 'Overskirts drawn up to reveal quilted petticoats, piled up hair and tiny hats came back into fashion,' Vanda Foster explains, 'and, in particular, the polonaise, an overskirt looped up to form three large puffs over the hips.'[25] This was exactly how Dolly Varden had been dressed by Hablot Browne, and by Frith. 'The novelty par excellence,' the *Englishwoman's Domestic Magazine* reported in June 1871, 'is the "Dolly Varden" costume, which is a pretty, coquettish copy of the noted picture of Dolly Varden, which was among Mr Charles Dickens's collection and sold at his death.'[26] A straw hat should be worn with it, trimmed to correspond. Dolly Varden, already thoroughly modern in the 1770s, as Dickens imagined her, was still thoroughly modern a hundred years later. Frith could be said to have understood rather better than Dickens himself what it was that kept her young.

---

22   Frith, *My Autobiography*, I, 311–13.
23   My account of her last laugh draws heavily on Vanda Foster, 'The Dolly Varden', *Dickensian*, 73 (1977), 19–24.
24   *Queen*, 16 July 1870; quoted by Foster, 'The Dolly Varden', p. 19.
25   Foster, 'The Dolly Varden', pp. 20–21.
26   *Englishwoman's Domestic Magazine* (June 1871); quoted by Foster, 'The Dolly Varden', pp. 21–22.

CHAPTER 5

Space, Movement, and
Sexual Feeling in *Middlemarch*

In Chapter 9 of *Middlemarch*, Dorothea Brooke, accompanied by her uncle and sister, visits her future home at Lowick Manor.

> The building, of greenish stone, was in the old English style, not ugly, but small-windowed and melancholy-looking: the sort of house that must have children, many flowers, open windows, and little vistas of bright things, to make it seem a joyous home. In this latter end of autumn, with a sparse remnant of yellow leaves falling slowly athwart the dark evergreens in a stillness without sunshine, the house too had an air of autumnal decline, and Mr Casaubon, when he presented himself, had no bloom that could be thrown into relief by that background.[1]

Mr Casaubon, rather alarmingly, is in camouflage. He seems unable, or unwilling, at this crucial moment in his life, to stand forth, to assume a shape. It is not that he is invisible, but that he remains, even upon presentation of himself, utterly indistinct.

We might gain some sense of what indistinctness meant to Eliot from a late and unpublished essay, 'Notes on Form in Art' (1868). The essay includes an account of form in general, as manifest in life as well as in art.

> Form, then, as distinguished from merely massive impression, must first depend on the discrimination of wholes and then on the discrimination of parts. Fundamentally, form is unlikenesss [...] Even taken in its derivative meaning of outline, what is Form but the limit of that difference by which we discriminate one object from another? — a limit determined partly by the intrinsic relations or composition of the object, and partly by the extrinsic action of other bodies upon it.[2]

Form, in life as in art, makes itself known, first, by external difference, or unlikeness; and secondly, by the degree of organization of internal complexity. No object can be considered to have form unless it reveals both its difference from other objects, and a sufficient diversity of parts to require the exercise of an ordering principle. Mr Casaubon's inability to assume a distinct shape suggests that he has

---

1   George Eliot, *Middlemarch*, ed. by David Carroll (Oxford: Oxford University Press, 1998), p. 74. Henceforth *M*.
2   Eliot, 'Notes on Form in Art', in *Selected Critical Writings*, ed. by Rosemary Ashton (Oxford: Oxford University Press, 1992), pp. 354–59 (pp. 355–56).

already failed on the first count. Whether or not he will succeed on the second remains to be determined.

Eliot, of course, subsequently goes to extraordinary lengths, in some of the most acute and intensely felt passages in her novel, to credit him with an internal complexity which deserves sympathetic understanding. But it may be too late. We need to take full account of the damage done to Casaubon by his enduring indistinctness. The damage is done by the contrast established in Chapter 9 between Casaubon and Will Ladislaw. As the party proceed towards the church, Celia takes advantage of Casaubon's momentary absence to remark that she has seen 'some one quite young coming up one of the walks': not a gardener, as Mr Brooke proposes, but a gentleman with a sketch-book (*M* 70). Celia's deliberate and reiterated emphasis on youth establishes the gentleman with a sketch-book as a potential rival to Casaubon. On their return from the church, the visitors make a circuit towards a fine yew-tree. 'As they approached it, a figure, conspicuous on a dark background of evergreens, was seated on a bench, sketching the old tree' (72). Unlike Casaubon, this figure immediately stands out. It manifests that difference which is the first condition of form. Only when the two sisters have taken in the form thus made does Eliot allow Casaubon to identify the gentleman with the sketch-book as his second cousin, Will Ladislaw. Ladislaw is able to impress upon them his youthful desirability twice over, and on the second occasion for a significant interval, before it can be diminished by a name.

Eliot's guide in aesthetic matters in general, and quite possibly the provocation to a study of form in nature and in art, was John Ruskin.[3] I do not mean to propose a source either for her essay or for her novel in Ruskin. But I do think that there is much to be learnt indirectly about the novel, in particular, by considering, for example, his meditation on the difference between seaweed and ribbons, in *The Seven Lamps of Architecture* (1849):

> The loosest weed that drifts and waves under the heaving of the sea, or hangs heavily on the brown and slippery shore, has a marked strength, structure, elasticity, gradation of substance; its extremities are more finely fibred than its centre, its centre than its root: every fork of its ramification is measured and proportioned; every wave of its languid lines is lovely. It has its allotted size, and place, and function; it is a specific creature. What is there like this in a riband? It has no structure: it is a succession of cut threads all alike; it has no skeleton, no make, no form, no size, no will of its own. You cut it and crush it into what you will. It has no strength, no languor. It cannot fall into a single graceful form. It cannot wave, in the true sense, but only flutter: it cannot bend, in the true sense, but only turn and be wrinkled. It is a vile thing; it spoils all that is near its wretched film of an existence. Never use it.[4]

For Ruskin, as for Eliot, form involves difference and a high degree of organized complexity: strength, structure, elasticity, and gradation of substance. Strength and

3   'The truth of infinite value that he teaches,' Eliot had written in a review of volume III of *Modern Painters* in 1856, 'is *realism* — the doctrine that all truth and beauty are to be attained by a humble and faithful study of nature': *Selected Critical Writings*, p. 248.
4   John Ruskin, *The Seven Lamps of Architecture*, in *Works*, ed. by E. T. Cook and Alexander Wedderburn, 39 vols (London: Longmans, Green, 1907), VIII, 148–49.

structure do not imply rigidity. Ruskin approved of languor; he might even have approved of Will Ladislaw, a creature specific enough, and yet built on decidedly languid lines. The ribbon, by contrast, is a 'vile thing' lacking both external difference and internal complexity. Formlessness, in Ruskin's view, was matter for social and moral as well as aesthetic discrimination. Ribbons, after all, were likely to be worn by woman of a certain class and a certain susceptibility. Ruskin cannot have thought Dickens's *Barnaby Rudge* any less 'monstrous' for the deplorable fact that it included 'a certain quantity of ordinary operatic pastoral stuff, about a pretty Dolly in ribands, a lover with a wooden leg, and an heroic locksmith'.[5]

What is at stake, in Chapter 9 of *Middlemarch*, is a woman's choice in marriage. The concept of form has allowed Eliot to be extraordinarily frank in assessing the prospects of the two men who want to marry Dorothea Brooke. Mr Casaubon, considered either as a member of the human race, or as a man, has no distinctive shape. He does not stand out. In the short term, mutual delusion may conceal this disability. For Casaubon, however, the game is already up. He will not reproduce himself. Hard though Eliot subsequently tries to rehabilitate him, she cannot undo the impression created with such meticulous brutality in Chapter 9. Casaubon is a born loser. He does not stand a chance against Will Ladislaw. The disability apparent before a marriage made possible by mutual delusion becomes doubly apparent after it. In Chapter 21, in what should have been the full flush of honeymoon, Casaubon returns from a day in the Vatican Library to find Dorothea and Will Ladislaw engaged in lively conversation. His immediate response is a surprise 'quite unmixed with pleasure': he knows perfectly well that he is in the presence of a rival whose superiority in the longer term is no longer in question. 'Mr Casaubon was less happy than usual, and this perhaps made him look all the dimmer and more faded; else, the effect might easily have been produced by the contrast of his young cousin's appearance.' Eliot takes the opportunity to emphasize Will's 'sunny brightness', and the dynamism of the utterly distinctive shape he cuts: 'Surely, his very features changed their form; his jaw looked sometimes large and sometimes small; and the little ripple in his nose was a preparation for metamorphosis.' Ladislaw is Ruskin's seaweed in human guise, his shapeliness exhibiting 'a marked strength, structure, elasticity, gradation of substance.' To Dorothea, and perhaps to Eliot herself, every wave of his languid lines is lovely. 'Mr Casaubon, on the contrary, stood rayless' (*M* 196).

Frankness was in the air, in 1871, when Eliot took the decision to incorporate a burgeoning story about one 'Miss Brooke' into a novel which until that point had mainly featured Vincys and Featherstones. Darwin published *The Descent of Man and Selection in Relation to Sex*, which expands upon the theories advanced in *The Origin of Species*, and upon their consequences for an understanding of the evolution of humankind. The struggle which shapes sexual selection, he had explained in

5   Ruskin, 'Notes on the Present State of Engraving' (1872), in *Works*, XXII, 467. See David Trotter, 'Dickens and Frith', in *William Powell Frith: Painting the Victorian Age*, ed. by Mark Bills and Vivien Knight (New Haven, CT, and London: Yale University Press in association with Guildhall Art Gallery, City of London, 2006), pp. 29–39; reprinted as Chapter 4 in this book.

The Origin of Species, is not for existence in relation to 'other organic beings' or to 'external conditions', but, rather, 'between the individuals of one sex, generally the males, for the possession of the other sex.' Victory, here, depends less on 'general vigour' than on the development (by the male of the species) of an array of 'special weapons'; while for the unsuccessful competitor, the outcome is not death, but few or no offspring.[6] The 'sexual struggle', he argued in *The Descent of Man*,

> is of two kinds; in the one it is between the individuals of the same sex, generally the males, in order to drive away or kill their rivals, the females remaining passive; whilst in the other, the struggle is likewise between the individuals of the same sex, in order to excite or charm those of the opposite sex, generally the females, which no longer remain passive, but select the more agreeable partners.

The Descent of Man offers, among other things, a detailed and graphic account of the secondary sexual characteristics (the special weapons) developed by the males of many species in order either to overcome other males or to charm the more agreeable among the females: and of the uses to which these characteristics have been put, by insects, animals, and human beings. The uses, one might note, are conscious uses.

> When we behold two males fighting for the possession of the female, or several male birds displaying their gorgeous plumage, and performing strange antics before an assembled body of females, we cannot doubt that, though led by instinct, they know what they are about, and consciously exert their mental and bodily powers.[7]

'Primitive' cultures appear to have constituted for Darwin a benchmark of the sexual struggle at its most intense. 'How low in the scale of nature the law of battle descends,' he observed in *The Origin of Species*, 'I know not; male alligators have been described as fighting, bellowing, and whirling round, like Indians in a war-dance, for the possession of the females.'[8] In *The Descent of Man*, looking high rather than low in the scale of nature, he was in no doubt that 'as savages still fight for the possession of their women, a similar process of selection has probably gone on in a greater or less degree to the present day.' Indeed, he seemed to think that modern men and women, too often swayed by 'mere wealth or rank', could by conscious sexual selection do rather more than they were in the habit of doing, not only for the 'bodily constitution and frame' of any offspring they might have, but for their intellectual and moral qualities as well.[9] To be sure, the 'rather more' no longer included, as it might once have done, the elimination of rivals. Eliot, too, was clear on this point: Sir James Chettam, finding that Dorothea has chosen Casaubon, 'was not so well acquainted with the habits of primitive races as to feel that an ideal combat for her, tomahawk in hand, so to speak, was necessary to the

6   Charles Darwin, *The Origin of Species* (London: Dent, 1971), p. 87.
7   Darwin, *The Descent of Man and Selection in Relation to Sex*, 2nd edn (London: John Murray, 1894), pp. 614, 211.
8   Darwin, *Origin*, p. 87.
9   Darwin, *Descent*, pp. 596–97, 617.

historical continuity of the marriage-tie' (*M* 57). Understood as a whole, however, the novel suggests very strongly that the pursuit of sexual rivalry, if not through war-dances and tomahawks, then through a display of plumage (and the 'strange antics' to go with it) remained an important part of modern life. It was Darwinism, with its insistent emphasis on variability as the key both to natural and to sexual selection, which shaped Eliot's understanding of form in life. Mr Casaubon's lack of difference ought to rule him out as a mate for the strongly differentiated Dorothea. Where women are concerned, Eliot wrote in the Prelude to *Middlemarch*, the 'limits of variation' are really much wider than anyone would imagine from the sameness of their coiffure and 'the favourite love-stories in prose and verse' (4).[10]

Eliot's consistent frankness in *Middlemarch* about the basis of sexual selection has cut remarkably little ice with her critics. The almost universal assumption is that the novel's portrayal of sexual love is neither convincing nor emancipatory. The objections levelled against it are that Will Ladislaw represents an implausible object of desire; and that Dorothea Brooke remains damagingly unaware of, and thus unable to control, her own sexuality. They have been framed, oddly enough, in terms of the very Darwinism whose presence in the text the critics seem unwilling to acknowledge. On the one hand, we are told, in effect, that Ladislaw will lose out in the sexual struggle because his plumage is inadequate (inadequate in the minds of generations of readers, if not in that of the author); on the other, that Dorothea does not know how to set about choosing for herself an agreeable partner.

Why, Carol Siegel asks in the course of a forceful restatement of the first of these complaints, does marriage to Will Ladislaw not prove a 'satisfying solution' to Dorothea Brooke's problems? The problem with Will, Siegel continues, is that his 'presence' in the narrative 'promises so much' and yet 'yields so little.' Both the promise and the ultimate failure lie 'in the register of the erotic'. Siegel puts the blame squarely on the stuffy conventions of domestic realism. There is an awareness of the erotic as a possibility in *Middlemarch*, she argues, but it comes 'from the text itself, from the places where the erotic inheres not in physically accessible space but in memory and speculation, in half-told stories such as that of Will's grandmother, Julia, and in evocation of other literary texts, such as Shakespeare's sonnets.' Will Ladislaw's presence in the text as an erotic being is only ever intertextual; he masquerades as the 'delightful androgyne whose love inspires and elevates the soul of his admirer "like to the lark at break of day arising" (sonnet 29).'[11] Siegel demonstrates in convincing detail that reference to Shakespeare enabled Eliot to make Ladislaw attractive; at least up until the point at which he dwindles into a prospective husband. The Dorothea who breaks off their first embrace to say that

---

10   Pointing out the Darwinian provenance of the term 'variation', Gillian Beer goes on to argue that the emphasis on plurality rather than singleness is 'crucial to the developing argument of *Middlemarch* which, with all its overtly taxonomic ordering, has as its particular deep counter-enterprise the establishment of individual diversity beneath ascribed typologies': *Darwin's Plots: Evolutionary Narrative in Darwin, George Eliot and Nineteenth-Century Fiction* (London: Routledge, 1983), pp. 149–54.

11   Carol Siegel, ' "The Thing I Like My Sister May Not Do": Shakespearean Erotics and a Clash of Wills in *Middlemarch*', *Style*, 32 (1998), 36–59 (pp. 39–42, 53).

she will take trouble to learn what everything costs (*M* 762) does not appear to have her eye on delightful androgyny. According to Siegel, intertextuality is where the fun is, or once was; the resumption of domestic realism has put an end to all that. Oddly, her argument separates the 'text itself' from the conventions which are generally thought in large measure to constitute it: those of domestic realism. I shall argue here that a great deal transpires, including much that ought to count as erotic, in the 'physically accessible space' which it is domestic realism's business to represent.

Sally Shuttleworth's objection is that the novel grants Dorothea a 'strongly passionate sexual nature', and then forbids her to understand its 'workings'. It insists throughout on the desirability of integrating intellect with ardour, but then makes an exception where sexuality is concerned. Shuttleworth shows that Eliot's understanding of the relations between mind and body was shaped by the psychological theories of Herbert Spencer and G. H. Lewes. These theories were developed within an evolutionary framework. Both Spencer and Lewis believed that the history of the human race revealed a gradual development from simple to complex structures of thought and feeling, and that the index to this development was the growth of moral consciousness. When preparing the final volume of Lewes's *Problems of Life and Mind* for publication after his death, Eliot added a passage whose burden was that the growth of moral consciousness would in due course produce 'in many highly wrought natures a complete submergence (or, if you will, a transference) of egoistic desire, and an habitual outrush of the emotional force in sympathetic channels.' Eliot, Shuttleworth remarks, would appear to have Dorothea firmly in mind here.[12] The passage reads like a commentary on Dorothea's response to the sight of Will Ladislaw kneeling at Rosamond Lydgate's feet. Fury at Will and scorn for Rosamond gradually recede as, in the early hours of the morning, she gazes out of the window at the world beyond the entrance-gates of Lowick Manor. 'She was a part of that involuntary, palpitating life, and could neither look out on it from her luxurious shelter as a mere spectator, nor hide her eyes in selfish complaining' (*M* 741). Dorothea would appear to have evolved beyond all kinds of 'egoistic desire', including that which informs sexual selection: her anger at Will had been quite specifically an anger at his display of himself, his obtrusion into her life, his refusal to stay among the crowd (740). This degree of evolution contrasts strikingly with the childishness often attributed to her at moments of sexual crisis: when she and Will finally acknowledge their love for one another, they stand at the window 'with their hands clasped, like two children' (761); when they embrace for the first time, she sobs out in a 'childlike way' her readiness to do without new clothes and to learn what things cost (762). Dorothea either remains in ignorance of her own sexuality, or thinks and feels too much to want to exploit it.

When adult sexuality is represented in *Middlemarch*, Shuttleworth maintains, it seems to require the terms not of psychology but of psychiatry: to have sexual thoughts and feelings is to go mad. As she notes shrewdly, Dorothea gazing out at the world beyond the entrance-gates is shadowed by an 'obverse image' from

---

12   Sally Shuttleworth, 'Sexuality and Knowledge in *Middlemarch*', *Nineteenth-Century Contexts*, 19 (1996), 425–41 (pp. 427–29).

the psychiatric literature of the period: that of the hysteric. Her exchanges with Rosamond reduce her to a 'palpitating anxiety' (*M* 749): now it is a mind on the edge of breakdown which palpitates, rather than the world, and it does so in misery. Lydgate, who attends Dorothea after Casaubon's death, feels sure that she has been suffering from 'the strain and conflict of self-repression' (462). As Shuttleworth points out, his diagnosis draws on 'theories of hysteria as a form of repression, and particularly sexual repression'. The novel suggests that he may have reason to associate Dorothea with the insane women of the psychiatric literature. When Casaubon, having heard from Lydgate that he is likely to die, rejects her solicitude, her reaction is furious. 'In such a crisis as this,' we are told, 'some women begin to hate.' Dorothea does not, quite. 'But the struggle changed continually, as that of a man who begins with a movement towards striking and ends with conquering his desire to strike' (400). As Shuttleworth shows, there is enough incipient murderousness in Dorothea for Lydgate to associate her with Laure, the actress with whom he had once been in love, and who had murdered her husband.[13]

Shuttleworth and Siegel differ in topic and approach. But they share an assumption: that domestic realism is not up to the task of representing sexuality. In Shuttleworth's view, the portrayal of sexual love in *Middlemarch* is shaped through and through by the 'contradictions and ellipses' in the psychological and psychiatric discourse of the time. Domestic realism cannot be said to supplement or to revise that discourse. When it comes to sexual feeling, the novelist has (even) less to offer by way of wisdom than the psychiatrists. If literature does have something to offer, it is not through domestic realism, but through the disruption of domestic realism by melodrama. According to Shuttleworth, the 'melodramatic history' of Laure 'disrupts the onward flow of the tale of Middlemarch life,' and 'acts to trouble and destabilize the ensuing narrative.'[14] In what follows, I shall argue that it is precisely to the onward flow of the tale of Middlemarch life — a life made manifest in 'physically accessible space' — that we should look for a representation of sexual feeling.

Space

When Mr Casaubon presents himself, on the occasion of Dorothea's first visit to Lowick Manor, the 'background' against which he fails to stand out is that constituted by the house itself, by architecture. The house, however, is as indistinct, as hard to make out, as its owner. It lacks expressive shape. Where, the narrator asks, are the children, the open windows, and the vistas that would transform a commonplace building into a home? The shape lacking at Lowick would be the product of good architecture and good sexual selection. Without such shapeliness, Ruskin had insisted in *Sesame and Lilies* (1865), a home is not a home. No longer distinct from the outer world, it becomes little more than 'a part of that outer world which you have roofed over, and lighted fire in'.[15]

13   Ibid., pp. 431–32.
14   Ibid., pp. 436, 433.
15   Ruskin, 'Of Queens' Gardens', published with 'Of Kings' Treasuries' as *Sesame and Lilies* (1865), in *Works*, XVIII, 122.

Karen Chase and Michael Levenson have recently uncovered the fantasy of architectural form which lay at the centre of Victorian conceptions of domestic life. They focus on *The Gentleman's House* (1864), a lavish and influential treatise by the architect Robert Kerr. Kerr was a 'consummate professional', Chase and Levenson observe, who 'brought the technical language of architecture into the general conversation.'[16] The subtitle of his book is 'How to Plan English Residences, from the Parsonage to the Palace'. The topic he had in mind was the accomplishment through architecture of domestic harmony, at the parsonage level and above.

There is a certain triumphalism in Kerr's account of the evolution of the gentleman's house from the eleventh-century Anglo-Saxon hall, comprising one room only, a space shared promiscuously by human and animal, high-born and low-born, men and women, to the complex structures made possible by modern design and engineering. The history of architecture, in short, could be understood as the history of the introduction and development of a concept of form. Form is difference, distinctness. 'The spirit of manufacture, from which home is to be a refuge,' Chase and Levenson remark, 'enters the house in a disciplined squad of modern domestics, whose role is to protect home life from the disruptions they exemplify.'[17] Form is also a high degree of organized internal complexity. Modern architecture, Kerr claimed, is

> a science of delightful intricacy, which, when duly applied, even on the smallest scale, constitutes an edifice a thing of complete organisation, in which every part is assigned its special function, and is found to be contrived for that and no other; the express purpose of the whole being that exquisite result which is signified by our scarcely translatable phrase — *home comfort*.[18]

Form, as Eliot had written in 1868, 'must first depend on the discrimination of wholes and then on the discrimination of parts.'[19] In Kerr's ideal home, the lower-class parts (for the use of the servants) are to be discriminated from the upper-class (for the use of the family), and the male from the female. Chase and Levenson point out that his model dwelling divides 'along a vertical axis that bisects domestic space, running from the saloon through the fountain to the garden thoroughfare'. With one or two exceptions, everything to right of the imaginary line is primarily for the use of men, and everything to the left primarily for the use of women: 'the gentleman's house thus achieves that rational differentiation of the sexes to which it had long aspired.'[20] Form arose out of differentiation, and gave rise in turn to comfort.

Kerr might well have thought the cottages Dorothea Brooke would like her uncle to build by way of improving his estate beneath his attention. But it is worth nothing that the authority to whom Dorothea appeals (*M* 29), John Claudius Loudon, had designed cottages which, although simple in structure, exhibit differentiation

---

16   Karen Chase and Michael Levenson, 'Robert Kerr: *The Gentleman's House* and the One-Room Solution', in *The Spectacle of Intimacy: A Public Life for the Victorian Family* (Princeton, NJ: Princeton University Press, 2000), pp. 156–78 (p. 157).

17   Ibid., p. 165.

18   Robert Kerr, *The Gentleman's House*, 3rd edn (London: John Murray, 1871), p. 12.

19   Eliot, 'Notes on Form', pp. 355–56.

20   Chase and Levenson, 'Robert Kerr', p. 163.

along gender lines. For example, male and female children have separate bedrooms which are approached by separate routes.[21] There is form, in these dwellings, and with it the possibility of comfort. The dwelling described in the greatest detail in *Middlemarch*, Lowick Manor, lies somewhere between the parsonage and the palace. It, too, exhibits differentiation along gender lines. That its formal complexity will ever produce comfort seems doubtful.

The library, Kerr wrote, 'is primarily a sort of Morning-room for gentlemen rather than anything else. Their correspondence is done here, their reading, and, in some measure, their lounging; — and the Billiard-room, for instance, is not unfrequently attached to it. At the same time the ladies are not exactly excluded.' It is rather hard to imagine Casaubon playing billiards; but the ground-floor library is certainly his domain, a place of business and of scholarship (from which Dorothea will not be exactly excluded). His 'views of the womanly nature' (*M* 69) are sufficiently broad to include provision of a boudoir for his wife: a blue-green room on the upper floor with a view down an avenue of limes. According to Kerr, the boudoir 'is a Private Parlour for the mistress of the house [...] as the personal retreat of the lady, it leaves the Drawing-room — and the Morning-room if any — still occupied by the family and guests.'[22]

In *Middlemarch*, marital disputes provoke a retreat into mutually exclusive gendered space. On the morning after their return from the disastrous honeymoon in Rome, Mr Casaubon is to be found in his library interviewing the curate, while Dorothea, upstairs in the boudoir, gazes out on 'the still, white enclosure which made her visible world' (*M* 257). The sight of the miniature of Will Ladislaw's grandmother, a woman who 'had known some difficulty about marriage', sets Dorothea glowing again. At the further thought of the vivid conversations she had held with Ladislaw in Rome, guilt overwhelms her, and she hurries out of the room 'with the irresistible impulse to go and see her husband and inquire if she could do anything for him' (258–59). A sharply polarized space has become for Dorothea an arena for the compulsive rehearsal of anxieties concerning her choice of a mate.

In Chapter 42, after Casaubon has been informed by Lydgate that he is likely to die, and that his wife knows this, Dorothea goes out into the garden to console him, and is bitterly repulsed. As they re-enter the house, Dorothea disengages her arm from his. The direction he subsequently moves in will express his feelings about her.

> He entered the library and shut himself in, alone with his sorrow.
> She went up into her boudoir. The open bow-window let in the serene glory
> of the afternoon lying in the avenue, where the lime-trees cast long shadows.
> But Dorothea knew nothing of the scene. (*M* 399)

Each has retreated into 'inward misery', and at the same time into what one might think of as an extremity of gender identification: all male, all female. The issue rendered critical by this going to extremes is stark enough. The chapter had

---

21 John Claudius Loudon, *Encyclopaedia of Cottage, Farm, and Villa Architecture and Furniture*, new edn (London: Longman, Brown, Green, and Longmans, 1846), pp. 9–11, 1135–45.

22 Kerr, *Gentleman's House*, pp. 116, 114.

begun with Casaubon's realization that '[a]gainst certain facts he was helpless: against Will Ladislaw's existence, his defiant stay in the neighbourhood of Lowick, and his flippant state of mind with regard to the possessors of authentic, well-stamped erudition: against Dorothea's nature, always taking on some new shape of ardent activity' (391–92). The game is up, or almost up. It is not too late to plan a posthumous revenge. Dorothea, meanwhile, gripped by 'rebellious anger' (399), seems momentarily, as we have seen, on the verge of hysteria. Polarization has destroyed the variability which distinguishes her from other women. Once again, though, a reflux of feeling sends her out of the room in search of her husband (401).

Dorothea's blue-green boudoir has been the subject of a great deal of commentary. Is it the kind of space that becomes for the heroines of other Victorian novels a critical and enabling point of view on the world?[23] It is in the boudoir, in Chapter 80, after a night of agony brought about by the sight of Will Ladislaw at Rosamond Lydgate's feet, that Dorothea looks out at the traffic on the road beyond the entrance-gates and feels 'part of that involuntary, palpitating life' (*M* 741). This time, she leaves the room not guiltily to console her husband, but with unshakeable conviction, like one of the new breed of female philanthropists and rescue-workers, to 'save' a fallen woman (742).[24] This time, the retreat into 'inward misery' has proved a turning-point, as she finally transcends the egoism of desire. It might also be the moment at which, to pursue Carol Siegel's line of argument, intertextuality finally transcends domestic realism: the culmination of a counter-narrative which reproduces the progress made, from dejection through bitter resentment to acceptance, by another forestry-bound protagonist, in Coleridge's 'This Lime-Tree Bower, My Prison'?[25] Dorothea, as Will Ladislaw had been moved to remark, *is* a poem.

My feeling is that domestic realism keeps a pretty tight grip on the mapping of space in *Middlemarch*; rather, the mapping of space is the grip it keeps on the novel. The boudoir and the library, although on different floors and offering different outlooks, exist in relation to one another on a grid intelligible in the light of Robert Kerr's architectural fantasy. What the novel tells us, however, is that the most decisively gendered spaces on the grid are dead spaces. Mr Casaubon lives for the most part in his library, and the room becomes associated with the heart disease first made manifest within it. Dorothea finds only solitude in her boudoir, but little relief from her heart's dis-ease. Even the stories arising out of the miniature of Ladislaw's grandmother will remain sterile unless acted upon. The conclusion Dorothea draws from her look out of the window is that she should stop looking

23   I am thinking of Jane Eyre 'shrined' in the 'double retirement' of a window-seat: *Jane Eyre*, ed. by Margaret Smith (Oxford: Oxford University Press, 1993), p. 8. See Karen Chase, *Eros and Psyche: The Representation of Personality in Charlotte Brontë, Charles Dickens, and George Eliot* (London: Methuen, 1984), pp. 85–91. Few novels, Chase remarks, are as 'spatially *articulate*' as *Jane Eyre*: *Middlemarch* may be one of them.

24   David Trotter, 'Some Brothels: Nineteenth-Century Philanthropy and the Poetics of Space', *Critical Quarterly*, 44 (2002), 25–32; reprinted as part of Chapter 9 in this book.

25   Shifra Hochberg, 'The Vista from Dorothea's Boudoir Window and a Coleridgean Source', *English Language Notes*, 29 (1992), 41–46. The scene may also have a visual source or 'intertext'. See Joseph Nicholes, 'Dorothea in the Moated Grange: Millais's *Mariana* and the *Middlemarch* Window-Scenes', *Victorians Institute Journal*, 20 (1992), 93–124.

out of the window. 'Moving through space is less important for Jane [Eyre], than witnessing an expanse.'[26] The opposite is true, I hope to show, for Dorothea. The form produced by the gendering of space in Lowick Manor is too much form of the wrong kind.

The 'new shapes' of 'ardent activity' which so trouble Casaubon emerge in spaces which do not yet bear the marks of a gendered habit of occupancy. After his seizure, Casaubon, who has been forbidden to work in the library, receives visitors in a previously undescribed room on the upper floor. In the opening chapter of Book IV ('Three Love Problems'), Mr Brooke, the Chettams, and Mrs Cadwallader arrive to observe Simon Featherstone's funeral from the window of this room, while Casaubon, who at present has little taste for funerals, slips away, in defiance of doctor's orders, to the library. This displacement within the gendered household grid produces, if not a new angle of sight, then the abrupt admission, as into a camera obscura, of new shapes. But for her visitors Dorothea too would have been shut up in the library, and unable to witness a scene which, aloof though it is from the 'tenor of her life', makes a deep impression (*M* 305).

> This dream-like association with something alien and ill-understood with the deepest secrets of her experience seemed to mirror that sense of loneliness which was due to the very ardour of Dorothea's nature. (306)

Dorothea experiences a double alienation. The 'something alien and ill-understood' is both her own sexuality and the world she looks out at and down on from the upper-floor windows of Lowick Manor. 'And Dorothea was not at ease in the perspective and chillness of that height' (306). Her protest, in effect, is against too much external difference: that conscience should look out at and down on sexual feeling as the gentry look out at and down on the labourers in the field. However, the very mirroring of one alienation in another suggests that the form produced by architecture, at least, is permeable. The terms in which that permeability is described are worth noting.

> 'How piteous!' said Dorothea. 'This funeral seems to me the most dismal thing I ever saw. It is a blot on the morning. I cannot bear to think that any one should die and leave no love behind.'
>
> She was going to say more, but she saw her husband enter and seat himself a little in the background. The difference his presence made to her was not always a happy one: she felt that he often inwardly objected to her speech.
>
> 'Positively,' exclaimed Mrs Cadwallader, 'there is a new face come out from behind that broad man queerer than any of them: a little round head with bulging eyes — a sort of frog-face — do look. He must be of another blood, I think.'
>
> 'Let me see!' said Celia, with awakened curiosity, standing behind Mrs Cadwallader and leaning forward over her head. 'Oh, what an odd face!' Then with a quick change to another sort of surprised expression, she added, 'Why, Dodo, you never told me that Mr Ladislaw was come again!'
>
> Dorothea felt a shock of alarm: every one noticed her sudden paleness as she looked up immediately at her uncle, while Mr Casaubon looked at her. (307–08)

26 Chase, *Eros and Psyche*, p. 88.

Dorothea perceives the lack of love at Featherstone's funeral as a blot on the morning, a stain; a thought interrupted by her husband's entrance into the room. The thought is taken up, in effect, by Mrs Cadwallader, who has spotted a different kind of blot, a 'frog-face' among the mourners. Mrs Cadwallader is the spokesperson for the perspective and chillness granted by social 'height'. She has already complained about the rich Lowick farmers, who are in her view 'monsters' because there is no way to class them (306). The frog-face is a further monstrosity, a genetic blot. We might recall, at this point, that Mrs Cadwallader has been characterized from the outset as the voice not only of social status — 'her feeling towards the vulgar rich was a sort of religious hatred' (55–56) — but also, in her perpetual concern with 'the Miss Brookes and their matrimonial prospects' (56), as the voice of sexual selection. Celia Brooke has no sooner confirmed the frog-face's oddity than, substituting as it were one lens for another in the camera obscura, she spots something even odder: Will Ladislaw's presence among the mourners. The second discovery bears, of course, upon the 'deepest secrets' of Dorothea's experience. It reintroduces into Lowick Manor a difference brought about not by architecture but by variation within the species: the difference between Will and the husband who cannot avoid noticing her sudden, demonstrative paleness. The paleness is also a blot of a kind, a stain.

The permeabilities registered with quite astonishing subtlety in this scene are evidence that the production of new forms — of forms demonstrating variability — may require a certain engagement with formlessness. One of its effects is to identify Will Ladislaw with Joshua Rigg, the man with the frog-face, and Featherstone's illegitimate son and, it turns out, his heir.[27] Mrs Cadwallader supposes that Rigg must be of 'another blood'; before long, Ladislaw's habit of stretching himself at full length on the rug in houses where he feels at home will raise suspicions concerning his 'dangerously mixed blood' (*M* 435).

Joshua Rigg's queerness is a matter of class. The problem lies not so much in his 'high chirping voice' and 'vile accent' (*M* 319) as in the status Featherstone's money will enable him to claim, a status he is not felt to have earned either by birth or by endeavour. Indeed, he has already begun to merge into a class above the one he was born into. His 'nails and modesty', we are told, 'were comparable to those of most gentlemen; though his ambition had been educated only by the opportunities of a clerk and accountant in the smaller commercial houses of a seaport' (387). Joshua Rigg is a clerk masquerading as minor gentry: the epitome of social mobility.

The petty bourgeoisie in general, and clerks in particular, had long been the focus of a Cadwallader-like religious hatred of the vulgar rich, of those who had got above themselves.[28] The hatred arose during the transition from the Hungry Forties, when the perceived threat came from a turbulent working class, to the prosperous Fifties, when the perceived threat came from an emergent mass culture.

27   The point is made by R. L. P. Jackson in a perceptive discussion of the scene: 'A History of the Lights and Shadows: The Secret Motion of *Middlemarch*', *Cambridge Quarterly*, 26 (1997), 1–18 (p. 13).
28   I describe this hatred and its implications at greater length in *Paranoid Modernism: Literary Experiment, Psychosis, and the Professionalization of English Society* (Oxford: Oxford University Press, 2001), ch. 3.

The anxiety it expressed was an anxiety about imitation. Joshua Rigg threatens only when he starts behaving like a gentleman, with regard to fingernails and modesty. Such behaviour disguises the external difference which gives one shape to a gentleman and another to a clerk. Imitation produces a formlessness which the religious hatred of social aspiration grasped as monstrosity: as strange blood, as an unclassifiable frog-face.

Joshua Rigg's fictional ancestor is Uriah Heep, in Charles Dickens's *David Copperfield* (1849–50). Heep, a man of conspicuously humble birth, begins as an articled clerk to lawyer Wickfield, but aims higher. He means to become Wickfield's partner, and if possible his son-in-law; and he recognizes David, who has himself been brought low in the world, but is making up ground rapidly, as a rival in both respects. His aim is to resemble David, and then to take his place. The aspiration it encodes is rendered as a physical formlessness or monstrosity which from the outset arouses in David a profound loathing. His face may not be frog-like, but his touch most certainly is.[29] Uriah — like Joshua Rigg in Mrs Cadwallader's eyes — is repellent first, and harmful second. His loathsomeness precedes anything that could possibly be construed as wrong-doing. The differences the two men erase by imitation are restored in and through the disgust their monstrosity arouses.

Dickens tended to arrange spectacular purgative expulsions for his petty-bourgeois imitators. The scene in *David Copperfield* in which Mr Micawber exposes Heep's treachery, like the scene in *Bleak House* in which Mr Bucket sends the Smallweeds and Chadbands packing, is almost euphoric in its sense of a wrong righted and an unmanageable feeling got rid of.[30] Eliot, by contrast, seems altogether relaxed about Joshua Rigg. Rigg sells the property he has inherited and returns to his seaport to run a money-changer's shop. He had meant, when he had property, 'to do many things, one of them being to marry a genteel young person; but these were all accidents and joys that imagination could dispense with' (*M* 488). Eliot did not share Dickens's fear that the petty bourgeoisie would seize power. For her, Rigg is of genetic rather than social or political interest.

Peter Featherstone had wanted a copy of himself.

> The copy in this case bore more of outside resemblance to the mother, in whose sex frog-features, accompanied with fresh-coloured cheeks and a well-rounded figure, are compatible with much charm for a certain order of admirers. The result is sometimes a frog-faced male, desirable, surely, to no order of intelligent beings. (*M* 386–87)

The frog-features have the merit, from a scientific and literary point of view, of providing evidence of the variation of species. Rigg is, for better or worse, different (from those born and bred in Middlemarch). Eliot's interest lay not in the bad features, but in the process of variation which gave rise to them, and which might

29   Charles Dickens, *David Copperfield*, ed. by Nina Burgis (Oxford: Oxford University Press, 1983), pp. 307–08.
30   Ibid., 610–21; *Bleak House*, ed. by Nicola Bradbury (Harmondsworth: Penguin Books, 1996), pp. 943–48. There are similar scenes in Thackeray: for example, *The History of Pendennis*, ed. by J. I. M. Stewart (Harmondsworth: Penguin Books, 1972), pp. 714–19.

just as well give rise to good ones. Will Ladislaw's features, too, are unmistakeably the product of variation. Indeed, they express variability: the little ripple in his nose, we remember, seems like 'a preparation for metamorphosis' (196). Will's main trait, Chase observes, 'is his ability to vary his traits.'[31]

Will Ladislaw and Joshua Rigg converge once again in Chapter 47, when Will attends a service at Lowick church in the hope of seeing Dorothea: that is, in order to display himself. Against the background of stolid parishioners, Rigg's frog-face seems like 'something alien and unaccountable' (*M* 443). As Jackson notes, the phrasing connects this abrupt manifestation back to the scene at Featherstone's funeral, in Chapter 34, when Dorothea had found the 'deepest secrets of her experience' mirrored in 'something alien and ill-understood' in the world outside (306).[32] It may be that in order to renew both self and society one has to engage in some measure with that which does not at first appear to have a form except in pure difference. Returning to his seaport, and money-changing, Rigg remains, like Will Ladislaw, a figure of shape-shifting, of metamorphosis.[33] Mrs Cadwallader, so alert to intruding frog-faces, had in that earlier scene associated Will's fitness for sexual selection with a certain indeterminacy of rank and function. 'A very pretty sprig,' said Mrs Cadwallader, drily. 'What is your nephew to be, Mr Casaubon?' (309). His fitness, as Chase points out, will depend not only on his looks, but on his ability to assume the responsibilities of an 'ardent public man' (782). Formlessness deliberately assumed may yet become the basis of a new and better kind of form. 'The free play in Will's life as a dilettante is the freedom to accept metamorphosis until its work is done.'[34]

Movement

In *Middlemarch*, it is not space which constitutes new form — the form made possible by metamorphosis — but movement through or into space: a space which is itself constituted, or re-constituted, by movement. In assessing the force of movement, we need to start where the novel does, with that difference between Dorothea and Celia which, as Helena Michie has persuasively demonstrated, structures the first half of the novel.

> When the two girls were in the drawing-room alone, Celia said —
> 'How very ugly Mr Casaubon is!'
> 'Celia! He is one of the most distinguished-looking men I ever saw. He is remarkably like the portrait of Locke. He has the same deep eye-sockets.'

31   Chase, *George Eliot: Middlemarch* (Cambridge: Cambridge University Press, 1991), 69. I am greatly indebted to Chase's account of Ladislaw's career as the novel's 'most serious use of Darwinian insight into the understanding of character within history': pp. 67–72.
32   Jackson, 'A History', pp. 13–14.
33   Franco Moretti points out that in Jane Austen's novels, which he sees as among other things an imaginary act of nation-building, narrative complication always takes place, not in the 'introverted, rural England' where the heroines were brought up and where they will live with their husbands, but in cities like London and Bath, or in seaports: *Atlas of the European Novel, 1800–1900* (London: Verso, 1998), pp. 18–19.
34   Chase, *George Eliot's Middlemarch*, pp. 70–71.

'Had Locke those two white moles with hairs on them?'

'Oh, I daresay! when people of a certain sort looked at him,' said Dorothea, walking away a little. (*M* 19)

Celia, as Michie puts it, views the world through a 'corporeal lens'. She lets us see the flaws and infirmities Dorothea has chosen not to notice. The contrast between the sisters is a contrast not only between modes of appearance and conduct, but between modes of perception. It enables Eliot to 'resolve the literary problem of representing a heroine who is simultaneously innocent and desirable, sexually repressed and highly erotic.' For a while, at least. As Ladislaw looms larger and larger in Dorothea's life, so Celia recedes. 'At this point of exchange between Celia and Will, when the impulse of disruptive sexuality is passed from sister to lover, Celia becomes frozen into an almost parodic rendition of herself.' [35]

We need, however, to note not only what the sisters see and say, but what they do. Celia's commentary on Mr Casaubon's moles makes it clear that she knows he is not a fit mate for Dorothea. Dorothea, infuriated by the commentary, *does* something. She speaks in anger, and then, apparently as the outcome of speech, or of the feeling which has animated speech, walks away a little. That walking away a little is performative rather than purposeful. She is not going anywhere. It supplements speech, and it fills a lack in speech. It does what speech cannot do: occupy, or take possession of, space. It enacts force: the force of feeling; the force of Dorothea's knowledge, already, in excess or contradiction of the words she has spoken, of Mr Casaubon's disability. The force will stay with her, while Celia becomes frozen into a parody of herself: characterized increasingly by the 'comfortable staccato' of her voice, or by movement which is never anything other than merely purposeful (*M* 459–60).

The contrast established in this scene between Dorothea and Celia is a contrast established by the skilful deployment of one of the basic techniques of domestic realism: the provision of speech-tags ('she said', 'he exclaimed', and so on) which embed what the characters say in the environment (the space and time) delineated by the narrative voice. For the most part, in nineteenth-century fiction, speech-tags served the relatively straightforward purpose of identifying the speaker. Some novelists, however, did put them to a particular use. Dickens, for example, in his early novels, developed the habit of interrupting his characters at intricate length.[36] In *Middlemarch*, Eliot constructed out of speech-tags a bridge between what is said and an action which exceeds or contradicts what is said; rather, she does so, as is domestic realism's privilege, in relation to some characters but not in relation to others. The syntactic pattern established in Dorothea's response to Celia's commentary on moles is a persistent one. It enables some characters to occupy or command space in a way that others do not. Those characters make their presence felt by the follow-through of speech into movement, of word into deed. For them,

35   Helena Michie, *Sororophobia: Differences among Women in Literature and Culture* (Oxford: Oxford University Press, 1992), pp. 42, 46.

36   Mark Lambert, *Dickens and the Suspended Quotation* (New Haven, CT: Yale University Press, 1981).

space becomes an arena for the display of plumage; that is, of vigour, of sexual fitness.

The only other character who moves as Dorothea moves, with feeling but without purpose, as a supplement to the lack in speech, is Will Ladislaw. They are alike in the shape of their movements even when they are alike in nothing else. That compatibility serves, one might hazard, as the novelist's account of the basis of appropriate sexual selection. In Chapter 22, as the Casaubons are preparing to leave Rome, Will visits Dorothea to say farewell, at a time when he knows Casaubon will not be there. His use of the arena available to him begins to explain why Casaubon might be thought to stand 'rayless' beside him. His first performance for Dorothea's benefit is a protest against her melancholy. '"You are too young — it is an anachronism for you to have such thoughts," said Will energetically, with a quick shake of the head, habitual to him' (*M* 206). The thoughts, as he immediately makes clear, are those relating to the 'stone prison' which awaits her at Lowick. They also relate, evidently, to the difference between an ancient husband and his youthful wife (and her equally youthful admirer). It is the former who must be reckoned the anachronism. Will eclipses his rival momentarily by that quick shake of the head, by the force of the carry-through from word into deed. He fears that he may have 'gone too far' (206). But Dorothea, attending rather to the tone of his utterance than to its content, and possibly not unappreciative of the movement which accompanies it, answers with a 'gentle smile' (207). Before long the smile will be reinforced by a 'remonstrant energy' the equal of his (207), and by movement. '"And there is one thing even now that you can do," said Dorothea, rising and walking a little way under the strength of a recurring impulse' (210). That 'one thing' is to stop criticizing Casaubon's scholarship. Will's criticisms, of course, have always been a protest against her choice of husband. He would do well to pay less attention to her request than to the rising and walking away a little which accompanies it.

In *Middlemarch*, the syntactic pattern evident in the initial deployment of speech-tags itself constitutes, as the novel develops, narrative pattern. In Chapter 37, after returning to Middlemarch to act as Mr Brooke's secretary, Will visits Dorothea at Lowick, and they immediately resume the conversation they had held in Rome (*M* 341). Once again, he protests against her imprisonment (342). Once again, he shakes his head backwards, and then lays into Casaubon's practice as a scholar. Dorothea responds with rather more than a gentle smile.

> 'I should like you to stay very much,' said Dorothea at once, as simply and readily as she had spoken in Rome. There was not the shadow of a reason in her mind at the moment why she should not say so.
> 'Then I *will* stay,' said Ladislaw, shaking his head backward, rising and going towards the window, as if to see whether the rain had ceased. (345)

Siegel understands the punning on 'will' as a connection to Shakespeare's sonnets: as evidence that Ladislaw's very being is intertextual.[37] But the conventions of domestic realism also play their part, here. They connect what Ladislaw says ('Then I *will* stay') not to Shakespeare, but to a certain occupation of space, a performance:

---

37   Siegel, '"This Thing…"', p. 52.

a shake of the head backwards, and a movement with only the slightest pretence of ostensible purpose ('as if to see whether the rain had ceased').

In Chapter 39, Dorothea surprises Mr Brooke and his secretary at work in the library at Tipton Grange. On her announcement, Ladislaw 'started up as from an electric shock, and felt a tingling at his finger-ends' (*M* 363). His response prompts the narrator to some thoughts about variability in sexual selection: about the subtle effects which 'make a man's passion for one woman differ from his passion for another as joy in the morning light over valley and river and white mountain-top differs from joy among Chinese lanterns and glass panels' (364–65). Dorothea's allure is clearly not of the Chinese lantern and glass panel variety. It provokes him, once Mr Brooke has left the room, to more than words. '"I may not have another opportunity of speaking to you about what has occurred," said Will, rising with a movement of impatience, and holding the back of his chair with both hands' (366). What he has to tell her is that Casaubon, consumed by sexual jealousy, has barred him from Lowick. The bitterness of their rivalry can no longer be concealed. It arouses in Will a new display: an impatient arising.

Since its theme is courtship, the narrative pattern constituted by these performances asserts itself only when Dorothea and Will are alone together; when they are in company, for example at Lydgate's house (*M* 407), or in church at Lowick (444), both feel constrained. After Casaubon's death, Will calls at Lowick Manor to say goodbye. Dorothea elects to see him in the drawing-room:

> The drawing-room was the most neutral room in the house to her — the one least associated with the trials of her married life: the damask matched the wood-work, which was all white and gold; there were two tall mirrors and tables with nothing on them — in brief, it was a room where you had no reason for sitting in one place rather than in another. (508)

This lack of association, this lack of a reason to sit in one place rather than another, releases the room from the immobilizing effects of gender polarization. Neutrality makes courtship conceivable again. Indeed, Will only just saves himself from falling at Dorothea's feet.

> 'I shall never hear from you. And you will forget all about me.'
>
> 'No,' said Dorothea, 'I shall never forget you. I have never forgotten any one whom I once knew. My life has never been crowded, and seems not likely to be so. And I have a great deal of space for memory at Lowick, haven't I?' She smiled.
>
> 'Good God!' Will burst out passionately, rising with his hat still in his hand, and walking to a marble table, where he suddenly turned and leaned his back against it. The blood had mounted to his face and neck, and he looked almost angry. (511)

The speech-tag, itself unusually animated ('burst out'), is the bridge to an embedding description of most unusual length and particularity. Will rises, and walks away, and stands upright, the blood mounted to his face and neck. His arousal, here, may be the closest the Victorian novel ever came to describing an erection. Not having to sit in one place rather than another allows you to make yourself fully felt.

There is to be one further farewell, in Chapter 62, in the library at Tipton Grange. Will is reminded of their meeting in Rome, Dorothea of the time he came to say goodbye to her at Lowick. His getting up and going to the window is itself reminiscent of a previous encounter in the library at Tipton (*M* 593). The novel has established a network of courtship scenes in which the drama of sexual selection takes place. Will and Dorothea perform for each other, but there can be no doubt that (as Darwinian theory would lead one to expect) his performance is the more brazen. It is also the more consistent. Will's arisings are to some extent habitual. They punctuate, for example, his painful interview with Bulstrode in Chapter 61 (584–86). Even on that occasion, however, what provokes them is the need to keep his honour unblemished if he is to stand a chance with Dorothea (586). They are *for* Dorothea, then, if not always provoked by her.

There follows the mutual self-revelation, at Lowick Manor. It crosses Dorothea's mind that she cannot receive Will in the library, 'where her husband's prohibition seemed to dwell' (*M* 757). The prohibition has already been lifted, I would suggest, through her frank acknowledgement of the fitness of her chosen mate. 'There was nothing that she longed for at that moment except to see Will: the possibility of seeing him had thrust itself insistently between her and every other object; and yet she had a throbbing excitement like an alarm upon her — a sense that she was doing something daringly defiant for his sake' (758). Their encounter is constituted by a by now familiar pattern of expressive but purposeless movements. The movements lift the spell: they take possession of the space once possessed by Casaubon. There is a certain brutality in this, and the brutality provides an unspoken context for the first embrace, which critics and readers have found so disappointing (762). The embrace is, admittedly, detumescent. But it may be that Eliot, having been so Darwinianly frank throughout the novel, having in this scene allowed Will and Dorothea to make their presence fully felt by movement through and into space, really did not need to do anything more.

CHAPTER 6

On the Nail:
Functional Objects in
Thomas Hardy's *The Woodlanders*

This essay is dedicated to the proposition that in some Victorian novels, and most notably in Thomas Hardy's *The Woodlanders* (1887), the purely functional object makes difference — of class, gender, race, or ethnicity — palpable. The functional object has a purpose, evidently: it is not yet bric-à-brac, which in turn is not yet waste-matter, or formlessness. Unlike bric-à-brac and waste-matter, it does not emerge fully into representation, in Victorian fiction. But its reticence can be made to count. Neither significant nor insignificant, neither symbol nor reality-effect, it obtrudes just sufficiently into the scene to prompt an otherwise inconceivable understanding of difference as difference.

Roughly speaking, in literature as in life, an object presents itself to us in one or more of four aspects: material substance, process of manufacture, function, and appearance. In life, the functional object is an object at once utterly ubiquitous and utterly unremarkable. There is nothing at all precious about the substance of which it is formed. A machine made it, or a person acting mechanically. It does not bear witness to human creativity or expertise. Even the function, which justifies its existence, must be reckoned as mundane. Indeed, it is at its least noteworthy precisely when justifying its existence. For a functional object, when functioning, eschews the glamour of not having a function: the glamour of redundancy, excess, waste. No wonder there are relatively few of them in literature, which overdoses on redundancy, excess, and waste. No wonder criticism has had little or nothing to say about them even when they do put in a rare appearance.

There is now a rich tradition of sophisticated, far-reaching enquiry into material culture in the Victorian age, and in modernity in general.[1] Within that tradition,

1   Asa Briggs, *Victorian Things* (London: Batsford, 1988); Thomas Richards, *The Commodity Culture of Victorian England: Advertising and Spectacle, 1851–1914* (Stanford, CA: Stanford University Press, 1990); Andrew H. Miller, *Novels Behind Glass: Commodity Culture and Victorian Narrative* (Cambridge: Cambridge University Press, 1995); Deborah Cohen, *Household Gods: The British and Their Possessions* (New Haven, CT: Yale University Press, 2006); Elaine Freedgood, *The Ideas in Things: Fugitive Meaning in the Victorian Novel* (Chicago, IL: Chicago University Press, 2006); John Plotz, *Portable Property: Victorian Culture on the Move* (Princeton, NJ: Princeton University Press, 2008). See

the object of study has for the most part been conceived of as the product of a double abstraction: first, of form and function from material substance; secondly, of meaning from form and function. How, and why, did stuff become absorbed into those discourses concerning value which constitute a culture's sustained reflection upon itself and its arrangements? The terms in which this enquiry has hitherto been conducted — product, commodity, good, possession, fetish, gift — continue to illuminate the poetics and politics of matter's self-transcendence in modern literature. Those terms remain productively faithful to their ultimate origin in the political and economic theories of Karl Marx, for whom wood held little or no philosophical interest until it took shape as a table, and began to get ideas about its status as a commodity.[2] They define for us what it was that people living in a particular place at a particular time thought remarkable about the material substance, process of manufacture, function, or appearance of a particular object or objects. In recent research, I have tried to describe what happens to objects when they abruptly cease to be remarkable by falling out of circulation: when they disappear from discourses of value.[3] Here, I want to explore in a speculative fashion the fate in literature of an object which was never in any way remarkable in the first place.

The unremarkable object I have in mind is an ubiquitous and everlasting piece of ironmongery: the common household nail, which Webster defines as a 'slender and usually pointed and headed fastener designed for impact insertion'. The standard nineteenth-century nail was not forged, but cut from iron strips or rods, either by a machine in a factory, or by hand in a workshop attached to a house or cottage.[4] A person acting mechanically made it, out of cheap material, to the same pattern, for purchase in bulk. Buried (often up to its neck) in some other substance, it advertises neither function nor appearance. It is not likely to get ideas above its station. In what

also: Susan Stewart, *On Longing: Narratives of the Miniature, the Gigantic, the Souvenir, the Collection* (Durham, NC: Duke University Press, 1993); Bill Brown, *A Sense of Things: The Object Matter of American Literature* (Chicago, IL: Chicago University Press, 2003); Peter Schwenger, *The Tears of Things: Melancholy and Physical Objects* (Minneapolis, MI: Minnesota University Press, 2006); Glenn Willmott, *Modernist Goods: Primitivism, the Market, and the Gift* (Toronto: University of Toronto Press, 2008); Elizabeth Outka, *Consuming Traditions: Modernity, Modernism, and the Commodified Authentic* (Oxford: Oxford University Press, 2009); and Bill Brown, 'Objects, Others, and Us (The Refabrication of Things)', *Critical Inquiry*, 36 (2010), 183–207. The most notable attempt to think back in the opposite direction, from form and function to material substance, is Isobel Armstrong's comprehensive and consistently illuminating *Victorian Glassworlds: Glass Culture and the Imagination, 1830–1880* (Oxford: Oxford University Press, 2008).

2   Karl Marx, *Capital*, trans. by Ben Fowkes, 3 vols (Harmondsworth: Penguin Books, 1976), I, 163–64.

3   David Trotter, 'Household Clearances in Victorian Fiction', in *The Uses of Phobia: Essays on Literature and Film* (Oxford: Wiley-Blackwell, 2010), pp. 17–28. Reprinted as Chapter 2 in this book.

4   Hugh Bodey, *Nailmaking* (Botley: Shire Publications, 2008). Working conditions in the industry became the subject of a number of commentaries, some of which, notably those by Friedrich Engels and John Ruskin, have in their turn been commented on. See Valentine Cunningham, ' "In the Darg": Fiction Nails the Midlands Metal-Worker', in *British Industrial Fictions* ed. by H. Gustav Klaus and Stephen Knight (Cardiff: University of Wales Press, 2000), pp. 36–53. My concern here is with the finished product only. See Friedrich Engels, *The Condition of the Working Class in England*, ed. by E. J. Hobsbawm (St Albans: Granada, 1969), pp. 228–29; John Ruskin, in *Works*, ed. by E. T. Cook and Alexander Wedderburn, 39 vols (London: Longmans, Green, 1907), XXIX, 173 — 5.

follows, I will examine this functional object's existence at or on occasion slightly above the threshold of representation in a variety of nineteenth-century novels; and then consider how and why it might be thought to articulate difference in Hardy's *The Woodlanders*.

Nails in Victorian Fiction

Nails, like pretty much any other sort of object, can of course serve as a plot device, and thus rise momentarily above their station. In Gothic, and other varieties of romance, specimens prised from a wall or floorboard sometimes come in handy for genre-specific activities such as the picking of locks or digging of holes in prison walls. William Godwin's Caleb Williams, for example, finds himself shackled to the floor of a cell in one such establishment, barely able to see the hand before his face.

> But my eyes, after a practice of two or three weeks, accommodated themselves to this circumstance, and I learned to distinguish the minutest objects. One day, as I was alternately meditating and examining the objects around me, I chanced to observe a nail trodden into the mud floor at no great distance from me. I immediately conceived the desire of possessing myself of this implement; but, for fear of surprise, people passing perpetually to and fro, I contented myself for the present with remarking its situation so accurately that I might easily find it again in the dark. Accordingly, as soon as my door was shut, I seized upon this new treasure, and having contrived to fashion it to my purpose, found that I could unlock with it the padlock that fastened me to the staple in the floor.[5]

Caleb here acts the *bricoleur*, making art out of whatever lies, literally, to hand. The nail's new function — to pick a lock — arises directly out of the failure of its old one: out of its having strayed so far from the purpose for which it was designed as to end up trodden into a mud floor. Thus re-purposed, it is for Caleb not just an 'implement', but a 'treasure'; and for Godwin, too, since it allows him neatly to advance the plot of his novel. Sir Walter Scott's Waverley, similarly confined, seems merely to want to discover what's going on outside.

> At length, upon accurate examination, the infirm state of his wooden prison-house appeared to supply the means of gratifying his curiosity, for out of a spot which was somewhat decayed he was able to extract a nail. Through this minute aperture he could perceive a female form, wrapped in a plaid, in the act of conversing with Janet. But, since the days of our grandmother Eve, the gratification of inordinate curiosity has generally borne its penalty in disappointment. The form was not that of Flora, nor was the face visible; and, to crown his disappointment, while he laboured with the nail to enlarge the hole, that he might obtain a more complete view, a slight noise betrayed his purpose, and the object of his curiosity instantly disappeared, nor, so far as he could observe, did she again revisit the cottage.[6]

5   William Godwin, *Caleb Williams*, ed. by David McCracken (Oxford: Oxford University Press, 1970), p. 199.

6   Sir Walter Scott, *Waverley; or, 'Tis Sixty Years Since*, ed. by Claire Lamont (Oxford: Oxford University Press, 1981), p. 180.

Waverley, too, acts the *bricoleur*. Scott, however, aims to do more than neatly advance the plot. The mythic parallel, rather oddly (or perhaps slyly) casting the brawny protagonist as Eve, attributes redundancy to the human condition, rather than to the level of skill demonstrated in the pursuit of any particular practice. In both cases, romance, distinguishing systematically between life and literature, has found a use in literature for that which no longer has a use in life.

In domestic fiction, which does not distinguish systematically between life and literature, nails feature for the most part descriptively: as objects on which to hang other objects, usually objects of considerable personal meaning and value such as mirrors, portraits, scriptural texts, keys, lanterns, watches, coats, hats, bonnets, shawls, and so on — up to and including the occasional gun or blunt implement.[7] The nail itself, mentioned strictly in passing, does no more rhetorically than indicate, by its insignificance, the significance the object it supports has in one way or another accumulated through narrative. Its existence, or rather its being mentioned at all, creates a hierarchy. It is there so that we may notice disparities of material substance, process of manufacture, function, and appearance between the nail and the burden it carries: sometimes to grotesque effect, as, for example, in *Jude the Obscure* (1896), when the body of little Jude is found hanging suspended from one by a piece of box-cord.[8]

Like all other domestic objects, nails do, of course, lapse sooner or later into waste. Delays can occur, however, in their lapsing into formlessness. Useless, but not yet fully disposed of, they persist as bric-à-brac, as that which possesses form without function. They may come to our attention, in that capacity, by the damage they inflict on human or animal flesh. In *The Golden Bough* (1890–1915), Sir James Frazer records instances of a form of contagious magic active in a variety of cultures which involved treatment of the cause rather than the effect of a wound: 'If a horse wounds its foot by treading on a nail, a Suffolk groom will invariably preserve the nail, clean it, and grease it every day, to prevent the foot from festering'.[9] Charles Dickens even managed to incorporate the decay of ironware into a secular myth of the death and resurrection of organic and inorganic substance. In Chapter 18 of *Bleak House* (1852–53), Esther Summerson describes a visit to Mr Boythorn's converted parsonage in Lincolnshire, with its orchard and garden straight out of a seventeenth-century country-house poem.

7   Though it is quite likely that the most frequent reference of all in Victorian fiction is to the biblical story of Jael (Judges 4. 17–21), the Jewish woman who entertained an enemy general in her tent with a view to nailing his head to the ground with a tent-peg, which crops up metaphorically in novels as diverse as Charlotte Brontë's *Villette* (1847), Rhoda Broughton's *Cometh Up as a Flower* (1867), Anthony Trollope's *The Last Chronicle of Barset* (1867), Wilkie Collins's *Man and Wife* (1870), and Olive Schreiner's *The Story of an African Farm* (1883); and many more besides. It is not hard to understand why a metaphor combining sexuality, violence, altruism, and female self-assertion should have appealed strongly to Victorian writers. But I have taken the view that a tent-peg is not a nail, as that commodity was and is generally understood, known and used.

8   Thomas Hardy, *Jude the Obscure*, ed. by Patricia Ingham (Oxford: Oxford University Press, 1985), p. 354.

9   Sir James Frazer, *The Golden Bough: A Study in Magic and Religion*, ed. by Robert Fraser (Harmondsworth: Penguin Books, 1994), p. 42.

But, indeed, everything about the place wore an aspect of maturity and abundance. The old lime-tree walk was like green cloisters, the very shadows of the cherry-trees and apple-trees were heavy with fruit, the gooseberry-bushes were so laden that their branches arched and rested on the earth, the strawberries and raspberries grew in like profusion, and the peaches basked by the hundred on the wall. Tumbled about among the spread nets and the glass frames sparkling and winking in the sun, there were such heaps of drooping pods, and marrows, and cucumbers, that every foot of ground appeared a vegetable treasury, while the smell of sweet herbs and all kinds of wholesome growth (to say nothing of the neighbouring meadows where the hay was carrying) made the whole air a great nosegay. Such stillness and composure reigned within the orderly precincts of the old red wall, that even the feathers hung in garlands to scare the birds hardly stirred; and the wall had such a ripening influence that where, here and there high up, a disused nail and scrap of list still clung to it, it was easier to fancy that they had mellowed with the changing seasons, than that they had rusted and decayed according to the common fate.[10]

The phrase 'vegetable treasury' wonderfully encapsulates nature's capacity to create not just sustenance, but meaning: an abundance in which use-value is hard to distinguish from exchange-value. Functional objects such as the nail high up on Boythorn's old red wall only caught Dickens's eye, I suspect, once they had ceased to function; this one has run up an additional flag of redundancy in the shape of the scrap of list which still clings to it, thus raising it decisively above the threshold of representation. Withheld from formlessness by benevolent neglect, and by that token established as bric-à-brac, the nail happily testifies to the superior power, if not of nature, then of myths of nature. It would be 'easier to fancy' that it had mellowed with the changing seasons than that someone had simply forgotten to remove it from the wall. A myth inaugurated in the realm of nature, among marrows and cucumbers, achieves its completion in the realm of culture, in Chapter 63 of *Bleak House*, when George Rouncewell, approaching his brother's midlands foundry, confronts a 'treasury' not vegetable but mineral, an abundance of iron: 'mountains of it, broken-up, and rusty in its age; distant furnaces of it glowing and bubbling in its youth'.[11] In both instances, bric-à-brac retains its specificity just long enough to stimulate myth-making.

Nails which had not yet ceased to function were to prove extremely useful to those writers whose aim was to insist through descriptive detail on the scope and intricacy of working-class experience. The nails on which things hang are not so much objects as relations in space and time. They orientate us. The nail with a lantern on it, or a key, contributes as vividly to the theatre of memory as it does to a phenomenology of the built environment. In the opening chapter of Elizabeth Gaskell's *Mary Barton* (1848), John Barton recalls the last time he saw his sister-in-

---

10   Charles Dickens, *Bleak House*, ed. by Nicola Bradbury (Harmondsworth: Penguin Books, 1996), p. 288. The 'Story of the Bagman's Uncle' includes some 'worn-out mail coaches' with their interior linings stripped out, 'only a shred hanging here and there by a rusty nail': Charles Dickens, *The Posthumous Papers of the Pickwick Club*, ed. by Robert L. Patten (Harmondsworth: Penguin Books, 1972), pp. 779–80.

11   Dickens, *Bleak House*, p. 952.

law Esther, whose good looks and restless spirit have apparently led her astray. 'She comes in, she goes and hangs her bonnet up on the old nail we used to call hers, while she lived with us'. The hanging of the bonnet on the nail had once been, and will never again be, an orientation, an allegiance. Barton subsequently rips the nail out of the wall, in his fury against Esther, and tosses it into the street.[12]

Hardy seems invariably to have associated nails with hats (*Jude the Obscure* being the exception which proves the rule). Descriptive detail consistently adds texture and depth to his narration of humble lives led in humble dwellings. In *Under the Greenwood Tree* (1872), for example, the house in which gamekeeper and timber-steward Geoffrey Day lives with his daughter Fancy merits several paragraphs of dense description. By no means the least striking of the details included is that concerning headwear: 'The ceiling was carried by a huge beam traversing its midst, from the side of which projected a large nail, used solely and constantly as a peg for Geoffrey's hat; the nail was arched by a rainbow-shaped stain, imprinted by the brim of the said hat when it was hung there dripping wet'.[13] It would not in any way diminish Geoffrey to observe that nothing more need be said about him (though plenty is). In *The Trumpet-Major* (1880), the preparation of an inn for a wedding abolishes a collective theatre of memory.

> By the widow's direction the old familiar incrustation of shining dirt, imprinted along the back of the settle by the heads of countless jolly sitters, was scrubbed and scraped away; the brown circle round the nail whereon the miller hung his hat, stained by the brim in wet weather, was whitened over; the tawny smudges of bygone shoulders in the passage were removed without regard to a certain genial and historical value which they had acquired.[14]

What has been lost, under the whitewash, is not just a specific history, and the value inherent in it, but insignificance itself: the capacity to say all that needs to be said without saying anything at all. Hardy indicates the extent of the loss by allowing an archaic sense of the genial — pertaining to marriage and generation — to persist beneath the modern connotation of jolliness. Something of this order is also at issue in *The Mayor of Casterbridge* (1886) when Henchard visits the 'weather-prophet' Fall in his cottage a few miles outside town. Fall's invitation to enter is 'responded to by the country form, "This will do, thank ye," after which the householder has no alternative but to come out'. So Fall places his candle on the dresser, takes his hat from a nail, and joins Henchard in the porch, shutting the door behind him.[15] The 'country form', here, includes that long-established conjunction of hat and nail, and the genial and historical value to which it has given rise. As so often in Hardy, and so rarely in the fiction of his contemporaries, hat and nail are equals. The

12   Elizabeth Gaskell, *Mary Barton*, ed. by Macdonald Daly (Harmondsworth: Penguin Books, 1996), pp. 114–15.
13   Thomas Hardy, *Under the Greenwood Tree*, ed. by Simon Gatrell (Oxford: Oxford University Press, 1985), p. 93.
14   Thomas Hardy, *The Trumpet-Major*, ed. by Linda M. Shires (Harmondsworth: Penguin Books, 1997), p. 115.
15   Thomas Hardy, *The Mayor of Casterbridge*, ed. by Keith Wilson (Harmondsworth: Penguin Books, 1997), p. 185.

object supported does not eclipse the object supporting. Intent on the illumination of humble lives from within, Hardy has done unique justice to the 'humility of things', in Daniel Miller's phrase: their capacity to enable or constrain even when, or especially when, unnoticed.[16]

In Godwin, Scott, and Dickens, the object which has strayed from its customary function in life, but not yet fallen to the level of waste, acquires a unique meaning in literature. In Gaskell, and far more extensively in Hardy, by contrast, the attention given to customary function *in general* raises even the humblest of those objects which have not strayed from it, and therefore do not count as bric-à-brac, just — barely — to the threshold of representation.

The Woodlanders

Begun seven months after the completion of *The Mayor of Casterbridge*, *The Woodlanders* turned out to be a very different kind of story. Early in 1886, Hardy had developed a new understanding of the novel as literary form. The novel, he claimed, should render society not as an aggregate of individuals, but as 'one great network or tissue' which 'quivers in every part when one point is shaken'.[17] The emphasis should be put on ideas. 'Characters' there are, of course, in *The Woodlanders*, but they exist by mental and moral attitude, rather than through the expressiveness of gesture and physical attribute. It has become customary to define this change of approach by means of the novel's reference to the visual arts. During its composition, Hardy shifted his allegiance from Dutch genre painting — the subtitle of *Under the Greenwood Tree* had been 'A Rural Painting of the Dutch School' — to Impressionism.[18] In 1892, he was to observe that 'in getting at the truth, we get only at the true nature of the impression an object, etc., produces on us, the true thing itself being still, as Kant shows, beyond our knowledge'.[19] What implications might this abandonment of Dutch School realism have had for the interest he took in the common household nail?

In Chapter 2 of *The Woodlanders*, Barber Percomb, arriving in Little Hintock after dark, immediately seeks out Marty South, whose luxuriant chestnut hair would make a perfect wig for his most profitable client, Mrs Charmond, the lady of the manor. Marty, viewed by firelight through the cottage's open window, is hard at work on the consignment of spars — wooden pegs used to fasten down thatch — that her father, who lies ill upstairs, has promised the local timber-merchant, Mr George Melbury. Such an abrupt opening into the innermost recesses of the rural

16   Daniel Miller, 'Materiality: An Introduction', in *Materiality*, ed. by Daniel Miller (Durham, NC: Duke University Press, 2005), pp. 1–50 (p. 5).

17   Florence Emily Hardy, *The Early Life of Thomas Hardy: 1840–1891* (London: Macmillan, 1928), p. 232.

18   J. B. Bullen, *The Expressive Eye: Fiction and Perception in the Work of Thomas Hardy* (Oxford: Clarendon, 1986), ch. 7; Ruth Bernard Yeazell, *Art of the Everyday: Dutch Painting and the Realist Novel* (Princeton, NJ: Princeton University Press, 2008), pp. 153–61.

19   Florence Emily Hardy, *The Later Years of Thomas Hardy: 1892–1928* (London: Macmillan, 1930), p. 178.

economy was not without precedent. George Eliot's *Adam Bede* (1859) had begun with the afternoon sun slanting into the 'roomy workshop of Mr Jonathan Burge, carpenter and builder, in the village of Hayslope, as it appeared on the eighteenth of June, in the year of our Lord 1799'.[20] Hardy, however, wanted characteristically to complicate without delay the picture of stalwart yeoman virtues young Mary South, like Adam Bede before her, might have been thought to present. He did so by inserting a paragraph's worth of supplementary description in the manner of Balzac.

> Beside her, in case she might require more light, a brass candlestick stood on a little round table, curiously formed of an old coffin-stool, with a deal top nailed on, the white surface of the latter contrasting oddly with the black carved oak of the substructure. The social position of the household in the past was almost as definitively shown by the presence of this article as that of an esquire or nobleman by his old helmets or shields. It had been customary for every well-to-do villager, whose tenure was by copy of court-roll, or in any way more permanent than that of the mere cotter, to keep a pair of these stools for the use of his own dead; but changes had led to the discontinuance of the custom, and the stools were frequently made use of in the manner described.[21]

Hardy appropriates Percomb's glance through the window in order to draw attention to the presence in the interior of an object the barber has in all likelihood not noticed at all: the coffin-stool. The stool's conversion from ceremonial to everyday use indicates that the Souths have recently come down in the village world. Descriptive detail, embellished by authorial commentary, has told us something about the family's 'social position' that we would not otherwise know. Hardy, like Balzac and Eliot before him, provides the key to the meaning locked up in his picture. But we might also note that the interpretative effort does indeed prove effortful: two further lengthy sentences are required to screen off the aspect of the coffin-stool (its appearance) to which descriptive detail has drawn attention, and fully illuminate another (its function). Converting an object into a symbol can be hard work.

There is further, even more intense single-mindedness to come. Point of view involves an attitude as well as an angle of vision, and it turns out that Barber Percomb at the window has altogether barred himself from seeing the obvious. The scene made possible by his presence as an observer has been framed precisely so as to exclude him: although he does not see it that way. Hardy, we might begin to suspect, understands subjectivity itself as just such an exclusion.

> In her present beholder's mind the scene formed by the girlish spar-maker composed itself into an impression-picture of extremest type, wherein the girl's hair alone, as the focus of observation, was depicted with intensity and distinctness, while her face, shoulders, hands, and figure in general were a blurred mass of unimportant detail lost in haze and obscurity. (*W* 41)

20   George Eliot, *Adam Bede*, ed. by Stephen Gill (Harmondsworth: Penguin Books, 1980), pp. 1–2. Eliot, of course, defends her own practice of domestic realism in this novel by comparison with the 'rare, precious quality of truthfulness' she had found in 'many Dutch paintings' (p. 179).
21   Thomas Hardy, *The Woodlanders*, ed. by David Lodge (London: Macmillan, 1974), p. 40. Henceforth *W.*

In the winter of 1886, Hardy had absorbed from an exhibition of paintings by the 'impressionist school' at the Society of British Art the principle that 'what you carry away with you from a scene is the true feature to grasp; or, in other words, *what appeals to your own individual eye and heart in particular* amid much that does not so appeal, and which you therefore omit to record'. This principle, he thought, might prove 'even more suggestive in the direction of literature than in that of art'.[22] It is generally taken to have proved more than suggestive in the direction of the novel he was then revising for book publication. For the focus of Hardy's observation now rests not so much on Marty's hair as on the nature and scope of Percomb's single-mindedness (for this will be a novel full of obsessives).

In the next chapter, Hardy, as though to assert mastery over the new method, creates an 'impression-picture' of his own. Marty South, realizing that Giles Winterborne does not want her, cuts off her long auburn locks: 'Upon the pale scrubbed deal of the coffin-stool table they stretched like waving and ropy weeds over the washed white bed of a stream' (*W* 51). The coffin-stool returns, this time as mere studio backdrop to the tableau of tresses. It has been prepared metonymically, by the substitution of part ('pale scrubbed deal') for whole, for its role as the vehicle of metaphor ('washed white bed of a stream'). Its objecthood, we might say, has been sacrificed to the meaning — or aura of meaningfulness — metaphor generates. Who might benefit from the meaning thus generated? Certainly not Marty. Percomb, perhaps, had he been there; but he is not. Hair, of course, especially abundant female hair, exerted considerable fascination over Victorian writers and painters.[23] But the waving and ropy weeds do not really do much for fetishization. The metaphor is gratuitous: meaning for the sake of meaningfulness.

Clearly, *The Woodlanders* does constitute a 'reaction against the techniques of *The Mayor of Casterbridge*', as Bullen puts it, in its abiding preoccupation with mental and moral attitude, with consciousness.[24] But it also develops, I think, a further reaction, against itself: against the view that 'in getting at the truth, we get only at the true nature of the impression an object, etc., produces on us' or, more broadly, against the hermeneutic imperative built into (or so Hardy seems to have believed) Dutch genre painting and Impressionism alike. Consider, once again, that old coffin-stool 'with a deal top nailed on, the white surface of the latter contrasting oddly with the black carved oak of the substructure'. What most fully eludes commentary in this description, either on Hardy's part or on that of his critics, is the nail which secures the stool's top to its substructure. The nail, by its having been required at all, marks a difference: the difference between modern white deal top and ancient black oak substructure. It marks that difference by all that it is (material substance, process of manufacture, function, appearance) at once. By remaining all that it is at once, and

---

22   Florence Hardy, *Early Life*, p. 241.

23   See, for example, Galia Ofek, 'Sensational Hair: Gender, Genre, and Fetishism in the Sensational Decade', in *Victorian Sensations: Essays on a Scandalous Genre*, ed. by Kimberly Harrison and Richard Fantina (Columbus: Ohio State University Press, 2006), pp. 102–14. The episode runs counter to a long tradition of *toilette* description, which I explore in 'Modernist *Toilette*: Degas, Woolf, Lawrence', in *Uses of Phobia*, pp. 77–96.

24   Bullen, *Expressive Eye*, p. 169.

in no one individual aspect in any way demonstrative, it resists interpretation. Its significance lies in its insignificance. For all that difference does is to happen. The functional object described aligns itself, so to speak, with social difference, with social mobility: it does not represent, or symbolize; it is not a metaphor. The nail which secures the top of the coffin-stool to its substructure is difference happening (and thus, in fact, a *lack* of security).

Why should the common household nail have served as the kind of functional object that this novel in particular sought to align with social difference and social mobility? *The Woodlanders* is a novel about wood; and about woods, and about the people who work in woods. It would not be an insult to Hardy to suggest that the characters in it are wooden. He himself describes them often enough as marionettes, or automata. When we first meet Marty South, like Giles Winterborne a woodlander born and bred, she is working with wood.

> On her left hand lay a bundle of the straight, smooth hazel rods called spar-gads — the raw material of her manufacture; on her right a heap of chips and ends — the refuse — with which the fire was maintained; in front a pile of the finished articles. To produce them she took up each gad, looked critically at it from end to end, cut it to length, split it into four, and sharpened each of the quarters with dexterous blows, which brought it to a triangular point precisely resembling that of a bayonet. (*W* 40)

It is passages such as this which provoked Elaine Scarry to argue that for Hardy 'human character' found its 'deepest registration' in the reciprocal alterations of person and world which constitute the activity of work. 'Marty South's cottage', Scarry writes, 'with its luminous tones of amber, brown, and red and its textures of willow wood, ash wood, hazel wood, leather, and human hair, is unified through the concentrating agency of the labouring act, human intelligence inscribing itself into the surfaces of the vegetable, animal and human materials accumulated there'.[25] But that concentrating agency has already produced, I would argue, the ghost of a difference more fundamental than labour itself. For Marty, splitting a gad and then dexterously sharpening each of the quarters in turn, has in effect manufactured a set of wooden *nails*. The instrument to which Hardy compares the product of this dexterous sharpening is an instrument made of iron: a bayonet. The ghost of difference (of not-wood) takes shape as soon as the piece of iron securing the coffin-stool's top to its substructure appears at — or just over — the horizon of the narrator's gaze.

We are often told that *The Woodlanders* is a novel about the invasion of an enclosed world by outside forces at once emancipatory and destructive: Felice Charmond, with her wealth, and the ways of an actress; Edred Fitzpiers, with his philosophy and philandering; even Barber Percomb, whose 'rather finical style of dress' indicates conclusively that he does not 'belong to the country proper' (*W* 35). The woodland succumbs to not-wood: according to Giles Winterborne, Felice's husband, who originally bought Hintock House as a place to retire to, had been 'a rich man engaged in the iron trade in the north' (257). Mr Charmond, clearly,

---

25   Elaine Scarry, *Resisting Representation* (Oxford: Oxford University Press, 1994), pp. 54–55.

has a lot to answer for. But not everything. Where the woodland is concerned, the outside is already inside — or, indeed, beneath. Grace Melbury, standing under the tree into which Winterborne has climbed, bill-hook in hand, finds herself close enough to him to see 'the expression of his face, and the nails in his soles, silver-bright with constant walking' (124–25). Their ultimate near-reconciliation will take place in the charcoal-burner's cottage in the depths of the Hintock woods to which Winterborne, now homeless, has retreated. Like Barber Percomb before her, Grace gazes in through an open window, as the light fades: 'A fire burnt on the hearth, in front of which revolved the skinned carcase of a very small rabbit, suspended by a string from a nail' (327). Again, there is nothing to be said about the nail. It seems, all in all, rather less significant than the size of the rabbit which will constitute poor Giles's supper. My argument is that such insignificance tells, in this wooden novel, as not-wood happening.

I have tried hard to re-describe, rather than merely to interpret, these fleeting manifestations of ironmongery. An interpretation looms, nonetheless, a re-reading even, if we take the hint about Mr Charmond's career in the iron trade. The general view has been that the novel investigates modernity's inexorable colonization of a hitherto remote territory (to the colonizers, a wilderness) populated by traditional communities (to the colonizers, near-primitives). By this account, the hint dropped about Mr Charmond might serve the same purpose as the standard observation in adventure stories from R. M. Ballantyne's *The Coral Island* (1858) to Joseph Conrad's *The Shadow-Line* (1917) concerning the lack of ironmongery in 'native' architecture. The first sight of an 'Oriental capital which had as yet suffered no white conqueror' prompts amazement in Conrad's narrator that 'in those miles of human habitations there was not probably half a dozen pounds of nails'.[26] There are, of course, as we have seen, many dozen pounds of nails in the miles of human habitations distributed throughout Hardy's Wessex. Long before the arrival of Mr Charmond and his northern wealth, the rural economy had been (on a small scale) industrial, capitalist, and exploitative. Or so the novel might now be taken to say.

Such a re-reading in the light of Wessex's embedded ironmongery seems to me worthwhile, if perhaps unremarkable. But the novel's true distinctiveness may in fact lie in its attempts to evade interpretation altogether: something a text addressed to an identifiable audience in accordance with understood generic conventions could only ever hope to accomplish intermittently. Penny Boumelha, discussing *The Woodlanders* in relation to two other 'pastorally influenced novels of marital choice', *Under the Greenwood Tree* and *Far from the Madding Crowd*, finds in it two elements which create a distinctive 'sense of disturbance': 'the peculiarly unstable character of class and sexuality, and the prevalence of obsession'. The relationships between the main protagonists in this novel are, as Boumelha points out, very specifically socio-economic. To a greater extent even than in *Under the Greenwood Tree* and *Far from the Madding Crowd*, class difference proves 'as central to the generation of

26 Joseph Conrad, *The Shadow-Line*, ed. by Jeremy Hawthorn (Oxford: Oxford University Press, 2003), pp. 39–40. See also R. M. Ballantyne, *The Coral Island*, ed. by J. S. Bratton (Oxford: Oxford University Press, 1990), p. 288.

desire and its thwarting or fulfillment' as gender difference. To say that Wessex was always already industrial, capitalist, and exploitative is to say that class and gender positions had become unfixed long before the arrival of Edred Fitzpiers and Felice Charmond. Hardy's topic, Boumelha concludes, is the interdependence of class and erotic mobility.[27] And while his new impressionist method was well suited to the portrayal of obsessiveness verging on mania, it could not handle the rapidity with which raptures flare and fade among the restless inhabitants of a Wessex no longer wholly in place 'under the greenwood tree' — or 'far from the madding crowd'. That is where the nails, refusing to signify, tell. I will conclude with a brief re-description of two scenes in which socio-erotic mobility happens across a difference made palpable by descriptive detail. To interpret these details would be to disable them.

The first scene, in Chapter 9, concerns the faltering of Melbury's long-held ambition to marry Grace to Giles Winterborne, even though an expensive education has now raised her above him. The Melburys have arrived early at the party Giles is throwing in honour of Grace's return to Little Hintock, and offer to help prepare the food.

> 'And I'll help finish the tarts,' said Grace cheerfully.
> 'I don't know about that,' said her father. ''Tisn't quite so much in your line as it is in your step-mother's and mine.'
> 'Of course, I couldn't let you, Grace!' said Giles, with distress.
> 'I'll do it, of course,' said Mrs Melbury, taking off her silk train, hanging it up to a nail, carefully rolling back her sleeves, pinning them to her shoulders, and stripping Giles of his apron for her own use. (*W* 102–03)

The equality established in Hardy's previous fiction between nail and garment no longer applies. The restlessness apparent in this penetration into the 'recesses' of Giles's 'awkwardly built premises' (102), this exchange of capacities and feelings across a social and physical distance thereby all the more vividly marked, is a force (for good or evil) with which the novel's protagonists will have to contend — including Giles, the most woodlandy woodlander of them all.

The second scene worth noting concerns the final stage of Grace's next return to Little Hintock, in Chapter 29, as the elegant wife of the gentleman-physician Edred Fitzpiers. Gazing out of the window of the hotel at Sherton Abbas, she sees Giles hard at work with his cider-press in the back-yard.

> He had hung his coat to a nail of the outhouse wall, and wore his shirt-sleeves rolled up beyond his elbows, to keep them unstained while he rammed the pomace into the bags of horsehair. Fragments of apple-rind had alighted upon the brim of his hat — probably from the bursting of a bag — while brown pips of the same fruit were sticking among the down upon his fine round arms, and in his beard. (*W* 205)

Grace's renewed desire for Giles, at this moment, could be taken as a renewed

27   Penny Boumelha, 'The Patriarchy of Class: *Under the Greenwood Tree, Far from the Madding Crowd, The Woodlanders*', in *The Cambridge Companion to Thomas Hardy*, ed. by Dale Kramer (Cambridge: Cambridge University Press, 1999), pp. 130–44 (pp. 140–42).

desire, after eight weeks of European tour with the terminally nonchalant Fitzpiers, for woodland ways. Giles, immersed in apple-detritus, seems like a fertility-god. But the stimulus lies not so much in the knowledge that she has had her fill of restlessness as in the knowledge that he may just be getting the hang of it. For she has come upon him in a 'debatable land', neither orchard nor woodland, on the very 'margin' of Wessex apple-country. Here, Giles lives a nomadic existence, wandering happily and profitably from place to place with his press. He has begun to differ from himself, hanging his coat from the nail of an outhouse wall. In Godwin, Scott, or Dickens, the nail would have had to have rusted, or fallen out of the wall, in order to become interesting. In Hardy, it speaks, if it speaks at all, from within its original function.

CHAPTER 7

Gissing's Fry-Ups:
Mess, Waste, and the
Definition of Working-Class Culture

No English novelist ever served a more strenuous apprenticeship in the trade of novel-writing than Arnold Bennett. The letters he wrote in the 1890s, while preparing himself for the composition of his first novel, *A Man from the North* (1898), display a wide-ranging knowledge of English, French, and Russian literature. In his view, Turgenev, 'the Bach of fiction', reigned supreme, with the Goncourts and Maupassant not far behind; George Moore came a respectable fourth. Naturalism, evidently, loomed large in Bennett's understanding of the ways in which a writer might be modern. The most important lesson it taught him was in the use of detail. 'You find fault with Maupassant,' he told George Sturt, the wheelwright-novelist, 'for his wealth of irrelevant (à vous entendre) detail. Frankly, I think you would do well to follow him some way in this. I don't think his detail *is* irrelevant.' There were, of course, 'mountains of detail' in *Anna Karenina*, as he admitted. But Naturalist fiction had surpassed even Tolstoy, he thought, in this respect: rather than embed event in descriptive detail, it made of descriptive detail an event. Such descriptive events need not (and perhaps ought not) aspire to the status of an emblem. Bennett was glad to find in *Germinie Lacerteux* 'no tortured symbolism of incident (a growing evil in these latter days)'. The point was to use descriptive detail eventfully, without thrusting it in the reader's face. The whole art, he came to realize, lay in the selection of the right kind of detail. Thus the Goncourts had withdrawn an 'adorably done' account of a Caesarean operation from *Germinie Lacerteux* because it seemed to them too realistic: 'comme trop vrai'.[1]

Such discretion notwithstanding, the kinds of detail for which Naturalism became notorious included the surgical and the pornographic. English commentators were not slow to condemn its intrusions into the operating theatre and the brothel. Bennett himself expressed outrage when a commentator drew parallels between an episode in *The Old Wives' Tale* (1908) and Maupassant's 'La Maison Tellier', a

---

[1] Arnold Bennett, *Letters*, ed. by James Hepburn, 4 vols (Oxford: Oxford University Press, 1966–86), II, 29, 9, 38, 56.

story about whores.[2] There is, however, one kind of detail which enabled French, Russian, and English writers alike to extend significantly the range and intensity of their descriptions without committing too much realism. The kitchen looms large in the work of the generation of the 1880s in France, Russia, and England: larger than it had in the work of its mountainous predecessors; and larger by far, even in French literature, than the operating theatre and the brothel. Culinary event, I shall argue, was one of the ways in which that generation announced itself. It is one of the ways in which Maupassant commented implicitly on Flaubert and Zola, and Chekhov on Tolstoy and Turgenev. It is one of the ways in which George Gissing, who also made a name for himself during the 1880s, and was greatly admired by Bennett, put some distance between himself and *his* mountainous predecessors, Charles Dickens and George Eliot.[3] This chapter is a chapter at once about modern writing and about modern food.

Bad Food: Maupassant, Joyce, Chekhov

The novel which put digestion on the literary map was Emile Zola's *Le Ventre de Paris* (1873). Set in the market of Les Halles, the novel concerns the decline and fall of an amateur revolutionary. Florent, banished for his part in protests against the 1851 *coup d'état*, has broken the law by returning to Paris. He comes back to a society which has grown fat on quiescence. His starvation, amid plenty, figures an absolute moral and political need which cannot be met because it is unrecognizable. Abstemious as a young man, he had grown thinner and thinner, burnt up by self-denial, while his brother fattened.[4] Now, after 1851, and the restoration of empire, appetite is the only thing over which he exercises a measure of control. He lodges with his brother, a pork-butcher, and finds work as an inspector in the fish-market. He could grow fat in his turn. But he wills himself to stay thin. His moral and political need is a form of anorexia, a willed absence of desire, a perverse leanness (*R-M* I, 788). He finds the buxom women who surround him in Les Halles beautiful, but unattractive. The breasts of one, as still and taut as a belly, fail to arouse him (667); those of another exude a vapour seasoned by the stench of the markets (738–39). Alone among Zola's major protagonists, Florent is constituted by deficit rather than excess. He does not even rise to incontinence.

By no means the least anorexic thing about *Le Ventre de Paris* is the plot, a deliberately feeble tale of intrigue and betrayal. Narrative itself withers, like the thin man at its centre: its withering shows us thinness, so to speak, from the inside. What takes its place is descriptive detail. The artist Claude Lantier, who will reappear in *L'Œuvre* (1886), acts as a surrogate author, his eye for colossal still lifes justifying epic catalogues of produce. Huysmans cannot have been alone in regarding these

---

2   Ibid., pp. 317, 319.

3   Bennett published an admiring essay on Gissing in the *Academy*, in December 1899; the essay is reprinted in *Fame and Fiction: An Enquiry into Certain Popularities* (London: Grant Richards, 1901), pp. 197–208. *Fame and Fiction* also includes an essay on Turgenev (pp. 211–30).

4   Emile Zola, *Les Rougon-Macquart*, ed. by Henri Mitterand, 5 vols (Paris: Gallimard, 1960–67), I, 643–44. Henceforth *R-M*.

natures mortes as Zola's greatest achievement.[5] Lantier's wanderings create Les Halles as a spectacle. Florent, however, his companion in *flânerie,* remains immune to spectacle. Florent's absolute need — converted into an absolute lack of appetite, a foreclosure of appetite — hollows out any inclination to linger over aesthetic delicacies. Recognizing in Florent's anorexia an implicit critique of Second Empire abundance, the fish-sellers of Les Halles conspire to revolt him to death (or at least to early retirement). They splash him with water; they spread refuse in his way (R-M I, 717). One of the buxom women finally provokes him beyond endurance by inserting a rotten skate among the pink salmon and creamy turbot on her slab (716). This is a bad moment, not only for Florent, but for spectacle, for descriptive detail, for the novel's complicity with modern painting. The rotten skate is the point at which fascination becomes aware of itself in its own excess.

Maupassant generalized the rotten skate. For him, particularly in the later work, fascination has always already become aware of itself in its own excess. His novels and stories make consistent use of a 'nutritional code' which translates the promptings of ambition and sexual desire, and the disgust consequent upon their satisfaction, into a serial encounter with foodstuff. In Maupassant, the dinner table is a mechanism for social and sexual advancement. What changes, between the early work and the late, is who eats whom. The female protagonists, easy meat in the early work, prove increasingly hard to swallow; while the male protagonists, omnivorous in the early work, suffer a catastrophic loss of appetite. 'From *mangeurs,* lovers of life and women, they become *mangés,* prey to an incurable disease that eats away at the very fibre of their being.'[6]

The change can be illustrated by a comparison between scenes in *Bel-Ami* (1885) and *Fort comme la mort* (1889). Towards the end of *Bel-Ami,* Duroy catches his wife Madeleine *in flagrante* with the upstart lawyer and politician Laroche-Mathieu. More revealing even than the pile of discarded clothes on the floor is the pile of left-overs on the sideboard: oyster shells, pieces of bread, the carcass of a chicken.[7] The adulterers have eaten each other up. What gives the nutritional code its particular force in this scene is Duroy's complicity. Wishing to divorce his wife, and marry the younger and wealthier Suzanne Walter, he has done everything he can to encourage the affair. From his point of view, Madeleine, like the oyster shells and the carcass, is so much waste-matter. Leftover food, a leftover wife: these are the measure of an organism's ability to renew itself by excluding whatever it does not require for its own immediate purposes. The idea of waste grounds the nutritional code. Substituting one form of detritus for another, it converts metonymy into metaphor, descriptive detail into generality. And Maupassant, himself complicit in Duroy's complicity, believes it.

In *Fort comme la mort,* in a scene which recapitulates and comments obliquely on the opening of *Bel-Ami,* Olivier Bertin, a fashionable painter, writing to a

5   Joris-Karl Huysmans, *Œuvres complètes,* 18 vols (Paris: Cres, 1928–34), I, 149–92.
6   Mary Donaldson-Evans, *A Woman's Revenge: The Chronology of Dispossession in Maupassant's Fiction* (Lexington, KY: French Forum, 1986), pp. 50–51.
7   Guy de Maupassant, *Romans,* ed. by Louis Forestier (Paris: Gallimard, 1987), pp. 454,

woman he loves hopelessly, describes the sudden impoverishment of his work as a failure of *flânerie*: the emptying out of a world once replete with subject matter has rendered his hermeneutic prowess null and void. Weary of the no longer fertile streets, already 'sickened', he enters a restaurant where bald, pot-bellied diners with moist foreheads swill and slump in an atmosphere of heat and sourness — and soon leaves, feeling even worse. Overripe fruit, overcooked vegetables, flabby bread, purulent cheese: something's not right with the bourgeois stomach. Bertin finds in this human stew evidence for, and an emblem of, his carefully nurtured secret knowledge of physical and moral decay.[8] One could say that Maupassant's later work endlessly recapitulates the story told in *Le Ventre de Paris*, the story of a thin man among fat men. For the most part, the thin men are thin because they are mad. Sometimes, as in *Fort comme la mort* and *Notre Cœur* (1890), his last novel, they have been driven mad, or half-mad, by emotional and sexual starvation. Olivier Bertin and his like do not merely observe the rotten skate among pink salmon and creamy turbot; they discover in its rottenness the exhaustion of their own desire to live. Paradoxically, their wastedness, their turning away from an overripe abundance, their secret knowledge of the rotten skate, identifies them as waste-matter. In Maupassant's later work, the social organism renews itself by flushing out or paring away these debilitated old men, this nausea which expresses by the violence of its rejection the very purulence it rejects.

The nutritional code comes under comprehensive review in that great bonfire of all the codes, James Joyce's *Ulysses* (1923). Two episodes, in particular, could be read as a sardonic commentary on Maupassant's touching faith in the intrinsic meaningfulness of food. In 'Lestrygonians', Leopold Bloom, his heart 'astir' with lust and hunger alike, decides to quell at least one of these appetites by dropping in to the Burton restaurant for some lunch. 'Stink gripped his trembling breath: pungent meatjuice, slop of greens.' He sees what Olivier Bertin had seen: men 'swilling'. 'A man with an infant's saucestained napkin tucked round him shovelled gurgling soup down his gullet. A man spitting back on his plate: halfmasticated gristle: no teeth to chewchewchew it. Chump chop from the grill. Bolting to get it over.' This is indeed the stomach of Dublin. 'Smells of men. His gorge rose. Spaton sawdust, sweetish warmish cigarette smoke, reek of plug, spilt beer, men's beery piss, the stale of ferment.' Like Bertin before him, Bloom can stand it no more. 'Look on this picture then on that. Scoffing up stewgravy with sopping sippets of bread. Lick it off the plate, man! Get out of this.'[9] Joyce, however, unlike Maupassant, provides a specific context (a narrative reason) for his hero's nausea. 'This,' Bloom has reflected a few pages before, 'is the very worst hour of the day. Vitality. Dull, gloomy: hate this hour. Feel as if I had been eaten and spewed' (*U* 208). It is, in fact, the very worst hour of Bloom's very worst day: the day on which, as he very well knows, his wife will commit adultery with Blazes Boylan. The meaning he attributes to half-masticated gristle is thus no more than a reflection of his state of mind. With an almost narcissistic fortitude, he has composed and re-composed the morbid tableaux in this gastronomic chamber of horrors — 'Scoffing up stewgravy with sopping sippets of bread' — until they engender the appropriate degree of self-hatred. Bertin's nausea, which has no immediate context, could be mistaken for a world-view. Bloom's could not: *its* immediate context becomes painfully obvious, when, after one or two further spasms of fear and loathing, he only just avoids what would have been a mortifying encounter with Blazes himself (234).

Bloom, of course, manages to avoid Boylan for the rest of the day. He returns home at night to a scene not wholly unlike the scene which greets Georges Duroy when he 'surprises' Madeleine with Laroche-Mathieu. Opening the kitchen dresser, he sees, among other things, 'four conglomerated black olives in oleaginous paper, an empty pot of Plumtree's potted meat, an oval wicker basket bedded with fibre and containing one Jersey pear, a halfempty bottle of William Gilbey and Co's white invalid port, half disrobed of its swathe of coralpink tissue paper' (*U* 788). These are the remnants of the meat, wine, and fruit Boylan selected at Thornton's, earlier in the day, in 'Wandering Rocks', and had sent round to Eccles Street (291–92). The point of the feast becomes apparent when Bloom climbs into bed beside Molly. 'New clean bedlinen, additional odours, the presence of a human form, female, hers, the imprint of a human form, male, not his, some crumbs, some flakes of potted meat, recooked, which he removed' (862–63). Like Duroy, Bloom has colluded in his wife's seduction by an upstart; unlike Duroy, he does not use this betrayal as an excuse to dispose of her. Madeleine may be reduced to a leftover; Molly is not. To Bloom, a mess is a mess, rather than a malfunctioning system. His response to the flakes of potted meat is complicated, but does not include the impulse to purge himself of waste-matter. 'Envy, jealousy, abnegation, equanimity' (864).

By the time Joyce got down to *Ulysses*, the nutritional code upon which Maupassant relied so heavily had become something of a museum piece: the object, rather than the instrument, of social and moral analysis. This process began at least as early as the 1880s. It is evident, I shall shortly suggest, in Gissing's novels. It is certainly evident in Chekhov's short stories. The meals in Chekhov's stories do not lend themselves to translation. They disrupt that global encoding of experience which made Maupassant's descriptions seem so eventful to Arnold Bennett (eventful, I have argued, to the point of symbolism). Chekhov's feeders, as vigorous in their way as Maupassant's, make a mess, not waste. On more than one occasion, Chekhov used their swilling and slumping to challenge the theory of waste proposed by an eminent precursor, Ivan Turgenev. Turgenev's idea was that social and economic change had created a category of 'Superfluous Men': men of wealth, breeding and refinement, who yet found themselves without a purpose in life, without a role. In novels like *Fathers and Sons* (1862) and *Virgin Soil* (1877), this human detritus floats uneasily on the gentle swell of Alexandrine reform. For Chekhov, however, the superfluity lay not so much in the men as in the idea: the theory which, in the 1880s, allowed an entire generation to explain its own inadequacy as the product of social and economic change.

'A Man of Ideas' (1885) describes a conversation, over lunch, on a stiflingly hot day, between prison superintendent Yashkin and his guest Pimfoff, a schoolteacher.

'A carafe of vodka, some stringy boiled beef and an empty sardine tin encrusted with grey salt are standing on the table.'[10] It is the prison superintendent, ironically, who turns out to be the man of ideas. Or rather of one idea. While baleful servitors ferry in fresh supplies of vodka and semolina pudding, Yashkin works his way through the entire catalogue of civilization's crowning achievements, describing each in turn as futile and redundant. In the gospel according to Yashkin, human endeavour is inherently wasteful. '"Everything's superfluous in this world!" Yashkin remarks suddenly' (ES 51). What could be more wasteful than the meal the two men have just consumed? 'Here we've been, stuffing and gorging ourselves, and what on earth for? No, it's all superfluous' (52). Yashkin's insight confirms a thought which has been gaining rapidly on the reader ever since that first glimpse of the empty sardine tin, a thought reinforced periodically by the meticulous notation of shameless belches and gurgles. A nutritional code operates in this story, translating descriptive detail into evidence for the point of view held from the outset by the more assertive of the two protagonists.

Or does it? During the meal, Martha, the cook, walks past the table carrying a bucketful of kitchen slops. 'A loud splash is heard, immediately followed by a dog's yelp' (ES 51). The cook's slow advance towards the midden solemnly enacts that interminable production and disposal of waste which, in Yashkin's gospel, constitutes human experience. And yet the nutritional code makes nothing of it. Neither man responds. The bucketful of slops is waste incarnate: that which a healthy organism expels in order to renew itself. The story, however, declines to convert metonymy into metaphor. Even Yashkin cannot quite bring himself to regard the redundancy of slops as proof of the redundancy of all human endeavour. For the signature this particular bucketful bears is that of contingency rather than system: a mess, a splash and a yelp. If there is anything superfluous, in this story, it is Yashkin's obsession with superfluousness. The story investigates paranoia: Yashkin's paranoia, and *our* paranoia, our complicity with a narrative code which translates an empty sardine tin into proof of the superfluousness of human experience.

Chekhov returned to the theme in one of his most elegantly complex stories, 'The Duel' (1891). Two years before, Layevsky, purportedly a man of ideas, had seduced Nadezhda, purportedly a woman of ideas, and taken her to live with him in the Caucasus, where he found work in the civil service. Now her pretensions bore him almost as much as the Caucasus. He speaks of himself as civilization's 'waste product': a failure, a 'superfluous man', like Bazarov, in Turgenev's *Fathers and Sons* (RM 36). Von Koren, a dandyish zoologist, offers a different point of view. He lays the blame for Layevsky's failure not on Layevsky himself, but on Turgenev: on the men of ideas whose obsession with waste has enabled a man of no ideas like Layevsky to pose as the victim 'of an era, of trends, of heredity, and all that stuff' (37). Von Koren articulates, with the authority accruing to scientific method, the

---

10   Anton Chekhov, *Early Stories*, trans. by Patrick Miles and Harvey Pitcher (Oxford: Oxford University Press, 1994), p. 49: henceforth *ES*. All quotations from Chekhov's stories are from this collection, or from *The Russian Master and Other Stories*, trans. by Ronald Hingley (Oxford: Oxford University Press, 1984). Henceforth *RM*.

critique of paranoia implicit in 'A Man of Ideas'. And yet, as the story develops, it is Von Koren, rather than Layevsky, who comes to resemble Yashkin; it is Von Koren who has a theory, Von Koren who generalizes wildly, Von Koren who acts as though Layevsky were indeed the victim of heredity. Von Koren envisages the duel he has provoked Layevsky into fighting as a form of pest-control; but his programme is thwarted, at the moment when he levels his pistol, by mishap (106). Chance, which Von Koren cannot even recognize, let alone manage, saves Layevsky. Indeed, it transforms him. His lucky escape persuades him to fall back in love (or at least in need, in affection) with Nadezhda. Von Koren, by contrast, will never change.

The story keeps its distance from Layevsky's muddling-through by an attention to theory, to scientific method; it keeps its distance from Von Koren's theory, from his scientific method, by an attention to mess, and in particular to the messes food makes. The scene in which Von Koren talks superfluousness to a hapless cleric, like the scene in which Yashkin talks superfluousness to Pimfoff, is framed by the preparation and eating of lunch (*RM* 34–38). Another meal, during the picnic which brings the antagonism between Von Koren and Layevsky to the boil, proves even messier. 'As happens on picnics, they floundered in a welter of napkins, bundles and surplus bits of greasy paper drifting about in the wind, they didn't know whose glass or piece of bread was where, they spilt wine on the rug and their knees, they scattered salt about' (55). Like the bucketful of slops in 'A Man of Ideas', these spillages and litterings bear contingency's signature. They are wasteful, but the wastefulness enhances, rather than diminishes, the pleasure the participants take in their fish stew; it is a good mess. The drifting paper and scattered salt prompt the thought that the distinction between good messes and bad messes may in some circumstances prove more useful than the distinction, for which Von Koren appears ready to kill Layevsky, between productivity and wastefulness, between order and disorder.

Food matters, then, in the work of Maupassant and Chekhov. Culinary event was one of the ways in which they made themselves modern. But the modernities it engendered were not the same. In Maupassant, a nutritional code permits us, should we wish, to convert metonymy into metaphor; thus, leftover food stands for the woman Georges Duroy is about to cast off. Each meal is potentially a feast, a ceremony, in so far as it expresses an otherwise inexpressible understanding of the basic requirements for social and moral order. Maupassant's heirs might be thought to include those anthropologists who have regarded food as a 'system of communication'.[11] In Chekhov, by contrast, meals are not feasts. They are anti-feasts: ceremony's negative image. They do not sustain social and moral order. They express accident, if anything. The empty sardine tin and the scattered salt resist

11   Roland Barthes, 'Towards a Psychosociology of Contemporary Food Consumption', in *Food and Drink in History*, ed. by Robert Forster and Orest Ranum (Baltimore, MD: Johns Hopkins University Press, 1979), pp. 166–73 (pp. 167–68). I am thinking of Claude Lévi-Strauss, *The Raw and the Cooked*, trans. by John and Doreen Weightman (New York: Harper and Row, 1969); and of Mary Douglas, 'Deciphering a Meal', *Daedalus*, 101 (1972), 61–81, and 'Food as a System of Communication', in *In the Active Voice* (London: Routledge and Kegan Paul, 1982), pp. 82–124.

conversion into metaphor; their resistance sets a limit to the power of the nutritional code, indeed of any code. They are properly the objects of a phenomenology rather than a semiotics. In his understanding of food, Chekhov has no heirs at all.

Class Eating

In Thomas Hardy's *A Pair of Blue Eyes* (1873), Stephen Smith, son of a master-mason, apprentices himself to an architect in Bombay. His expectation is that professional experience will make a gentleman of him, and a fit husband for the elegant, cultured Elfride Swancourt. On his return to England, he receives a warm welcome from his humble parents. Mrs Smith has scrubbed and dusted in his honour. Mr Smith has killed a pig, and promises a 'good supper of fry'. A visitor arrives. William Worm, who keeps the turnpike-gate, suffers from a form of tinnitus. He cannot clear his head of the fizz of food frying. 'Ay, I assure you that frying o' fish is going on for nights and days. And, you know, sometimes 'tisn't only fish, but rashers o' bacon and inions.' Worm is (and not by name only) a walking metaphor: the very incarnation of a humble diet. The steaming and hissing pork, together with the 'awkward' presence of William Worm, the buddha of fry-ups, forcibly remind Stephen that he has not yet completed his metamorphosis into a gentleman.[12] He begins to suspect that he will never win Elfride.

For an English writer of Hardy's generation, to write about food was to write about class. The 'supper of fry' had become, by its greasiness, by its saturating odour, the enactment and symbol of a proletarian life-style. There is, to be sure, a fish-and-chip shop (*le friteur*) in *Le Ventre de Paris* (*R-M* I, 784); but no special significance attaches to it. In England, by contrast, such establishments had long since earned themselves a sociology. In the early 1850s, Henry Mayhew estimated that there were around 300 fried-fish sellers in London, many of them itinerant. These unfortunates wore the atmosphere of their trade like a uniform.

> Even when the fish is fresh (as it most frequently is), and the oil pure, the odour is rank. In one place I visited, which was, moreover, admirable for cleanliness, it was very rank. The cooks, however, whether husbands or wives — for the women often attend to the pan — when they hear of this disagreeable rankness, answer that it may be so, many people say so; but for their parts they cannot smell it at all.[13]

A decade later, Walter Greenwood's ruminations on the working-class preference for fried rather than boiled fish led him to the topic of dripping. 'In every "general shop", in every rag and bone shop, in the high street, and in the hundred courts and filthy alleys that worm in and out of it, may be seen solid slabs of a tallowy-looking substance, and marked with a figure 6, 7, or 8, denoting that for as many pence a pound weight of the suspicious-looking slab may be obtained.' Thought by

---

12   Thomas Hardy, *A Pair of Blue Eyes*, ed. by Roger Ebbatson (Harmondsworth: Penguin Books, 1986), pp. 284–86, 292.
13   Henry Mayhew, *London Labour and the London Poor*, ed. by Victor Neuburg (Harmondsworth: Penguin Books, 1985), p. 70.

its purchasers to be the residue of roast and baked meats, the dripping was in fact, Greenwood took pleasure in stating, made of mutton suet and boiled rice, with a gravy of bullocks' kidneys 'stirred into the mess' in order to give it a 'mottled and natural appearance'.[14]

Workers in the Dawn (1880), the first of Gissing's slum novels, boasts a sociological prelude: a description of a stroll down Whitecross Street, in the East End of London, on market night. In *Dombey and Son* (1848), Dickens, no doubt with the findings of social investigators like Edwin Chadwick in mind, had invited his readers to follow the clergyman or doctor who, 'with his life imperilled at every breath', goes resolutely down into the dens of the poor.[15] Gissing, likewise, invites *his* readers to examine the 'unspeakable abominations' suggested by a gas-lamp flickering at the further end of a vile passage-way.[16] But Gissing goes further than Dickens. He supplements the glance down a passage-way with a survey of further unspeakable abominations: the butcher's display of rotten meat, the rag-seller's filthy bits of torn linen and draggled trimming, the sordid gin-palace. Equally sordid, though perhaps not quite as abominable, is the eating-house. 'Behind the long counter stand a man and a woman, the former busy in frying flat fish over a huge fire, the latter engaged in dipping a ladle into a large vessel which steams profusely; and in front of the counter stands a row of hungry-looking people, devouring eagerly the flakes of fish and the greasy potatoes as fast as they come from the pan, whilst others are served by the woman to little basins of stewed eels from the steaming tureen' (*WD* 4–6). The sizzling and steaming, the greasiness: this food repels, not because it tastes bad, but because it permeates; those who ingest it take it into their hair and clothes as well as into their stomachs; they take it, as William Worm had done, into their very being. Fried food is a condition rather than a nutrient. Metonymy becomes metaphor: you are what you eat; at least, you are what you eat on a Saturday night, 'the one evening in the week which the weary toilers of our great city can devote to ease and recreation' (3), when every meal is a feast, and every mouthful expressive. As in Maupassant, what converts metonymy into metaphor is the idea of waste. Fried food joins the cast-off clothes and the mounds of excrement in the obscene ceremony of waste which constitutes life in the London slums.

The sociological prelude to *Workers in the Dawn* could be said to recapitulate fifty years of philanthropic thinking about urban poverty. It begins where Chadwick had begun, in 1842, with the primal abomination: a mound of excrement at the further end of a narrow courtyard. The basic premise of the sanitary reformers was that proper drainage and proper ventilation would go a long way towards solving the problem of the slums. Gissing, peering down the vile passage-way, as Dickens had done before him, concurred. Gissing knew, however, as Chadwick and Dickens could not have known, that proper drainage and ventilation would never

14   Walter Greenwood, *Unsentimental Journeys: or, Byways of the Modern Babylon* (London: Ward, Lock, and Tyler, 1867), p. 13.

15   Charles Dickens, *Dombey and Son*, ed. by Peter Fairclough (Harmondsworth: Penguin Books, 1970), p. 737.

16   George Gissing, *Workers in the Dawn*, ed. by Pierre Coustillas (Hassocks: Harvester Press, 1985), p. 4. Henceforth *WD*.

be enough. For reasons that had as much to do with politics as with engineering, sanitary reform failed. The consequent shift of emphasis within philanthropic thinking about urban poverty can best be traced in the successive positions taken by James Kay-Shuttleworth, who (as James Kay) had contributed to Chadwick's *Report on the Sanitary Condition of the Labouring Population of Great Britain*, from the 1850s to the 1870s. A series of papers reissued in the 1862 record his disillusionment with the programme of sanitary reform which he and Chadwick had devised in the 1830s and 1840s. Thirty years of better drains had apparently had little effect on the terrible figures for child mortality in Manchester. Rather than solving the problem of slumland, better drains had simply revealed a further dimension within it; all they had done was to 'unmask' an innate moral depravity, 'the habits of an unlettered sensual population'.[17] However, this new concern with innate moral depravity did not altogether supersede an older concern with the predisposing effects of environment. If the unletteredness of the population had become a factor in its debilitating sensuality, then there was a remedy to hand. Education might yet achieve what sanitary reform had not. Writing in 1873 on 'The Laws of Progress, as Illustrated in the History of the Manual Labour Class in England', Kay-Shuttleworth felt able to report that, ten years on, respectability was finally beginning to settle on the class in question, or at least on its artisan elite.[18] Respectability amounted to the latest weapon in reform's armoury. It might not abolish the slums. But it would establish a firm distinction between those in the 'manual labour class' who wished to improve themselves and those who did not, and thus isolate and cordon off the latter. Indeed, evidence of the artisan elite's growing enthusiasm for self-improvement helped to make the case for further constitutional change in the run-up to the Reform Bill of 1867.[19]

Gissing's survey of Whitecross Street on a Saturday night articulates this shift of emphasis. The focus of his concern is not so much the mound of excrement as the pub, where men and women 'maul' each other with 'vile caresses', 'and all the time, from the lips of the youngest and the oldest, foams forth such a torrent of inanity, abomination, and horrible blasphemy which bespeaks the very depth of human — aye, or of bestial — degradation' (WD 6–7). The remedy for such bestial behaviour is not drains, but moral education — indeed, education of every kind. 'See how the foolish artisan's wife [...] lays down a little heap of shillings in return for a lump, half gristle, half bone, of questionable meat — ignorant that with half the money she might buy four times the quantity of far more healthy and sustaining food' (4). In the 1880s, diet became a philanthropic focus. School managers hoped that, by encouraging children to enjoy a cheap and nutritious diet of oatmeal, rice, and macaroni, they could educate the Foolish Artisan's Wife out

---

17   James Kay-Shuttleworth, *Four Periods of Public Education* (London: Longman, Green, Longman, and Roberts, 1862), pp. 149–53.
18   Kay-Shuttleworth, 'The Laws of Social Progress, as Illustrated in the History of the Manual Labour Class in England', in *Thoughts and Suggestions on Certain Social Problems: Contained Chiefly in Addresses to Meetings of Workmen in Lancashire* (London: Longmans, Green, 1873), pp. 3–39.
19   For example, J. M. Ludlow and Lloyd Jones, *Progress of the Working Class, 1832–1867* (London: Augustus Kelley, 1973). First published in 1867.

of her taste for questionable meat. By 1900, 'Why do not the poor use porridge?' had become, as one social worker put it, an 'ever-recurring question'.[20] Gissing may or may not have thought that porridge was the answer. But he clearly implies that ignorance about nutrition is one point at which philanthropy could usefully intervene in the Saturday night pageant of abominations. He recognized that the crowd thronging Whitecross Street was miscellaneous, 'comprehending alike the almost naked wretch who creeps along in the hope of being able to steal a mouthful of garbage, and the respectably clad artisan and his wife, seeing how best they can lay out their money for the ensuing week' (7). In the 1880s, social reform sought to peel the artisan and his wife away from the almost naked wretch along the line of respectability.

That the almost naked wretches did not seem aware of the extent of their own degradation was small comfort to Gissing. 'We suffer them to become brutes in our midst,' he concluded, 'and inhabit dens which clean animals would shun, to derive their joys from sources from which a cultivated mind shrinks as from a pestilential vapour. And can we console ourselves with the reflection that they do not feel their misery?' (WD 8). Like the fish-seller who does not realize that his clothes stink, the almost naked wretches do not know how brutal they are. Respectability will have to be injected into this more or less insensate social body from the outside. The novels Gissing wrote in the mid-1880s consider the effect that a 'cultivated mind' which does not shrink from pestilential vapours might have on life in the London slums. One of the few beacons of enlightenment in *Demos* (1886) is Westlake, a middle-class socialist and man of letters loosely based on William Morris. However, Gissing rapidly lost any faith he might once have held in the interventions of a cultivated mind. The literary consequence of this loss of faith was a strictly enforced detachment. In *Thyrza* (1887), slumland is 'decisively enclosed', Adrian Poole remarks, 'by the idiom of observation, of a generalised and distancing compassion'.[21]

Thyrza concerns the efforts of a wealthy young philanthropist, Walter Egremont, to bring literature — 'spiritual education' — to the 'upper artisan and mechanic classes': there is no point, he reckons, in disturbing the 'mud' at the very bottom of the social order.[22] The almost naked wretches are to be left to their own devices, while the respectable poor find further incentives to respectability in the life of the mind. Gissing modelled Egremont's initiative on projects such as the Working Men's College run by F. D. Maurice and the university extension courses which came into effect in the 1870s. The initiative founders upon the indifference to literature even of the respectable poor, and upon romantic entanglement: Egremont and his most promising student, Gilbert Grail, both love the same woman, Thyrza Trent. The novel's critique of middle-class meddling leaves room for, and is reinforced by, an examination of working-class habits and attitudes; like *Workers in the Dawn*, it

20   Quoted by Ellen Ross, *Love and Toil: Motherhood in Outcast London, 1870–1918* (Oxford: Oxford University Press, 1993), p. 36.
21   Adrian Poole, *Gissing in Context* (London: Macmillan, 1975), p. 78.
22   Gissing, *Thyrza*, ed. Jacob Korg (Hassocks: Harvester Press, 1974), p. 14. Henceforth *Th*.

conceives the zoning of London in gastronomic as well as spatial terms; like *Workers in the Dawn*, it imagines the slum as an agglomeration of waste-matter.

Chapters 1 and 2 take place in a house on the shores of Ullswater, where Walter Egremont explains his philanthropic scheme to Annabel Tyrell, daughter of a cultured man of letters. Chapter 3 introduces us to 'A Corner of Lambeth', where Gilbert Grail and Luke Ackroyd talk briefly, before Ackroyd dives into the 'small general' run by Mr and Mrs Bower. This is where Ullswater culture ends, and Lambeth culture begins. 'When the young man stepped through the doorway he was at once encompassed with the strangest blend of odours; every article in the shop — groceries of all kinds, pastry, cooked meat, bloaters, newspapers, petty haberdashery, firewood, fruit, soap — seemed to exhale its essence distressfully under the heat; impossible that anything sold here should preserve its native savour' (*Th* 26). Exhalation is the key to Lambeth culture: hybridity, loss of outline, murkiness, seepage. On the counter is a 'perspiring yellow mass' retailed under the name of butter (26). Mrs Bower, a thoroughly respectable woman who does not depend financially upon the shop (her husband is a foreman at Egremont & Pollard's oilcloth manufactory), has somehow merged with its oleaginous contents: dripping sweat, she declares that she's 'a-goin' like the butter' (27). Metonymy becomes metaphor.

Mr Bower, a 'petty capitalist', and as respectable as his wife, does some merging of his own when he visits the aptly named Mrs Butterfield, caretaker of a school building which Egremont wants to convert into a library. Mrs Butterfield is cooking onions when he arrives, and the smell of frying releases him from his 'pomposities of manner' into proletarian freemasonry. As she stirs the 'hissing mess' with a fork, he probes for details of the friendship between Egremont and Thyrza Trent (237–38). Zola had associated gossip with waste. In *Pot-Bouille* (1882), the tittle-tattle of servants further compounds the foul stench emanating from kitchens and blocked drains (*R-M* III, 99, 107, 250); in *Le Ventre de Paris*, Mlle Saget, who lives off the scraps from aristocratic tables, and whose stock in trade is 'filthy scandal', brings the protagonist down by her insinuations (*R-M* I, 834–35, 819). In his most Zolaesque moment, Gissing associates gossip with frying, with seepage and saturation, with waste-matter. Gossip is, literally, a smear. You are what you eat, and what you eat is what you peddle. Metonymy becomes metaphor.

When Egremont offers him a job as librarian, and release from wage-slavery, Gilbert Grail decides to take some air. He finds himself in Lambeth Walk, where the odours of naphtha and fried fish are 'pungent on the wind' (*Th* 111). Rehearsing half-articulated desires, he wanders out to the middle of Lambeth Bridge, and gazes across at the centres of political and cultural power on the opposite bank. 'He has gone out to "realise" the great joy which has befallen him,' John Goode observes, in a fine discussion of the scene, 'but he is drawn by an unknown power to this severe reminder that the other side is obscure, unreachable.'[23] The severe reminder is in a sense Grail's own metonymic and metaphoric attachment to grease: to the odours of naphtha and fried fish. The job from which librarianship would release

23   John Goode, *George Gissing: Ideology and Fiction* (London: Vision Press, 1978), pp. 103–04.

him is at a soap factory. 'The narrow street was redolent with oleaginous matter; the clothing of the men was penetrated with the same nauseous odour' (73). Like soap, like gossip, class *smears*. Grail's fondness for books will not secure his release from engulfing oleaginous matter.

The narrative compulsively repeats the smear, reinstating again and again the view from outside. On one occasion, Mrs Ormonde, Egremont's philanthropic friend, rescues Thyrza, who has fled after telling Egremont that she loves him, from Mrs Gandle's coffee-shop in the Caledonian Road. A lengthy description does for the Caledonian Road what the sociological prelude to *Workers in the Dawn* had done for Whitecross Street. 'You look off into narrow side-channels where unconscious degradation has made its inexpugnable home, and sits veiled in refuse' (*Th* 319). Inexpugnable: there is mud here which no cultivated mind, however robust, will be able to disturb. Small wonder, then, that Mrs Gandle should preside over a carnival of greasiness. 'Before the fire, bacon and sausages were frizzling; above it was spluttering a beef-steak. On a sink in one corner were piled eating utensils which awaited the wipe of a very loathsome rag hanging hard by' (320). It is the entrance of Mrs Ormonde, beyond doubt a lady, which opens up this scene for inspection. The 'feeders' who gaze at her in awe will never escape from the sound of frizzling and spluttering, just as Mrs Gandle will never escape from the sound of her own Dickensian surname. For them, there is no way out.

Thyrza cannot really be said to mark an advance on *Workers in the Dawn* in anything except disillusionment. Like Zola, like Maupassant, Gissing operates a nutritional code which relentlessly converts metonymy into metaphor: in this case, it converts a taste for fried food into inexpugnable degeneracy. Both novels seal slumland off in the sound and stench of frizzling. But I want to suggest that the very blackness of Gissing's disillusionment with the interventions of the cultivated mind led him, in *The Nether World* (1889), to conceive slumland in something close to its own terms. The sheer incongruity of middle-class attitudes and habits, in a place where unconscious degradation sits veiled by refuse, made him think again. Despairing of the 'man of ideas', Gissing, like Chekhov, took up with a phenomenology of lived experience.

Nether Worlds

This may seem an implausible claim. *The Nether World* is generally reckoned to be at once Gissing's most complex account of working-class culture, and his most blackly pessimistic. Critics stress his detachment from, or hostility to, the world it depicts. They have found hatred, rather than pity, in the depiction, in Chapter 12, of a Bank Holiday crowd.[24] And they have assumed that the corollary of detachment must be pessimism: the world from which Gissing distances himself can only be a

---

24 Rod Edmonds, 'The Conservatism of Gissing's Early Novels', *Literature and History*, 8 (1978), 48–69 (p. 58); Jacob Korg, *George Gissing: A Critical Biography*, 2nd edn (Brighton: Harvester Press, 1980), p. 114; David Grylls, *The Paradox of Gissing* (London: Allen and Unwin, 1986), p. 51; Gill Davies, 'Foreign Bodies: Images of the London Working Class at the End of the 19th Century', *Literature and History*, 14 (1988), 64–80 (p. 71).

world without hope.[25] A more recent emphasis on Gissing's interest in biomedical theories of degeneracy, and on their exemplification in *The Nether World* by the burly and voracious Clem Peckover, has reinforced the idea that the slumland he so caustically surveyed is beyond redemption.[26] On one side of the social and moral divide stands the cultivated mind, on the other an agglomeration of animate and inanimate matter.

My view, by contrast, is that Gissing's intensifying detachment encouraged him to make distinctions, for the first time, *within* slumland: to separate the respectably clad artisan and his wife from the scavenger, and to imagine how they might think and feel (about scavenging, among other things). *The Nether World* could quite justifiably have been called *Nether Worlds*. In it, Gissing explored the relation between respectability and self-respect which has begun over the last twenty years or so to preoccupy historians of working-class culture. 'Respectability,' as Peter Bailey put it in an essay published in 1979, 'is respectable again.' Once regarded as shorthand for bourgeois hegemony, it was now acquiring, Bailey thought, a new complexity.[27] Historians like Brian Harrison and Trygve Tholfsen had demonstrated that in mid-Victorian Britain significant numbers of working people thought of themselves as respectable, without thereby relinquishing a distinct and irreducible class identity, or abandoning their opposition to capitalism.[28] According to Geoffrey Crossick, the search for respectability among an artisan elite was often 'radical' and 'aggressive'. These men and women sought not just a negative freedom, from want and charity, but the positive freedom to make real choices about the kind of life they might lead.[29] Respectability meant independence, and the self-respect independence brought with it. More recently, Michael Mason has argued that among the working classes self-improvement in respect both to sexual conduct and to temperance was a direct result of increasing political radicalism.[30] Embourgeoisement may not have contributed as much to 'equipoise', Bailey concludes, as the ability of working people to sustain a 'satisfying inner life'.[31] In *The Nether World*, Gissing found terms for that (imperfectly) satisfying inner life.[32]

25   Poole, *Gissing in Context*, pp. 86, 91; Grylls, *Paradox*, p. 49.
26   Edmonds, 'Conservatism', pp. 50–53; Davies, 'Foreign Bodies', pp. 69–70; William Greenslade, *Degeneration, Culture and the Novel, 1880–1940* (Cambridge: Cambridge University Press, 1994), pp. 75–76.
27   Peter Bailey, '"Will the Real Bill Banks Please Stand Up?": Towards a Role Analysis of Mid-Victorian Working-Class Respectability', *Journal of Social History*, 12 (1979), 336–53 (p. 336).
28   Brian Harrison, *Drink and the Victorians: The Temperance Question in England, 1815–1872* (London: Faber and Faber, 1971); Trygve Tholfsen, *Working-Class Radicalism in Mid-Victorian England* (London: Croom Helm, 1976).
29   Geoffrey Crossick, *An Artisan Elite in Victorian Society: Kentish London, 1840–1880* (London: Croom Helm, 1978), pp. 136–37.
30   Michael Mason, *The Making of Victorian Sexual Attitudes* (Oxford: Oxford University Press, 1994), pp. 117–38.
31   Bailey, '"Real Bill Banks"', pp. 340–43. See also Gareth Stedman Jones, 'Working-Class Culture and Working-Class Politics in London, 1870–1900: Notes on the Remaking of a Working Class', in *Languages of Class: Studies in English Working-Class History, 1832–1982* (Cambridge: Cambridge University Press, 1983), pp. 179–238.
32   There are of course other ways to do this. David Green and Alan Parton, for example, have

The equivalent to Gilbert Grail, in *The Nether World*, is Sidney Kirkwood, an educated working man who, like Grail, must endure the occasional close encounter with the odours of naphtha and fried fish. When Clara Hewett, the woman he loves, finds a job as a waitress at the Imperial Restaurant and Luncheon Bar run by the Gandle-like Mrs Tubbs, Kirkwood fears that she has lost any chance of 'self-respect'. No wonder, since at the back of the restaurant stands a cooking-stove 'whereon frizzled and vapoured a savoury mess of sausages and onions'. Irritated by the 'fume of frying', Kirkwood loses himself in a 'fit of disgust' which is merely the accentuation of a familiar mood. 'To the Hewetts he had spoken impartially of Mrs Tubbs and her bar; probably that was the right view; but now there came back upon him the repugnance with which he had regarded Clara's proposal when it was first made.'[33] The repugnance which comes back upon him is a repugnance at the loss of self-respect entailed by what he regards as an immersion in matter.

In *The Nether World*, however, unlike *Thyrza*, there is an alternative to frizzling and vapouring — to hybridity, loss of outline, murkiness, seepage — *within* slumland. Kirkwood is a jeweller. 'The triumphant sunshine, refusing to be excluded even from London workshops, gleamed upon his tools and on the scraps of jewellery before him; he looked up to the blue sky, and thought with heavy heart of many a lane in Surrey and in Essex where he might be wandering but for this ceaseless necessity of earning the week's wage' (*NW* 90). In the novels of the mid-1880s, Gissing opposed countryside to slum as moral day to moral night. Here, however, the pastoralism, like the Dickensian faith in sunshine, is nothing if not self-conscious. When Jane Snowdon, Kirkwood's protégée, enjoys a brief holiday in rural Essex, she finds that the 'evil of the times' has left its mark there, too (165). What matters, then, is not what his tools reflect, but what they are: in a nether world characterized by murkiness and seepage, they alone have a shape, a discernible surface. To put it another way, the gleam matters phenomenologically. It is the self-respect Kirkwood derives from an occupation he will never be able to do without. His skill secures for him a positive as well as a negative freedom. He can choose where to live. He has rooms in a house in Tysoe Street, a street that 'begins reputably and degenerates in its latter half'. At one end is Wilmington Square, occupied in the main by jewellers, watch-makers and other craftsmen. Kirkwood has a good view of the Square from his window; in the opposite direction the street falls almost immediately under the 'dominion of dry-rot'. A brass plate on the door shows the inscription 'Hodgson, Dial Painter' (50). The brass plate, an assertion of shape and surface if ever there was one — an assertion of identity through or in shape and surface — answers the grease and the fumes, the mould and dry-rot, which everywhere else in slumland throw a veil of refuse over inexpugnable degradation. To put it another way, the tools and the brass plate enable us, by their outline, by their brightness, to reconceive the grease and the fumes — to conceive

made excellent use of Poor Law records to reconstruct the values and codes of slum-culture 'from the inside': 'Slums and Slum Life in Victorian England: London and Birmingham at Mid-Century', in *Slums*, ed. by S. Martin Gaskell (Leicester: Leicester University Press, 1990), pp. 17–91.

33   Gissing, *The Nether World*, ed. by John Goode (Hassocks: Harvester Press, 1974), pp. 30–31. Henceforth *NW*.

them phenomenologically, as a lack of outline and brightness, as mess rather than waste.

The gleam, like the grease and fumes, does become a metaphor. The novel's only philanthropist, Michael Snowdon, is a working man who has inherited a fortune from his petty capitalist son. Snowdon's idealism is of the kind which 'dazzles, inspires, raises to heroic contempt of the facts of life' (*NW* 179). Such dazzle amounts, we might think, to too much gleam: too abrupt an assertion of shape and surface. Clara Hewett, tiring of Mrs Tubbs, goes on the stage and, after brief success, is disfigured by a jealous rival. She returns to Clerkenwell, to the 'weltering mass' of the inhabitants of Farringdon Road Buildings. 'Gone for ever, for ever, the promise that always gleamed before her whilst she had youth and beauty and talent' (274). The weltering mass will cast its veil of refuse over the gleam. Aspiration is by no means futile; it has played its part, as the narrator acknowledges, in Clara's 'upward struggle in independence' (276). But, in the novel's economy, the more abstract a gleam, the greater the extent to which it relies upon an answering gleam in someone else's eyes, the more doubtful its worth. It is the metonymies which tell, which guarantee self-respect, in Gissing's account of the nether world.

Clara Hewett's brother, Bob, has a certain skill in metal-working. Early in the novel, he shows Kirkwood a medal he has cast. 'In his hand, which was very black, and shone as if from the manipulation of metals, he held a small bright medal' (*NW* 18–19). The brightness survives in the 'gleaming ring' proudly worn by his young wife, Penelope, or Pennyloaf, a gleam purchased by an artisan's dedication to his work (105). Bob Hewett's upward struggle in independence is defined not only by the gleam of metal, but by his clothes. Peter Bailey has found evidence of Gissing's interest in working-class attitudes towards respectability in the distinction he makes between workmen who wear collars and those who do not.[34] 'Bob's workshop was upstairs, and the companions with whom he sat, without exception, had something white and stiff round their necks; in fact, they were every bit as respectable as Sidney Kirkwood, and such as he, who bent over a jeweller's table' (69). As the gleam of metal answers grease and fume, so that collar answers the raggedness of the ragged classes (literally, the *Lumpenproletariat*). A collar asserts shape and surface, and thus identity, both by the material out of which it is made and by the way it gives definition to the human form. Rags do not. Clara's depressive mother seems 'wrapped up rather than dressed' (15–16); Mad Jack, a local feature, is 'not clad, but hung over with the filthiest rags' (43); the inhabitants of Shooter's Gardens, the worst slum in Clerkenwell, are 'soaked with grimy moisture, puffed into distortions, hung about with rotting garments' (248). These unfortunates stand condemned as much by their lack of outline as by the filth and rot they exude. Bob Hewett, who turns to crime, ends up dead and distinctly collarless in Shooter's Gardens, with Mad Jack watching over him (345–47). One might say that his brief and inglorious career is conceived phenomenologically, as an erosion of outline, a smearing and muddying.

There is no way out of the nether world. But there are ways out within it. Mad Jack's vision of a hell on earth (*NW* 345) is not, as has been suggested, the definitive

34   Bailey, '"Real Bill Banks"', pp. 347–48.

word of a choric figure.[35] Mad Jack is, after all, mad. Sidney Kirkwood, living in suburban Crouch End with Clara and the remaining Hewetts, knows hardship, but not hell on earth. His bitter experiences have taken their toll. 'In the matter of attire he was no longer as careful as he used to be; the clothes he wore had done more than just service, and hung about him unregarded' (370). The life he lives is, however, a life he has chosen: a life made possible by the gleam of metal, if not, any longer, of aspiration. Similarly, Jane Snowdon's escape from servitude is an escape into outline. 'No longer were her limbs huddled over with a few shapeless rags' (97). One place where her influence is felt is the second-hand clothing business run by Pennyloaf Hewett and two other women (387–88). The workshop is also a residence, and, like every other residence in slumland, horribly overcrowded. But it undeniably nurtures self-respect.

Gissing's achievement, in *The Nether World*, was to invent a phenomenology of slum textures: of metal and grease, of collar and rag. That phenomenology enables us to imagine what self-respect might have looked like to men and women who knew they would never achieve what the middle classes understood by respectability. It is a remarkable achievement. Furthermore, having invented a phenomenology of slum textures, Gissing took great care to ensure that it could not be mistaken for a 'view from the inside'. The narrator's detachment sets a limit to the penetrative force of phenomenology. So, I think, does the person of Clem Peckover.

The novel's opening chapter introduces us to Clem, and to her domestic slave, Jane Snowdon. The first hint of Clem's presence, as Jane descends to the kitchen, is gastronomic. 'Through the half-open door came a strong odour and a hissing sound, plainly due to the frying of sausages' (*NW* 5). Appetite, and an unapologetic enjoyment of power, characterize Clem as a 'noble savage'. 'Civilisation,' the narrator intones, 'could bring no charge against this young woman; it and she had no common criterion' (6). The meal proceeds. 'The sausages — five in number — she had emptied from the frying-pan directly on to her plate, and with them all the black rich juice that had exuded in the process of cooking — particularly rich, owing to its having several times caught fire and blazed triumphantly' (6). There follows the meticulous application of mustard and pepper, and the crushing of thick slices of bread into the 'black grease' (7). The narrator cannot conceal his admiration for the skill with which Clem conveys the pieces of sausage to her mouth by means of the knife alone (7). Only after disposing of the last trace of 'oleaginous matter' (8) does she turn her full attention to the cringing Jane.

Metaphor clusters around Clem. She is an animal, a Red Indian, a 'rank, evilly-fostered growth' (*NW* 7–8). If the metaphors convince, then we have no choice but to regard her as Gissing's version of a degenerate. But those sausages are pure metonymy. They are what Clem does, and does well, not what she is. Their context is not theories of degeneracy, but the campaign for dietary reform; they resist improvement by oatmeal. Porridge was 'work'us stuff', the classic institutional diet; meat, and especially meat as meat-like as Clem's sausages, represented freedom of

---

35   Poole, *Gissing in Context*, p. 92; Grylls, *Paradox*, p. 49.

choice.[36] Clem eludes metaphor by the sheer 'gusto' with which she attacks her food, and Jane. Eating and torturing people are the things she likes doing best in the world. She has chosen, and the choice is her identity. She embodies 'fierce life independent of morality' (8). The narrator does not admire the scorn she expresses for middle-class notions of respectability. But he gives the fierceness its due. He invites us to distinguish not between order and disorder, but between a good mess and a bad mess. To Clem, the sausages represent a good mess; to him, they represent a bad mess. He can identify them as a bad mess, to his own way of thought, without at the same time assimilating the mess-maker to the mess, and implying, as the narrator of *Workers in the Dawn* or *Thyrza* might well have done, that the entire heap of ordure could with advantage be flushed down some imaginary all-purpose drain.

Clem's most important quality is her determination to create an 'independent life' for herself *within* the world she already knows. 'She had no desire whatever to enter a higher class than that in which she was born; to be of importance in her familiar circle was the most she aimed at' (*NW* 259–60). At the theatre, her concern is not to occupy a 'superior place', but to extinguish her neighbours in the pit by a 'lavish' style of costume and the purchase of something expensive to eat and drink (260). There is a form of self-respect, here, which shadows that earned after a very different fashion, arduously, and at great cost, by Sidney Kirkwood and Jane Snowden. At one point, Gissing juxtaposes these two forms of self-respect — the form which has adapted middle-class decorum to a life in the slums, and the form which refuses even to recognize that decorum — across a break between chapters. At the end of Chapter 34, Kirkwood tells Jane Snowdon, who loves him, that he feels honour bound to marry the ruined and helpless Clara. 'For an instant, while Sidney was still speaking, she caught a gleam of hope in renunciation itself, the kind of strength which idealism is fond of attributing to noble natures' (318). Gissing catches the gleam's ambiguity with perfect tact: it is entirely admirable, all that the middle-class philanthropist could hope for, and yet not enough to live by. Chapter 35 opens with Clem Peckover, now married to Jane's father, Joseph Snowdon, at breakfast. 'Clem, also in anything but *grande toilette*, was using a knife for the purpose of conveying to her mouth the juice which had exuded from crisp rashers' (319). Jane has chosen to live by the faintest of gleams, Clem by juice. This juxtaposition, Chekhovian in its moral density, seems to me one of the finest moments not only in Gissing's writing, but in the totality of nineteenth-century representations of the nether world. It is true that Gissing cannot quite bring himself to allow Clem to get away with it. The last news we have of her is that she has been accused of attempting to poison her mother (373). But the sausages are what stays in the mind: an outrage against oatmeal, a metonymy which will never succumb to metaphor, a dark self-respect. Good mess or bad?

---

36 Ross, *Love and Toil*, p. 32.

CHAPTER 8

Lesbians before Lesbianism:
Sexual Identity in Early
Twentieth-Century British Fiction

Towards the end of Radclyffe Hall's *The Unlit Lamp* (1924), the heroine, Joan
Ogden, who has grown miserably old in a small provincial town, overhears two
young women discussing her. She recognizes them as women of the same 'type' as
her: unattached, independent, sexually ambiguous. They dress like her, and wear
their hair cut in a similar style. But they seem to inhabit a different world: *their* lamps
have definitely been lit. Unlike her, they are aggressively intelligent and purposeful,
'not at all self-conscious in their tailor-made clothes, not ashamed of their cropped
hair.' At once envious of, and terrified by, their success, Joan has to acknowledge
that she belongs to another age. Her place in the evolution of feminism is that of
the 'pioneer' who 'got left behind.' She is, as one of her tormentors remarks, 'what
they used to call a "New Woman".'[1]

It is a powerful scene because it notices both the anguish of the old New Woman,
the superseded pioneer, and the boldness of the really new New Woman, who
would not seem half so formidable were she not so fiercely determined to put the
past behind her. When they identify her as a superseded pioneer, Joan Ogden's
tormentors bring to bear on the development of feminism an intricate genealogy
whose scope and function are no longer self-evident. They define themselves in
relation to their immediate precursors, rather than in relation to an understanding
of the development of British society as a whole. This genealogical habit has, to
date, attracted little attention. I believe that the habit merits attention, not because it
will deliver a ready-made account of the development of modern British feminism,
but because it offers a unique insight into the ways in which early twentieth-
century British feminists imagined their opportunities and purposes, that is, the
ways in which they created an identity for themselves.

One might begin to reconstruct that genealogy, in very rough terms, by positing
three 'waves' of feminist activity. The first, consisting of women born in the 1860s
and 1870s, peaked in the 1890s. Its concern with education, and with the economic
and sexual emancipation of women inside (and sometimes outside) marriage,

---

1   Radclyffe Hall, *The Unlit Lamp* (London: Virago, 1981), pp. 284–85.

found a vivid focus in the New Woman novels of the 1890s, and their successors, the 'marriage problem' or 'sex' novels of the Edwardian era.[2] The second wave, consisting of women born in the 1870s and 1880s, peaked in the 1900s. Its main concern with the economic and political destinies of women who had chosen not to marry led to campaigns to improve living and working conditions, and to secure the vote.[3] These, one might call the Newer Woman. New and Newer Women were sometimes suspected of lesbianism, as we shall see, but did not necessarily think of themselves as lesbians, and were not necessarily thought of in those terms. The third wave, peaking in the 1920s, divided from their precursors by the abyss of the First World War, and conscious that some of the political and economic battles had been at least half-won, found a focus in androgynous modernity, and in the emergence of a lesbian subculture.[4] These were the Newest Women of all. The opportunities and purposes I have sketched were not, of course, the only ones available to feminists. But some women did recognize them, and by that recognition instituted a genealogical habit whose outcome was a radically made-over identity: an identity constructed genealogically, in relation not to what wholly resembles it, or wholly opposes it, but to what partly resembles it.

New Historicism, the form of analysis currently dominant in literary and cultural studies, has tended to attribute to 'discourse' a decisive function in the determining of identity, and to rupture or crisis a decisive function in the determining of social change.[5] Current explanations of the emergence of a lesbian subculture in the 1920s thus favour a crisis (the war) and a discourse (the classificatory schemes of the new sexology). For example, Sandra Gilbert and Susan Gubar argue that the war made possible an 'unprecedented transcendence of the profounder constraints imposed by traditional sex roles': they instance the 'erotic release' experienced during it by lesbian writers such as Radclyffe Hall, Amy Lowell, Gertrude Stein, and Vita Sackville-West.[6] Other scholars have argued that an identity of any kind, sexual or otherwise, cannot be known until it has been articulated. Thus, it is said,

2   On New Woman novels, see, inter alia: A. R. Cunningham, 'The "New Woman" Fiction of the 1890s', *Victorian Studies*, 17 (1973), 177–86; Gail Cunningham, *The New Woman and the Victorian Novel* (London: Macmillan, 1978); and Kate Flint, *The Woman Reader, 1837–1914* (Oxford: Oxford University Press, 1993), pp. 294–316. On the Edwardian 'marriage problem' or 'sex' novel, see David Trotter, *The English Novel in History 1895–1920* (London: Routledge, 1993), pp. 197–213.

3   Martha Vicinus, *Independent Women: Work and Community for Single Women, 1850–1920* (London: Virago, 1985). For novels about working women and about the suffrage campaigns, see Trotter, *English Novel*, pp. 44–48.

4   For representations of the Newest Woman, see Mary Louise Roberts's wide-ranging and incisive account of *la femme moderne* in *Civilization without Sexes: Reconstructing Gender in Post-War France, 1917–1927* (Chicago, IL: Chicago University Press, 1994).

5   In literary studies, New Historicism is still associated primarily with the description and analysis of Renaissance literature. For an anthology of representative approaches, see *New Historicism and Renaissance Drama*, ed. by Richard Wilson and Richard Dutton (London: Longman, 1992). Its spread to other fields is charted in *New Historical Literary Study: Essays on Reproducing Texts, Representing History*, ed. by Jeffrey N. Cox and Larry J. Reynolds (Princeton, NJ: Princeton University Press, 1993).

6   Sandra M. Gilbert and Susan Gubar, *No Man's Land: The Place of the Woman Writer in the Twentieth Century*, vol. II: *Sexchanges* (New Haven, CT: Yale University Press, 1989), pp. 299–300.

Victorian feminists could not or would not alter their 'romantic vocabulary' so as to incorporate desire for another woman; later generations, however, maturing after 1920, found themselves able to 'discuss their sexual identity in a new sexual language.'[7] That language was provided by the male sexologists (Richard von Krafft-Ebing, Havelock Ellis, Edward Carpenter) who invented the category of the third sex: 'inverts' concealing the soul of a man in a woman's body. Radclyffe Hall, by appropriating and revaluing the stereotype of the 'mannish lesbian' in *The Well of Loneliness* (1928), became the first British writer to articulate female homosexuality.[8]

There is evidence to support both arguments. 'And then again the war made everything different!' is the refrain of Marie Belloc Lowndes's *Lilla* (1916), and of a great number of other novels and memoirs: the things made different included sexual attitudes and behaviour.[9] Hall said that the war's death-dealing had finally given a 'right to life' to women like Stephen Gordon, the heroine of *The Well of Loneliness*.[10] Similarly, a right to life could also be claimed by appropriating, and transvaluing, the classifications of the sexologists. In 1915, the feminist Frances Wilder wrote to Carpenter to tell him that she had at once recognized herself in his account of an 'intermediate' sex, part male, part female. Wilder attributed her 'strong desire to caress & fondle' a female friend to a 'dash of the masculine' in her own temperament.[11] Clearly, both war and sexology made some difference (a big difference) to some women who were beginning to think of themselves as lesbians. But all the difference to all such women? Did the strong desires experienced by such as Frances Wilder always have to be categorized and named before they could be known?

A number of recent studies have shown that the scope of lesbian self-awareness in Britain, both before and after the First World War, greatly exceeded the scope of sexological knowledge.[12] If we are to do justice to that self-awareness, we will have to discard or refine the preoccupations — with crisis, with discourse — engendered by the New Historicism. It is at this point that the genealogies sketched by a writer like Radclyffe Hall may prove of some assistance. In particular, they may help us to rethink the question of agency. The crisis model of personal and social change tends to obscure agency. Thus when Gilbert and Gubar claim that to literary women 'the soldier's sacrifice at times seemed to signal a cultural wound or fissure

---

7   Carroll Smith-Rosenberg, *Disorderly Conduct: Visions of Gender in Victorian America* (Oxford: Oxford University Press, 1985), p. 284. For a similar analysis, see Jeffrey Weekes, *Sex, Politics and Society: The Regulation of Sexuality since 1800* (London: Longman, 1981), p. 115.

8   Esther Newton, 'The Mythic Mannish Lesbian: Radclyffe Hall and the New Woman', in *Hidden from History: Reclaiming the Gay and Lesbian Past*, ed. by Martin Bauml Duberman, Martha Vicinus, and George Chauncey (New York: Meridian, 1989), pp. 281–93. See also Jonathan Dollimore, *Sexual Dissidence* (Oxford: Oxford University Press, 1991), pp. 48–52.

9   Marie Belloc Lowndes, *Lilla: A Part of Her Life* (London: Hutchinson, 1916), p. 159.

10   Radclyffe Hall, *The Well of Loneliness* (London: Virago, 1982), p. 275.

11   Quoted by Newton, 'Mythic Mannish Lesbian', p. 286. See Ruth F. Claus, 'Confronting Homosexuality: A Letter from Frances Wilder', *Signs*, 2 (1977), 928–33.

12   Terry Castle, *The Apparitional Lesbian: Female Homosexuality and Modern Culture* (New York: Columbia University Press, 1993); Suzanne Raitt, 'Charlotte Mew and May Sinclair: A Love-Song', *Critical Quarterly*, 37 (1995), 3–17.

through which radically new social modes might enter,' it is hard to be sure who is doing what to whom, and how.[13] The discourse-model does address the question of agency, but in somewhat static terms. Thus sexology is said to create a position ('invert', say) that can be occupied, by the woman who desires other women, and revalued in and through occupation. The genealogical model, by contrast, envisages a process of partial imitation, a continual adjustment of sameness and difference within a shared history. Joan Ogden is strictly speaking a Newer Woman who partially resembles the New Women who befriend and teach her: like them, she does not wish to marry; unlike them, she is interested in politics. Her young rivals misidentify her as a New Woman, brusquely conflating the categories of New Woman and Newer Woman in order to emphasize their difference from all that has gone before them. The circulation of identities does not stop there, however. For Joan's response to their emphasis on difference is to make herself more like them, to dress as they dress. Her imitation of them, were they ever to notice it, would show them to themselves in a new light. The play of reciprocal gazes, of reciprocal fantasies, continually modifies identity along the movable borderline of partial resemblance. And the novel itself actively contributes to the circulation of identities by exploring the sameness within the difference upon which the Newest Woman insist too rigidly. It re-establishes, in its account of Joan Ogden's youth and early adulthood, the very distinction between New and Newer Women they have, for their own genealogical purposes, collapsed. That account imagines homosexual identity as a choice made, or entered into, over a period of time and within some quite punitive constraints, between the erotic possibilities available in a society that did not as yet contain a recognizable lesbian subculture.

This essay has been written, like *The Unlit Lamp*, from Joan Ogden's point of view. It tries to reconstruct some of the social and erotic possibilities available to women who would appear not to have read Edward Carpenter, in pre-war and wartime Britain. My main focus will be on the fiction of the period (Newer Woman fiction, if you like), which has had a great deal less attention paid to it than the New Woman novel of the 1890s or the experimental fiction of the 1920s.[14] I shall look first at a number of notably serious-minded feminist writers, including Rose Allatini and 'Cicely Hamilton' (Cicely Mary Hammill), then at L. T. Meade, a prolific author of best-selling romances. Some of these writers, and some of the 'odd' women they portray, might have regarded themselves as lesbians. What matters is that, in a period without assertive sexual or literary subcultures, both polemical and mass-market fiction sustained a range of narratives in which women desired and were desired by other women.

---

13   Gilbert and Gubar, *Sexchanges*, p. 309.
14   On gender and female modernism, see Suzanne Raitt, *Vita and Virginia: The Work and Friendship of Vita Sackville-West and Virginia Woolf* (Oxford: Oxford University Press, 1993); and, more generally, *The Gender of Modernism: A Critical Anthology*, ed. by Bonnie Kime Scott (Bloomington, IN: Indiana University Press, 1990). Jane Eldridge Miller's *Rebel Women: Feminism, Modernism, and the Edwardian Novel* (London: Virago, 1994) gives exemplary attention to female modernism's Edwardian precursors.

Such narratives tell us more about collective fantasy than they do about individual behaviour. Of course, it is hard to establish how they might have been read at the time. Although my main concern here is with the fiction and the collective fantasies it might be said to articulate, I will approach the question of readerships by discussing, in the third and final section of the essay, an openly lesbian writer, 'Christopher St John' (Christabel Marshal), who published before Radclyffe Hall, but nonetheless clearly hoped and expected that she would be read by lesbians.

The point of examining fiction published in the first two decades of the century is not simply to fill a gap in the historical record. In a curious way, the scandalous homosexual couples of the 1920s, real and fictional, reiterate the scandalous heterosexual couples of the 1890s, real and fictional. Both arrangements established an alternative to social and sexual norms in and through the very form of renegade partnership. In each case, two people unite against the world, and find in their union a cultural politics. The arrangement, and the thinking that surrounds it, are essentially dyadic: in that respect, it mirrors, or even reproduces, the orthodoxy to which it is opposed. The world against which two people unite is itself made up of couples. But the lives and writings I discuss here tell a different story. During the 1900s and 1910s, the advantages and disadvantages of singleness became a major issue. Single women flourish in the fiction of the period in a way they rarely did before, and have rarely done since. Furthermore, in radical life as well as in radical books, the renegade couple found powerful rivals not only in the solitary woman, but also in the group of women, and even, on occasion, the female threesome. What we find in the lives and books of the Newer Women is a range of possibilities which in some respects exceeds those available both to the New Women and to the Newest Women. Indeed, the monadic and triadic thinking they articulate remains as provocative today as it must have been when it was originally formulated.

Independent Women in Pre-War and Wartime Fiction

Rose Allatini's *Despised and Rejected*, published in 1917 under the pseudonym A. T. Fitzroy and immediately banned on the grounds that it was likely to prejudice the recruiting of persons to serve in His Majesty's Forces, and their training and discipline, is a novel about homosexuality and about pacifism. In a Europe polarized by military conflict, pacifism offered Allatini an analogy for the sexual 'intermediacy' that was by then one self-definition available to gay men and women. When war breaks out, Dennis Blackwood and his male lover both become conscientious objectors and are duly arrested and charged. It is clear that Allatini, like Frances Wilder, had been reading Edward Carpenter. A journalist friend of Dennis's claims that men who stand 'mid-way between the extremes of the two sexes' are the 'advance-guard' of a more enlightened civilization.[15] The novel's understanding of male homosexuality, in short, justifies the stress some historians have put on the efficacy of scientific discourse.

One of Dennis's closest allies is Antoinette de Courcy, whose life has been shaped by her passion, now exhausted, for an older woman, Hester Cawthorn. Hester, with

15   Rose Allatini (A. T. Fitzroy), *Despised and Rejected* (London: GMP, 1988), p. 348.

her 'masculine-looking' walking stick and the brim of her felt hat turned down to shade her 'thin, sombre face', fascinates Antoinette from the moment of their first meeting, in a drearily conventional family hotel. The walking stick, the felt hat, and the sombreness are all there is to see, or to know, about Hester. Yet for Antoinette this is enough. Hester's indifference to the codes governing dress and manner represent a microscopic tear in the fabric of bourgeois life. Her singleness, among men and women whose main business it to be or to become a couple, represents another microscopic tear. If those men and women take account of Hester at all, it is as an oddity, a lack (or the sign of a lack). But the lack acquires, in and through this very neglect and the vague unease it sometimes provokes, a definite moral and erotic charge. Hester's 'fierce reserve', the 'sensitiveness' lying behind a 'brutally direct manner', give her in Antoinette's eyes a 'compelling and magnetic dignity'. Eroticism, here, is the call of one singularity to another. It is genealogical: the ambiguous acknowledgement of a pioneering Newer Woman by someone still young enough to become in due course one of the Newest. Antionette feels that no 'irritation or annoyance' can ever touch her as long as she wraps herself around with memories of Hester: the 'world of men' will always prove disappointing by comparison.[16]

Antoinette's love for Hester, although no more than a prelude to the main action, is the novel's most memorable event. And this despite a distinct shortage of explanatory contexts. Dennis Blackwood may define himself as a member of the 'intermediate sex', but neither Hester nor Antoinette does; and while his struggle with the military authorities provides a political analogy and support for his newly affirmed sexual orientation, it does nothing for Antoinette. The cultural fissures opened by the war do not bring her erotic release. How, then, are Hester and Antoinette able to acknowledge one another? How do we recognize them for what they are? Some of the book's first readers would have recognized Hester, I believe, and through Hester the nature of Antoinette's love, because they had already encountered her like in Newer Woman fiction.

The conventions of domestic realism, dominant in the nineteenth-century British novel, insisted that the marriage of hero and heroine in the final chapter should complete both their identities and the narrative. Edwardian women writers sometimes modified those conventions so as to incorporate a minor character whose uncompromising independence the heroine admires but does not in the end want for herself. These characters are superfluous, both in social terms (they never marry) and in narrative terms (they fade away as the wedlock plot sweeps hero and heroine on to their own and the novel's resolution). Yet they often stay in the mind rather longer than the happy couple. Their unfulfilment is both a dead end and a new beginning, since some readers might imagine for them, under different circumstances, another story, a different resolution. They inhabit a virtual narrative that might be said to exist in the minds of readers for whom the wedlock plot has little or no interest.

In that virtual narrative, deprivation and lack acquire a positive charge. For

---

16   Ibid., pp. 12, 44, 51, 65–66, 69.

these superfluous women are by no means unlit lamps. Elspeth Macleod, in Alice
Stronach's *A Newnham Friendship* (1901), expresses a familiar enough view when
she encourages Carol Martin, who lives with a random assortment of secretaries,
journalists, and landscape gardeners in a 'Women's Barracks' in the East End of
London, to marry. 'Don't be one of them, dear friend. Don't be a neutral.'[17] But a
neutrality deliberately chosen can scarcely be considered a sign of weakness. Carol
Martin's choice of the women's barracks has created a new identity.

Edwardian writers had a great deal to say both about the formal institutions
that have since been described by social historians (women's colleges, settlement
houses) and about the more loosely defined communities of the boarding house
and the club. Their novels gave independent working women not only a physical
presence, but an address. Hilda Forester, in Olive Birrell's *Love in a Mist* (1900),
wants the heroine to live with her and a journalist friend in their Bloomsbury flat,
which serves as both home and meeting place; Jehane Bruce, in Violet Hunt's *The
Workaday Woman* (1906), throws Bohemian parties in hers, at which the relations
of the sexes are 'a little altered', and the women gain character at the expense of
the men.[18] Bloomsbury, in central London, was freelance territory, a place where
things were a little altered. Dolf Wyllarde's *Pathway of the Pioneer* (1906), set in a
Bloomsbury boarding house, describes an informal society called 'Nous Autres',
whose members include a freelance journalist, an actress, a typist and shorthand
clerk, a post office clerk, a music teacher, and a musician who plays in the Ladies'
Catgut Band. Sally Richards, the wartime typewriter girl in Violet Tweedale's *The
Heart of a Woman* (1917), may have given her woman's heart in the traditional fashion
to the man who employs her, but she also belongs to a club whose membership
consists entirely of 'free lances, unmarried working women of advanced opinions
and pronounced celibacy'.[19] These young freelances are all Newer Women.

It is important to recognize that 'Nous Autres' could be reconfigured as an
audience, and their attitude to narrative thus made explicit. In 'A Conjugal Episode',
a late story by one of the most successful New Woman novelists, George Egerton
(Mary Chavelita Dunne), published in *Flies in Amber* (1905), the narrator, visiting
Paris, takes a room in a house owned by a woman separated from her husband,
and so enters a female community consisting of the landlady, the landlady's two
sisters, and her closest friend.[20] In the husband's absence, the women fantasize,
momentarily, about becoming men, about dressing in men's clothes. When he
reappears, the community disperses. But this account of the triumph of heterosexuality is framed in an interesting way: the narrator tells her tale, in London,
to three friends, all working women, gathered in the Bloomsbury flat belonging
to one of them. The framing narrative recalls the many occasions in *fin-de-siècle*
fiction when male listeners assemble to hear a tale brought back from the unknown:

---

17   Alice Stronach, *A Newnham Friendship* (London: Blackie and Son Limited, 1901), p. 385.
18   Olive Birrell, *Love in a Mist* (London: Smith, Elder, 1900), pp. 228, 247; Violet Hunt, *The
Workaday Woman* (London: T. Werner Laurie, 1906), p. 35.
19   Violet Tweedale, *The Heart of a Woman* (London: Hurst and Blackett, 1917), p. 225.
20   George Egerton, 'A Conjugal Episode', in *Flies in Amber* (London: Hutchinson, 1905), pp.
102–42.

Kipling's soldiering stories, Wells's *The Time Machine*, James's *The Turn of the Screw*, Conrad's *Heart of Darkness*. These occasions at once threaten the men assembled, by disclosing the uncanny, and confirm them in their privileged access to a knowledge too dangerous to be revealed to women and children. The occasion of 'A Conjugal Episode', by deliberate contrast, confirms women in their access to a knowledge too dangerous to be revealed to men, and so challenges the male reader in his narrative as well as his sexual pride. What the three friends witness, and so actualize, is a narrative ordinarily restricted to the virtual: the story of the homosocial and homosexual fantasies threaded through the triumph of heterosexuality.

Again, this was a challenge renewed by the next generation of writers. In G. B. Stern's *Children of No Man's Land* (1919), a group of working women (a secretary, a chauffeuse, two caterers, and a biologist) debate the impact of the war on the 'sex problem'. These freelances see themselves as belonging to a 'transition period', and they certainly revise traditional ideas concerning femininity (one of them crops her luxuriant hair while they talk). As in 'A Conjugal Episode', the occasion of the debate matters as much as its content. As the women debate the sex problem, a group of men, lubricated by whisky and soda, gathers to discuss *them*. Male clubland still goes about its business; but it has met its match (or its mirror image).[21]

One answer to the heterosexual couple was the group or club. Another was the defiant singularity adopted by such as Hester Cawthorn. The one thing which unites Joan Ogden and her detractors, in *The Unlit Lamp*, is the knowledge that femininity can be redefined by the conscious manipulation of social symbolism: dress, bodily styling, gesture. There was much to be gained, as well as lost, by these minor violations of custom. Joan's first instinct, after the shock of humiliation has worn off, is to head straight for the outfitter and buy some properly masculine neckties, a grey flannel suit, and a soft felt hat.[22] Neckties were a feminist issue.

No one was more aware of the defining qualities of social symbolism than the actor and writer Cicely Hamilton. Hamilton was instantly attracted to the suffrage movement because it looked set to 'shaken and weaken the tradition of the "normal woman".' But she lost faith when she discovered that its leaders were intent, in effect, on preserving the normal woman. They insisted too much, for her taste, on 'the feminine note'. 'In the Women's Social and Political Union the coat-and-shirt effect was not favoured; all suggestion of the masculine was carefully avoided, and the outfit of a militant setting forth to smash windows would probably include a picture-hat'. Hamilton's feminism involved, among other things, the disruption, not of political meetings, but of the 'costume-code' that defined traditional femininity.[23] To the innocent eye, one form of protest could look much like the other. A character in Beatrice Harraden's *Interplay* (1908) mistakenly identifies a fellow passenger as a suffragette on the basis of her red tie and 'severe hat'.[24] The Pankhursts might not have been amused.

21   G. B. Stern, *Children of No Man's Land* (London: Duckworth, 1919), pp. 226–52.
22   Hall, *Unlit Lamp*, p. 285.
23   Cicely Hamilton, *Life Errant* (London: Dent, 1935), pp. 65, 75.
24   Beatrice Harraden, *Interplay* (London: Thomas Nelson, 1908), p. 131.

The coat-and-shirt effect was one to which a number of writers gave imaginative substance. Discreetly masculine garb adorns a long line of neutrals from the protagonist of Menie Muriel Dowie's *A Girl in the Karpathians* (1891) through to Edith Haynes, in Hamilton's war-novel *William: An Englishman* (1919), a 'tall young woman in tweed coat and skirt', as fiercely reserved, and as compelling, as Hester Cawthorn.[25]

If tweed, with its connotations of masculinity, was one way to disrupt the costume-code, then colour, particularly bright or discordant colour, was another. Joan Ogden learns non-conformity from older feminists like Beatrice Lesway, a schoolteacher who lives in Bloomsbury. Beatrice's untidiness and garish clothes make her almost, but not quite, a figure of fun. 'Her whole appearance left you bewildered; it was a mixed metaphor, a contradiction in style, certainly a little grotesque, and yet you did not laugh.'[26] Mixture and contradiction make her hard to interpret, but easy to distinguish. The extraordinary clothes worn by the artist Yvonne Irdwine, in Margaret Legge's *The Rebellion of Esther* (1914), 'purples and greens and scarlets and yellows all mixed anyhow,' give her, too, a distinctive illegibility. Equally striking is the 'singular effect' of the mackintosh, golf cap, and dogskin riding gloves worn by Anne Yeo, in Ada Leverson's *Love's Shadow* (1908).[27] Leverson contrasts Anne's passionate, prickly devotion to Hyacinth Verney with the boredom of marriage and the banality of adulterous intrigue. When Hyacinth decides to marry, Anne retires to a Bloomsbury boarding house. What makes these women compelling (more than a joke) is that the decision they have taken, to be odd, affects every aspect of their lives. Colourfulness and tweed, overstatement and understatement, set in motion a genealogical 'reading'. They are the point from which a well-informed reader might have embarked upon a virtual narrative.

Woman to Woman: L. T. Meade and the Fantasy of Seduction

L. T. Meade married when she was twenty-five, and had three children. She does not appear to have identified herself as a lesbian. But her innumerable and in most respects entirely conventional romances return again and again to the portrayal of women whose compelling dignity is overtly erotic, and therefore a site of virtual narrative. These women are utterly imperious, unlike the freelances of the Newer Woman novel, whose love for them sometimes serves as a measure of their imperiousness. They dominate the narratives in which they appear. Meade began to publish in the 1870s, and made her name in the 1880s as the author of school stories. Thereafter, she was prolific in that genre and several others. A discussion of two books published in 1898, the first a New Woman novel, the second a story about terrorists, will show how she adapted the conventions of disparate genres to the portrayal of a new type of heroine.

25   Menie Muriel Dowie, *A Girl in the Karpathians* (London: George Philip & Son, 1891), p. 17; Cicely Hamilton, *William: An Englishman* (London: Skeffington & Son, 1919), p. 153.
26   Hall, *Unlit Lamp*, p. 200.
27   Margaret Legge, *The Rebellion of Esther* (London: Alston Rivers, 1914), p. 35; Ada Leverson, *Love's Shadow* (London: Richards, 1908), p. 299.

The Cleverest Woman in England develops the sensational aspects of New Woman fiction so popular during the first half of the 1890s. Dagmar Olloffson, the child of an unhappy marriage, dedicates herself to campaigning for the emancipation of women, both as a writer and as a public speaker. She falls in love with Geoffrey Hamlyn, a staunch conservative and bitter opponent of women's rights. They strike a bargain: neither will interfere with the other's convictions. Dagmar becomes an assiduous wife and mother, while continuing to speak and write on behalf of the 'Cause'. She converts half their Bloomsbury house into a shelter for battered and fallen women. She is, as she herself puts it, a 'contradiction'.[28] Tragically, one of the women she has rescued from distress brings smallpox into the house, and Dagmar dies. The novel celebrates her as a pioneer, while at the same time demonstrating, luridly, the dangers of political commitment.

Meade dramatizes Dagmar's divided loyalty by contrasting her love for her husband with her more ambiguous feelings for Imogen Pryce, a suffragette whom she has long befriended. The marriage comes as a shattering blow to Imogen, whose jealousy thereafter irradiates the action. Geoffrey huffily tells Imogen that, although they both love Dagmar deeply, they should not put themselves in 'the same category'. But the palpable strength of Imogen's feelings makes it hard to put her into any other category. The very closeness of the names by which Dagmar calls her husband and her friend (Geoff, Genny) suggests that one might quite easily be substituted for the other. 'I do not love you as I ought,' Imogen tells Dagmar.[29] The expression of her true, forbidden feelings for Dagmar is the book's most vivid event.

Scenes between husband and wife quickly fall into the same pattern: a disagreement about politics, followed by an embrace. The embrace, however, lacks erotic charge. 'He knelt by her, she laid her head on his breast. A moment later she had dropped asleep.' Although Dagmar's affection for Geoffrey is genuine, and frequently reiterated, she does not appear to desire him passionately. Dagmar and Imogen make the more promising couple. 'Now I — sometimes I think I am too big, there is too much of me; but you are *petite*, Imogen, altogether the sort of woman that a man would fall in love with.' Their encounters, punctuated by false moves and eruptions, are suffused with an ambiguous eroticism.

> 'Sit down by me, Imogen, for a moment.'
> Imogen obeyed. Dagmar kept her hands folded lightly in her lap. Imogen, who was always fond of touching those she loved, tried to take possession of one of the hands, but Dagmar very decidedly repulsed her.
> 'What did you do that for?'
> 'I don't want you to hold my hand. I have told you before that it is terribly effeminate.'
> 'Ah, you can little guess what I feel for you.'

It is the indeterminacy starkly rendered by Imogen's passion that unsettles Dagmar, provoking her to uncharacteristic abruptness. The only description she can find for them is 'effeminate', a quality as repellent to her in a woman as it would be in

28   L. T. Meade, *The Cleverest Woman in England* (London: Ballantyne, Hanson, 1898), p. 19.
29   Ibid., pp. 25, 116.

a man, and as hard to define. Imogen determines the rhythm of these encounters: her caress elicits from Dagmar no more than a gesture of rejection; but that very rejection, its abruptness a virtual acknowledgement of desire, emboldens her to declare herself.

> Imogen stood behind her friend, pushing back her soft hair, and laying her cool fingers on the white broad forehead.
>
> Dagmar submitted to the caress in utter weariness, then irritation, altogether foreign to her nature, seized her, and she sprang up.
>
> 'Oh, don't touch me just now, Genny, I can't quite bear it, I have gone through a good bit. The fact is, I am in a dilemma, and only you can put me straight.'
>
> 'Then I will, darling, to my heart's blood.'[30]

That irritation, so foreign to Dagmar's nature, is, by its very foreignness, an intenser feeling than any to which Geoffrey moves her. His desire remains unacknowledged. Dagmar knows that Imogen is a lesbian, even if she cannot, or will not, say as much. Addressed, implicitly, as a lesbian, Imogen responds with a declaration, with her 'heart's blood'. Although the novel holds her indirectly responsible for Dagmar's death, it never portrays her as a monster or a joke. Imogen's desire is the true measure of Dagmar's imperiousness.

The Cleverest Woman in England is sober stuff, however, by comparison with one of the six other novels Meade published that year, *The Siren*. Vera, the siren in question, is half English, half Russian (Dagmar Olloffson is half English, half Swedish). A brutal public flogging received in Siberian exile converts her to Nihilism. Her mission is to secure the fortune of her wealthy English father, Colonel Nugent, then assassinate him and the Tsar with bouquets of poisoned roses. In England, she proves an immense success and, eventually learning to love and respect her father, longs to exchange Russian magnetism for English respectability. But the memory of the flogging keeps her loyal to the cause. There can be no compromise between a daughter's love and a terrorist's dedication. She commits suicide.

By far the most compelling passages in this routine thriller concern Vera's arrival in English society and her mass seduction of Colonel Nugent's household. First to go is Frank Norreys, the fiancé of Nugent's niece, Wilmot. He is soon followed by Wilmot, and her mother, Lady O'Brien. Vera's mission requires her to exercise her 'powers of fascination' to the full: 'walking over hearts,' she calls it. However, whereas Nugent and Norreys submit instantly, the two women put up a fierce resistance, and their capitulation, when it comes, is thus the more heartfelt, the more charged. Lady O'Brien is struck immediately by Vera's wonderful eyes: 'when they look at you they make you feel queer.' Vera's frank avowal of will-to-power finally overwhelms her.

> She kissed Lady O'Brien as she spoke. That kiss thrilled through the widow almost as if it had been bestowed by a lover. She took one of Vera's hands and held it tightly.

---

30   Ibid., pp. 217, 18, 161, 243.

The kiss widows Lady O'Brien more effectively than her husband's death, obliterating heterosexuality. Wilmot, too, aware of Norreys's fascination with Vera, hates her power. But Wilmot's hatred fades mysteriously on the eve of her wedding.

> 'If you will I should love it; and yet sometimes, Vera, I hate you so much — so much.'
> 'No, no, Wilmot, you cannot hate me.'
> 'I do not now; I love you with passion. Oh, yes, come and sleep with me.'
> 'I will come to you soon after midnight, not before. I must go now.'[31]

Vera's terrorist mission, like Dagmar Olloffson's commitment to women's rights, expresses her imperious will. That imperiousness provides a context in which the writer can imagine the seduction of one woman by another.

Meade remained extraordinarily prolific. By the Edwardian period, she was averaging about ten books a year. Although the bulk of her output is dull stuff, her taste for the lurid did allow her to develop extensive fantasies about powerful women. Lady Darnley, for example, in *A Maid of Mystery* (1904), a standard crime story, has compelling reddish-brown eyes that are 'not nice', and holds the heroine's hand in 'a sort of caressing manner which I could not escape from without marked rudeness.'[32] The caress, as urgent in its way as Imogen Pryce's, creates a degree of excitement for which burglary may provide the occasion, but surely not the cause. There is no possible connection between Meade's novels and the 'new sexual language' elaborated at more or less the same time by Edward Carpenter. But they, too, I would suggest, made lesbianism visible.

Another Story: Christopher St John and Her Circle

The suffragette, journalist, and author Christabel Marshall became, on the title pages of her books as well as in the memoirs of her friends, Christopher St John. In 1899, when she was in her mid-twenties, she met and fell in love with Ellen Terry's daughter, Edy Craig. St John and Craig lived together, at first in London, then in Small Hyth, in Kent, until the latter's death in 1947. During the First World War, they were joined in Small Hyth by Clare Atwood, a painter. Bernard Shaw encouraged St John to write a history of that 'unique' *ménage-à-trois*. She never did. But Vita Sackville-West's 'Triptych' is an informative beginning.[33]

The lesbian trio dissimulates lesbianism. It pre-empts any suspicion of 'marriage', of coupling. To that extent, it may seem, and may well have been, a defensive measure, possibly a self-denial. But it also creates possibilities, ways of thinking and acting, which were to be foreclosed by the lesbian couples of the 1920s. The presence of a third ensures that passionate love between women cannot settle into an imitation of heterosexual marriage, a fixed distribution of masculinity and

---

31 Meade, *The Siren* (London: F. V. White, 1898), pp. 129, 112, 105, 137, 144–45.
32 Meade, *A Maid of Mystery* (London: F. V. White, 1904), p. 162.
33 Vita Sackville-West's 'Triptych' was published in Eleanor Adlard, ed., *Edy: Recollections of Edith Craig* (London: Muller, 1949), pp. 118–25, together with further recollections by St John, Cicely Hamilton, Sheila Kaye-Smith, and others. See also Julie Holledge, *Innocent Flowers: Women in the Edwardian Theatre* (London: Virago, 1981), ch. 8.

femininity. According to Sackville-West, these three 'strong personalities' had managed to live at 'close quarters' for many years without overshadowing each other.[34] St John and Atwood played full parts, as writer and designer, in the plays and pageants directed by Craig, who may or may not have been the model for Miss La Trobe, in Virginia Woolf's *Between the Acts* (1941). Whatever the basis of this enduring triangular arrangement, it was certainly regarded at the time as distinctly, and richly, unorthodox.

St John was a writer, and avowed her lesbianism in her writing. The semi-autobiographical *Hungerheart* was published in the same year (1915) and by the same publisher (Methuen) as D. H. Lawrence's *The Rainbow*. While *The Rainbow* was banned, largely on account of its depiction of a lesbian affair, *Hungerheart*, although far more radical in its sexual politics, attracted little attention. It is a first-person narrative, set in the final decades of the nineteenth century, and describes the emotional and spiritual development of a young woman (a Newer Woman, in my classification), Joanna Montolivet. Joanna, also known as John and John-Baptist, notices that while men have both a male life and a life as a human being, women find themselves excluded from 'common humanity' as 'merely females'. Rejection of the 'merely female' life shaped by marriage and maternity frees her to love women.[35]

Joanna's first, overwhelming passion is for Lady Martha Ladde, who inspires 'heroic, erotic, infantine, splendid' daydreams, and on whose pillow she leaves red roses and poems. Lady Martha's appeal lies not only in her beauty, but, more interestingly, in her 'insolent, off-hand manner'. Social status has liberated her from convention. She wears whatever she likes ('a rose-coloured felt hat and rough tweed clothes of a masculine cut'), and behaves as she pleases.[36] This is, if you like, the Newer Woman's crush, the Newer Woman's genealogical passion. It mixes two images from the fictional repertoire: freelance and siren, femininity played down and femininity played up. Young Joanna finds the combination of the freelance's felt hat and tweed with the siren's imperiousness utterly irresistible.

After Lady Martha, Joanna falls for a succession of opaquely exotic or refractory women who both grant and withhold, recognize and disavow, so enabling her to desire them along the borderline of partial resemblance. 'It was *to love* I yearned more than *be loved*, and I was entirely free from sexual instincts.' To define sexual feeling as an instinct is to at once to relegate it to the impersonal (the array of sexological categories) and to reclaim for the personal (the crucially formative, the moral, the political) a range of ambiguously fantasized erotic feelings. What connects Joanna's lovers is that they are all the same as her, and yet different. Identity emerges in the circulation of sameness and difference. The ones who arouse the strongest emotions are Lady Martha and the stormily compelling Giovanna Ludini, who reaches to her 'innermost parts'. Giovanna recognizes Joanna's desire, only to ignore it. 'Perhaps she has withheld herself from me because she is contaminated with innumerable unknown loves. Yet how fair and innocent is her white forehead!

---

34   Sackville-West, 'Triptych', p. 123.
35   Christopher St John (Christabel Marshall), *Hungerheart* (London: Methuen, 1915), p. 58.
36   Ibid., pp. 61–62.

I caress it despairingly with my fingers.'[37] Giovanna has been touched, as another siren, Dagmar Olaffson, had been touched; but she, too, will not touch others. In fact, the two women touch in name only, through the echo of Giovanna in Joanna, without consummation.

The novel never resolves the tension between sameness and difference. Indeed, it finds in that irresolution a structure for lesbian eroticism. Joanna eventually becomes a Catholic. The 'insupportable rapture' stirred by a vision of the Virgin Mary displaces the supportable (if barely so) raptures stirred by heroic-erotic daydreams.[38] However, the pattern of Joanna's relationship with the nun who is her spiritual adviser reproduces that of her relationships with the other more worldly women in her life. Spiritual conversion seems less like the climax towards which the narrative has always been moving than one more rapture in a sequence of raptures. The structure of this *Bildungsroman* is serial, not developmental. Each new lover is introduced abruptly, with a minimum of context, and disappears as soon as the rapture dies down; the rhythm of Joanna's life is the rhythm, or a-rhythm, of serial eroticism.

Sameness and difference circulate not only within the text, but also between the text and its readers. It is surely St John speaking through Joanna when she addresses a reader who both is and is not feminine. 'Brotherly minds of mine, neglected in the study of womanhood, this was written for you!'[39] *Hungerheart* makes actual the virtual narrative of the Newer Woman novel. Homosexual desire is no longer a subordinate clause within the sentence of the wedlock plot. It is itself a sentence; or, rather, a series of clauses, a parataxis.

Hungerheart was St John's only novel. Thereafter, she turned to biography, writing lives of two prominent New Women: Christine Murrell, the first woman to be elected to the Council of the British Medical Association (1924) and to the General Medical Council of Great Britain (1933); and the composer Ethel Smyth.[40] Published after the era of the Newer Woman had ended, both books fall outside the scope of this essay. But they contain some significant emphases. In both, St John casts herself as the Newer Woman who both resembles and differs from the New Woman. She remembers Murrell as the kind of mixed metaphor that Joan Ogden, in *The Unlit Lamp*, sees in Beatrice Lesway: 'a woman of massive frame, a virile woman, whose irreproachably feminine clothes seemed incongruous.'[41] Similarly, the imperious Smyth 'usually wore a rough tweed coat and skirt, a cap of the same material, or a "boater".'[42] Like Lady Martha Ladde, these are women who both understate and overstate femininity.

37   Ibid., pp. 88, 248–49.
38   Ibid., pp. 283–84. On lesbian converts to Catholicism, see Joanna Glasgow, 'What's a Nice Lesbian like You Doing in the Church of Torquemada: Radclyffe Hall and Other Catholic Converts', in *Lesbian Texts and Contexts: Radical Revisions*, ed. by Joanna Glasgow and Karla Jay (London: Onlywomen, 1990), pp. 241–54.
39   St John, *Hungerheart*, p. 98.
40   St John, *Christine Murrell, M.D.: Her Life and Her Work* (London: Williams and Norgate, 1935); St John, *Ethel Smyth: A Biography* (London: Longmans, 1959).
41   St John, *Christine Murrell*, p. xvii
42   St John, *Ethel Smyth*, p. 42.

Neither had much time for dyadic thinking and living. Murrell lived for thirty years, in a succession of London flats and a house in Surrey, with Honor Bone. Both were graduates of the London School of Medicine for Women, and they established a joint practice in Bayswater in 1903. Their 'professional partnership' could be said to have set the pattern for their personal partnership. Murrell, however, proved too energetic for the semi-invalid Bone, and in 1925 Marie Lawson came to live with them in their Surrey home: this time, the friendships were based on 'chemical' rather than professional affinity.[43] Again, the decision to form a *ménage-à-trois* is suggestive, although there is even less biographical evidence here than in the case of St John, Craig, and Atwood. Smyth, by contrast, claimed in her memoirs that she had given up heterosexuality for work. The space cleared in her life by that renunciation filled with passionate '*engouements*', with a serial eroticism comparable to Joanna Montlivet's. Smyth's *engouements*, like Joanna's, often involved women of higher social standing. Her 'almost insane' passion for the Princesse Edmond de Polignac, for example, turned on her beloved's aristocratic insouciance. 'Grave, natural, don't-care-ish, the soul of independence — in short, all the things I like.'[44]

St John's biographies of Christine Murrell and Ethel Smyth constitute a genealogical testament: the Newer Woman's last word on the New Woman. They demonstrate that, for one early twentieth-century feminist, at least, genealogy had become not only a habit, but an article of faith. St John moved towards, and into, homosexual identity by living and writing along the borderline of partial resemblance.

---

43   St John, *Christine Murrell*, pp. 35, 102.
44   Quoted by St John, *Ethel Smyth*, pp. 123–24.

CHAPTER 9

Feminist Nausea

The aim of this essay is very loosely to associate different kinds of writing undertaken by middle-class women for the purpose of advancing the social, political, and cultural emancipation of themselves and of others both like and unlike them. The essay builds in part on previous research into the framing of identity through the self-conscious performance of gender in fiction and memoirs published from the 1890s to the 1920s.[1] Its subject is the variety of uses to which women writers were able to put an ontological feeling of nausea: a feeling about existence as such. The feminists of the era found themselves challenged in their being as well as in their consciousness. In order to establish that these uses were indeed various, I have chosen to focus on women with starkly contrasting purposes in mind. My first two sections concern published and unpublished writings by successive generations of nineteenth-century female philanthropist: philanthropy having become by the 1860s a means of emancipation for middle-class women, inside or outside marriage.[2] I turn then to 'Naturalist' or 'cynical' tendencies in the New Woman novels of the 1890s, and their successors, the 'marriage problem' novels of the 1900s and after.[3] It should be possible, I believe, to reconstruct the genealogy of the sophisticated *nauséaste* (or specialist in nausea) who features as the narrator of some of Katherine Mansfield's early stories. For one thing both sets of writers had in common was a lively interest in, and respect for, a feeling customarily regarded as without meaning or value.

Some Brothels

In October 1863, a Mission Hall and Soldiers' Institute opened for business in Aldershot, in Hampshire. Aldershot was and is a military town, and in the 1860s it

---

1   'Lesbians before Lesbianism: Sexual Identity in Early Twentieth-Century British Fiction', in *Borderlines: Genders and Identities in War and Peace, 1870–1930*, ed. by Billie Melman (London: Routledge, 1998), pp. 193–211. Reprinted as Chapter 8 in this book.

2   Frank Prochaska, *Women and Philanthropy in Nineteenth-Century England* (Oxford: Clarendon Press, 1980); *The Voluntary Impulse: Philanthropy in Modern Britain* (London: Faber and Faber, 1988); 'Philanthropy', in *The Cambridge Social History of Britain*, 3 vols, ed. by F. M. L. Thompson (Cambridge: Cambridge University Press, 1990), III, 357–93.

3   All scholars of the period owe a debt to the path-breaking work of Martha Vicinus. See, in particular, *Independent Women: Work and Community for Single Women, 1850–1920* (Chicago, IL: University of Chicago Press, 1985). On the New Woman novel, see Sally Ledger, *The New Woman: Fiction and Feminism at the Fin de Siècle* (Manchester: Manchester University Press, 1997).

boasted a plentiful supply of souls in need of saving. Some of those souls belonged to the prostitutes who had long been the inevitable concomitant of a standing army. In 1864, the men who ran the Institute's Refuge Committee organized a series of midnight meetings during which strenuous efforts were made to convince these 'outcast women' of the error of their ways. Sarah Robinson, who worked at the Institute, saw at once that such meetings were next to useless. The motives which prompted outcast women to attend them did not, for the most part, include an overwhelming urge to be cast back in again. Robinson wanted to try a different approach. 'I shut myself up for some hours to pray and think it over,' she recalled in her autobiography, *A Life Record* (1898), 'until my own course, at least, seemed clear, *to go into the girls' own rooms*.'[4] She meant to be public in private, to reform discreetly.

We know how and to what effect Robinson went into the girls' own rooms both from her own account, and from the account given by Ellice Hopkins, whom she met in 1868 in Portsmouth, where they established a Soldiers' Home, and who subsequently became known in her own right as a resourceful and indefatigable rescue worker.[5] Robinson's account centres, as so much of the nineteenth-century social reform and slum-visiting literature did, on a rite of initiation: on the revelatory, life-changing moment of encounter between philanthropy's subject and its object. What feelings were at play, on the philanthropist's part, in that encounter?

'Most of the girls were in their beds,' Robinson observed of her first foray into an Aldershot brothel, 'and on the whole received me kindly; but, after a long morning's visiting, I had to hurry back to my room, and for over an hour was violently sick.' As so often in the social reform literature, nausea, at once a gut-feeling and a thesis about the irreparability of the human predicament, configures the philanthropic encounter. The rhetorical function it serves is to establish the philanthropist's singularity as a social being or social performer. The nausea she feels sets her apart both from the lower-class men and women whose behaviour has induced it, and from the upper-class men and women who have never known anything like it. 'I could not write the things I saw and heard,' Robinson said, 'and prayed to *forget* them' (*LR* 137–38). The need to forget sights and sounds which cannot be forgotten at once impedes philanthropy and in some sense keeps it going.

Nausea, so absolute a rejection of the world as it is, and yet so singular, enabled Robinson to avoid the feelings a pious young woman could reasonably be expected to feel on entering an army brothel: curiosity, fear, helplessness. For example, her account of the philanthropic encounter rather interestingly elides its physical circumstance.

> The biggest public-houses owned whole blocks of buildings, each room accommodating two girls, some living luxuriously, others miserably poor, from fourteen years of age up to thirty; some fearfully diseased, unable to leave their beds, supported by the kindness of others. (*LR* 138)

4   Sarah Robinson, *A Life Record* (London: James Nisbet, 1898), p. 137. Emphasis in original. Henceforth *LR*.
5   And this despite her partial disablement. She suffered from curvature of the spine, and spent most of her adult life buckled into a surgical 'support': Jennie Chappell, *Noble Work by Noble Women* (London: S. W. Partridge, 1900), p. 70.

Robinson passes immediately from the building to its inhabitants. She sets aside the figure of the prostitute, discovering in its place individual women with ambitions and dilemmas of their own. Singularized herself by nausea, she is on the look-out for singularity in others. Fearlessness followed by vomiting (followed by a resumption of fearlessness) connects public to private self in ways that were not otherwise readily conceivable for middle-class women in mid-nineteenth-century Britain. The vomit tells her that it is she, and not someone else, who has gone into the girls' own rooms.

The feeling is always already social in that it derives from changes in the understanding of public and private space. According to Ellice Hopkins, Robinson began her work in Aldershot at a time when the prostitutes 'herded together in colonies, as many as a hundred inhabiting a row of small tenements, all communicating with one another internally, by means of passages, and named after the public-house which generally formed the corner house; a state of things which I am thankful to say no longer exists.'[6] Hopkins apprehends, or imagines, something elided in Robinson's account: the den, the row of tenements communicating with one another internally by a passage. This passage evidently fascinated her. In *Active Service; or, Work Among Our Soldiers*, a book written in order to raise money for the Soldiers' Home at Portsmouth, Hopkins further reported that when Robinson began her work in Aldershot the prostitutes 'used to congregate in colonies of 70 to 100 together, occupying whole courts or large blocks of buildings named after the public-house that owned them, and threaded on the inside by long intricate passages connecting the whole.'[7] In Hopkins's eyes, it is the passage threading the tenements together on the inside which makes the space of the brothel utterly distinctive: a space like no other, a labyrinth, a den. We might almost be in Kafka's burrow.[8] There is a literary imagination at work here: an imagination intent on a 'poetics of space'.[9] This imagination does not engage in reverie.[10] Rather, it bears directly on historical circumstance. The space Hopkins has delineated is also a time: a 'state of things' which thankfully no longer exists. Her imagination works with, and in, history. We need to conceive it historically.

Martin Daunton has described how the steep rise in the price of urban land between the 1780s and the 1810s led to a more economical use of the space available. The existing built-up area — notably the courtyards at the rear of houses on the main streets — was exploited ever more intensively through in-filling and sub-division. Developments on the edge of towns and cities reproduced the pattern prevailing in the central districts. 'The result,' Daunton concludes, 'was a promiscuous sharing of

6   Ellice Hopkins, *The Visitation of Dens: An Appeal to the Women of England* (London: Hatchards, 1874), p. 8. Henceforth *VD*.

7   Ellice Hopkins, *Active Service; or, Work Among Our Soldiers*, rev. edn (London: Hatchards, 1874), p. 11.

8   Franz Kafka, 'The Burrow', in *The Great Wall of China and Other Works*, ed. and trans. by Malcolm Pasley (Harmondsworth: Penguin, 1991), pp. 185–218.

9   Hopkins was the accomplished if derivative author of a novel — *Rose Turquand*, 2 vols (London: Macmillan, 1876)—and a volume of poems: *Autumn Swallows: A Book of Lyrics* (London: Macmillan, 1883).

10   Gaston Bachelard, *The Poetics of Space*, trans. by Maria Jolas (Boston, MA: Beacon Press, 1994).

facilities in the private domain of the house, a cellular quality of space in the public domain, and a threshold between public and private which was ambiguous and permeable.'[11] Friedrich Engels, writing about Manchester in 1844, found it virtually impossible to convey to his readers the idea of the 'tangle' of dwellings created by this kind of layout.[12] Such was the space, Ellice Hopkins imagined Sarah Robinson entering in Aldershot in 1863.

During the course of the nineteenth century, Daunton observes, the 'cellular' layout of these courts, which made it difficult to distinguish between public and private space, gave way to a 'more open texture'. Individual dwellings were sealed off into privacy, while the public domain became a neutral space, or 'connective tissue' made sterile and anonymous. The threshold between public and private had been redrawn in such a way as to render it less permeable. The change arose in part at least from a concern for public order, since cellularity was a threat at once to hygiene and to respectability. It opened up the city, Daunton observes, 'in order to make it visible for inspection.'[13] In Richard Sennett's terms, the aim was to 'purify' or to 'suburbanise' space, both in new inner-city developments and in the suburbs themselves, and so define it as entirely functional.[14] Baron Haussmann was shortly to realize that aim to spectacular effect in his restructuring of Paris. In Aldershot, in 1863, Sarah Robinson could be thought to have entered not just a space, but a time. The disambiguation enforced by the recent opening up of the city had made the brothel — this domain held between the public and the private, between commerce and domesticity — doubly fascinating. It was there, or in rather in going to and fro between different spaces and different times, between the good new open city and the bad old closed city, that one might become independent. Such are the uses to which disorder — and, I would add, nausea — can be put.

Robinson's success in the brothels of Aldershot persuaded Hopkins to try the same tactics in the brothels of Portsmouth; and she, too, had her rite of initiation, her nauseating rebuff. On her first visit, everything seemed to be going well. She engaged a group of women in earnest discussion, eventually persuading them to kneel and pray with her. Leaving them, she felt that she had at least made an impression. 'The door had not been closed two seconds behind me, as I left, when I heard shrieks of horrid laughter from all four, and fragments of indecent jests, which I in vain strove not to hear.' She went home 'literally bruised and bleeding'. It is worth noting that bricks and mortar played a large part in her conception of the brutal rebuff she had been dealt. She felt, she wrote, as though she had just dashed herself against a 'dead wall'. 'My prayer seemed to have gone no higher than the ceiling' (*VD* 11).

What these metaphors indicate is a considerable investment on Hopkins's part in the poetics of space: an investment which, given its scope and durability, we

11   Martin Daunton, 'Housing', in *Cambridge Social History of Britain*, II, 195–250 (p. 202).
12   Friedrich Engels, *The Condition of the Working Class in England*, ed. by E. J. Hobsbawm (St Albans: Granada, 1969), p. 81.
13   Daunton, 'Housing', pp. 203–04.
14   Richard Sennett, *The Uses of Disorder: Personal Identity and City Life* (New Haven, CT: Yale University Press, 2008), p. 83.

might even suspect of yielding pleasure. It is the act of entering the labyrinth which compels her. This is a visitation manual, a how-to book. 'Having fixed upon the house to be visited, do not knock at the front door any more than you would in visiting a public-house, but go boldly in and knock at the door of one of the upstair rooms' (*VD* 18–19). What is engrossing about the brothel is that it is a domain in which the distinction between public and private has not yet been stabilized, set firmly in place. Do not knock at the front door, Hopkins advises, but boldly go in. The boldness, as of a person entering a public house, was the performance which subdued nausea by acknowledging it.

The going to and fro really made itself felt when the difference in outlook to be negotiated was social as well as moral. A fascinating footnote in *The Visitation of Dens* indicates that the rescue workers did not yet quite know what to do when it came to the 'upper class' of brothel: the kind, that is, which boasted a lockable front door and a servant to open and close it. In such establishments the boundary between public and private had been set at the entrance to the building, and rendered relatively impermeable by protocol. Here one could not go boldly in. The solution Hopkins proposes is an even more deliberate and structured resort to class identity. 'I should suggest all the formalities of a regular call being observed; to dress in one's very best, and to send up one's card, having, if possible, obtained the name, but if not, asking for the lady of the house, and stating that one calls on business' (*VD* 19–20). For the philanthropist, there might well have been a gain, here, in the resumption of formalities. Hopkins and her fellow workers would no doubt have preferred to dress in their very best. But the gain would also be a loss, I suspect: a loss of the occasion to go boldly in.

My argument has been that the philanthropic encounter in which rescue work began was represented by those who undertook it as provoking diverse emotions, and that if we want to understand the motives of such as Sarah Robinson and Ellice Hopkins we must find a way to discriminate among them, and to set them in relation. In addressing this issue, I have sought to avoid the model of affect which has dominated recent thinking about attitudes to the slum. That model is a Freudian model, and it assumes that the loathing so vividly expressed at times by social reformers for the physical and moral state of the slum is proof of fascination. The model collapses one expression of feeling into another in accordance with a more or less unvarying formula which will not permit analysis either of desire or of disgust in its own right.[15]

If pleasure concerns us, the kind of pleasure to be derived from going boldly into a labyrinth or den, we might turn not to Freud, but to Georges Bataille: the 'idiosyncratic scholar, essayist, and pornographer', as one historian describes him (admiringly, I think).[16] Bataille has to his credit a life-long obsession with waste-matter, with entropy. So crucial to his thinking was this obsession that he wrote an entry on 'formless' (the *informe*) for the *Critical Dictionary* he published in

15   See David Trotter, 'The New Historicism and the Psychopathology of Everyday Modern Life', *Critical Quarterly*, 42 (2000), 36–58. Reprinted as Chapter 1 in this book.
16   James Clifford, *The Predicament of Culture: Twentieth-Century Ethnography, Literature, and Art* (Cambridge, MA: Harvard University Press, 1988), p. 125.

Documents, the ethnographic and surrealist journal which began to appear in 1929. The formless, in Bataille's usage, is not just a term for that which has lost its form. It is rather an operation, at once social and aesthetic, to produce lack of form. It is an act of declassification and declassing which brings things down in the world by ruthlessly exposing their materiality. 'To affirm [...] that the universe resembles nothing at all and is only *formless*, amounts to saying that the universe is something akin to a spider or a gob of spittle.'[17] The formless is hugely productive.[18] According to Freud, disgust is a symptom, the expression of an otherwise voiceless desire; according to Bataille, it is an exercise, not necessarily pleasurable in itself, whose declassifying and declassing effects create a kind of pleasure.

I do not, of course, want to reduce Ellice Hopkins's prostitutes to a gob of spittle. But I do think that the declassing involved in not dressing in one's very best and going boldly into a brothel as though it were a public house was also a declassifying, an erasure of the lines drawn in social space. The formless is not the prostitute, but the den or labyrinth she inhabits, where she must be sought. Rescue work had to be performed among the lowest of the low, and Hopkins knew that it required a self-lowering. 'If you are content to go to this work in the ordinary prayerful frame of mind in which go into our districts,' she wrote, 'you will be simply paralysed by the evil around you. This work has emphatically to be done on the knees' (*VD* 17–18).

The conditions in which the prostitutes lived in when Robinson and Hopkins began visiting them clearly provoked a revulsion that was as much spiritual as physical. Those conditions could not but be understood as the emblem of humankind's fallen state. But the revulsion also constituted, through the violence of the declassing and declassifying it had inflicted, a kind of ontological grounding. Enduring formlessness, socially and physically on their knees, Robinson and Hopkins at the same time imagined a different way of life for themselves.

The Rhetoric of Ontological Feeling

Towards the end of the century, as sociological enquiry meshed with rescue work in pursuit of a secular vision of reform, it became possible to articulate more fully the terms of an engagement with formlessness. I want now to suggest that we can grasp those terms in a certain hesitation, in the records kept by members of the next generation of female philanthropists, between metaphor and metonymy.

Beatrice Potter (later Webb) joined the Soho Committee of the Charity Organization Society (COS) in April 1883. In December 1884, she agreed to co-manage Katherine Buildings, in the Aldgate area of London, which the East End Dwellings Company had built to house casual labourers and their families, with Ella Pycroft, a country doctor's daughter. Potter had to abandon her role as a rent collector in November 1885, when her father suffered a stroke, and the following year began work as an assistant to Charles Booth, who was laying the foundations

---

17   Georges Bataille, 'Formless', in *Encyclopaedia Acephalica*, ed. by Alastair Brotchie (London: Atlas Press, 1995), pp. 51–52.
18   *Formless: A User's Guide*, ed. by Yve-Alain Bois and Rosalind E. Krauss (New York: Zone Books, 1997).

for his massive sociological study of London life and labour. Potter's conversion from social work to social enquiry, and her subsequent advocacy of state and municipal socialism, was in large measure a reaction against her experiences as a COS visitor and rent collector. She objected to the emphasis on discipline and surveillance. The COS never granted assistance without rigorous prior investigation; a visitor was sent to interview each family, and a case report drawn up. A committee made the final decision. Form 28, carried by all COS visitors, declared that help was only available to those who sought to help themselves. 'Persons of drunken, immoral or idle habits cannot expect to be assisted unless they can satisfy the committee that they are really trying to reform.'[19] The intention was to abolish indiscriminate alms-giving, and to encourage habits of independence and foresight among the 'deserving' poor. The effect, Potter complained, was to transform charity workers into 'amateur detectives'. The COS had failed to learn the lesson learnt by the sanitary reformer Edwin Chadwick when, in the 1840s, he abandoned his long-running campaign to distinguish the respectable from the unrespectable poor, and began instead to advocate 'positive municipal action in the provision of drainage, paving, water supply, open spaces, improved dwellings, hospitals and what not.'[20]

Potter and Pycroft kept a 'record' of the inhabitants of Katherine Buildings, in which they logged basic information (employment, number of children, dates of arrival and departure, etc.) and explanatory remarks (the reasons for terminating a lease).[21] The record shows Form 28, as it were, in action; but not unequivocally. For the nauseous feeling which sharpens social and moral discrimination at the same time casts doubt on its legitimacy, its basis in fact. A phrase which crops up again and again is 'clean and apparently respectable'. Sometimes the bad sorts were easy to spot. Abraham Morris, a Jewish tailor with a disabled and 'disgustingly dirty' wife, did not last long. 'Room in filthy condition & children uncared for & half starved. Constantly in arrears. Neighbours complained of number of animals kept & smells. Gave them notice to quit — forced them to leave by threat of distraint' (KB 25). In this case, the dirt and the stench add up to something more than a failure to pay the rent, something not far short of an index to depravity. These are metonymies poised on the edge of metaphor. Mrs Morris's noxious dirt, for example, eclipses the disablement which may well have contributed to it. Yet the emphasis remains largely on physical circumstance, and on what it is reasonable to expect people to make of it.

Keeping animals was always likely to get you into trouble, in Katherine Buildings. One woman, whose husband was a clerk in the Tower of London, brought some

19   Carole Seymour-Jones, *Beatrice Webb: Woman of Conflict* (London: Allison and Busby, 1992), p. 79.
20   Beatrice Webb, *My Apprenticeship* (London: Longmans, Green, 1926), pp. 200–05.
21   *Katherine Buildings: Record of the Inhabitants during the Years 1885–1890*, British Library of Political & Economic Science, Miscellaneous Collection 43. Henceforth *KB*. Potter kept the record until November 1885, when she gave up rent-collecting in order to look after her father, and Pycroft took over. Scholars have made surprisingly little use of it. See Rosemary O'Day, 'Before the Webbs: Beatrice Potter's Early Investigations for Charles Booth's Inquiry', *History*, 78 (1993), 232–33; and Lewis, *Love and Toil*, p. 72.

bantams back from a visit to Ireland. She promised to send the bantams to the Tower, but instead sent them to the back room, where they disgustingly occupied a washstand. Her mistake, perhaps, was to create an opportunity for metaphor: animals on the floor bespeak necessity, animals on a washstand innate brutishness. 'Rough, coarse woman, very well to do — Didn't like to be honest' (*KB* 115). So *they* had to go, even if they did pay the rent on time. Other fatal indications of lack of social and moral worth apparently included too much scar-tissue. The Bardons, a young couple, 'clean but doubtfully respectable', wanted to move the wife's mother into the Buildings. 'Her landlord advised me not, & her appearance would have been enough. She accounted for the numerous scars on her face by saying that she had always lived in dark places, & so knocked herself about!' The Bardons promptly left, to be near the mother in her dark place (148).

In other cases, the criterion of moral depravity proved too clear-cut a criterion to resist. Robert Grimstone, a pork butcher in steady employment, came to the Buildings with his mulatto wife. Both were respectable, industrious, and sober, even if they did leave their room in an untidy state. But Potter and Pycroft still considered evicting them on the grounds that Grimstone's mother had once kept a 'gay-house', or brothel. 'Asked them to pledge themselves not to see her. Husband refused — "His mother had been a good mother to him, he wasn't going to shut the door in her face."' Family loyalty, and a class-specific notion of good mothering, mattered more to people like Grimstone than 'respectable' behaviour. Since the brothel-keeper, loyal in her turn, stayed away from Katherine Buildings, the Grimstones were not thrown out (*KB* 39). They had had a narrow escape. Susan Farmer, a 'clean, strong, hardworking' widow with a son and five daughters, was less fortunate. 'Found the whole family were "gay".' The son and two of the daughters had illegitimate children. Another daughter was a prostitute. When Susan Farmer's husband was dying, he made her promise not to marry again. Being a woman of her word, she did not marry the man she subsequently lived with. Since he never gave her enough money, she refused to speak to him again. 'Told me this with pride — Impossible to make her see the wrong of it' (239). Like Robert Grimstone, Susan Farmer lived, with a consistency one cannot help admiring, by the light of a moral code. It just wasn't a middle-class code. For the most part Potter remained faithful to metonymy, to judgements based on physical circumstance, and what had been made of it. Sometimes, however, the lure of moral abstraction proved too hard to resist. In November 1886, she went back to Wentworth Buildings, the other East End block she had managed with Ella Pycroft, during Pycroft's absence on holiday. She described in her diary the loathing she felt at the incessant physical mingling, the social and sexual promiscuity, of slum-life. 'Even their careless, sensual laugh, the coarse jokes and unloving words depress one as one presses through the crowd, and almost shudders to touch them.' Potter found the proximity of meeting-places to lavatories in Wentworth Buildings particularly offensive.[22] Metonymic contiguity — the lavatory next to the meeting-place — has been parlayed into a

22   Webb, *Diary*, ed. by Norman and Jeanne Mackenzie, 2 vols (London: Virago, 1986), I, 185–86. For a comparable response, see Edith Hogg, 'On the Fur-Pullers of South London', *Nineteenth Century*, 42 (1897), 734–43.

damning metaphoric substitution: sociability is excremental. No doubt it involved an ample provision of gobs of spittle.

For an alternative view of life in Katherine Buildings, one more consistently attuned to the value of metonymy, we can turn to an example of the new kind of fiction which was making its mark in the late 1880s. The *Record* indicates that a 'literary woman' had rented a room in the summer of 1886 'for purposes of observation' (*KB* 99). This was Potter's cousin Margaret Harkness, whom she had known since childhood, and in whom she confided during her time at Katherine Buildings.[23] Harkness's own record of the inhabitants of Katherine Buildings sets the scene of her first novel, *A City Girl*, published in 1887 under the pseudonym of 'John Law', which ostentatiously adopts their point of view. 'Several times in the week ladies arrived on the Buildings armed with master-keys, ink-pots, and rent-books. A tap at a door was followed by the intrusion into a room of a neatly-clad female of masculine appearance.' The rent-collector comes fully equipped both with bourgeois moral standards and with the micro-technology of discipline and surveillance. Her intrusiveness is subtly underlined by her appearance, itself a symbolic transgression of the line which separates 'masculine' from 'feminine' behaviour. Harkness did acknowledge that one or two of the more 'superior' tenants had taken some at least of those standards to heart, and consequently kept themselves very much to themselves. But she understood that the Buildings were popular precisely because they permitted the full flowering of social intercourse. 'The children played about the court, the mothers gossiped in the doorways, the men smoked and talked politics on the balconies.'[24] Social promiscuity, sickening to Potter, did not trouble Harkness at all.

Naturalism

In March 1887, Potter shared a railway carriage with Sir George Trevelyan. 'I begged him to go into a smoking carriage [...] for had I not in the pocket of my sealskin not only a volume of Zola, but my case of cigarettes! neither of which I could enjoy in his distinguished presence.' The novel was *Au bonheur des dames* (1883), in which Zola 'did' department stores. Sir George eventually settled down with *The Princess Casamassima* (1886), Henry James's most ambitious attempt at an unpoetic subject. Potter continued to read Zola with enthusiasm. She even felt on occasion the 'vulgar wish to write a novel'. But sociology seemed to her the more 'worthful' exercise of powers, and she devoted the rest of her life to developing the necessary expertise.[25] Zola was a writer as deeply committed to the accumulation of metonymic detail as he was to all-encompassing metaphor. Something like a phobic picturesque established itself in Naturalist fiction by means of the elaborate descriptive passages which were from the outset understood to constitute one of its most easily identifiable features.[26]

23   Webb, *Diary*, I, 139.
24   John Law (Margaret Harkness), *A City Girl* (New York: Garland, 1984), pp. 9, 13, 11.
25   Webb, *Diary*, I, 198, 298.
26   David Trotter, 'Naturalism's Phobic Picturesque', in *The Uses of Phobia: Essays on Literature and Film* (Oxford: Wiley-Blackwell, 2010), pp. 40–58.

The perceived indecency of Zola's fiction meant that fulsome endorsements were hard to come by. Yet the New Woman writers who began to make themselves felt during the 1880s found that they could not ignore it altogether. Most nineteenth-century British novels implicitly or explicitly divide the human lifespan into a long rise stretching to the age of 60 or so, and a short (physical) decline. Naturalist fiction envisaged instead a rapid physical rise to the moment of reproduction in the twenties, then a redundancy accelerated by the gradual emergence of some innate physical or moral flaw. Its standard degeneration plot seemed to many British women writers to fit the case of modern British middle-class manhood only too well. 'Doctors-spiritual must face the horrors of the dissecting-room,' declared Sarah Grand (Frances McFall), one of the leading New Woman novelists, in the preface to *Ideala: A Study of Life* (1888).[27] In the bestselling *The Heavenly Twins* (1893), the heroine's husband discovers to his dismay that her sitting room is lined with books on subjects such as anatomy and pathology. 'He could not have been more horrified had the books been *Mademoiselle de Maupin*, *Nana*, *La Terre*, *Madame Bovary*, and *Sappho*; yet, had women been taught to read the former and reflect upon them, our sacred humanity might have been saved sooner from the depth of degradation depicted in the latter.'[28] Grand's major preoccupation was with a woman's need for economic, sexual, and spiritual independence within, and conceivably beyond, marriage. In her view, the French realists were the only writers to take full measure of the degradation middle-class marriage had become for a wife dependent in every way on a corrupt and tyrannical husband. For her, as for Zola, individual degeneracy both produced and was produced by the decline and fall of nations. In *The Beth Book* (1897), she proposed political contexts for the intense physical and moral loathing the heroine comes to feel for her husband in the feminist campaigns against vivisection, and for reform of the Contagious Diseases Acts and of the divorce laws.[29]

To be more precise, Beth's loathing for her husband, Dan, a doctor, begins as physical and ends as moral, or even political. He issues detailed bulletins concerning the ailments of his female patients. 'Of two words Dan always chose the coarsest in talking to Beth, now that they were married, which had made her writhe at first.' Equally loathsome is his habit of sitting up until all hours with his cronies, smoking and drinking, and debating 'lewd topics'. As their lives interpenetrate, so Beth's disgust deepens. She objects to his smoking in her bedroom, indeed to his presence in her bedroom. She suffers from 'the smell of alcohol and tobacco, of which he reeked, and from which he took no trouble to purify himself.' When she catches him opening her letters, she endures 'one of those attacks of nausea and shivering which came upon her in moments of deep disgust'. In comparison with these defilements, the social and sexual indignities to which he subjects her —

---

27   Sarah Grand, *Ideala: A Study of Life*, 3rd edn (London: Richard Bentley, 1889), p. viii.

28   Sarah Grand, *The Heavenly Twins* [1893] (Ann Arbor: University of Michigan Press, 1992), p. 104.

29   I describe these contexts, and what Grand made of them in the novel, in *Cooking with Mud: The Idea of Mess in Nineteenth-Century Art and Fiction* (Oxford: Oxford University Press, 2000), pp. 267–86.

withholding an allowance, an affair with a patient — seem mere pinpricks.[30] To be sure, there is *some* moral complaint in the mixture, about 'lewd topics', and so on. But the nausea which turns Beth decisively against Dan is physical. It is the disgust provoked by Dan's reek which once again surges through her when she discovers a dog strapped to the table in his surgery. The feeling, forcefully articulated in the 1890s by a militant political campaign against vivisection, now has public as well as private force. Beth leaves home. Ontological feeling has decided her fate: her feminism.

Cynics

Rather oddly, in view of Dan's behaviour, Beth never sues for divorce. She simply leaves both Dan and nausea behind to live on her own in London. By the 1890s, however, conduct likely to cause acute mental suffering, such as to injure health and endanger reason, had long since amounted to cruelty in the estimation of the law.[31] Beth could well have petitioned successfully for legal separation. Many abused wives did.

'The case is an exceedingly filthy one,' *The Times* observed about *Craigie* v. *Craigie* (1895), 'and most of its details are utterly unfit for publication in a newspaper.'[32] Reginald Walpole Craigie, a clerk at the Bank of England, had married Pearl Richards on 16 July 1887. He was 29, she 19; they had one son, born on 16 August 1890. Early in 1891, she left him, and returned to her father's house. The petition she filed on 12 April 1894 listed sixteen charges against him, including habitual adultery, physical violence, and consistent unkindness. He had, among other things, sworn at her, hit her, thrown her books into the fire, and infected her with venereal disease. The most explosive charge was that contained in paragraph 18 of the petition. 'That on numerous occasions when the said Reginald Walpole Craigie has been in bed with me he has insisted, notwithstanding my strong and repeated objections, on my taking part in filthy and disgusting practices which were most offensive to me and rendered me ill.' On 15 June 1894, the petitioner was asked to furnish further and better particulars of the nature of these practices. On 4 July 1894, Reginald Craigie responded by claiming that his wife had condoned any acts of adultery and cruelty he might have committed. He also claimed that 'on several occasions the Petitioner, while refusing to render the Respondent marital intercourse as hereinafter mentioned, herself suggested and offered to take part in the practices in the said paragraph 18 of the said petition referred to.' [33] Pearl Craigie, accompanied by her father and a nurse, gave evidence at the trial. She was awarded a decree nisi, with costs.

After she left her husband in 1891, Craigie began to develop a career as a writer, adopting the pseudonym 'John Oliver Hobbes'. In the early 1890s, she published a

30   Sarah Grand, *The Beth Book* (London: Virago, 1980), pp. 355, 380–81, 344, 381–82.
31   Trotter, *Cooking with Mud*, pp. 278–86.
32   'Probate, Divorce, and Admiralty Division', *The Times*, 4 July 1895, p. 12.
33   *Craigie* v. *Craigie* (1895): PRO divorce files, J77/534/16319.

series of novellas which understandably take as their subject courtship and marriage, or more often mis-marriage. These novellas reflect upon the anxieties endured by many women at the time, and they do so in ways which vary significantly the formula of the New Woman novel. The difference lies in their tone: a cynicism which feeds off, and displaces, expressions of physical loathing.[34] The first of these tales, *Some Emotions and a Moral* (1891), announces in its opening sentence the moral around which emotions are to circulate: '"Ideals, my dear Golightly, are the root of every evil. When a man forgets his ideals he may hope for happiness, but not till then."'[35] Golightly, an idealist to the end, commits suicide rather than seduce his best friend's wife. But it is the women, in Craigie's tales, not the men, who go lightly, or go Wilde: who learn through bitter experience that ideals are at the root of every evil. Craigie could not stop imagining female cynics. There must be as much heartless flirtation in her books as in those of any other writer in an age dedicated to heartless flirtation. For her, marriage was cynicism's laboratory. She was by no means alone in that belief among women writers of the period.

Prominent in the turn-of-the-century school of cynicism were Violet Hunt and Ada Leverson. The heroine of Hunt's *A Hard Woman* (1895) is a professional flirt, hardened by pride and some impressively metallic dresses. One of her flirtations goes disastrously wrong, leaving her penitent and heavily in debt. Her husband forgives her, but he has himself fallen in love with another woman, a 'type-writer girl' and aspiring actress who lives in a slum occupied by 'professional independent women', 'free lances'.[36] The result is a stand-off between two types of modern woman, and unhappiness all round. Hunt championed the second type in *The Workaday Woman* (1906), and the first in *Sooner or Later: The Story of an Ingenious Ingenue* (1904), which vents the bitterness she felt after two unsatisfactory relationships with older men. Ada Leverson married young, and unhappily; when her husband emigrated to Canada, she did not go with him. Such action as there is in her novels tends to involve muddled courtship, mis-marriage, and the petering out of minor flirtations. The tone of *Love's Shadow* (1908), the first in a trilogy chronicling the marriage of Edith and Bruce Ottley, is light, and sometimes marvellously waspish, but the plot turns on the bullying of women by morally and intellectually inferior men: Bruce Ottley, a humourless bore and hypochondriac, was based on Leverson's husband, Ernest. Born in the 1860s, united by the experience of sexual and emotional intimidation, Craigie, Hunt, and Leverson were feminists, but not New Women.

When one character in Craigie's *A Study in Temptations* takes a gloomy view of the world, another advises him not to get his nose in an artificial manure heap and think he is studying nature. '"If you take Zola for your gospel and the gospel for fiction, God must help you".'[37] Getting her own nose in an artificial manure heap was a temptation Craigie knew well, and one which, like Sarah Grand, she for the most part avoided. However, the sensationalism for which Craigie had little time

34   Trotter, *Cooking with Mud*, pp. 286–89.
35   John Oliver Hobbes (Pearl Craigie), *Tales* (London: T. Fisher Unwin, 1894), p. 2.
36   Violet Hunt, *A Hard Woman*, 2nd edn (London: Chapman and Hall, 1896), pp. 35, 138.
37   Hobbes, *Tales*, p. 216.

flourished unapologetically — and with it a new figure, a figure from Zola — in the work of Eliza Gollan (1856–1938), who published as 'Rita'. Rita's *A Husband of No Importance* (1894), the story of a wife who devotes herself full-time to literature, was an overt attack on the New Woman novel. She achieved popular success with *Souls* (1903), a satire, more violent in tone than Craigie's or Leverson's, on the corruption of High Society. *Saba Macdonald* (1906) draws on the bitter experiences of her unhappy first marriage, to a German composer of popular music. But it is in the authentically rancid *Queer Lady Judas* (1905) that the female *nauséaste* puts in her first appearance in English fiction. Cécile de Marsac, widow of a Parisian *roué*, arrives in London to establish herself, under the name of Madame Beaudelet, as a beautician and *masseuse*. Her first client, the spectacularly ugly Lady Judith Vanderbyl, turns out to be Lady Judas, famous *modiste*. The two women form an alliance in loathing. The disgust they feel for the physical and moral foulness their expertise helps to alleviate or obscure, and for their own part in the deception, is unrelenting. Nausea constitutes their horizon. 'This is a book OF WOMEN, FOR WOMEN, BY A WOMAN,' Rita declared in the preface. 'They may hate it for its truth, but each and all in their "looking glass" hours will acknowledge that it is true. For his own sake, and for the sake of some cherished illusions, no "mere man" should be bold enough to read it.' [38] Whether it amounts to a feminist book is another question.

In the summer of 1909, Katherine Mansfield was deposited by her mother, who had travelled from New Zealand for the purpose, in the little Bavarian spa town of Bad Worishofen. She shortly moved out of her hotel into the Villa Pension Muller, which was to provide the setting and the title of her first collection of stories, *In a German Pension* (1913). Mansfield's cousin and friend, Elizabeth von Arnim, had already made a successful literary career out of witty assaults on German arrogance, philistinism and misogyny. Von Arnim's first marriage, to a German nobleman who died in 1910, was troubled by differences of age and nationality, and by her distaste for childbearing: feelings which found expression in the dark and lucid *The Pastor's Wife* (1914). Her second, even more disastrous marriage, to Earl Russell, provided the theme of the yet darker *Vera* (1921). Von Arnim's friendship with Mansfield connects the school of cynics to female modernism.

In Von Arnim's novels, the Germans are for the most part buffoons, albeit buffoons intent on world domination. Mansfield chose the same targets. But she wasn't simply out to bash the Hun. Several of the pension stories were first published in *The New Age*; and they belong, as Lee Garver has shown, to the journal's critique of Fabian socialism's centralizing tendencies. Mansfield was certainly no Beatrice Webb. What the narrator of *In a German Pension* most objects to among her fellow guests is a perceived fondness for state regulation, and for motherhood in all its forms. Garver compares the political attitudes implicit in her own behaviour to the individualist feminism advocated by Mansfield's friend — and *New Age* contributor — Beatrice Hastings.[39] The politics of *In a German Pension* should not

---

38   'Rita' (Eliza Gollan), *Queer Lady Judas* (London: Hutchinson, 1905), p. ii.

39   Lee Garver, 'The Political Katherine Mansfield', *Modernism/Modernity*, 8 (2001), 225–43.

be over-stated. But there is plenty of attitude in the sly observations. That attitude I would describe as a cynicism produced by and in turn producing (nauseous) ontological feeling. Mansfield was against the kinds of social and moral purification programme, currently taking a statist and even eugenic turn in Britain as well as in Germany, of which Ellice Hopkins and Sarah Robinson had been the product, and which they had by their going to and fro implicitly put to the test. The descriptive detail in her stories is a way of observing that since such programmes never work in physical terms — and we have nausea to tell us that they do not — they are unlikely to work in social, political, and moral terms either. Mansfield's Germans preach cleanliness, but are themselves in the most literal sense unclean. The very first story in the collection, 'Germans at Meat', gives us soup on a waistcoat, a woman who picks her teeth with a hairpin, and a man who cleans his ears with a table napkin. Surfaces and apertures become a contaminated space where self and world mix promiscuously. The story reverts at the end to Von Arnim territory, with banter about invasion scares and England's degeneracy. But its bodily emphasis has opened up a margin for the expression of less easily classifiable anxieties. Subsequent stories explore that margin, presenting, among other *frissons*, a tie dunked in coffee, and a waiter who cleans his nails with the edge of a concert programme.[40] This is ontological thinking. And it forms the basis for an individualist feminism.

The narrator of *In a German Pension* would qualify on most counts as a *nauséaste*. Her nausea goes against the grain of what we now take to be the preoccupations and methods of the most innovative women writers of the time. Thus, the reaction provoked by Germany in the Mansfield's narrator is very different from that provoked in Dorothy Richardson's Miriam Henderson, in *Pointed Roofs* (1915). Germany proves to be less of an ordeal for Miriam, who has gone there to teach English, than might have been expected: and certainly not the land of spillage and self-evacuation depicted by Mansfield. The success of her first class signifies not so much in itself as because it removes 'an obstacle to gladness which was waiting to break forth.'[41] Gladness waiting to break forth is very much the subject of the early volumes of *Pilgrimage*, and Germany counts only insofar as it hinders or encourages the breaking forth.

At one point, Miriam has her hair washed by an intimidating German woman. Gripped by nausea, she places her head in the bowl. 'Then her amazed ears caught the sharp bump-crack of an eggshell against the rim of the basin, followed by a further brisk crackling just above her. She shuddered from head to foot as the egg descended with a cold slither upon her incredulous skull.' The sound of the egg breaking is wonderfully rendered, as if by some extraordinary disembodied act of attention. But the shudder does not last long. By the time the egg reaches it, Miriam's skull is already 'incredulous': no longer a surface upon which the world leaves its mark, but a seat of consciousness. Soon 'warmth' and 'ease' return to her 'clenched body'. She emerges from the ordeal 'glowing and hungry', identified

40   Katherine Mansfield, 'Germans at Meat', in *Collected Stories* (Harmondsworth: Penguin Books, 2001), pp. 683–87; 'The Sister of the Baroness', in *Collected Stories*, pp. 691–96 (p. 693); 'The Modern Soul', in *Collected Stories*, pp. 711–21 (p. 717).
41   Dorothy Richardson, *Pilgrimage*, 4 volumes (London: Virago, 1979), I, 56.

once again by appetite, not revulsion. Miriam's appetite for life swallows Germany whole. Sitting in a Delikatessen, surrounded by the girls from her school, she feels 'securely adrift'.[42] In Mansfield's stories, by contrast, no one is ever *securely* adrift.

These differences of emphasis perhaps lay behind the scepticism Mansfield expressed on occasion about women writers like Richardson and May Sinclair. The scepticism is evident enough, for example, in her review of Sinclair's *Mary Olivier: A Life* (1919). *Mary Olivier* is a book about desire, about getting what you want. Desire, which seeks out difference, makes Mary different. 'Restlessness. That was desire. It must be.' When all her potential lovers have proved unsatisfactory, or left her, and her mother, who claimed her from them, has died, she still does not give up on desire. Instead, she converts desire itself into a form of fulfilment. 'She had gone through life wanting things, wanting people, clinging to the thought of them, not able to keep off them and let them go.' Now she rejects other-generated 'ecstasy' in favour of self-generated 'happiness'. The advantage of this arrangement, the novel concludes, is that there 'isn't any risk' to it.[43]

Mansfield expressed astonishment at the fervour with which Mary Olivier pursues happiness, 'running into the room where Papa on his dying bed is being given an emetic, to see if it is on the counterpane, running out to see if it is in the cab that has come to take Aunt Charlotte to the Lunatic Asylum, and then forgetting all about it to stare at "Blanc-mange going round the table, quivering and shaking and squelching under the spoon".'[44] Mansfield felt, I think, that this strident 'passion for life' is in fact curiously passionless; and that Mary Olivier, because she never really sees the horror of mad Aunt Charlotte or vomiting Papa (and it took a true aficionado to spot the disgusting blanc-mange, which plays a *very* small part in the novel), never sees life at all. To Mansfield, such experiences were important in themselves, and not merely as obstacles to gladness. Mary Olivier, whose favourite authors are Shelley and Whitman, finds 'a secret and terrible enchantment' in 'the ugliest facts'.[45] By contrast, Mansfield's protagonists find only ugliness in the ugliest facts.

There is some evidence to suggest that, had she lived longer, Mansfield would have become the most formidable cynic of them all. '*Je ne parle pas français*', a story first published in 1920 by the Heron Press in an edition of one hundred copies, is the next best (or worst) thing to a manifesto for cynicism. The narrator is a twenty-six-year-old Parisian, Raoul Duquette, author of three books: *False Coins*, *Wrong Doors* and (quintessential Mansfield topic) *Left Umbrellas*. Sexually initiated at the age of ten by an African laundress, Duquette is thoroughly corrupt, an idler, a gigolo, a pimp, and bisexual to boot. The story concerns his encounter with an English friend and lover, Dick Harmon, and a woman called Mouse, whom Dick has brought to Paris, and abruptly abandons; it is she who cannot speak French. Duquette promises to return to the hotel in which Mouse has been abandoned,

42   Ibid., I, 60, 88.
43   May Sinclair, *Mary Olivier: A Life* (London: Virago, 1980), pp. 228, 378, 380.
44   Mansfield, 'The New Infancy', reprinted in *The Gender of Modernism*, ed. by Bonnie Kime Scott (Bloomington: Indiana University Press, 1990), p. 312.
45   Sinclair, *Mary Olivier*, p. 289.

but never does. Sarah Henstra has engagingly compared Duquette to Dr Matthew Dante O'Connor, the drunken, conniving, transvestite narrator of Djuna Barnes's *Nightwood* (1936). The critical consensus, Henstra notes, is that these male narrators imagined by women should be understood as 'examples of masculinity gone awry, against which the awakening feminist consciousness of the stories asserts itself'. But such readings cannot account for the 'vexed interplay' in their utterances of 'mischief, exhilaration, discomfort, and sorrow'. Better, Henstra argues, to regard those utterances as performative than as symptomatic. 'Barnes and Mansfield have created in Matthew and Raoul narrative voices that expose and challenge the social and discursive limits on the construction of the self.'[46] This is persuasive and illuminating. But it does not quite take fully enough into account the most striking formal feature of '*Je ne parle pas français*'.

The story cordons off narrative from description. It begins and ends in description. Duquette sits in a dirty little café, observing in a self-conscious fashion the owner seated on a stool with her face perpetually to the window, and the scarcely more active waiter.

> When he is not smearing over the table or flicking at a dead fly or two, he stands with one hand on the back of a chair, in his far too long apron, and over his other arm the three-cornered dip of dirty napkin, waiting to be photographed in connection with some wretched murder. 'Interior of Café where Body was Found.' You've seen him hundreds of times.

Thus far, the story is no story at all, but an exercise in the phobic picturesque, and one that concludes with a flourish Zola would surely have approved of. Tempted to create a *vignette*, the writer reaches over to the next table for some writing materials. 'No paper or envelopes, of course. Only a morsel of pink blotting-paper, incredibly soft and limp and almost moist, like the tongue of a little dead kitten, which I've never felt.' The all-seeing literary imagination founders in the abject touch of something soft and limp and moist: something as formless as a gob of spittle. What literature comes down to, in and through description, is radical ordinariness. Or almost comes down to. Duquette notices at the bottom of the page of blotting-paper (already it is a page, not a morsel, not mere matter), written in green ink, the phrase 'Je ne parle pas français'. At once, meaning blossoms, and with it the prospect of further narrative. 'There! It had come — the moment — the *geste*.' The phrase recalls Duquette's first meeting with Mouse, and the whole sorry business of abandonment and failure of nerve. It seems that the story will end in melancholia. But there is a final narrative: a twist, cynically, *against* narrative. A vengeful descriptiveness plunges us back into the abject, into nausea.

> I must go. I must go. I reach down my coat and hat. Madame knows me.
> 'You haven't dined yet?' she smiles.
> 'No, not yet, Madame.'
> I'd rather like to dine with her. Even to sleep with her afterwards. Would she be pale like that all over?

---

46 Sarah Henstra, 'Looking the Part: Performative Narration in Djuna Barnes's *Nightwood* and Katherine Mansfield's "*Je ne parle pas français*"', *Twentieth Century Literature*, 46 (2000), 125–49 (p. 126).

> But no. She'd have large moles. They go with that kind of skin. And I can't
> bear them. They remind me somehow, disgustingly, of mushrooms.[47]

Ontological feeling could not have announced itself more clearly. This really is
what the world looks like when you stop having ideas about it.

'Je ne parle pas français' is a manifesto for cynicism, and one which should by now
have received a great deal more attention than it has done. It proposes two distinct
portraits of the artist: as melancholic, immured in the past; and as nauséaste, face to
face, at altogether too close a range, with the present. It asks us to assess the uses of
narrative, perpetually à la recherche du temps perdu, against those of ontological feeling
as evinced in and by description. There is no easy choice, of course. But Mansfield
has made it abundantly clear what is at issue. And it is descriptive levelling, not
the geste, or significant moment, which has the last word. A strange consistency
of revulsion links ambiguous, cynical Raoul Duquette back to Lady Judas, and
Lady Judas in turn further back to the abused wives of New Woman fiction, who
themselves arise indirectly out of the exploits of Sarah Robinson, Ellice Hopkins,
and Beatrice Potter, who took formlessness on. Books of women, for women, by
women?

---

47 Mansfield, 'Je ne parle pas français', in Selected Stories, ed. by Angela Smith (Oxford: Oxford
University Press, 2002), pp. 142–67 (pp. 143–45, 167). This is the story's conclusion as printed in the
Heron Press editions. Most subsequent editions, including the Penguin Collected Stories, have lowered
the curtain after Duquette's 'No, not yet, Madame.'

CHAPTER 10

Dis-Enablement:
Subject and Method in the
Modernist Short Story

The novel is a literary form largely given over to affirmative action of one kind or another. For three hundred years or more, in the West, it has staunchly affirmed bourgeois individuals of all ages, genders, and temperaments in the richness of their political, social, moral, cultural, sexual, emotional, and psychopathological being. To be storied is never not an honour, and the novel has long been, and probably remains, despite severe competition, the most versatile and the most sympathetic mode of story-telling around. Even for psychopaths, it's a no-brainer. Dead or alive, there'll be more to you, considered as a person in a book, at the end of the ordeal than there was at the beginning. The novel may be tough on Ahab, and tough on the causes of Ahab (capitalism, paranoia, an aggravating whale), and tougher still on the customary boat-load of innocent bystanders; but when the mayhem stops there's almost certain to be an Ishmael bobbing about in a coffin among the wreckage. Or a Dorothea quietly performing those 'unhistoric acts' on which the 'good of the world' partly depends.[1] To this day, and even during its recurrent spasms of bleakness or postmodernity, the novel has continued to hand out redemption like free matchday programmes, or bus-passes for the elderly. Who could stay nihilist for 500 pages? The secret of the novel's age-old self-renewal as a literary form is that it can easily be understood to affirm categories as well as persons: nation, class, ethnicity, creed, sexual orientation. And it has always been hospitable to perceived outsiderdom. Despite its own best (or worst) instincts, it just can't stop affirming.

Or so it must have appeared, towards the end of the nineteenth century, as the Victorian age drew to a close in Britain and the United States. So it certainly appeared to Henry James, in 'The Art of Fiction' (1884), contemplating what a novel would have to include and exclude for the British public to consider it a success. 'One would say that being good means representing virtuous and aspiring characters, placed in prominent positions; another would say that it depends on a "happy ending", on a distribution at the last of prizes, pensions, husbands, wives, babies, millions, appended paragraphs, and cheerful remarks.'[2] The novel affirms, it

---

1   George Eliot, *Middlemarch*, ed. by David Carroll (Oxford: Oxford University Press, 1997), p. 785.
2   Henry James, 'The Art of Fiction', in *The House of Fiction: Essays on the Novel*, ed. by Leon Edel

might be said, because its enduring subject is enablement. Novels describe exactly what it is that makes it possible for someone to do something she or he could not otherwise have done. In nineteenth-century fiction, the something done is as often something known or felt as something enacted. But the focus remains on what has made that something possible: the stamina, the courage, the circumstances, the historical conditions, the luck.

There were, of course, alternatives. The Naturalist fiction which began to appear in the 1860s and 1870s, at first in France, and subsequently in America and across Europe, added a new pattern to the small stock of curves describing the shape lives take (or adapted an old one from classical tragedy): the plot of decline, of physical and moral exhaustion.[3] Most nineteenth-century novels implicitly or explicitly divide the human life-span into a long rise stretching to the age of sixty, measured in social and moral terms, and a short (physical) decline. Naturalist fiction envisaged instead a rapid physical rise to the moment of reproduction in the twenties, then a long redundancy accelerated by the emergence of some innate physical or moral flaw. In his Rougon-Macquart novels (1871–93), which describe the effects of heredity and environment on the members of a single family, tracing the passage of a genetic flaw down the legitimate line of the Rougons and the illegitimate line of the Macquarts, Emile Zola figured this long redundancy as the reduction of meaning to matter. The action chronicled in the bleakest of them — *L'Assommoir* (1877), *Nana* (1880), *La Bête humaine* (1890) — takes the form of a relentless decline into utter degradation: a downward spiral which can only be measured, ultimately, in physical terms, as bodily breakdown and decay. Naturalist fiction's subject is disablement, or dis-enablement. It perversely refuses to acknowledge that social and moral meaning accrue regardless even in the meanest of existences. Gervaise Coupeau, *L'Assommoir*'s anti-heroine, a laundress who ends up as a prostitute, does not hold back on the self-abjection. 'But her career, as presented, has fairly the largeness that, throughout the chronicle, we feel as epic,' as James put it, 'and the intensity of her creator's vision of it and the dense sordid life hanging about it is one of the great things the modern novel has been able to do.'[4] From that point of view, the lively interest Naturalism took in accumulations of dense sordid life could be understood simply to have reinforced the novel's inherent capacity to affirm. James may have felt that the genre's recent investment in bad blood and even worse luck had proved no less metaphysical than its enduring complicity with the providential (good blood generates even better luck).[5]

(London: Rupert Hart-Davies, 1957), pp. 23–45 (p. 27).

3   Philip Fisher, 'Acting, Reading, Fortune's Wheel: *Sister Carrie* and the Life History of Objects', in *American Realism: New Essays*, ed. by Eric J. Sundquist (Baltimore, MD: Johns Hopkins University Press, 1982), pp. 259–77 (p. 271).

4   James, 'Emile Zola', in *Documents of Modern Literary Realism*, ed. by George J. Becker (Princeton, NJ: Princeton University Press, 1963), pp. 506–34 (pp. 527–28). The essay was first published in the *Atlantic Monthly* in August 1903.

5   For some compelling reflections on these matters, see Fredric Jameson, 'The Experiments of Time: Providence and Realism', in *The Novel*, ed. by Franco Moretti, 2 vols (Princeton, NJ: Princeton University Press, 2006), II, 95–127.

Naturalism is generally thought to have run its course by around 1900, though it remained for some time thereafter a matter of interest for some American writers. But narrative disenchantment — amounting on occasion to a disenchantment with narrative — had broadly set in. In literary fiction, at least, there were to be no further distributions at the end of prizes, pensions, husbands, wives, and so on. The disenchantment, however, was by Naturalist standards pretty mild. James's heroes and heroines, who learn to know dense sordid life of a kind, are no strangers to providence. Leopold Bloom, humiliated by the prospect of his wife's imminent infidelity, stays away from home all day: to return a sadder but in some ways wiser man, having done things he would not otherwise have done, his marriage quite conceivably in better shape at the end of the day than it was at the beginning. Nick Carraway, the Ishmael bobbing about in the wreckage at the end of *The Great Gatsby*, even manages to glimpse an 'orgastic future'.[6]

It's possible, of course, to have too much of the good thing which is getting things done. Might we not also need to dis-affirm? That is, to know what it feels like when that which might make it possible for us to do something just does not happen, as time and time again in the past it hasn't, in all likelihood; as for one last time in the future it definitely won't. My proposition here is that one task the short story took on, at the turn of the century, when it achieved a new commercial and critical eminence as a literary form, was dis-affirmation. Roland Barthes had a short story in mind (Flaubert's 'Un Cœur simple') when he remarked on modern literature's apparent conviction that meaning had somehow become incompatible with existence.[7] Lukács agreed. The novel, he wrote, was the 'epic' of an age in which that incompatibility could no longer be ignored.[8] However, it might still be the business of such a form zealously to seek meaning out in existence, as James had indicated in his commentary on Zola, and, if it was not to be found, make it up. The short story can be less forgiving. Like Leopold Bloom, Waythorn, in Edith Wharton's 'The Other Two' (1904), feels such intense 'physical repugnance' at the thought that his wife has invited another man into his house that he resolves to stay out all day. In this case, the man is his wife's ex-husband, and merely wishes to see the child of that previous marriage. But the intrusion none the less puts an end once and for all to his 'joy of possessorship'.[9] 'The Other Two' comfortably outdoes *Ulysses* in dis-affirmation.

To dis-affirm — to render meaning incompatible with existence — is to take a lively interest in instances of what I shall term dis-enablement. By dis-enablement, I mean that first radical discomfiture in a person's experience which allows us to deduce both the precariousness of an established identity, and the likelihood (or more often unlikelihood) of its eventual repair and rehabilitation. Such discom-

6   F. Scott Fitzgerald, *The Great Gatsby*, ed. by Ruth Prigozy (Oxford: Oxford University Press, 1998), p. 144.
7   Roland Barthes, 'The Reality Effect', in *The Rustle of Language*, trans. by Richard Howard (Oxford: Blackwell, 1986), pp. 141–48 (p. 148).
8   Georg Lukács, *The Theory of the Novel*, trans. by Anna Bostock (London: Merlin Press, 1978), p. 56.
9   Edith Wharton, 'The Other Two', in *Collected Stories* (New York: Carroll and Graf, 1988), pp. 16–31 (p. 21).

fitures work loose the intricate combination of inner and outer resource which has hitherto made it possible for a person to lay claim to acknowledged (social, moral, or other) accomplishment. The short story dis-affirms by studying dis-enablement. Characters in novels often suffer agonizing discomfiture: Bloom does when he leaves home in the morning, and then again when he catches sight of Blazes Boylan on his way to the Ormond Hotel; Lambert Strether does, in James's *The Ambassadors*, when he realizes that Chad Newsome and Madame de Vionnet are lovers. In the longer form, the discomfiture itself is not the whole story; in the shorter, it is. Or so it became, at any rate, in a wide range of short fictions written between around 1890 and around 1930. Some of the most compelling stories written by American, British, and Irish writers during that period are stories about the dis-enablement of professional patriarchy: of that combination of social status, gender-privilege, and expertise which made it possible for middle-class men to think themselves entitled to behave in a particular way. Waythorn, in 'The Other Two', is a broker who has invested in marriage. He regards marriage as a foundational enhancement — not just desirable, but necessary — of his moral being. It is the stage upon which he performs as himself (even when he dines at his club, he is a husband dining at his club). As professional patriarch, Waythorn was soon to find himself in good (or at least plentiful) company. A list of notable stories on the subject would include Joyce's 'The Dead', Fitzgerald's 'An Alcoholic Case', Ernest Hemingway's 'Indian Camp', D. H. Lawrence's 'The Prussian Officer', Virginia Woolf's 'Solid Objects', Elizabeth Bowen's 'Making Arrangements', and William Carlos Williams's 'Old Doc Rivers'. Dis-enablement, moreover, was not a fate reserved exclusively for middle-class men in the short fiction of the period. Middle-class women had to endure their fair share of it. There was no shortage, for example, of short fiction about spinsters. In order to demonstrate the range as well as the quality of this preoccupation with dis-enablement, I will discuss short stories by two writers who would not in other respects bear much comparison: one, an American, and a man, flourished in the 1890s; the other, Anglo-Irish, and a woman, first became known in the 1920s. Stephen Crane's 'An Episode of War' was published posthumously in the *Gentlewoman* in December 1899, and then in *Last Words* (1902). Elizabeth Bowen's 'The Secession' appeared in *Ann Lee's* (1926).

What these stories demonstrate, I believe, is that dis-enablement had become for some writers both a subject and a method. According to Frank O'Connor, the short story is at its best as a literary form when it dramatically reconfigures the novel's intricate mesh of temporal and causal relationships.

> The short story represents a struggle with Time — the novelist's Time; it is an attempt to reach some point of vantage from which past and future are equally visible. The crisis of the short story *is* the short story and not as in a novel the mere logical inescapable result of what has preceded it. One might go further and say that in the story what precedes the crisis becomes a consequence of the crisis — *this* being what actually happened, *that* must necessarily be what preceded it.[10]

10   Frank O'Connor, *The Lonely Voice* (Hoboken: Melville House, 2004), p. 103.

A novel's crisis is the knowledge produced, for reader and protagonist alike, by the consequences of a first radical discomfiture. It occurs when and where we know that they know that they have been dis-enabled. Such knowledge is affirmative, since all knowledge affirms in the knowing, if not in what is known. By contrast, the crisis of a short story does not necessarily produce affirmative knowledge. That is, it can be represented either as producing or as not producing affirmative knowledge. In Romantic tradition, crisis always and uniquely produces knowledge; even, or especially, if it has at the same time produced fragmentation, the expressive shard or scrap. O'Connor's idea of a vantage-point from which past and future are equally apparent belongs to that way of thinking. However, a past and a future equally apparent are a past and a future equally uninformative. According to O'Connor, the vantage-point created by the crisis of a short story encourages us to deduce cause from effect — but a cause which can only be deduced from its effect has no predictive value at all. Such knowledge does not enable. Having failed to predict the present crisis, the past can scarcely be thought to have anything to tell us about its future consequences. The stories I will now examine both represent crisis as a suspension of narrative itself: as ignorance rather than knowledge. The vantage-point turns out to be a blank space, a gap between paragraphs.

Crane's original title for 'An Episode of War' was 'The Loss of an Arm', which would not only have given the story's plot away, but also obscured its richly provocative emphasis on the dis-enabling consequences of (or are they somehow are predisposition to?) disablement. 'An Episode of War' opens in mid-ceremony.

> The lieutenant's rubber blanket lay on the ground, and upon it he had poured the company's supply of coffee. Corporals and other representatives of the grimy and hot-throated men who lined the breastwork had come for each squad's portion.
>
> The lieutenant was frowning and serious at this task of division. His lips pursed as he drew with his sword various crevices in the heap until brown squares of coffee, astoundingly equal in size, appeared on the blanket. He was on the verge of a great triumph in mathematics and the corporals were thronging forward, each to reap a little square, when suddenly the lieutenant cried out and looked quickly at a man near him as if he suspected it was a case of personal assault. The others cried out also when they saw blood upon the lieutenant's sleeve.[11]

The lieutenant is a man known to us in and through his rank, his position within the hierarchy constituted by the chain of command in an army at war. His identity is primarily *social*. But there is more to him than that: a symbolic surplus, over and above the social identity established by rank, of *moral* identity. That moral identity resides in the care — the frowning seriousness — with which he divides up the coffee. The gesture of the 'great triumph in mathematics', reiterated daily, has built moral upon social authority into an extravaganza of self-enablement. The triumph is more than fairness and efficiency require. It is this symbolic excess, rather than the lieutenant's body, which suffers a radical discomfiture when the bullet (the little

---

11   Stephen Crane, 'An Episode of War', in *Prose and Poetry* (New York: Library of America, 1984), pp. 671–75 (p. 671). Henceforth *EW.*

piece of hard matter) breaks his arm. He has been at once disabled and dis-enabled. Matter has taken its revenge upon symbolism, upon efforts to deduce meaning from existence, upon the project of identity.

'A wound gives strange dignity to him who bears it' (*EW* 671). Does it? And, if so, would that be a dignity worth having? The lieutenant retires from the fray.

> As the wounded officer passed from the line of battle, he was enabled to see many things which as a participant in the fight were unknown to him. He saw a general on a black horse gazing over the lines of blue infantry at the green woods which veiled his problems. An aide galloped furiously, dragged his horse suddenly to a halt, saluted, and presented a paper. It was, for a wonder, precisely like an historical painting. (672–73)

He was *enabled* to see many things... If there is a dignity accruing to physical damage, then it might perhaps derive from the superiority of the knowledge available to the observer of a scene over that available to a participant in it. Does such knowledge *re-enable*? Crane seems to doubt that there is any equilibrium in the withdrawal from experience. For the lieutenant's retreat has removed him, by a kind of hallucination, twice over: from both the place and the time of battle. He sees the front-line not as it is seen by a general distant from it in space, but as the general distant from it in space will be seen by a painter distant from him in time. He can only understand the battle which caused his retreat as the present (perceptual) effect of a future (aesthetic) effect for which there has as yet been no cause. You wouldn't bet on his re-enablement.

After various minor adventures, which rather conspire to make him feel that he doesn't know 'how to be correctly wounded' (*EW* 674), the lieutenant encounters a surgeon. This the story's conclusion.

> The lieutenant had been very meek but now his face flushed, and he looked into the doctor's eyes. 'I guess I won't have it amputated,' he said.
> 'Nonsense, man! nonsense! nonsense!' cried the doctor. 'Come along, now. I won't amputate it. Come along. Don't be a baby.'
> 'Let go of me,' said the lieutenant, holding back wrathfully. His glance fixed upon the door of the old school-house, as sinister to him as the portals of death.
> And this is the story of how the lieutenant lost his arm. When he reached home his sisters, his mother, his wife, sobbed for a long time at the sight of the flat sleeve. 'Oh well,' he said, standing shamefaced amid these tears, 'I don't suppose it matters so much as all that.' (*EW* 674–75)

The story's crisis has taken place, without our knowledge, in the narrative gap preceding the final paragraph, during which the lieutenant's arm has been amputated. Could we have seen it coming? To be sure, the lieutenant's figuring of the school-house door as the 'portals of death' does not bode well. But we are more likely at a first reading to understand such hyperbole as the last gasp in a struggle for supremacy between experts, than as an imminent revelation. In that futile clamour, an entire symbolic order fails. The crisis, manifest in and as a failure of narrative, is then no more than a recognition of the fact that meaning has become incompatible with existence. We cannot imagine a way to be correctly wounded. Wounding *is*. The story, dis-enabling itself, says just that. The lieutenant's concluding remark convinces us neither that the amputation matters, nor that its not mattering won't prove fatal.

'The Loss of an Arm' would indeed have been too explicit a title for 'An Episode of War'. Elizabeth Bowen ran no such risk when she came up with 'The Secession' as a term broadly suggestive of the crisis which will affect the thirty-something protagonist of a story about tourists in Rome. To secede is to go apart: 'to withdraw from fellowship in any affair,' as Samuel Johnson put it. When the withdrawal is that of a group or party from an alliance, federal union, or majority view, it can, of course, have the most fateful consequences. The *OED* also notes an archaic sense: retirement from an accustomed neighbourhood, or from public view. A seventeenth-century bishop is quoted as claiming that Jesus's flesh was 'bereft of natural life' by the 'secession' of his unspotted soul. Clearly there will be no loss of anything as literal as an arm in this story. Its title reeks, ever so subtly, of secret implication.

The story begins with the Pension Hebe's most recent arrival settling in, a scene as ceremonious, if a lot less public, than the lieutenant's distribution of coffee.

> Seen in any light, the English lady recorded in her diary, the Roman streets are very mysterious, and seen from above (her window commanded everything, and she paid a supplementary ten lire a day for the city's generosity) the roofs and gardens of Rome are scarcely less so. She had arrived at the blank hour of eleven, and she spent the remainder of her morning spread-eagled on her window-sill, looking out from a height which would have made another woman dizzy at a panorama which should have abashed her.[12]

The English lady, like the lieutenant, is at first identified by rank alone. Again, the exercise of rank generates a symbolic surplus: moral identity built upon social. Wealth has bought the English lady a view of Rome, which a certain recklessness or triumph of intellect then doubly commands in 'joy of possessorship'. Bowen, however, seems no more concerned than Crane had been to convert this radiance of identity into a point of view or reflecting consciousness. The entry in the English lady's diary is almost ostentatiously unrevealing. We won't learn for several paragraphs that she is called Miss Selby, and until a good deal later yet that her first name is Lena. The narrative voice — 'looking out from a height which would have made another woman dizzy at a panorama which should have abashed her' — circles its object warily, if not with a certain fastidiousness.

Miss Selby awaits, in her turn, a further arrival: Mr Humphrey Carr, a retired schoolmaster, who some years previously 'spoke' to her about marriage, and might yet do so again in Rome, under the more immediate pressure of their shared passion for antiquity. Propriety demands that Mr Carr remain in the public eye by taking a room at the Pension Hebe, where, in a mathematical triumph of his own, he divides his attention scrupulously between Miss Selby and three American ladies. '*When Miss Selby began to wish that she had sent Humphrey to another hotel, to spend her days in his less distributed society, it is not known; but certainly she never betrayed*

---

12   Elizabeth Bowen, 'The Secession', in *Collected Stories* (Harmondsworth: Penguin, 1983), pp. 160–69 (p. 160). Henceforth *S*.

herself' (*S* 162). Discomfiture has set in. The coupling of intrusive emphasis with a studiously impersonal construction ('*When* ... it is not known ...') enacts the wariness the narrative voice will continue to display towards its subsequent aggrandisement into crisis. Indeed, we first learn about the degree of Miss Selby's discomfiture from commentary on Mr Carr's state of mind.

> Ever since he had come to Rome he had been like this; something had died as he entered the salon of the Pension Hebe and she rose up to greet him from among her friends. He could not discharge himself of what he had come out to say: it was no longer there. It was horrible that this should be so, that nothing was to happen to her here, in Rome. (163)

The 'point of view' invoked here is not just Mr Carr's, but that of James's late stories about confirmed bachelors who turn out to be the only person in the world to whom nothing is ever to happen. We are about as far away from Miss Selby as we could be in a discussion of her most bitter disappointment. The nothing which is to happen to her in Rome will somehow have to be articulated *as* nothing.

As the impossibility of her desire becomes apparent, so point of view passes conclusively from Miss Selby to Humphrey Carr and Mildred Phelps, one of the American ladies, to whom he has become increasingly attracted. The story's crisis takes place during an expedition the three of them make, with the other American ladies, to Hadrian's Villa, across the Campagna. On the way back, in a tram, Humphrey and Mildred slump exhausted, while Miss Selby talks on indefatigably.

> Often the roar of the tram would rise to drown her voice, but they still saw her lips alive, her brain glowing through her features, while her dark glance flitted, stabbed and flitted from face to face. She made the gestures of gathering up some brightness and slowly for their approbation letting it trickle through her fingers. The American ladies, wound up in their veils, passively and smilingly marvelled at her. Afterwards, they said it had been a swan song.
>
> That Miss Selby kept a diary (as a record, not as an outlet), entered her most trivial expenses in a notebook, and wore her keys round her neck, all proved that she was very methodical. From the account-book, it was gathered that not a five-centesimi piece could have gone its way unconsidered; and from the diary that not a glance, a half-smile, an intonation, not the slightest interchange between any of them, had escaped her. She had charted the atmosphere of her company; she had been meticulously accurate. (*S* 167)

The crisis — Miss Selby's absolute disappearance — takes place in the gap Bowen has introduced between paragraphs. Does it involve her unspotted soul's secession from the flesh? We never find out. Another impersonal construction ('... it was gathered that ...') intervenes to remind us that this story does not deal in intimacy. It dis-enables itself in order to state that secession (whatever that might involve) *is*. Alerted to the significance of Miss Selby's diary, we re-read the story, looking for clues. At a second reading, the references to the diary salted away within it do indeed have a predictive value. But it is already, of course, too late. Cause can only be grasped, after the event, as effect. As O'Connor puts it, *this* being what actually happened, *that* must already have done so. As in 'An Episode of War', the gap between paragraphs is a cut which severs meaning from existence.

Poetic tautness and clarity are so essential to the short story, Bowen once wrote, that the form 'may be said to stand at the edge of prose.'[13] 'The Secession', like 'An Episode of War', has been taken to that edge. Novelists, too, sometimes work between as well as within paragraphs. Leo, one of the two child protagonists in Bowen's *A House in Paris* (1935), gets conceived between paragraphs, during a dirty weekend in Romney. His mother, not yet knowing that she is a mother, observes that this crisis in the lives of two lovers, each already engaged to someone else, had 'finished the past but did not touch the future'.[14] It does neither. In a novel, it wouldn't. Had she been in a short story, had she been reading a short story, she would have known what it means to finish the past without touching the future.

---

13   Bowen, 'Introduction' to *The Faber Book of Modern Stories* (London: Faber and Faber, 1944), reprinted in *The New Short Story Theories*, ed. by Charles E. May (Athens: Ohio University Press, 1994), pp. 256–62 (p. 256).
14   Bowen, *The House in Paris* (London: Vintage, 1998), pp. 151, 160.

CHAPTER 11

Fascination and Nausea:
Finding Out the Hard-Boiled Way

In crime fiction, Auden said, the corpse must shock 'not only because it is a corpse but because, even for a corpse, it is shockingly out of place, as when a dog makes a mess on a drawing-room carpet'.[1] The really bad thing about murder, from one point of view, is that it makes a mess in a clean place. And yet that messiness, in Auden's view so crucial to stories about murder, so productive, rarely features in the explanations put forward for the broad and enduring appeal of crime fiction. Why?

The general view would seem to be that the shock detective fiction delivers is strictly hermeneutic. What we confront when the detective arrives at the scene of the crime is not a corpse, not a ruined carpet, but a ripening enigma. The enigma provokes interpretation rather than nausea: as the pursuit of meaning heats up, any shock we might initially have felt soon evaporates. Lodged securely in the empire of signs, tracking an infallible exegete through mean streets and even meaner discourses, we await closure. Most commentators feel that the detective story has proved resoundingly successful as a genre because it does what all stories do, only better: it masterfully produces, and at the same times trains us to produce, by its exuberant display of hermeneutic attitude, the 'fictive concords' which systematize existence.[2] Crime fiction has come to be regarded as 'the epistemological genre *par excellence*':[3] as a paradigm (an allegory) of narrative itself — or of the disciplinary techniques of surveillance and classification which, some would say, characterize the world we live in. In none of these accounts of the genre's weighty responsibilities does the corpse feature *as a corpse*, as a mess in a clean place.

One might think that there would be a difference, where corpses are concerned, between 'classic' and 'hard-boiled' detective fiction. Holmes, after all, has little affinity with decomposition, with waste-matter. Were there to be a Baker Street dog, Mrs Hudson would surely dispose of its messes without interrupting his

---

1   W. H. Auden, 'The Guilty Vicarage', in *The Dyer's Hand* (London: Faber and Faber, 1948), p. 151.
2   The phrase 'fictive concords' is Frank Kermode's: *The Sense of an Ending: Studies in the Theory of Fiction* (Oxford: Oxford University Press, 1967), pp. 7, 18.
3   Brian McHale, *Constructing Postmodernism* (London: Routledge, 1992), p. 147. According to Peter Huehn, the genre 'thematizes narrativity itself as a problem, a procedure, and an achievement': 'The Detective as Reader: Narrativity and Reading Concepts in Detective Fiction', *Modern Fiction Studies*, 33 (1987), 451–66 (p. 451).

cocaine-daze. The hermeneutic foreplay which precedes each of his adventures is an announcement that, in Baker Street, sublimation is always already in progress. It textualizes, or narrativizes, matter (an abrasion, the scrape of mud on a boot). The corpses, too, are always already textual. They have been edited by assassination. Uncommon reader that Holmes is, a resident 'interpretive community' of one, or grudgingly two, they do not remain opaque (mere matter) for long. And they do not bring out an equivalent opacity in the interpreter; he knows doubt, on occasion, but never nausea, never shock. The fascination which stirs in him is chastely epistemological.

Raymond Chandler's Philip Marlowe, by contrast, *does* have a certain affinity with waste-matter. Murder might very well happen to him, and does happen repeatedly to his friends and associates. He might very well become redundant, he would have us believe, at any time, in one way or another. The best he can hope for, even on the least taxing of assignments, is to get messed up. Bent cops, old buddies, *femmes fatales*, barmen: they all have a shot at it. One way or another, in story after story, he will end up feeling that he has been treated like shit. Marlowe's problem is that he cannot distinguish himself sufficiently from the mess on the drawing-room carpet. And yet the commentaries insist that, in the 'hard-boiled' as in the 'classic' version of the genre, the detective's task is not crime-prevention, but surveillance and control. The detective, it is said, 'fulfils the demands of the function of knowledge rather than that of lived experience: through him we are able to see, to know, the society as a whole, but he does not really stand for any genuine close-up experience of it.'[4]

The emergence in post-war American writing of a 'metaphysical' or 'anti-detective' detective fiction has reinforced the tendency to view the genre it imitates and burlesques in abstract terms.[5] 'Stories of detection and quest, emblems of the search-and-seizure mentality of the revelational plot (or, more aptly, plotted revelation), have been redesigned in contemporary fiction to conform to a modesty of aims enforced by an irremediably cryptic world.'[6] When those stories re-emerge in and through their deconstruction in books like Thomas Pynchon's *The Crying of Lot 49* (1966) and Paul Auster's *The New York Trilogy* (1985–86), and in commentaries on Pynchon and Auster, they do so precisely as *emblems*. Reading them again, with Oedipa Maas or Daniel Quinn in mind, we recognize in them little except the 'search-and-seizure mentality' which supposedly informs them. Thus there is an entire tradition of commentary on *The New York Trilogy* which represents detective fiction as no more than an embodiment of the literary and ideological closure Auster so elegantly refuses.[7] The criticism, unlike the book itself, it should

---

4   Fredric Jameson, 'On Raymond Chandler', in *The Critical Response to Raymond Chandler*, ed. by J. K. van Dover (Westport, CT: Greenwood Press, 1995), pp. 65–87 (pp. 69–70).
5   Michael Holquist, 'Whodunit and Other Questions: Metaphysical Detective Stories in Post-War Fiction', *New Literary History*, 3 (1971), 135–56; William V. Spanos, 'The Detective and the Boundary: Some Notes on the Postmodern Literary Imagination', *Boundary 2*, 1 (1972), 147–68.
6   Arthur M. Saltzman, 'De(in)forming the Plot', in *Designs of Darkness in Contemporary American Fiction* (Philadelphia: University of Pennsylvania Press, 1990), pp. 52–95 (p. 52).
7   These commentaries are too numerous to list. But see Saltzman, 'De(in)forming the Plot', pp.

be said, ignores mess altogether. Mess cannot be deconstructed (that is its great virtue).

This essay is dedicated to the proposition that Auden got it right: the corpse must shock, the detective (even, for a moment, the detective) must be shocked. My aim is not to produce a survey or a re-evaluation of the genre. It is, rather, to read a handful of 'hard-boiled' detective stories against the grain of a criticism which can no longer see a representation of material event for the discursive structure (the 'mentality') informing it.[8]

Floaters

After a few genteel preliminaries, Dorothy Sayers's *Whose Body?* (1923) unveils a body in a bath, in the suburban apartment belonging to an architect, Mr Thipps (henceforth 'poor little Thipps').

> The body which lay in the bath was that of a tall, stout man of about fifty. The hair, which was thick and black and naturally curly, had been cut and parted by a master hand, and exuded a faint violet perfume, perfectly recognisable in the close air of the bathroom. The features were thick, fleshy and strongly marked, with prominent dark eyes, and a long nose curving down to a heavy chin. The clean-shaven lips were full and sensual, and the dropped jaw showed teeth stained with tobacco.

This, seen from Wimsey's point of view, but without as yet any comment from him, is the closest the corpse comes to materiality. Its metamorphosis from material trace into sign-system begins almost immediately, as Wimsey deploys his monocle 'with the air of the late Joseph Chamberlain approving a rare orchid' (p. 18), and then accelerates, in Chapter 2, as he reviews the evidence in the company of Parker of Scotland Yard. Wimsey has seen something Parker hasn't: a further, recessed materiality (wax in the ears, dried soap in the mouth, filthy toenails). The point of the embedded dirt, like that of the violet perfume and the long nose, is to emphasize by its opacity the speed and sureness with which Wimsey converts matter into sign. The clues are of two kinds: marks of sameness (race and class affiliation), which help to identify the victim; and marks of difference, which, by revealing what has been done to the victim's body (the way in which it has been edited), help to identify the killer. The dead body in the bath has become a set of signifiers whose signified is the identity of the killer. Chapter 2 ends with Wimsey's delighted recognition that 'we're up against a criminal — *the* criminal — the real artist and blighter with imagination.'[9] He has looked straight through the victim (a blighter with no imagination, presumably) to an outline of the criminal (*the* criminal).

56–70; and Jeffrey T. Nealon, 'Work of the Detective, Work of the Writer: Paul Auster's *City of Glass*', *Modern Fiction Studies*, 42 (1996), 91–110.
8   Slavoj Žižek attempts something similar, to ingenious effect, in 'Two Ways to Avoid the Real of Desire', in *Looking Awry: An Introduction to Jacques Lacan through Popular Culture* (Cambridge, MA: MIT Press, 1991), pp. 48–66. I discuss the bodies in 'classic' detective fiction in *The English Novel in History, 1895–1920* (London: Routledge, 1993), pp. 220–27.
9   Dorothy Sayers, *Whose Body?* (London: Coronet Books, 1989), pp. 17–18, 33–35.

As Slavoj Žižek points out, the scene which confronts the detective, like that which confronts the psychoanalyst, is often a 'false image' put together by the criminal in order to conceal or distort the evidence of his or her involvement in the crime. 'The scene's organic, natural quality is a lure, and the detective's task is to de-nature it by first discovering the inconspicuous details that stick out, that do not fit into the frame of the surface image.' The detective's domain, Žižek adds, and the analyst's, is the domain of *meaning*, not of 'facts'. The crime-scene is by definition 'structured like a language'. And since the identity of a signifier depends on its difference from other signifiers, the absence of a trait can have a positive value. 'Which is why the detective's artifice lies not simply in his capacity to grasp the possible meaning of "insignificant details", but perhaps even more in his capacity to apprehend absence itself (the non-occurrence of some detail) as meaningful.'[10] Grasping the scene of the crime as a text edited by the murderer, the detective is able to apprehend him in and through his own deceptions, his own cunning, his fatal fondness for sly footnotes.

This is well said. But it fails to take account of the almost inevitable presence at the scene of someone other than the detective, someone who does not have the right hermeneutic attitude. In the interval between Wimsey's first glimpse of the body in the bath and his application of the monocle, poor little Thipps leaves the room. '"If you'll excuse me," he murmured, "it makes me feel quite faint, it reely does"'.[11] Poor little Thipps is about to barf. His nausea brings into play, at the very moment of detection, a curiosity about matter which Wimsey's brilliance soon overshadows, but never quite eclipses. If the monocle-flourishing detective authorizes the pleasure and comfort we take in 'plotted revelation', then the queasy bystander reminds us of our vulnerability to shock.

In 'hard-boiled' fiction, Žižek adds, the detective loses the distance that would enable him 'to analyse the false scene and to dispel its charm'.[12] The detective's affinity with mess prevents him from converting matter into sign. To be sure, he is not likely to heave. But the scene charms him. It could conceivably charm him to the point of revulsion; its 'organic' quality, so hard to de-nature, could conceivably produce in him an 'organic' response. Acknowledging that potential affinity, 'hard-boiled' stories try harder than their 'classic' counterparts to make an inaugural mess. One indication of this concerted effort is their regular deployment of floaters. Floaters, the result of death by drowning, disrupt the conversion of matter into sign. They are, as everyone must know by now, hard to fingerprint, and thus to identify. They evade the very technique which first associated detection (and detective stories) with the romance of scientific reason, of power/knowledge. The lady Philip Marlowe finds in a lake turns out not to be the lady he thought she was.

> The depths cleared again. Something moved in them that was not a board. It rose slowly, with an infinitely careless languor, a long dark twisted something that rolled lazily in the water as it rose. It broke surface casually, lightly, without haste.

10   Žižek, 'Two Ways', pp. 53, 57.
11   Sayers, *Whose Body?*, p. 18.
12   Žižek, 'Two Ways', p. 60.

The floater is a slow intrusion from a world beyond this one: it has to be prised out of or detached from an element which is not the earth we tread or the air we breathe. It is an immanent shapelessness.

> The thing rolled over once more and an arm flapped up barely above the skin of the water and the arm ended in a bloated hand that was the hand of a freak. Then the face came. A swollen pulpy grey white mass without features, without eyes, without mouth. A blotch of grey dough, a nightmare with human hair on it.

Marked off within the text as a separate paragraph, falling below the threshold at which devices like punctuation can be expected to work properly ('A swollen pulpy grey white mass...'), this account reaches a discursive limit. The scene into which the floater emerges is very definitely not 'structured like a language'. The distinctions which found the symbolic (inside/outside, nightmare/reality) no longer obtain. The water may possess a 'skin', but the corpse which rolls out of it does not. Once again, a hermeneutically challenged bystander offers a point of view other than that of the detective. 'The man called Andy got a dusty brown blanket out of the car and threw it over the body. Then without a word he went and vomited under a pine-tree.' In this case, furthermore, Marlowe himself proves vulnerable, albeit belatedly. He has a nightmare about a blotchy, water-logged corpse, about putrescence.[13]

Floaters are perhaps too much of a gift to writers trying to hard-boil discursive structure out of the crime scene. Marlowe's nightmare with human hair on it re-surfaces in Joseph Koenig's *Floater* (1986), where a Florida fisherman gets rather more than he had bargained for.

> Forgetting about alligators, he stepped onto some flat rocks and snagged the floating object. It was the body of a woman — about fifty, he guessed. He didn't care to look at it closely. Something had nibbled at the arms and legs, and the torso was bloated and distended. He tried to nudge it to shore but barely moved it. Then he noticed a dark mass clinging to what was left of an arm just below the surface. He poked at it with the rod, and the body submerged and bobbed ponderously.[14]

This corpse, too, gets a paragraph to itself. But the fussy notation of separate movements (stepping onto the flat rocks, nudging, poking) ensures that the floater will not float in anyone's dreams. The fisherman has been endowed with the detective's more-or-less stalwart indifference to organicism, if not his interpretative zeal. Nobody barfs.

Altogether more effective are the floaters whose retrieval punctuates Thomas Harris's *The Silence of the Lambs* (1988). Clarice Starling's first assignment is to take fingerprints from one, in a funeral parlour in West Virginia. Nobody barfs: but only because kindly old Jack Crawford, head of the Behavioral Science section at the FBI, has brought his Vicks VapoRub with him. This corpse yields a rich crop

13 Raymond Chandler, *The Lady in the Lake* (Harmondsworth: Penguin Books, 1952), pp. 47–48, 53, 90.
14 Joseph Koenig, *Floater* (New York: The Mysterious Press, 1986), p. 153.

of further clues: the broken fingernails, the pattern of the flaying, the position of the entry wound, and, above all, the death's head moth lodged in the throat. But its metamorphosis from material trace into sign-system remains incomplete. Just as Marlowe has nightmares about the lady in the lake, so the memory of the funeral parlour comes back to Starling, in tension with the 'savage pleasure' of problem-solving, at once overwhelming her and re-kindling her rage. The corpse endures, not only as a set of signifiers, a spectacle deceptively staged by an assassin, but as affect, as shock. This floater floats. It becomes a rhythm, a refrain: 'when Catherine Martin floats, when the next one floats, and the next one floats.'[15] At such moments the savage pleasure of problem-solving collapses in on itself.

Floaters are the genre's admission that matter shocks and that shocks matter. Even when the corpse does not float, it must make a mess, and people must respond to that mess as they usually respond to messes, with disgust. Auden got it right, and Hollywood has acknowledged that he did by incorporating what one might call the barf-scene into the conventions of *film noir*. There is a memorable one in Richard Marquand's *Jagged Edge* (1985), for example, when the District Attorney first enters the bedroom where a publishing magnate's wife lies battered to death. By now, the convention is so well established that the Coen brothers' *Fargo* (1996) even includes a meta-barf-scene. Police chief Marge Gunderson, inspecting the overturned car which contains one of the victims in a multiple homicide, announces that she is going to barf; but what turns her stomach is morning sickness, not the sight of blood.

The corpse is detective fiction's first and only object, its defining obstacle: the veil of matter whose piercing, with the help, it may be, of archives and laboratories, announces that gnosis has begun. Thereafter, out of earshot of commonplace retching, of the reader's retching, the 'cognitive hero' enters a virtual reality where even the beatings and the seductions are patterns thrown on a screen, events staged by the first and only assassin (the implacable Other).[16] Is she, or he, subject enough to survive? Fictional detectives have to be more characterful than fictional spies or fictional cowboys: interiority is expected of them. They go to work with their subjecthood, and *on* their subjecthood, for they must not be deflected from the hermeneutic endeavours upon which, in a fallen world, truth and justice depend. The sublimation which converts a dead body into a set of clues significantly prefigures the detective's long and arduous sublimation of his or her own body: of desire and rage, of fear and loathing. Here, too, however, the sublimation may not be complete. Clarice Starling answers all of Dr Hannibal Lecter's probing questions, except the last one. 'The other thing I wonder is... how do you manage your rage?' (*SL* 163). It is a question to which the *genre* has no answer. I want to define that inability by examining the detective's relation to authority, and to desire.

---

15   Thomas Harris, *The Silence of the Lambs* (London: Mandarin, 1990), pp. 79, 307, 175. Henceforth *SL*.
16   Wladimir Krysinski, *Carrefours de signes: essais sur le roman moderne* (The Hague: Mouton, 1981), p. 168.

Fathers

The Silence of the Lambs and Chandler's *The Big Sleep* are coming-of-age sagas in which the protagonist has to win approval in the eyes of the father (society), without compromising his or her independence. But which father? In each case, there is a good father, wise and incorruptible; and a bad father, wise and corrupt. The good father has the power to grant or withhold a recognition which is not his alone, and which does not issue directly from him. He is childless (he has not yet appointed his successor). His wish is for the survival of the race, of the social order. The bad father grants or withholds personal recognition: whatever he gives issues directly from him, in the form of wealth or information. He has been recklessly fertile: his misbegotten children are always already wreaking havoc. His wish is to populate the universe, for the duration of his own life, with people who interest him: he knows, and gives shape to, neediness (desire and rage, fear and loathing).

In *The Big Sleep*, the good father is genteel, solitary Taggart Wilde, the District Attorney, for whom Marlowe once worked; the bad father is General Sternwood, begetter of two uncontrollable daughters, and source of dubious largesse. In *The Silence of the Lambs*, the good father is genteel, solitary Jack Crawford; the bad father is Dr Hannibal Lecter, confessor to serial killers, and source of vital information. Wilde and Crawford see a place for their protégés in the system they uphold. Sternwood and Lecter identify and exploit neediness. The power of these stories is that they divert the rite of passage into and through a relation with the bad father in which fascination grips with ever-increasing intensity until it finally reaches and exceeds its limit. Both open with a visit to the bad father.

In Chapter 1 of *The Big Sleep*, Marlowe arrives at General Sternwood's Bel-Air mansion. 'I was everything the well-dressed private detective ought to be. I was calling on four million dollars.'[17] The narrative enacts with almost pedantic thoroughness the intensity of Marlowe's engrossment by wealth, and by the corruption wealth entails. He passes through the grandiose hall, where Carmen Sternwood flirts with him, and falls against him, round the lawn behind it, to the greenhouse where the General sits, in absolute recession, at the heart of darkness. The greenhouse is the mansion's primary cell, a 'deep' space adapted for its owner's exclusive use, a shrine; to reach it from the street, Marlowe must negotiate a whole series of 'shallow' intermediary zones.[18] And yet the shrine's occupant does not exactly emanate power. 'Here, in a space of hexagonal flags, an old red Turkish rug was laid down and on the rug was a wheel chair, and in the wheel chair an old and obviously dying man watched us come [...]' (*SL* 13). The syntax mimics a roundabout and carefully policed approach to the source; but the source is dry. At once shrunken and diffuse, impotent and promiscuous, General Sternwood exercises power by metastasis. It is too late, we soon gather, for cognitive heroism. What mediates Marlowe's encounter with corrupt authority is not the romance

---

17   Chandler, *The Big Sleep* (Harmondsworth: Penguin Books, 1948), p. 9. Henceforth *BS*.
18   I derive this understanding of the social relations embodied in the structure of a building, very crudely, from Bill Hillier and Julienne Hanson, *The Social Logic of Space* (Cambridge: Cambridge University Press, 1984).

of reason, but fascination and nausea. The orchids surrounding the wheelchair, through which he must force a path, make him feel sick. 'The plants filled the place, a forest of them, with nasty meaty leaves and stalks like the newly washed fingers of dead men' (13). Here, at this proleptic crime-scene (or morgue-scene), the cognitive hero almost barfs. Indeed, cognition is not really the issue. There is nothing to interpret. Marlowe goes to the bad father, a shameless hedonist, to receive acknowledgement of his own desire for wealth and power; but the bad father has already given all he has to give, or almost all. Those nasty meaty leaves mark fascination's limit: the point at which it becomes aware of itself, for the first time, in its own excess.

In Chapter 2 of *The Silence of the Lambs*, Clarice Starling arrives at the Baltimore State Hospital for the Criminally Insane to interview Hannibal Lecter. Lecter's cell is the most recessed room in the most recessed part of a recessed institution. Like General Sternwood, he has been immobilized (though not for very long). To reach this primary space, and have her own desires and hatreds acknowledged by the shamelessly desiring and hating bad father, Starling, like Marlowe, must placate the functionaries (Dr Chilton, of the 'fast grabby eyes'), and pass through the intermediate zones (*SL* 11–12). Marlowe has to cope with orchids, Starling with Miggs, who flicks semen at her as she returns from Lecter's cell (23). Again, there is not much scope for cognitive heroism. As Lecter recognizes, cognition, the ostensible purpose of Starling's visit, is not really the issue. Like the orchids, Miggs's mess marks a limit: fascination's limit in, or at, nausea.

If these stories begin with the bad father, in deep space, already at the limit, they conclude with the dispersed violence of his errant children. Here, too, the vocabulary of revulsion intrudes where one might not necessarily have expected it. On his first visit to the Sternwood mansion, Marlowe looks out over the oilfields which are the source of the family fortune. 'The Sternwoods, having moved up the hill, could no longer smell the stale sump water or the oil, but they could still look out of their front windows and see what had made them rich' (*BS* 25–26). At the end of the story, the saving distance articulated by sight collapses. Marlowe goes down among the stinking oilfields to confront, in one of Chandler's most Conradian moments, the General's wild child, Carmen.

> The wells were no longer pumping. There was a pile of rusted pipe, a loading platform that sagged at one end, half a dozen empty oil drums lying in a ragged pile. There was the stagnant, oil-scummed water of an old sump iridescent in the sunlight.
> 'Are they going to make a park of all this?' I asked.
> She dipped her chin down and gleamed at me.
> 'It's about time. The smell of that sump would poison a herd of goats. This the place you had in mind?'
> 'Uh-huh. Like it?' (209)

The sump, we learn later, contains the body of Rusty Regan, the General's other 'son': by now, presumably, a 'horrible decayed thing', as Vivian Sternwood will put it (218). That the sump conceals what Marlowe has been looking for from the start matters less, at this point, than that it should nauseate him. There will be time enough, after nausea, to find out who ended up where. For the encounter with the bad father and his works is not about truth and justice; it is about fascination, and fascination's excess.

Clarice Starling must confront Hannibal Lecter's most malevolent 'son', Jame Gumb, in his burrow: a maze of underground rooms containing a variety of horrible decayed things.

> In absolute black the hiss of steam pipes, trickle of water.
> Heavy in her nostrils the smell of the goat. (*SL* 332)

The stench reminds Starling, as it reminds Marlowe, that she has looked too hard for too long, that at some time or another, in some way, she has colluded with the bad father who knows exactly what she needs. As with the floater in *The Lady in the Lake*, an interruption to the narrative, a surplus of rhetorical effect over syntax, administers shock to the reader (somewhat portentously, in this case).

In *The Big Sleep* and *The Silence of the Lambs*, the good father supervises the hermeneutic process which is generally taken to characterize the genre of detective fiction. Marlowe does his detecting for Wilde's benefit (*BS* 108–09), Starling for Crawford's (*SL* 151–52). With the bad fathers, another scheme comes into play, one the genre is not thought to favour. In this case, complicity establishes a dialectic of fascination and nausea which forms (or deforms) the protagonist more comprehensively than involvement in the hermeneutic process, or in disciplinary techniques of surveillance and control. The dialectic, we might note, outlasts the tale told; it prevents closure. The bad father's even worse children die, or are put away; the bad father survives.

Quasi-celibacy

The dialectic activated by Marlowe's encounter with General Sternwood takes shape in his subsequent encounters with Vivian and Carmen, who together constitute a split or doubled *femme fatale*. Žižek points out that the detective's fate (his acknowledgement of the scope and intensity of his own desires) is usually decided at the moment when the *femme fatale* suffers her final breakdown. This moment, when her power of fascination suddenly 'evaporates', leaving him (and us) with little but disgust, confirms either his triumph or his collapse. What awaits her beyond hysteria is the death drive at its purest. 'When the woman reaches this point, there are only two attitudes left to the man: either he "cedes his desire", rejects her, and regains his imaginary, narcissistic identity (Same Spade at the end of *The Maltese Falcon*), or he *identifies* with the woman as symptom and meets his fate in a suicidal gesture (the act of Robert Mitchum in what is perhaps the crucial *film noir*, Jacques Tourneur's *Out of the Past*).'[19] In *The Big Sleep*, Chandler separates the fascination from the disgust. From the moment Vivian Sternwood first arranges her legs on the *chaise-longue*, she is 'worth a stare' (*BS* 22). Carmen, on the other hand, occasions neither 'embarrassment' nor 'ruttishness', even when stark naked (40). Her collapse,

19 Žižek, 'Two Ways', pp. 65–66.

when it comes, renders her utterly abject: she froths at the mouth, and wets herself (211). The intensity of the disgust Marlowe feels for Carmen enables him to preserve his narcissism intact, while still remaining vulnerable, it may be, or might be under somewhat different circumstances, to a stare-worthy woman like Vivian. Marlowe's erotic status, like that of many other private eyes, male and female, is one of quasi-celibacy. These men and women are sexually suspended: to vivid effect.

Reasons have been advanced for attributing Marlowe's suspension to homosexuality.[20] In Chapter 24 of *The Big Sleep*, Marlowe finds Carmen Sternwood in his bed, naked. 'It's so hard for women — even nice women — to realize that their bodies are not irresistible' (*BS* 153). When he declines the offer, she hisses at him, 'her mouth open a little, her face like scraped bone' (153), and calls him a 'filthy name'. 'I couldn't stand her in that room any longer. What she called me only reminded me of that' (154). Later, after she has gone, seeing the imprint of her 'small corrupt body' on the sheets, he tears the bed to pieces savagely (155). The next morning, he wakes up with a 'hangover' from women. 'Women made me sick' (156). This sickness at women could be taken to indicate a 'homosexuality' specific to Philip Marlowe rather than a generic requirement.

I would argue, on the contrary, that Marlowe's revulsion from Carmen is a development of the dialectic of fascination and nausea established by his encounter with the bad father. Marlowe is fascinated by the bad father's corrupt wealth, and by the corruption, sexual and otherwise, of his two daughters. Vivian and Carmen Sternwood are figures of transgression, of a non-pathological desire which has assumed responsibility for its own fate. The novel's evident fascination with homosexuality is a fascination with a sexuality identified, by the culture which disowns it, and by Chandler himself, as transgressive. The 'horror' some people feel at homosexuality, Chandler wrote, is like a woman's fear of scorpions. The bonds which 'hold us to sanity' are fragile, and constantly under threat from 'repulsive insects' and 'repulsive vices' alike. 'And the vices are repulsive, not in themselves, but because of their effect on us. They threaten us because our own normal vices fill us at times with the same sort of repulsion.'[21] If, as seems likely, the 'filthy name' Carmen calls Marlowe is 'faggot', then she thereby associates herself with the repulsive insects and repulsive vices which threaten his hold on sanity (on narcissism). Carmen herself, with her hissing and her scraped-bone look, resembles a snake rather than a scorpion. Her bestiality and the filthy name she calls Marlowe constitute her as the point at which fascination (those 'normal vices', perhaps) becomes aware of itself in its own excess. Vivian Sternwood describes Proust to Marlowe as a 'connoisseur in degenerates' (*BS* 58). So was Chandler. Chandler used the idea of 'the homosexual' to define degeneracy: that excess of non-pathological desire which must be pathologized, through the nausea it produces, if 'normal vices' are to remain normal. The genre demanded it of him.

20   Michael Mason, 'Marlowe, Men and Women', in *The World of Raymond Chandler*, ed. by Miriam Gross (London: Weidenfeld and Nicolson, 1977), pp. 90–101.
21   Chandler, letter of 9 July 1949 to Dale Warren, in *Selected Letters*, ed. by Frank MacShane (London: Jonathan Cape, 1981), p. 185.

Marlowe's curious quasi-celibacy is very much at issue in the scene in the Fulwider Building, when he overhears Lash Canino, Eddie Mars's hitman, killing honourable, diminutive Harry Jones. The building itself is as 'nasty' (*BS* 166) as General Sternwood's orchids.

> The fire stairs hadn't been swept in a month. Bums had slept on them, eaten on them, left crusts and fragments of greasy newspaper, matches, a gutted imitation-leather pocket-book. In a shadowy angle against the scribbled wall a pouched ring of pale rubber had fallen and had not been disturbed. A very nice building. (167)

Marlowe does not frequent mean streets and nasty lobbies in order to feed a 'habit of loathing'.[22] He frequents them because he believes he will find there an acknowledgement of his own desires. What he finds instead is waste-matter, a mess which could quite easily be a mess he himself has already made (the ring of pale rubber already 'pouched'). He finds a pathologized version of his own desires. And yet he is not quite ready to quit. In this 'very nice' building, something 'very nice' happens. The delicious guilt Marlowe feels as a man dies on the other side of a flimsy partition is as intense a pleasure as any he experiences in the novel. William Marling has compared the Fulwider Building to one of Deleuze and Guattari's 'celibate machines': a mechanization of experience which produces unpredictable and uncontrollable autoerotic intensities compounded of pleasure and pain.[23] Marlowe subsequently discharges the intensity stored autoerotically during Jones's murder when he shoots Canino. 'But his gun was still up and I couldn't wait any longer. Not long enough to be a gentleman of the old school. I shot him four times, the Colt straining against my ribs' (194).

Jones's murder strikes an odd note. Canino carries a gun, but instead of pulling the trigger, like any other Chandler hoodlum, he persuades Jones to drink from a bottle of poisoned whisky which he just happens to have with him. It is as though he seduces Jones to death. 'The purring voice was now as false as an usherette's eyelashes and as slippery as a watermelon seed' (*BS* 170). The connection I would make, taking a hint from Vivian Sternwood's reference to Proust, is with the scene in *À la recherche* when the narrator overhears the Baron de Charlus seducing Jupien. He cannot believe how noisy they are: it is almost as though a murderer and his resuscitated victim were taking a bath together, in order to wash away the traces of the crime. He concludes that pleasure is the one thing in life as vociferous (as intense) as pain, especially when it involves an immediate concern for cleanliness.[24] Proust's narrator overhears a seduction which sounds like a murder; Marlowe overhears a murder which sounds like a seduction. The implication of both scenes is that the intensity of a transgressive experience can only be measured by the mess it makes. Entering the room where Harry Jones lies, after Canino's departure, Marlowe sees

---

22   Tom S. Reck, 'Raymond Chandler's Los Angeles', in *The Critical Response*, pp. 109–15 (p. 111).
23   William Marling, *The American Roman Noir: Hammett, Cain, and Chandler* (Athens: University of Georgia Press, 1995), pp. 213–16.
24   Marcel Proust, *Remembrance of Things Past*, trans. by C. K. Scott Moncrieff and Terence Kilmartin, 3 vols (Harmondsworth: Penguin Books, 1983), II, 631.

that he has vomited on his overcoat (171). Like the narrator in *À la recherche*, the hard-boiled detective is there, on our behalf, to experience rather than to know: to measure out from a point inside it the dialectic of fascination and nausea.

CHAPTER 12

Fanon's Nausea

In the 1930s, Jean-Paul Sartre mounted a campaign against the philosophy of consciousness which constitutes one of the more flamboyant episodes in the steadily lengthening history of modern and postmodern anti-humanism. Sartre's encounter with the writings of Husserl and Heidegger enabled him to declare that consciousness 'has no "inside"', that it is no more than an existence for ever 'beyond itself'. 'We are delivered from Proust,' he felt ready to announce in 1939. 'We are likewise delivered from the "internal life".'[1] One of the instruments he hoped to set to the task of deliverance from the internal life was nausea.

Nausea, Sartre argued, is the 'taste' of contingency. Nausea is what the world is like when you stop having ideas about it. Roquentin, in *Nausea* (1938), is, as it were, a *nauséaste*: a man overcome by revulsion, permanently beyond himself, sick with sickness. 'The grey thing has just appeared in the mirror. I go over and look at it, I can no longer move away.'[2] What he sees in the mirror is his own image, evidently; but the image no longer functions *as* an image, no longer presents him to himself. It has failed to acknowledge the search for meaning and value which is the great aim of consciousness, and its only justification. Roquentin is brought face to face with physiognomy's obverse. The mirror lowers him, outside of himself, into his own estranged flesh.[3] This wrenching self-estrangement later develops into a nauseous ontology, when the root of a chestnut tree at which Roquentin happens to be gazing suddenly loses its 'harmless appearance' as an abstract category, as an identifiable object in the world. The root decomposes in front of him. The 'veneer' of shape and identity melts, 'leaving soft, monstrous masses, in disorder — naked, with a frightening, obscene nakedness' (*N* 183). Where consciousness hollows out a negativity into which it can withdraw, being (physiognomy's obverse) coagulates and solidifies into a mass or mess 'glued to itself'. In *Being and Nothingness* (1943), Sartre installed slime (*le visqueux*) as the ultimate glue, the nauseous essence of being. Slime, he wrote, appears to us not only as an object or substance, but as a

1   Jean-Paul Sartre, 'Intentionality: A Fundamental Idea of Husserl's Phenomenology', trans. by Joseph P. Fell, *Journal of the British Society for Phenomenology*, 1 (1970), 4–5 (p. 5). Another major essay from the same period concludes with the thought that 'there is no longer an "inner life"': Sartre, *The Transcendence of the Ego: An Existentialist Theory of Consciousness*, trans. by Forrest Williams and Robert Kirkpatrick (New York: Noonday Press, 1957), p. 93.
2   Sartre, *Nausea*, trans. by Robert Baldick (Harmondsworth: Penguin Books, 1965), p. 30. Henceforth *N*
3   Alain Buisine, *Laideurs de Sartre* (Lille: Presses Universitaires de Lille, 1986), pp. 95–99.

relation, in which we are always already implicated, to the world. To exist is to get stuck. Slime, in which we are always already stuck, is the world's 'ontological expression'.[4]

A pretty feeble expression, if we are to believe commentators like Emmanuel Levinas, who by the late 1940s had begun to argue that Sartre did not go nearly far enough in his denunciations of the philosophy of consciousness. Levinas thought that the contingencies laid bare by horror are a whole lot nastier than those laid bare by mere nausea. It is of his or her subjectivity, he argued, that the subject is stripped, in horror. 'The subject is depersonalized. "Nausea", as a feeling of existence, is not yet depersonalization; whereas horror turns the subjectivity of the subject, its particular nature as *being*, inside out.'[5] Horror, so to speak, trumps nausea; and has itself since been trumped again and again, in that further raising of the depersonalization stakes we call poststructuralism, by a rich variety of purgatives (*différance*, discourse, the abject, and so on). The result is that we read Sartre, Merleau-Ponty, de Beauvoir, Bataille, Leiris, Caillois, and Malraux, if we read them at all, as an anticipation of, or feint towards, Derrida, Foucault, and Kristeva.[6] We return to Paris in the 1930s primarily in order to find contexts for Paris in the 1960s and 1970s. It might well be, however, that Sartre and his contemporaries demand a reconsideration in terms which are neither exactly their own nor exactly those of poststructuralism.

Paris in the 1930s was the scene of a remarkable cross-fertilization of French culture by German philosophy, by Hegel and Husserl. Husserl features dramatically, in relation to an apricot cocktail, in Simone de Beauvoir's description of the birth of existentialism in 1932. De Beauvoir, Sartre, and Raymond Aron are sitting in the Bec du Gaz on the Rue Montparnasse. They order the speciality of the house, an apricot cocktail. Aron, who has been at the French Institute in Berlin studying Husserl, points to his glass. The great thing about being a phenomenologist, he says, is that you can make philosophy out of an apricot cocktail. 'Sartre,' de Beauvoir observes grandly, 'turned pale with emotion at this. Here was just the thing he had been longing to achieve for years — to describe objects just as he saw and touched them, and extract philosophy from the process.'[7] What made this extraction of philosophy possible was the concept of intentionality: consciousness is always and everywhere consciousness *of*. 'Sensible things,' Merleau-Ponty observed, 'as they come under our scrutiny at the same time as the body, become the philosopher's themes for analysis. As Husserl said, through the perception we have of them, things are given to us in the flesh — carnally, *leibhaftig*.'[8] According to Levinas,

4   Sartre, *Being and Nothingness: An Essay on Phenomenological Ontology*, trans. by Hazel E. Barnes (London: Routledge, 1969), pp. xli, 604–11.
5   Emmanuel Levinas, *De l'existence à l'existant* (Paris: Fontaine, 1947), p. 100.
6   This is the case, for example, with Denis Hollier's elegant and instructive *Absent without Leave: French Literature under the Threat of War*, trans. by Catherine Porter (Cambridge, MA: Harvard University Press, 1997).
7   Simone de Beauvoir, *The Prime of Life*, trans. by P. Green (Harmondsworth: Penguin Books, 1965), p. 135.
8   Maurice Merleau-Ponty, 'The Philosophy of Existence', in *Texts and Dialogues: Maurice Merleau-Ponty*, ed. and trans. by Hugh J. Silverman and James Barry (Atlantic Highlands, NJ: Humanities Press, 1992), pp. 129–39 (p. 132).

who studied with Husserl in Freiburg in 1928, and first wrote about him in 1930, the advantage of phenomenology was that it put the philosopher 'near to things'.[9] Phenomenology's 'phenomenon' is not an appearance distinct from essence, but rather the very way in which essence appears. Appearance must be understood as a 'positivity', Sartre observes: 'its essence is an "appearing" which is no longer opposed to being but on the contrary is the measure of it'. The phenomenon is the 'relative–absolute': relative, in that its appearance presupposes someone to appear to; absolute, in that it transcends the consciousness it appears to, revealing itself 'as it is'.[10]

However, the emphasis laid by Husserl's French disciples on nearness and carnality cannot obscure the fact that for them the appeal of the concept of intentionality lay as much in what it said about consciousness as in what it said about the world. It is by constituting the world through its intentional acts, Husserl argued, that consciousness fully possesses itself. Levinas and Sartre found in Husserl a philosophy of freedom (of self-possession through choice), rather than a philosophy of embeddedness. By this account, the apricot cocktail would only have begun to matter if Aron, flexing his intentionality, had thought to dump it all over the egregious Sartre: the intentional act gives meaning to its object. For Levinas and Sartre, meaning thus remains in the gift of a consciousness able to grasp it by freely reflecting on itself. Merleau-Ponty tried harder than most to grasp the interpenetration of organism and environment, their chiasmic carnality. But he, too, laid as much emphasis on the freedom of consciousness as on its inherence in the world. The problem on which *The Phenomenology of Perception* (1945) concentrates, in terms derived from Husserl, is 'how the presence to myself (*Urpräsenz*) which establishes my own limits and conditions every alien presence is at the same time depresentation (*Entgegenwärtigung*) and throws me outside myself.' How can the self be open to phenomena which transcend it, by belonging to a natural and social world, and yet which exist only to the extent that they are taken up and lived by it?[11]

Existential phenomenology imagines organism and environment as the two instantiations, reciprocally defined, of an interminable circularity. It is no surprise, therefore, that Aron's apricot cocktail should rapidly have been overshadowed, as a philosophical event, by the lectures Alexandre Kojève gave on Hegel's *Phenomenology*

9   Levinas, *Ethics and Infinity*, trans. by Richard A. Cohen (Pittsburgh, PA: Duquesne University Press, 1985), pp. 30–31. Phenomenology, Sartre said, ensured the investigator's 'proximity' to the object of investigation: *Sketch for a Theory of the Emotions*, trans. by Philip Mairet (London: Routledge, 1994), p. 23.
10 Sartre, *Being and Nothingness*, p. xxii.
11 Merleau-Ponty, *The Phenomenology of Perception*, trans. by Colin Smith (London: Routledge and Kegan Paul, 1962), p. 363. During the preparation of the *Phenomenology*, Merleau-Ponty examined a number of Husserl's unpublished manuscripts in the Husserl Archives in Louvain: H. L. van Breda, 'Merleau-Ponty and the Husserl Archives at Louvain', in *Texts and Dialogues: Maurice Merleau-Ponty*, pp. 150–61. It is worth pointing out that the discussion of *Urpräsenz* and *Entgegenwärtigung* occurs in a chapter devoted to the 'existential modality of the social'. 'We must return,' Merleau-Ponty argues, 'to the social with which we are in contact by the mere fact of existing, and which we carry about inseparably with us before any objectification' (p. 362).

of Spirit at the École des Hautes Études between 1933 and 1939.[12] Merleau-Ponty attended.[13] So did Georges Bataille, now best known as the leading exponent of a 'heterology' or 'science of the wholly other' which would be the theory of that which theory expels, of that which revolts it. Poststructuralism has sought to keep this programmatically impure science pure for its own use by removing any trace of dialectic (of the reciprocal definition of *Urpräsenz* and *Gegenwärtigkeit*). We are told that the formlessness which is heterology's 'object' does not negate dialectically, but rather by lowering, by putrefaction, by entropy.[14] Who could doubt that Bataille's analysis of formlessness and of expenditure without return is indeed the basest of base materialisms?

It should also be said, however, that Bataille's preoccupation with lowering and dispersal engenders its own opposite: a preoccupation with the 'virile integrity' of the 'full existence'.[15] As he put it in 'Sacrifices' (1933), knowledge of the arbitrariness of existence does not by any means invalidate the 'immediate reality' of the self's 'imperative presence' in the world: 'this lived experience *equally* constitutes an inevitable point of view, a direction of being required by the eagerness of its own movement.'[16] In 'The Psychological Structure of Fascism', also written in 1933, Bataille opposed the basely heterogeneous *Lumpenproletariat* not just to a homogeneous bourgeoisie, but to the 'imperative' heterogeneity of the demagogue, in terms drawn from Hegel (or at least from Kojève).[17] It is not my intention to argue that Bataille's materialism was dialectical through and through.[18] But I do think that a preoccupation with 'virile integrity' and 'imperative presence' looms rather larger in his writings than the current emphasis on *l'informe* and *la dépense* might suggest. To take up with the theory of the subject to which Kojève's lectures and Aron's apricot cocktail gave rise, in terms other than those generated by the

12   Alexandre Kojève, *Introduction to the Reading of Hegel: Lectures on The Phenomenology of Spirit*, assembled by Raymond Queneau, ed. by Allan Bloom, trans. by James H. Nichols (Ithaca, NY: Cornell University Press, 1969).

13   On the Hegelianism of Merleau-Ponty's early work, see Barry Cooper, 'Hegelian Elements in Merleau-Ponty's *La Structure du comportement'*, *International Philosophical Quarterly*, 15 (1975), 411–23; and, more generally, James Schmidt, 'Lordship and Bondage in Merleau-Ponty and Sartre', *Political Theory*, 7 (1979), 201–27.

14   See, for example, Yve-Alain Bois and Rosalind E. Krauss, *Formless: A User's Guide* (New York: Zone Books, 1997), pp. 67–73.

15   Georges Bataille, 'The Sorcerer's Apprentice', trans. by Betsy Wing, in *The College of Sociology (1937–39)*, ed. by Denis Hollier (Minneapolis: University of Minnesota Press, 1988), pp. 12–23 (p. 18.) This lecture, delivered at the College of Sociology in 1937, partly by way of a response to Kojève's scepticism about the whole project, offers a not wholly un-dialectical account of the relation between will and chance (organism and environment).

16   Bataille, 'Sacrifices', in *Visions of Excess: Selected Writings, 1927–1939*, ed. by Allan Stoekl, trans. by Allan Stoekl with Carl R. Lovitt and Donald M. Leslie (Minneapolis: University of Minnesota Press, 1985), pp. 130–36 (p. 131).

17   Bataille, 'The Psychological Structure of Fascism', in *Visions of Excess*, pp. 137–60 (p. 146): 'If the heterogeneous nature of the slave is akin to that of the filth in which his material situation condemns him to live, that of the master is formed by an act excluding all filth: an act pure in direction but sadistic in form.'

18   For that, see Georges Didi-Huberman, *La Ressemblance informe ou le gai savoir visuel selon Georges Bataille* (Paris: Macula, 1995).

philosophy of the 1960s and 1970s, is to take up, for better or worse, not only with identity's dispersal, but with its concentration.

This is true even of the remarkable studies of disabling affect which existential phenomenology conducted as part of its programme to take philosophy closer to things: Heidegger's analysis of fear and anxiety, in *Being and Time* (1927);[19] Levinas's analyses of shame, in 'De l'évasion' (1935), and of fatigue, in *De l'existence à l'existant* (1947);[20] Sartre's analyses not only of nausea, in *Nausea* and *Being and Nothingness*, but of hatred, in *The Transcendence of the Ego* (1937), and of fear and horror, in *Sketch for a Theory of the Emotions* (1939).[21] These feelings in some way disable or exceed consciousness. They are as close as we can reasonably expect to get to what the world is like when you stop having ideas about it. They blossom as meaning and value fade. And yet they are not, as the phenomenologist might perhaps have hoped, a complete emptiness. 'If we are really to be seized by horror,' Sartre says, 'we have not only to mime it, we must be spell-bound and filled to overflowing by our own emotion, the shape and form of our behaviour must be filled with something opaque and weighty that gives it substance.'[22] It would be more accurate to say that nausea fills Roquentin than that it empties him. The chestnut tree presses itself weightily on him, as the carcase had once pressed itself on Baudelaire: 'my nostrils overflowed with a green, putrid smell.'[23] The weight is in the synaesthesia. For *Nausea* is not a novel about nausea, but a novel about a man who becomes a *nauséaste* — and thus the very man to write a novel about nausea. So it's not goodbye to Proust, after all, or to the internal life. Nausea, Maurice Blanchot observed, sticks to Roquentin's consciousness, as it sticks in the reader's.[24] The chestnut tree does what the apricot cocktail failed to do. In nausea, being gets glued not only to itself, but to a person. An identity (de)forms. Merleau-Ponty, who despite his Hegelianism had a preference for rather less dramatic encounters between Self and Other, would have imagined this process geologically, as a sedimentation.[25] These ideas of weight, stickiness, and sedimentation constitute a vivid if radically incomplete sketch for a theory of the subject.

Heidegger, Levinas, and Sartre pursue their analyses of disabling affect in the name of ontology. 'Being,' Sartre claims, 'will be disclosed to us by some kind of immediate access — boredom, nausea, etc., and ontology will be the description of the phenomenon of being as it manifests itself; that is, without intermediary.' Such

19   Martin Heidegger, *Being and Time*, trans. by John Macquarrie and Edward Robinson (Oxford: Blackwell, 1962), pp. 228–35.
20   Levinas, *De l'évasion* (Montpellier: Fata Morgana, 1982); *De l'existence*, pp. 41–52.
21   Sartre, *Transcendence of the Ego*, pp. 62–68; *Sketch*, pp. 66–91.
22   Sartre, *Sketch*, p. 76.
23   Sartre, *Nausea*, p. 183.
24   Maurice Blanchot, 'The Novels of Sartre', in *The Work of Fire*, trans. by Charlotte Mandell (Stanford, CA: Stanford University Press, 1995), 191–207 (p. 196). Blanchot attributes the remark to Sartre himself.
25   Merleau-Ponty's understanding both of the sedimentations the world leaves in consciousness, and of the sedimentations which consciousness leaves in the world, would require an essay to itself. For a preliminary analysis of the trope, see Jerry H. Gill, *Merleau-Ponty and Metaphor* (Atlantic Highlands, NJ: Humanities Press, 1991), p. 25.

disclosures, he goes on, are what Heidegger would call a 'surpassing towards the ontological'. Anxiety, fatigue, and the rest are where the world most bluntly makes itself felt to consciousness. And yet these feelings have a nasty habit of disclosing under analysis a condition a long way short of universal. Viscosity, for example, which in Sartre's account starts off as the world's ontological expression, as the 'agony of water', soon develops into something rather more particular. 'The honey which slides off my spoon on to the honey contained in the jar first sculptures the surface by fastening itself on it in relief, and its fusion with the whole is presented as a gradual sinking, a collapse which appears at once as a *deflation* [...] and as *display* — like the flattening out of the full breasts of a woman who is lying on her back.' Viscosity, as Sartre imagines it, is gendered: the product of the way in which a man might look at a woman. Viscosity, he continues, is 'a soft, yielding action, a moist and feminine sucking': 'it lives obscurely under my fingers, and I sense it like a dizziness'. Significantly, and no doubt in recognition of the tendency of his own argument, Sartre concludes his analysis of viscosity and the nausea it provokes with an acknowledgement that being is no longer the issue. 'Ontology abandons us here; it has merely enabled us to determine the ultimate ends of human reality, its fundamental possibilities, and the value which haunts it.'[26] Sartre's surpassing *towards* ontology has become, whether he wanted it to or not, a surpassing *of* ontology, a surpassing towards culture. It is in the failure of the ontological project — in the work which it makes possible and indeed necessary, but which it cannot itself complete — that cultural phenomenology (a phenomenological description of culture rather than of being) might find its *point d'appui*.[27] To define that opportunity, I turn now from Sartre to Frantz Fanon, who found himself unable to do without the ontological project, and unable to do anything with it.

Encounters

If a single term could be said to anchor Heidegger's discussion of *Mitsein* (Being-with), in *Being and Time*, it is probably *begegnen*: to meet, to encounter. And yet it is not at all clear that *Mitsein*, in his understanding of it, requires anything it would be appropriate to describe as an encounter with the Other: with that which is not the Same, not the Self. The empirical presence or absence of others may matter to us as individuals, Heidegger argues, but it is ontologically meaningless.[28] Thus, the priority of the Same (of *Dasein*'s relation to Being) remains unchallenged, despite all those rousing skirmishes with the alien. This ontological confirmation of the principle of identity has long been regarded as existentialism's chief deficiency. When Levinas took Heidegger on, in *Time and the Other* (1947), he did so by imagining death as that which destroys solitude, as an event 'made of alterity'.[29] But

26   Sartre, *Being and Nothingness*, pp. xxiv–xxv, 607–09, 615.
27   Theodor Adorno spoke of 'the evolution of phenomenology, which once was animated by the need for contents and became an invocation of being, a repudiation of any content as unclean': *Negative Dialectics*, trans. by E. B. Ashton (London: Routledge, 1973), p. 7. On the inception of a 'cultural phenomenology', see the Introduction to this book.
28   Heidegger, *Being and Nothingness*, pp. 153–68.
29   Levinas, *Time and the Other*, trans. by Richard A. Cohen (Pittsburgh, PA: Duquesne University

existential phenomenology could also be put to a different kind of test. What, at a particular time in a particular place, might the empirical presence or absence of a particular Other actually amount to?

One empirical encounter which took place right under phenomenology's nose was that recorded by Frantz Fanon, in Chapter 5 of *Black Skin, White Masks* (1952). It has recently become an important focus for postcolonial theory, most notably in Homi Bhabha's *The Location of Culture* (1994), and in *The Fact of Blackness*, the proceedings of a conference held at the Institute of Contemporary Arts in London in 1995.[30] 'Why Fanon?' Stuart Hall asks. 'Why, after so many years of relative neglect, is his name once again beginning to excite such intense intellectual debate and controversy? [...] And why is it around the text *Black Skin, White Masks* that the renewed "search for Fanon" is being conducted?'[31] The answer to those pertinent questions is not, and will never be, 'a renewed "search for Sartre"'. And yet Sartre is in there somewhere, because he is everywhere in *Black Skin, White Masks*, as inspiration and antagonist.[32] In Martinique, Hall points out, to be against colonialism was to be '*for* French Republican ideology, with its rallying cry of liberty, equality and fraternity'. Fanon may have removed himself from all that, but he did not necessarily leave it behind.[33] The part cultural phenomenology can play in this debate is to clarify what poststructuralism has obscured: the specificity of the terms Fanon drew from Sartre.

According to Fanon, the black person's desire is a detour around the obstacle placed in its path by a white racism which systematically denies or misrecognizes it. To define that detour, he imagines, as primal scene and everyday occurrence, an encounter between a white child and a black man (himself). The encounter has three moments. The first moment seems to take place on the street, or perhaps in a railway station.

> 'Look, a Negro!' It was an external stimulus that flicked over me as I passed by. I made a tight smile.
> 'Look, a Negro!' It was true. It amused me.
> 'Look, a Negro!' The circle was drawing a bit tighter. I made no secret of my amusement.
> 'Mama, see the Negro! I'm frightened!' Frightened! Now they were beginning to be afraid of me. I made up my mind to laugh myself to tears, but laughter had become impossible.

The reduction to 'Negro' obliterates what Fanon terms the black man's 'corporeal

Press, 1987), p. 74.

30   Homi Bhabha, *The Location of Culture* (London: Routledge, 1994); *The Fact of Blackness: Frantz Fanon and Visual Representation*, ed. by Alan Read (London: Institute of Contemporary Arts, 1996). 'The Fact of Blackness' is the title of Chapter 5 of *Black Skin, White Masks*: or rather, it is a somewhat skimped translation of the title Fanon gave his chapter, 'L'expérience vécue du Noir'. For an illuminating account of the implications of the original terms, see Ronald A. T. Judy, 'Fanon's Body of Black Experience', in *Fanon: A Critical Reader*, ed. by Lewis R. Gordon, T. Denean Sharpely-Whiting, and Renee T. White (Oxford: Blackwell, 1996), pp. 53–73.

31   Stuart Hall, 'The After-Life of Frantz Fanon', in *The Fact of Blackness*, pp. 14–31 (p. 14).

32   Sonia Kruks, 'Fanon, Sartre, and Identity Politics', in *Fanon: A Critical Reader*, pp. 122–33.

33   Hall, 'After-Life', p. 31.

schema', replacing it with an 'epidermal schema', a black skin upon which the outline of racist stereotype has been inscribed. The description's second moment concerns what happened to him after he found that he could no longer laugh himself to tears at racism's absurdity. It turns on a feeling of sickness which has something (but not everything) to do with the self-division in and around stereotype.

> In the train I was given not one but two, three places. I had already stopped being amused. It was not that I was finding febrile coordinates in the world. I existed triply: I occupied space. I moved toward the other ... and the evanescent other, hostile but not opaque, transparent, not there, disappeared. Nausea ...

The third moment involves a return to consciousness, a partial recovery.

> On that day, completely dislocated, unable to be abroad with the other, the white man, who unmercifully imprisoned me, I took myself far off from my own presence, far indeed, and made myself an object. What else could it be for me but an amputation, an excision, a hemorrhage that spattered my whole body with black blood? But I did not want this revision, this thematization.[34]

In this third moment, the emphasis shifts from (banal) nausea to (dramatic) imprisonment and injury, and then, tentatively, to possible resistance. Fanon has removed himself from nausea, but he has not, as the rest of the chapter demonstrates, left it behind.

One way to make sense of Fanon's colonial encounter would be to describe its first and third moments as a reflection on the extraordinary pages in *Being and Nothingness* which demonstrate how the Other's gaze at once enables and disables identity. Reading these pages, Fanon must surely have been struck by the violence Sartre routinely attributes to that gaze. The Other's look solidifies and alienates, decentralizes and decomposes, strips bare and destroys. The Other, equipped in Sartre's imagining of it with gun and torch, 'comes searching for me so as to constitute me at a certain distance from him'; the Self constituted at that distance is a soldier on the battlefield, stalked by those he stalks, or fleeing in panic.[35] Who'd be a Self? But there is, of course, a large difference, on which Fanon's analysis turns. In the colonial encounter the white person's gaze disables without enabling. It takes away the black person's individualizing corporeal schema (his or her being), and produces in return a reductive stereotype. 'The black man,' Fanon memorably remarks, 'has no ontological resistance in the eyes of the white man.'[36] Fanon thus re-reads Sartre, whose discussion of the gaze is itself a re-reading of Hegel's discussion of the dialectic of master and slave. Stuart Hall has suggested that Fanon's dialogue is with Hegel (or at least Kojève's Hegel) rather than with Sartre, and that his appropriation of the master/slave trope informs the whole argument of *Black Skin, White Masks*, in ways which are not necessarily to its advantage. [37] I

---

34   Frantz Fanon, *Black Skin, White Masks*, trans. by Charles Lam Markmann (New York: Grove Weidenfeld, 1967), pp. 111–12.
35   Sartre, *Being and Nothingness*, pp. 252–302. It is worth noting that Sartre also uses the metaphor of haemorrhage, though in relation to the world rather than the Self (pp. 257, 261).
36   Fanon, *Black Skin, White Masks*, p. 110.
37   Hall, 'After-Life', pp. 29–30.

think that Hall is right about this, but that something else of Sartre remained, for Fanon, all the same, something else apart from a vividly re-worked Hegelianism. Fanon's understanding of the real violence inflicted in the colonial encounter at once refutes and reproduces Sartre's understanding of the ghostly violence inflicted in the ontological encounter.

Why Fanon? Poststructuralism's answer is that Fanon combines an analysis of racial and cultural violence with an analysis of 'subject-formation'.[38] As Homi Bhabha has observed, Fanon sought to integrate a Hegelian-Marxist dialectic and a phenomenological affirmation of Self and Other into a psychoanalytic understanding of the ambivalence of the Unconscious. Bhabha's Fanon is the Fanon who refracts alienation through psychoanalysis, the Fanon who responds to the pressure of racism on the ambivalence of psychic identification with an 'agonizing performance of self-images'. For Bhabha, the colonial encounter is thick with relativity, and colonial identity a 'perverse palimpsest': a hybrid construction, an intricate layering of narcissism and paranoia.[39] There, nothing at all transcends the consciousness it appears to, revealing itself as it is. By this account, Fanon's writing theorizes the 'knowledge of the practice of action': the state (the temporality) of the day-to-day struggle for freedom. Its address is not so much to the 'bi-polar antagonism' between white person and black person as to the 'heterogeneous, differential conditions' which constitute the 'liminal "subject" or body of the colonized people in the performative act of insurgency'.[40] There is much to be said, as I shall show, for Bhabha's exact focus on liminality and performance. But his analysis will always have a problem with nausea, because nausea introduces a 'bi-polar antagonism' into the supposedly heterogeneous and differential temporality of the day-to-day struggle for freedom.

How much of a problem becomes apparent in Bhabha's only extended description of the primal scene's second (nauseous) moment. I quote his quotation from *Black Skin, White Masks* in full, because it is itself a poststructuralist artefact.

> When it undergoes resistance from the other, self-consciousness undergoes the experience of desire ... As soon as I desire I ask to be considered. I am not merely here and now, sealed into thingness. I am for somewhere else and for something else. I demand that notice be taken of my negating activity in so far as I pursue something other than life ...
>
> I occupied space. I moved towards the other ... and the evanescent other, hostile, but not opaque, transparent, not there, disappeared. Nausea.[41]

According to Bhabha, it is from the 'overwhelming emptiness' of nausea that Fanon deduces the black person's demand for and the white person's unconscious disavowal of the 'negating, splitting moment of desire'. Fanon's nausea, in short, is no more and no less than a commentary on desire and its suppression. Bhabha goes to extraordinary lengths to deny the primacy of nausea. The two paragraphs in the

38   Henry Louis Gates, 'Critical Fanonism', *Critical Inquiry*, 17 (1991), 457–70 (p. 458).
39   Bhabha, 'Interrogating Identity', in *The Location of Culture*, pp. 40–65 (pp. 41–46).
40   Bhabha, 'Day by Day ... With Frantz Fanon', in *The Fact of Blackness*, pp. 187–205 (pp. 188–89).
41   I give the passage as Bhabha has it: 'Interrogating Identity', p. 51. His only reference is to p. 112 of *Black Skin, White Masks*; in fact, the first paragraph of his quotation derives from p. 218.

quotation above are in fact from separate chapters in *Black Skin, White Masks*. By fusing them, without any acknowledgement that he has done so, Bhabha makes it appear that Fanon's invocation of nausea arises directly out of an invocation of desire. Furthermore, the invocation of desire, which occurs in a later section on 'The Negro and Hegel', in Chapter 7, is Hegelian through and through; in transferring it, Bhabha has stripped its Hegelianism from it by silent elision.[42] And the ellipses which enable him to graft one passage onto another have been introduced at the expense of Fanon's own ellipsis: the ellipsis which endows the concept on which the argument turns with a certain additional significance. 'Nausea ...'

It seems to me that we should understand Fanon's nausea not as the failure or thwarting of desire, but as an emotion in its own right. Fanon does not move towards the Other in the hope that his desire will be acknowledged, and that the Other will acknowledge his or her desire for him. Nausea propels him forward into the Other. The distance between subject and object collapses. According to Sartre, an emotion like horror arises 'when the world of the utilizable vanishes abruptly'.[43] Fanon had thought to use his laughter to turn the tables on the white man, but he cannot. Instead, nausea brings him, as it brought Roquentin, right up against the Other, who has thus come too close to see, too close to imitate, too close to mock. Bhabha's analysis, founded on notions of liminality and performance, cannot conceive that closeness. What has happened, I think, in this abrupt disappearance of the white man's utilizable physiognomy, is that ontology has finally begun, for Fanon; it has begun, as it began for Roquentin, in nausea. Fanon has been thrust forward by nausea into physiognomy's obverse, which is not relative, but relative-absolute, transcending the consciousness to which it appears. In the colonial encounter, he gets an inaugural taste of facticity, and the 'form' of his behaviour fills at once with something opaque and weighty. He has become a *nauséaste*. End of performance (for the moment).

Or perhaps for ever. According to Sartre, a feeling like horror or nausea only arises 'against the background of a complete alteration of the world'. In horror or nausea, an 'overwhelming and definitive quality' of the horrible or the nauseous 'makes its appearance'.[44] It is Fanon's nausea which sticks to him, which forms a formless (an informal) identity, in the spatter of black blood. The appearance of the relative-absolute in nausea, against the background of the world's complete transformation, is the (un)making of him. And yet Fanon is not Roquentin, because his inaugural taste of facticity enfolds an inaugural taste of racism. Nausea, which could happen anywhere to anyone, happened to *him* in the colonial encounter. For him, the taste of facticity is also inescapably a taste of stereotype ('Look, a Negro!'). For him, ontological alienation is at the same time a cultural alienation provoked by an overwhelming and definitive quality of the white person's hatred for the black person. In the colonial encounter, real violence thus enacts and is enacted by ghostly

---

42   Thus, for example, Bhabha cuts the following sentence off at the semi-colon. 'I demand that notice be taken of my negating activity in so far as I pursue something other than life; in so far as I do battle for the creation of a human world — that is, of a world of reciprocal recognitions.'
43   Sartre, *Sketch*, pp. 90–91.
44   Ibid., pp. 88, 82.

violence. It is the reproduction of one kind of sickness by another, as much as the difference remaining between them, which makes possible a new knowledge of the practice of action. Nausea, which could happen any time in any place, at random, *had* to happen when and where it did, to Fanon, because it is colonialism's necessity. It defines that which produced it: the colonial encounter.

If we take Fanon's nausea seriously, as a reflection on and with Sartre, then we must acknowledge that the encounter is, in its second moment at least, ontological. Human experience includes among its possibilities, indeed among its probabilities, an encounter with the relative-absolute, a taste of facticity. Analysis of the taste of facticity is one occasion when it does make sense to speak of 'human experience'. And yet, as we have seen, Fanon's colonial encounter is a surpassing of as well as a surpassing towards ontology. For its third moment acknowledges dialectically that the relative-absolute confronted during the course of the encounter as a whole is a relative relative-absolute, mediated by racism: a disclosure of cultural necessity rather than of chance. Fanon rejects the 'application' of Sartre's ontology to black experience, 'because the white man is not only the Other, but also the master, whether real or imaginary'. But he only does so at the very end of the chapter containing his description of the colonial encounter, and then in a footnote. In the description itself, nausea stands out, as a turn of the narrative, and as a concept trailing its own ellipsis. In the remarkable pages which follow the description, nausea again stands out; rather, it doubles. There is the ontological nausea provoked in the street and in the train by the vanishing of the utilizable, and there is the cultural nausea provoked in retrospection by the thought of the narrowness and triviality ascribed to black experience by the white gaze: *and both persist*. The spatter of black blood does not mark the supersession of ontology by (cultural) politics, of idealism by disillusionment. It is rather the point at which the corporeal schema and the epidermal schema cross bindingly over each other without touching: the surpassing of ontology remains a surpassing towards ontology. Fanon says that, reflecting on his primal scene and everyday occurrence, he came reluctantly to accept on the 'level of the intellect' an identity constructed out of bits and pieces of relative otherness: tom-toms, cannibalism, and the rest. 'But I rejected all immunization of the emotions. I wanted to be a man, nothing but a man.'[45] We should not re-immunize those emotions by filtering them through poststructuralism.

Colonial Facts and Fantasies

Ambivalence is the key term in Bhabha's theory of the colonial encounter. He finds it, for example, in the stereotype, that racist 'marking of the subject' which Fanon encountered not only on the street, but in children's fiction, where white angels routinely slay black demons. Bhabha argues that the stereotype is, despite

---

45   Fanon, *Black Skin, White Masks*, pp. 138, 112–13. It is only fair to Bhabha to point out that he does draw attention, in 'Day by Day ...', to the 'nauseous' repetition of Fanon's colonial encounter throughout *Black Skin, White Masks* (p. 201); but his unwillingness or inability to theorise nausea prevents him from grasping exactly what is at stake in the repetition.

appearances, an uncertain expression of power, at once overweening and anxious, at once definitive and endlessly repeated.[46] Thus the ambivalence of colonial practice and discourse may under certain circumstances become the weakness around which or against which insurgency gathers. As Robert Young puts it, Bhabha's achievement is to have recast ambivalence in and as an 'enabling form'.[47] There is, however, a problem here, to which Young also draws attention, in that Bhabha relies heavily on Freud for a definition of ambivalence. The problem is that psychoanalysis imports into the study of historical event an understanding of ambivalence not as the catalyst of change, but as an inertial pleasure, a compulsive repetition. At his most Freudian, Bhabha envisages the 'twin figures' of narcissism and paranoia repeating 'furiously' in the 'other scene' of colonial authority. This furious hesitancy is comparable, he argues, to the *fort/da* game described in *Beyond the Pleasure Principle*.[48] The *fort/da* game is in Freudian theory a figure of compulsive repetition: the child plays it because, in his mother's absence, it is all he has, all he can do. By this account, the colonial subject (colonizer or colonized) who agrees to perform thereby also agrees *not* to bring the performance to an abrupt end.

Young resolves the difficulty by arguing that Bhabha's eclecticism is itself a 'teasing mimicry', a sly civility designed, like the sly civilities it expounds, to provoke and disorientate. The ambivalence of colonial discourse might be thought to emerge not at the time of its enunciation, but at the time of its analysis by the present-day historian; there, in the historian's restless eclecticism, it produces its political effect.[49] Plausible though the argument is, it does not quite meet the whole case. Bhabha may regard history-writing as itself an effect of Orientalism, but he has not relinquished historiographical ambitions. His essay on aspects of the Indian Mutiny, for example, engages quite explicitly with the 'more traditional' arguments of historians like Ranajit Guha and Eric Stokes. Indeed, what emerges from these enquiries is a kind of counter-teleology. If nineteenth-century Orientalism foreshadows and finds its justification in orthodox twentieth-century history-writing, then the experience of its victims and opponents foreshadows and finds its justification in poststructuralism.[50] A counter-teleology which grounds itself in the

46   Bhabha, 'The Other Question: Stereotype, Discrimination and the Discourse of Colonialism', in *The Location of Culture*, pp. 66–84.

47   Robert Young, *White Mythologies: Writing History and the West* (London: Routledge, 1990), p. 147. See also Stephen Slemon, 'The Scramble for Post-Colonialism', in *De-Scribing Empire: Post-Colonialism and Textuality*, ed. by Chris Tiffin and Alan Lawson (London: Routledge, 1994), pp. 15–32 (pp. 23–24).

48   Bhabha, 'Of Mimicry and Man: The Ambivalence of Colonial Discourse', in *The Location of Culture*, pp. 85–92 (p. 91); 'The Commitment to Theory', in *The Location of Culture*, pp. 19–39 (p. 25). See also 'The Postcolonial and the Postmodern: The Question of Agency', in *The Location of Culture*, pp. 171–97 (p. 183).

49   Young, *White Mythologies*, pp. 152, 155–56. In *Colonial Desire: Hybridity in Theory, Culture and Race* (London: Routledge, 1995), Young argues that contemporary cultural theory unknowingly repeats the patterns of thought through which culture and race were defined in the nineteenth century.

50   Bhabha, 'By Bread Alone: Signs of Violence in the Mid-Nineteenth Century', in *The Location of Culture*, pp. 198–211 (p. 207); 'The Postcolonial', p. 173. The 'more traditional' arguments are: Ranajit Guha, *Elementary Aspects of Peasant Insurgency* (Delhi: Oxford University Press, 1983); and

analysis of nineteenth-century governmental discourses can and should be held to account for the methods it brings to bear on them.

One of the founding texts of Bhabha's counter-teleology is a 'negotiation' which took place under a tree outside Delhi, in May 1817. Anund Messeeh, an Indian catechist, a 'mimic man' trained by British missionaries to disseminate the Christian faith, came across a group of converts earnestly debating the wisdom of the Gospels.

> 'These books,' said Anund, 'teach the religion of the European Sahibs. It is THEIR book; and they printed it in our language, for our use.' 'Ah! no,' replied the stranger, 'that cannot be, for they eat flesh.' — 'Jesus Christ,' said Anund, 'teaches that it does not signify what a man eats or drinks. EATING is nothing before God. *Not that which entereth into a man's mouth defileth him, but that which cometh out of the mouth, this defileth a man*: for vile things come forth from the heart. *Out of the heart proceed evil thoughts, murders, adulteries, fornications, thefts; and these are the things that defile.*'[51]

The ambivalence at issue here is the ambivalence introduced by translation. Who exactly do these Christian thoughts translated into Hindustani belong to? Is it decisive that the Gospels (Matthew 15. 1–20) elevate the claims of innate moral sense above the claims of culturally specific dietary laws? And for whom might it be decisive? In that hesitation of authority over the text, over the validity and scope of the Western sign, misreading flourishes; and, around it, perhaps, resistance. Anund Messeeh's black-skinned interlocutors put on and take off their white masks at will, forcing him, it may be, to acknowledge through their playful performance his own liminality.

Bhabha's analysis skilfully teases out the subversiveness of the civility these less than whole-hearted converts to Christianity deploy in their negotiations with Anund Messeeh. They tell Anund that they propose to meet once a year for the purposes of religious debate. Next time, they add, they may even come to Meerut, where there is a Christian padre, to be baptized. However, while they accept Christian doctrine, they draw the line at certain aspects of Christian ritual. 'We are willing to be baptized, but we will never take the Sacrament. To all the other customs of Christians we are willing to conform, but not to the Sacrament, because the Europeans eat cow's flesh, and this will never do for us.'[52] It is, indeed, as Bhabha establishes, a wonderfully ambivalent performance: pious enough to keep

---

Eric Stokes, 'The Military Dimension: The Sepoy Rebels', in *The Peasant Armed: The Indian Revolt of 1857*, ed. by C. A. Bayly (Oxford: Clarendon Press, 1986), pp. 49–99.

51   The story is told in a report, under the general heading of 'Foreign Intelligence', entitled 'Visit of Anund Messeeh; and his Discovery of an extraordinary Body of Native Christians', in the London *Missionary Register*, 6 (1818), 17–20 (p. 18): emphasis in original. The report incorporates several documents: a letter from a Mr Fisher to a Mr Thomason, dated 6 May 1817, describing the scene under the tree outside Delhi; a letter from Anund Messeeh (not Messeh, as Bhabha has it) to Fisher, dated 12 May 1817, describing follow-up work among the believers, who have now returned to their villages; and a letter from a Lieutenant Macdonald to Thomason, dated 19 July 1817, validating Anund Messeeh's reports. Bhabha's lengthy quotation from the *Register* ('Signs Taken for Wonders', in *The Location of Culture*, pp. 102–22 (pp. 102–04)) is another poststructuralist artefact: it silently conflates Fisher's letter with Anund Messeeh's, Western voice with Eastern.

52   'Visit of Anund Messeeh', p. 19.

the missionaries happy, though some way short of a gratifying spiritual rebirth. Never quite sure that this almost-conversion had ever happened, the *Missionary Register* sought to verify it over and over again, by a compulsive repetition of testimony. And yet the threat posed explicitly to the Christian faith and implicitly to British rule in India lies less in the performance of civility than in the blunt dismissal of the Sacrament. Eating cow's flesh provokes nausea, in these people. That nausea has in effect destroyed the white person's ontological resistance to the black person's gaze. It has destroyed the white person's claim to a being and a spiritual wisdom which transcend cultural difference. Anund Messeeh's experiences would surely have indicated to anyone who thought about them that nausea was a more likely catalyst of rebellion than ambivalence.

Rebellion did come, of course, in 1857. Bhabha's boldest contribution to the history of British India is to identify rumour as the 'uncontrolled, yet strategic affect' of the political revolt once known as the 'Indian Mutiny'.[53] It was rumour's inherent ambivalence, Bhabha argues, the fact that it can neither be proved nor disproved, which, in 1857, spread a fatal uncertainty among the military and civilian authorities, and made insurgents out of sepoys.

The rumour in question concerned the passage of a chapati-shaped token from village to village, immediately after the introduction into the Native Infantries of the Enfield rifle and its notorious greased cartridge. Bhabha's text is the account of the episode in the first volume of Sir John Kaye's *History of the Indian Mutiny* (1864). 'Some saw in it much meaning,' Kaye concludes, after surveying the various views expressed at the time, 'some saw none. Time has thrown no new light upon it. Opinions still differ.'[54] For Bhabha, this enduring 'indeterminacy' represents a loss of colonial authority, and a 'new, hybrid space' in which rebellion had suddenly become conceivable, and in which it can be re-conceived more than a hundred years later. To put it another way: rhetorical effect (indeterminacy) produced, and still produces, political affect (panic, rebelliousness). According to Kaye, the chapati was a common symbol: its transmission from one village to the next was intended to carry off disease. But chapatis transmitted at a time of unrest shed their iconic status. Now they could mean anything. Rumour takes hold of them. 'It is "panic" that speaks in the temporal caesura between symbol and sign,' Bhabha argues, 'politicizing the narrative; the agency of politics obscurely contained in the contagion of chapati flour, or in the more revealing castratory fantasies of the former governor-general Ellenborough "to emasculate all the mutineers and to call Delhi Eunuchabad".'[55] Bhabha's excavation of the temporal caesura between symbol and sign is acute and provocative. But he has to strain to demonstrate its political consequences. Of the two examples he gives of the 'agency of politics', only one, the belief that the British planned to contaminate flour supplies with bone-dust, could be said to have had anything to do with the rumours surrounding

53   Bhabha, 'By Bread Alone', p. 199.
54   Sir John Kaye, *History of the Indian Mutiny*, ed. and completed by Colonel Malleson, 6 volumes (London: W. H. Allen, 1888–89), I, 420.
55   Bhabha, 'By Bread Alone', pp. 202, 203–04.

the chapatis. Ellenborough's threat was issued much later, in the autumn of 1857, and in the confident knowledge that the mutinous regiments surrounded in Delhi were on the point of surrendering. It is, indeed, the 'more revealing' example. What it reveals, however, is the efficacy not of ambivalence, but of hatred, of lust for revenge, of nausea.

The framing of Kaye's description of the chapati episode makes it clear that he, too, regarded hatred and nausea, not indeterminacies of meaning, as the catalyst of rebellion. In his account, the circulating chapatis are one indication among many of a widespread anxiety about British plots to defile the people. The focus of that anxiety was the introduction in native regiments of cartridges greased with animal fat. There was nothing in the least bit indeterminate about these cartridges, one end of which had to be bitten off by the rifleman. 'The contamination,' Kaye points out, 'was to be brought to his very lips; it was not merely to be touched, it was to be eaten and absorbed into his very body.' Little scope, here, for ambivalence, for plural meaning, for sly civility. 'It needed no ingenious gloss to make the full force of the thing itself patent to the multitude. It was not a suggestion, an inference, a probability; but a demonstrative fact, so complete in its naked truth, that no exaggeration could have helped it.' Kaye compares the outcry about greased cartridges to an outcry about leather headdresses in Southern India fifty years before. The cartridges, he concludes, were 'incomparably more offensive' to both Hindus and Muslims, 'more insulting, more appalling, more disgusting'. So offensive, in fact, that they proved the catalyst for an unprecedented outbreak of rancorous political and religious animosities.[56] That outbreak, provoked by disgust at British plots to defile the people, was surely the context for the rumours surrounding the chapatis. Political affect is to be found, not in the rumours, but in the disgust. Revulsion produces revolt. What transforms the sepoy into an insurgent is nausea rather than masquerade.

Dogs and Mad Englishmen: Leonard Woolf in Ceylon

By Bhabha's account, ambivalence enables the colonized by disabling the colonizer. The 'twin figures' of narcissism and paranoia repeating furiously in the other scene of colonial authority undo that authority by the ambivalence they engender in colonizer and colonized alike. I want now to consider, as a final example of the ways in which cultural phenomenology might deepen and extend the study of colonial practice and discourse in its historical contexts, some observations by a notoriously ambivalent colonizer, Leonard Woolf.

Woolf was appointed to the Colonial Civil Service in Ceylon (Sri Lanka) in October 1903, when he was twenty-three years old. He arrived in Ceylon in January 1904, and lasted out the full seven-year tour of duty, returning to England

---

56   Kaye, *History of the Indian Mutiny*, pp. 360–62. Kaye's history was completed by Malleson, whose summary of the incident confirms his emphasis. 'In a greater degree the annexation of Oudh and the measures which followed that annexation; in a lesser degree the actual employment of animal fat in the composition of the cartridges, constituted ample grounds for the distrust evinced by the Sipahis' (*History*, III, 236).

on leave in May 1911. Rather than resume his career in Ceylon, he married Virginia Stephen, in August 1912, thus transferring himself from the history of empire to the history of literature, where he has remained ever since. Woolf was an outstanding civil servant. Starting as a cadet, in Jaffna, in the north of the island, he soon demonstrated a passion for management and a relish for responsibility which ensured rapid promotion. He ended his years in Ceylon as Assistant Government Agent in Hambantota, in the south of the island, where he was in sole charge of a district of 1000 square miles with a population of 100,000. Because work was the only thing in his life, because he was so good at it, it became his identity. The formation of that identity is reasonably well documented, in the official diary Woolf kept in Hambantota, in letters to friends at home, and in autobiographical writings.[57]

In the first volume of his autobiography, Woolf presents the years in Ceylon as a coming of age, and as a coming of awareness about the nature and problems of imperialism. He had taken the post, he recalls, 'without any thought about its political aspect'. The man who arrived in Colombo, the capital of Ceylon, in January 1905, was a 'very innocent, unconscious imperialist'. The man who left, in May 1911, knew his own mind. The autobiography turns those years into a 'moral tale' about 'the absurdity of a people of one civilization and mode of life trying to impose its rule upon an entirely different civilization and mode of life'.[58] What brought about Woolf's change of heart? Where did this critique of colonialism *come from*?

From ambivalence, one might suppose, from a hesitation between desire and contempt, between narcissism and paranoia. After his arrival in Ceylon, Woolf developed an 'uneasily ambivalent' attitude to British rule, exaggerating his 'stern Sahib attitude' in order to conceal his increasing dislike of the 'whole system' from himself. He became 'more and more ambivalent, politically schizophrenic, an anti-imperialist who enjoyed the fleshpots of imperialism'.[59] However, there is no evidence that this political schizophrenia proved in any way decisive. It is clear from both the public and the private record that the stern Sahib attitude Woolf developed as Assistant Government Agent in Hambantota, towards the end of his time in Ceylon, saw off his own unease. There, he had no qualms about implementing British colonial policy. Ambivalence alone did not bring about his change of heart. For him, colonialism was both a masquerade and an encounter with facticity.

The two things Woolf took with him from England to help him rule the Empire were an edition of the complete works of Voltaire, in ninety volumes, and a fox-terrier called Charles. The 'moral tale' of his years in Ceylon is a tale about the

---

57   Since 1808, Government Agents in Ceylon had been required to keep a daily record of their activities. Woolf published the record he kept in Hambantota as *Diaries in Ceylon, 1908–1911: Records of a Colonial Administrator* (London: Hogarth Press, 1963). The letters he wrote at the time, many of them to Lytton Strachey, his closest friend, have been collected in *Letters*, ed. by Frederic Spotts (London: Bloomsbury, 1990). *Growing: An Autobiography of the Years 1904–1911* (London: Hogarth Press, 1961) is of course a reconstruction after the event; but it is based to a large extent on letters written at the time, to Strachey and others.
58   Woolf, *Growing*, pp. 25, 193.
59   Ibid., pp. 157, 159.

exercise of reason, in the classic Enlightenment manner, and a tale about a dog. The dog may well have been the more important factor in his critique of colonialism.

On their first day in Colombo, outside the Grand Oriental Hotel, Charles bounded up to a Sinhalese man standing on pavement, 'and committed a nuisance against his clean white cloth as though it were a London lamp-post': nobody seemed to mind very much. Shortly afterwards, overcome by heat and excitement, Charles was violently sick in the middle of the hotel courtyard. 'Three or four crows immediately flew down and surrounded him, eating the vomit as it came out of his mouth.'[60] Once again, nobody seemed to mind very much; a waiter looked on impassively. Woolf's nausea, like the nausea of the sepoy made to bite off the end of a greased cartridge, is mediated by the recognition that members of another race and culture do not share it, or even acknowledge it. Their failure to do so (their lack of revulsion) dissolves their ontological resistance. It is in itself revolting, because it shows them to be in their being merely an effect of custom and habit. They do not know what facticity is. Woolf's nausea arises in the crossing-over of the corporeal schema to which the Self still aspires, in the name of all races and cultures, and the epidermal schema which is the only language the Other appears to understand. Of course, one could argue that he has mistaken politeness, a reluctance to embarrass or offend the young Sahib, for indifference. Maybe the waiter and the man on the pavement were just being slyly civil, in the ways Bhabha has taught us to recognize. But there can be little doubt that Woolf's response to this primal scene and everyday occurrence was Sartrean. Charles's misadventures had persuaded him that nausea was the (colonial) world's 'texture'.[61]

Two further incidents, which took place while Woolf was in Jaffna, made him 'fully aware' for the first time of his position as a 'ruler of subject peoples'; he began to doubt whether he wanted 'to rule other people, to be an imperialist and proconsul'.[62] In each case, a complaint was laid against him by the Jaffna Tamil Association, and the Government Agent asked him to explain himself.

One complaint was that Woolf had struck a prominent Jaffna lawyer with his whip, as a gesture of contempt. Woolf managed to prove, to his own and his boss's satisfaction, that he had simply pointed something out to a colleague, and in doing so inadvertently touched the lawyer. In this case, the theatricality with which he performed his stern Sahib attitude, the grandness of his gesture, created the scope for misunderstanding. The lawyer, he concluded, 'was in the right, not right in believing that I would and had hit him in the face, but right in feeling that my sitting on a horse arrogantly in the main street of their town was as good as a slap in the face.'[63] This is the colonial encounter as Bhabha understands it: the mutual misrecognition of divided or heterogeneous identities.

However, if one incident turns on the meaning imputed to a gesture (on paranoia), the other turns on a nuisance (on nausea). Woolf had posted a notice in the veranda

60   Ibid., p. 22.
61   Woolf, *Sketch*, p. 82.
62   Woolf, *Growing*, p. 111.
63   Ibid., p. 114.

of government offices in Jaffna which forbade spitting. When one of the clerks spat on the veranda, Woolf felt sickened enough to force him to clean up the mess, even though he knew that the man's caste prohibited menial labour.[64] In this case, there was no room at all for ambivalence. These are nauseas produced within and perhaps by one of colonialism's defining institutions. Woolf sickens because spittle on the veranda is to him matter decisively out of place; this (ontological) taste of facticity is crossed by an equally sickening recognition of cultural difference, in the knowledge that spittle on verandas does not appear to trouble his Ceylonese subordinates at all. By contrast, what sticks in the clerk's throat is both the defilement produced by menial labour and his superior's failure to acknowledge it as a defilement. Again, ontology and culture cross over. In this crossing over, culture qualifies ontology's universalism, by obliging us to ask for whom the matter at issue is out of place, while ontology lends its intimacy with the relative-absolute to the knowledge of the practice of action in the colonial encounter. It is the crossing over of sicknesses which compels both protagonists to act, as it had once made insurgents of sepoys, in India in 1857. The clerk lodges a formal complaint. Woolf begins to wonder whether he really wants to be a ruler of 'subject peoples'.

Particulars

This essay has been written in the belief that the only way to describe cultural phenomenology is to do it. But it should be possible to draw one or two preliminary conclusions even from this small amount of doing.

Discussing the history of twentieth-century avant-gardes, Hal Foster has suggested that we need to *re*-connect with 'lost' practices in order to *dis*-connect from a current practice felt to be in some way 'misguided' or 'oppressive'. 'The first move (*re*) is temporal, made in order, in a second, spatial move (*dis*), to open a new site for work.'[65] To reconnect with the lost practice of existential phenomenology is to disconnect from a poststructuralism which, if not exactly oppressive, has perhaps come to be taken too much for granted (not least by Foster himself). And the reconnections are unlikely to stop at whatever happened in Paris in the 1930s. Kierkegaard's reading of Hegel, for example, is not without interest from this point of view.[66] And why stop at post-Kantian philosophy? The first cultural phenomenologist was surely Michel de Montaigne.[67]

Paris in the 1930s is thus not an origin, or a definitive emergence. It was the place and time at which certain questions came to be posed: about the uses of dialectic, about the relative-absolute, about presence and depresentation. We should approach the writers of that place and time in terms which are neither exactly their own nor

64   Ibid., pp. 111–12.
65   Hal Foster, *The Return of the Real: The Avant-Garde at the End of the Century* (Cambridge, MA: MIT Press, 1996), p. 3.
66   Gillian Rose, *The Broken Middle: Out of Our Ancient Society* (Oxford: Blackwell, 1992).
67   The first heterologist, Michel de Certeau might say: 'Montaigne's "Of Cannibals": The Savage "I"', in *Heterologies: Discourse on the Other*, trans. by Brian Massumi (Minneapolis: University of Minnesota Press, 1986), pp. 67–79.

exactly those of poststructuralism. A cultural phenomenology derived from that reconnection would be at once a surpassing towards and a surpassing of ontology, either in the direction of ethics,[68] or in the direction of aesthetics,[69] or in the direction of history. The programme of research I have outlined here would have as its object that surpassing towards and of ontology which can be understood to take place in historical event and historical utterance.

There would be something daft about a particularism so avid for particularity that it derived the fall of empires from canine vomit; and there would be something worse than daft about a particularism avid exclusively for the *abject*, and for the mild self-congratulation which abjectness seems to inspire in its devotees. I have chosen to concentrate here on the nauseous because the feeling it provokes can be shown to inform from end to end nineteenth- and twentieth-century British representations of the colonial encounter. What might interest us about nausea is its unfolding in event and utterance at once as random worldliness and as colonialism's bitter necessity: as the point at which particular and universal cross bindingly over each other without touching, or break dialectically apart. One could of course choose to explore in a similar fashion many other feelings in many other contexts. And there is no reason why cultural phenomenology should disavow or apologize for its own externality to other (and perhaps in some ways more ambitious) historicizing projects and methods. Its bottom line could be that the particular is, as matters and materialisms currently stand, a risk well worth taking.

68   As, for example, in the question Levinas asks of Merleau-Ponty, in 'On Intersubjectivity: Notes on Merleau-Ponty', in *Outside the Subject*, trans. by Michael B. Smith (London: Athlone Press, 1993), pp. 96–103 (p. 101): 'In the handshake that phenomenology attempts to understand on the basis of mutual knowledge [...] does not the essential, going beyond knowledge, reside in confidence, devotion and peace (with an element of the gift, going from myself to the other, and a certain indifference toward compensations in reciprocity and thus with ethical gratuitousness), which the handshake initiates and means, instead of being a simple code transmitting information about it?'
69   A direction illuminatingly taken, partly by way of a reading of Gillian Rose, by Isobel Armstrong, in 'Writing for the Broken Middle: The Post-Aesthetic', *Women: A Cultural Review*, 9 (1998), 62–96.

PART II

Narrative Space in Cinema

CHAPTER 13

The Space Beside:
Lateral Exposition, Gender, and
Urban Narrative Space in
D. W. Griffith's Biograph Films

The aim of this essay is to define and explore an episode in the development of the classical continuity system, with regard to what it might have to tell us about the construction of urban narrative space in (early) American cinema, and in particular about the gendering of that construction.

Lateral Exposition

According to the standard account, the classical continuity system — a specific set of guidelines for cutting shots together, whether by scene dissection or by montage — was firmly in place by 1917.[1] The outcome of American cinema's steadily increasing commitment to narrative, from around 1903 onwards, continuity editing made it possible to situate the spectator at the optimum viewpoint in each shot, and to keep that viewpoint on the move as the story developed. The optimum viewpoint is not that from which an action can be seen in its entirety, but that from which it can be understood in its essence. For cinema's 'turn' to narrative was not in any straightforward sense the outcome of an urge to tell stories. It involved, as Thomas Elsaesser and Adam Barker put it, 'the contradictory articulation of a logic of space and time, within the context of a new industrial commodity, the reel of film, itself standing for new experiences of spectatorship'.[2] Classical Hollywood cinema is, as David Bordwell puts it, 'a cinema of narrative *integration*, which absorbs cinematic techniques and engaging moments into a self-sufficient world unified across time and space.'[3]

1   David Bordwell, Janet Staiger, and Kristin Thompson, *The Classical Hollywood Cinema: Film Style & Modes of Production to 1960* (London: Routledge, 1985).
2   Thomas Elsaesser and Adam Barker, 'Introduction' to 'The Continuity System', Part 3 of *Early Cinema: Space, Frame, Narrative*, ed. by Thomas Elsaesser (London: BFI Publishing, 1990), pp. 293–317 (p. 293). On the transition to story films in American cinema, see Charles Musser, *The Emergence of Cinema: The American Screen to 1907* (Berkeley: University of California Press, 1990), pp. 337–69.
3   David Bordwell, *On the History of Film Style* (Cambridge, MA: Harvard University Press, 1997), p. 127.

One problem confronting a cinema bent on narrative integration, perhaps *the* problem, was how most effectively to co-ordinate the multiple spaces required by stories of any degree of complexity. 'There are two basic patterns,' as Kristin Thompson puts it, 'for editing multiple spaces together: joining contiguous spaces and cross-cutting (i.e. joining non-contiguous spaces).' From 1903 onwards, various methods were developed to demonstrate to the viewer that the spaces understood to be contiguous were indeed so: the movement of an identifiable character or object from one to another; direction matching, which ensures the intelligibility of such movement from the position of the viewer; and, from around 1909, eyeline matches, which cut from a character looking to what that look might encompass, though not from her or his point of view. The purpose of these methods was of course to establish the diegetic (if not actual) homogeneity of the self-sufficient world to which the multiple spaces belong. Cross-cutting, by contrast, moves between simultaneous events in non-contiguous locations.[4] In this case, the implied homogeneity of the film's self-sufficient world derives entirely from narrative structure: the story, and the story alone, will in the fullness of time establish a relation between one space and another.

Promoting film's 'increased narrativity' was, as Charlie Keil observes, the main objective of the 'group style' developed by American film-makers between 1907 and 1913, in the transition from a cinema of attractions to a cinema of narrative integration.[5] The more than 400 films D. W. Griffith made for the Biograph company during this period have most often been regarded as a laboratory for the development and testing of methods or 'patterns' by which actions spread across multiple spaces might be edited together in such a way as to generate and clarify narrative. Cross-cutting, in particular, became with Griffith, as Tom Gunning observes, a 'narrative structure', a means to shape the relations of time and space for various purposes: to create suspense, in races to the rescue; to disclose feeling, as when one person so occupies the thoughts of another that he or she comes into view, is actually 'seen', at the moment of the thought, in a distant place; or, polemically, in essays in social criticism, to establish a contrast between the conditions of wealth and poverty.[6] The pattern thus developed is always in some measure abstract. 'Griffith's cinema,' Elsaesser and Barker note, 'is a kind of orgy of metaphor: everything can be combined with everything else, stand for everything else, rhyme with everything else.' There is nothing in the image that cannot become the basis of an analogy.[7] Thus, for example, the person 'seen', in her or his distant place, becomes a metaphor for what the person seeing feels. Cross-cutting has the power to resolve heterogeneity.

4   Kristin Thompson, 'The Formulation of the Classical Style, 1909–1928', in *Classical Hollywood Cinema*, pp. 157–240 (pp. 203–12). Thompson reserves the term 'parallel editing' for cuts between events which do not occur at the same time. Other historians use the terms 'cross-cutting' and 'parallel editing' interchangeably. For simplicity's sake, I will observe Thompson's distinction here.

5   Charlie Keil, *Early American Cinema in Transition: Story, Style, and Filmmaking, 1907–1913* (Madison: University of Wisconsin Press. 2001), p. 127.

6   Tom Gunning, *D. W. Griffith and the Origins of American Narrative Film: The Early Years at Biograph* (Urbana: University of Illinois Press, 1991), pp. 186–207, 243–49.

7   Elsaesser and Barker, 'Introduction', p. 302.

To put it another way: cross-cutting creates space by the destruction of place. Each narrative space brought into relation with another by cross-cutting has to be understood as a zone. In cross-cut races to the rescue such as *The Lonely Villa* (1909) and *The Lonedale Operator* (1911), assailant and rescuer, each closing in space by space (yard by yard, or mile by mile, it's all the same) on their shared destination, only ever *pass through*, on their way to somewhere else, to where the victim is — or, rather, to where the victim awaits their arrival, since she too occupies a zone rather than a space (an expectancy). More or less the only furnishing of any note in the room where the victim awaits rescue is that which connects one zone to another (the telephone in *The Lonely Villa*), or time present to time future: the clock in *The Fatal Hour* (1908) whose hands will trigger the gun aimed at the female detective when they reach twelve. These are not inhabited environments.

Griffith did not in fact give up all that easily, as cross-cutting required him to, on the implied homogeneity of some of the multiple spaces through or across which he spread the action of his films. He did not always convert an inhabited environment into a zone, place into space. At the beginning of the transitional period, Keil notes, film-makers sometimes 'attempted to retain a sense of spatial wholeness by marking out contiguous spaces within a single set.' They might, for example, split the set and film it so that the division appears as a vertical bar running down the centre of the frame.[8] Griffith experimented with this device in early Biographs such as *The Devil* (1908), *An Awful Moment* (1908), *The Girls and Daddy* (1908), and *Those Boys* (1909). The split set, however, created its own problems. It was only appropriate to a handful of narrative situations; even then, it might either keep the action at too great a distance from the viewer to be readily intelligible, or, on the contrary, reveal too much too soon.[9] Gradually the practice of splitting the set into two rooms gave way to the practice of cutting from one room to another (that is, from one set to another: the scenes arising out of each set would have been shot together, at the same time, then the set struck and another mounted in its place). From 1909, room-to-room cutting became for the method or pattern by which Griffith rendered the homogeneity of the sub-spaces constituting a single narrative space (for example, the rooms in a house).

According to Barry Salt, Griffith developed in his first films for Biograph 'the practice of transferring part of the action of a scene into adjoining hallways and rooms even when this was not strictly necessary, although in his case what the actors were doing was certainly always relevant to the development of the story.' By 1911, Salt continues, that fondness for movement from room to room had become an obsession, as Griffith sought consistently to explore the 'space beside'.[10] *Three Sisters* (1911), for example, concludes with a climactic sequence of 28 shots alternating between three set-ups — a kitchen, a hall, and a bedroom — established as contiguous by movement from one to another. The house, Ben Brewster and

8   Keil, *Early American Cinema*, p. 106.
9   Joyce E. Jesionowski, *Thinking in Pictures: Dramatic Structure in D. W. Griffith's Biograph Films* (Berkeley: University of California Press, 1987), p. 27; Keil, *Early American Cinema*, p. 107.
10   Barry Salt, *Film Style and Technology: History and Analysis*, 2nd edn (London: Starword, 1992), pp. 98–99.

Lea Jacobs remark, is like a doll's house, 'the front wall of the three adjacent rooms being as it were transparent to the camera.' It only exists as a whole, they rightly add, by inference.[11] My argument will be that the inference the viewer can make about the homogeneity of narrative space, in front of Griffith's Biograph films, is often a strong one; and that we need to take account of, and examine the reasons for, its strength. In my view, the strength of the inference derives neither from mise-en-scène alone, nor from contiguity editing alone, but from a practice I shall term 'lateral exposition'. Lateral exposition is the art of the space beside.

Lateral exposition was a road not taken, or if taken, soon abandoned, by Griffith, and by American film-makers in general. The practice stubbornly insisted, at a time when the commercial and dramatic advantages of the synthesizing of narrative space had become too obvious to ignore, that the viewer should infer its homogeneity by mapping the images projected onto a 'world' whose internal relations can readily be grasped in detail as well as in outline (are, as it were, palpable). My claim here is that by examining what Griffith thought he might achieve in this fashion, and indeed what he *did* achieve in this fashion, we may be in a better position to understand an imaginative opportunity in and for cinema, not only during the transitional period, but subsequently. I shall concentrate on *Death's Marathon* (1913), one of the last films he made for Biograph, and, although by no means representative of his work there, a wonderfully vivid demonstration of what could be done, in describing the modern city, with the space beside.

Contexts

Griffith's experiment with lateral exposition had a bearing both on the emergence in the years before the First World War of an 'American' cinema, and on the strategies developed during that process at once to explore and to exploit ideas of femininity.

Tom Gunning has argued that by 1913 it had become possible to distinguish between national styles in narrative film-making, or at least between European and American 'models'. The European style of deep staging achieved a 'sort of formal perfection' around 1913 or 1914, Gunning suggests, as an alternative to cross-cutting, and to the kinds of scene dissection already apparent by then in Biograph and Vitagraph films. Conversely, American film-makers had for some years been making strenuous efforts to differentiate home-grown from foreign product. The greatest consequence of formation of the Motion Picture Patents Company in 1908 was the relative exclusion of foreign manufacturers: foreign share of the market dropped from 60% to about 10% by 1914. Gunning contrasts two methods for the development and clarification of narrative event: cross-cutting, in Griffith's Biograph films; and composition in depth, in Feuillade's *Fantômas* series of 1913–14.[12] Feuillade, as David Bordwell has shown compellingly, used

11   Ben Brewster and Lea Jacobs, *Theatre to Cinema: Stage Pictorialism and the Early Feature Film* (Oxford: Oxford University Press, 1997), p. 189.
12   Gunning, *D. W. Griffith*, pp. 195–204.

composition in depth to create a 'subtle choreography' which guides the viewer's attention to the 'key dramatic material' in a scene. Bordwell calls for greater nuance in our understanding of the supposed dichotomy between European and American film-making in these years.[13] The nuance is needed on Griffith's side as well as Feuillade's. I shall try to show that lateral exposition was a way to be American, and yet not wholly reliant on cross-cutting or scene dissection.

It may also have been a way to vary that representation of romantic love culminating in the lawful wedded union of 'suitable' partners which was from first to last the main ideological business of Griffith's film-making. It is generally thought that Griffith staunchly upheld a patriarchal view of the family which economic, social, and political developments had placed under severe threat, and that his characteristic narrative methods constitute a response to that threat. As Miriam Hansen has observed, many of the Biograph films 'register a traumatic breakdown of boundaries — between domestic and public space, between good and evil, between virgin and prostitute — and the work of the narrative usually consists of reaffirming these boundaries. Staged most forcefully through last-minute rescue races, the ideological project relies crucially on parallel narration, on subcodes of cross-cutting and accelerated editing.'[14] 'For Griffith,' Virginia Wright Wexman concludes, after noting how the themes identified with the campaign for women's suffrage 'found their way' into his films, 'parallel montage is a way of constituting the couple.'[15]

Scholars pursuing this line of argument have understandably chosen to focus on the feature films of Griffith's 'Gish period': *Birth of a Nation* (1915), *Intolerance* (1916), *Broken Blossoms* (1919), and *Way Down East* (1920).[16] Lilian Gish, whom Griffith recruited for Biograph in 1912 with her sister Dorothy, was to prove 'the perfect embodiment of the highest feminine principle as he understood it'.[17] Gish's persona was 'ideally suited', Wexman points out, to the (re)constitution of the lawfully wedded couple through a montage which alternates medium and long shots of a bustlingly active male rescuer with close-ups of a passive (tortured) female victim.[18]

It may well be to my purpose that Griffith's leading woman in *Death's Marathon* was not Lilian Gish, but Blanche Sweet. Sweet subsequently featured as the patriarch-

---

13   Bordwell, *On the History of Film Style*, pp. 9, 22.

14   Miriam Hansen, *Babel & Babylon: Spectatorship in American Silent Film* (Cambridge, MA: Harvard University Press, 1991), p. 223.

15   Virginia Wright Wexman, *Creating the Couple: Love, Marriage, and Hollywood Performance* (Princeton, NJ: Princeton University Press, 1993), p. 44.

16   Michael Rogin argues that the 'collapse of gender and social differences' apparent in the Biograph films prompted Griffith to generate a 'new and deeper system of differences' in *Birth of a Nation*: '"The Sword Became a Flashing Vision": D. W. Griffith's *The Birth of a Nation*', *Representations*, 9 (1985), 150–95 (p. 159). On *Intolerance*, see Hansen, *Babel & Babylon*, esp. pp. 218–41, and Rogin, 'The Great Mother Domesticated: Sexual Difference and Sexual Indifference in D. W. Griffith's *Intolerance*', *Critical Inquiry*, 15 (1989), 510–55; on *Broken Blossoms*, Nick Browne, 'Griffith's Family Discourse: Griffith and Freud', in *Home is Where the Heart Is: Studies in Melodrama and the Woman's Film*, ed. by Susan Gledhill (London: BFI Publishing, 1987), pp. 223–34; and on *Way Down East*, Wexman, *Creating the Couple*, pp. 48–63.

17   Richard Schickel, *D. W. Griffith: An American Life* (New York: Proscenium, 1984), p. 177.

18   Wexman, *Creating the Couple*, p. 47.

toppling heroine of *Judith of Bethulia* (1913). Griffith had originally intended that she should play Elsie Stoneman, in *Birth of a Nation*. Gish only secured the part when substituting for Sweet in a rehearsal of the scene in which Elsie is violently accosted by the mulatto Silas Lynch (George Siegmann). 'I was very blonde and fragile-looking,' Gish recalled. 'The contrast with the dark man evidently pleased Mr Griffith, for he said in front of everyone, 'Maybe she would be more effective than the more mature figure I had in mind.'[19] Blanche Sweet was neither white enough nor sweet enough to play Elsie Stoneman.[20] We might or might not be able to speak of a 'Sweet period' in Griffith's film-making. I shall propose here that in *Death's Marathon* the homogeneous narrative spaces constructed by lateral exposition made it possible for him to imagine a woman's part in marriage differently, and to subtle, if not radical, effect. I want to ask what the space beside might have done for Sweet's 'more mature' figure.

Thematized Space in the Early Biographs

The homogeneity of the spaces defined by lateral exposition in Griffith's Biograph films could of course only ever be a matter of inference. But the inference is often, as I have already suggested, a strong one. Charlie Keil speaks of the sense these films consistently generate of the 'emphatic contiguity' of adjacent spaces.[21] On what basis might Griffith have expected us to infer a house from an assortment of rooms?

There is plenty of evidence that Griffith meant to design, and to gain dramatic advantage from, film-sets that were socially as well as topographically intelligible. The social whole of which particular sub-spaces could be imagined as parts was as often as not the tenement block, and by implication the neighbourhood. Thus, by 1911, in films like *The Root of Evil*, the hallway or vestibule had emerged as the provocation to urban narrative. As Griffith used it, Russell Merritt notes,

> the vestibule was both a playing area and a proleptic space, a gateway that always denoted space beyond the margins of the frame. It was the [...] staging area for entry into adjacent rooms (including that Biograph specialty, the forced entry), a site for eavesdropping or spying, a space for greetings and farewells, and, above all, a space for chance encounters between characters headed in opposite directions.[22]

The vestibule had become the 'master image' of the Griffith tenement neighbourhood; and so it remained, in later films such as *The Musketeers of Pig Alley* (1912), and, indeed, the modern story in *Intolerance*. In these films, the staging of the action relies for its coherence on the viewer's knowledge of the organization of urban space for social purposes.

---

19   Lilian Gish, *The Movies, Mr Griffith, and Me* (Englewood Cliffs, NJ: Prentice-Hall, 1969), p. 133.
20   Rogin, '"The Sword Became a Flashing Vision"', pp. 163–64.
21   Keil, *Early American Cinema*, p. 88.
22   Russell Merritt, 'The Root of Evil', in *The Griffith Project*, vol. v, ed. by P. C. Usai (London: British Film Institute, 2001), pp. 192–94 (p. 193).

Griffith, it would seem, suspected that such knowledge might not be enough; or at least might not be enough when the narrative space in question was somewhat removed from the familiar terrain of the tenement neighbourhood. Barry Salt points out that by 1910 he had expanded his enquiry into the 'space beside' to include 'action spread backwards and forwards across what were effectively adjoining spaces in exterior scenes.'[23] Of particular interest from this point of view is the 'cave-man' epic *Brute Force* (1913). By mid-1913, Griffith was acutely restless at Biograph. The commercial and critical success of his 'Indian' films had nurtured in him the ambition to fabricate, as Joyce Jesionowski puts it, 'wholly realized social orders'. The 'Indian' films develop 'carefully crafted gestural systems' whose purpose is to realize the 'patterns of social interchange' regulating a specific community. The system in operation in *Brute Force* covers the full range of socially expressive behaviour, from grooming to genocide. Equally fabricated is the terrain, or milieu, within which the film's two warring tribes do battle. Griffith maps the positions occupied by the tribes at opposite ends of an evolutionary spectrum onto the ground they contest. A pair of shots renders each tribal home in terms of the evolutionary stage at which their inhabitants might be thought to have arrived. 'These comparative constructs,' Jesionowski explains, are connected on a 'grand left-to-right lateral' that spans the Stone Age world in shots of varying scale.[24] The contention over women between the two tribes moves backwards and forwards across this grand lateral so comprehensively as to constitute a world war. Narrative space, in this film, is symbolic through and through: to step to the left is to evolve, or at least to enact evolution.

The example of *Brute Force* would suggest that it sometimes took extreme measures to establish the homogeneity of non-urban narrative space. Where urban settings were concerned, Griffith appears to have felt, the viewer's grasp of the organization of space for social purposes would do the trick. That organization of space is the theme explored by the staging of the action in side-by-side spaces, by emphatic contiguity. By defining the use the Biograph films make of the space beside as lateral exposition, I have meant to bring out their argumentative side. The New York *Dramatic Mirror* described *A Corner in Wheat* (1910), Griffith's fierce (and fiercely experimental) indictment of speculation in commodities, not as a 'picture drama', but as 'an argument, an editorial, an essay on a subject of deep interest to all'.[25] *Death's Marathon* amounts, if not exactly to an editorial, then, through its exposition of narrative space — by making us think again about the organization of the urban environment for social purposes — at least to an argument or an essay (without ever ceasing to be a picture drama). This is something, I would argue, that Feuillade did not achieve, and perhaps could not have achieved, with the methods at his disposal.

23   Salt, *Film Style and Technology*, p. 99.
24   Jesionowski, *Thinking in Pictures*, pp. 113–14.
25   Quoted in Gunning, *D. W. Griffith*, p. 241.

Death's Marathon

Death's Marathon (1913), a domestic melodrama illustrative of modern urban experience, is best known for the cross-cut race to the rescue, or non-rescue, which brings the main action to a violent conclusion. A young woman (Blanche Sweet) chooses between two suitors. The marriage brings happiness at first, and a child, then disillusion. The husband (Henry B. Walthall) gambles heavily, and covers his losses by stealing from the company he runs with his ex-rival (Walter Miller).[26] The latter realizes what is going on, but covers the theft with his own money in order to protect the woman he still loves. Sinking deeper and deeper into debt, the husband decides that suicide is the only way out, and (rather oddly) calls his wife to inform her of the decision. She desperately tries to keep him on the phone while her old suitor races to the rescue. Griffith cuts between the gun-toting Walthall, to whom desperation has lent a certain suaveness, an agonized Sweet, and Miller's frantic mercy-dash.[27] Miller arrives too late. Sweet, rooted to the phone, takes the full force of Walthall's death. Griffith thus disabled the narrative system he had so authoritatively made his own. This is one piece of cross-cutting which most certainly will not reconstitute the couple.

Death's Marathon includes three primary interior spaces: an office suite (inner and outer); the main room of the family home, divided into two sections by a curtain; and a saloon in the club of which both men are members, where the husband gambles. There is a fourth interior space, loosely connected to the second: the bedroom in which, during the early years of the marriage, the wife fondly expects her husband's return home from work, their child in a cradle at her side. This fourth space is linked graphically to the film's only significant exterior: parkland where the proposal of marriage takes place.[28] In the proposal scene, Walthall insinuates himself around the post supporting the bower in which Sweet sits; when he arrives home after work, he insinuates himself around the post of the bed in which she lies. Bower and bedroom are spaces linked metaphorically to each other rather than metonymically to the spaces beside them. The contiguity emphasized here is one of time rather than space: in the trajectory of idealized marriage, coupledom has seamlessly given rise to parenthood. Though we are meant to suppose, I think, that the bedroom lies immediately to the right of the main room; the baby seems always to be on hand from that direction when its presence is required. That the trajectory of marriage as traditionally understood, with its rigid attribution of gender roles,

26   Since the characters in this film were not named in the intertitles or in Biograph publicity material, I shall identify them by reference to the actor or actress.

27   Walthall had played a comparably suicidal widower in *The Usurer* (1912). Blowing his brains out on screen was evidently something of a specialism.

28   There is a second exterior 'space', examined to illuminating effect by Tom Gunning. A shot of Sweet seated demurely in an elaborate garden renders by its 'dream-like aspect' the vision Miller has of her (the feelings he has for her). It is, as Gunning points out, 'one of the most deliberately subjective images Griffith had yet achieved at Biograph': 'Death's Marathon', in *The Griffith Project*, vol. VII, ed. by P. C. Usai (London: British Film Institute, 2003), pp. 55–66 (pp. 60–61). The image does not belong to the thematised homogeneous spaces established throughout the film by lateral exposition.

might in fact pass aslant rather than through the narrative spaces which constitute lived (urban middle-class) life is the basis of the argument Griffith made in *Death's Marathon*. If the onset of marriage is conceived as a sprint, then its dissolution may turn into a marathon.

The three primary interior spaces are all defined by scenes of arrival and departure, that is, by a certain relation between the inside and the outside of the building: cars draw up, people climb out and go in; people come out, climb into cars, and depart. That relation between inside and outside is the 'theme' which enables us to infer their homogeneity as spaces, and their function within the urban environment as a whole. The scenes at the club are set apart by the fact that they are staged in depth, and on the diagonal: the corner of the room in which the gambling takes place occupies the centre of the frame, and there is a further room beyond, in which activity is sometimes visible, and through which people enter and exit. In the scenes at the club, the relation between the interior and the exterior of the building is so mediated that it does not emerge as a theme. In the scenes played in the main domestic and business spaces, by contrast, it most certainly does.

The primary domestic space and the primary business space each consists of a pair of contiguous sub-spaces arranged laterally. The domestic space is an altogether odd construction. A curtain divides it into a more public section, on the left, which gives access, directly or indirectly, to the street, and which contains a desk and a telephone; and a more private section, on the right, connecting to the bedroom, and containing a dressing-table with a mirror on it. The main business interior is equally odd. It consists of an inner office, on the left, in which a great deal happens, including suicide; and an outer office, on the right, which, although replete with furniture, is never occupied. As in *Brute Force*, though for very different purposes, Griffith has devised a 'grand left-to-right lateral'. At the far left stands the inner office, from which the outer office can be entered by movement to the right; at the far right, the inner living-room, from which the outer living-room can be entered by movement to the left. Between the outer office and the outer living-room stretches an expanse of vestibule, pavement, and street which the film does not need to render because nothing of any significance in itself will take place there.[29]

The function of this arrangement of narrative space is to figure or make intelligible the relation between interior and exterior, which is also, according to the 'social logic' identified by Bill Hillier and Julienne Hanson in a wide range of architectural modes, the relation between a public and a private realm. The most important distinction that logic maintains, Hillier and Hanson argue, is between a 'deep' space within a building attainable only by passage through other spaces, and thereby adapted for its owner's exclusive use, as sanctuary or shrine; and the 'shallow' spaces (neutral, inclusive, open-ended) through which the visitor must

---

29   One consequence of the artificiality of this arrangement of sub-spaces is that they are rather hard to identify. Gunning, for example, describes the inner or right-hand domestic sub-space as a 'sort of hallway': 'Death's Marathon', p. 62. I don't think it can be, because it does not lead, directly or indirectly, to the street. A further complication is introduced by the fact that, as Gunning points out, the same set does service both for this inner sub-space and for the bedroom where Sweet and her baby await Walthall's return from work.

pass in order to attain it.[30] A deep space, we might say, is one in which power and desire renew themselves, and each other; or are finally found out. The area of transit which social elites have traditionally interposed between that deep space and the vulgar public street gives rise, by contrast, to actions which are in some measure inessential, to behaviour amounting to ceremony rather than to revelation.

In *Death's Marathon*, the inner office, at the far left of the film's grand lateral, is where dark deeds are done. Walthall takes money from the safe it contains (that recess within a recess), to feed his gambling-frenzy. When he later finds his way back there (as to a sanctuary, or anti-sanctuary), to kill himself, the room is in darkness, and he must grope his way into it, before lighting a lamp. The illumination from the lamp creates an isolated playing space for him in the foreground of the shot. The outer office, empty throughout, though well enough equipped with desks and telephones, is an area of transit (though never just a zone, since what takes place there is of significance in itself, albeit as ceremony rather than revelation). Visitors cross and re-cross this area of transit on their way to and from the deep space it permits access to.

On one occasion, a boy delivering a telegram to Miller in the inner office enters the outer office through the door in the rear wall of the set, takes an elaborate puff at his cigarette, deposits the cigarette neatly on the edge of a desk, and pushes open the door to the inner office. On his way out after having delivered the telegram, he retrieves the cigarette; we even catch a glimpse of him putting it to his lips again as he closes the door in the rear wall of the set. The business with the cigarette is, of course, entirely incidental. It does not advance the story. It establishes the shallow space of the outer office as precisely a space in which something other than the renewal of power and desire, something other than truth-telling, customarily occurs. That something is *performance*: an excess of symbolism over function. The business with the cigarette makes the telegram boy a boy who knows he is a telegram boy, and likes to know it. It is also, of course, business for the actor playing the telegram boy (Robert Harron): the kind of flourish which might just have caught a producer's attention.

When truth-telling rather than performance is at issue — when the story requires advancing — the outer office ceases to exist. The telegram Robert Harron has brought informs Miller that the firm will require its entire cash reserve for immediate use. Miller, who has witnessed Walthall's theft, acts swiftly to replace the stolen money with his own. Just as well, too. No sooner has he done so than the firm's backer (Lionel Barrymore) blusters directly into the inner office to confront the startled Miller, impatiently setting aside his hat and stick, and pulling off his gloves. These garments bring with them the vulgar public street. We have not witnessed Barrymore's passage through the outer office's shallow space, a space made vivid for us by Harron's business with the cigarette. Power goes straight to the point. Our sense of the threat posed by Barrymore depends on our understanding that he is not someone whose actions are bound by the social logic of space. That logic has been articulated for us by lateral exposition.

30   Bill Hillier and Julienne Hanson, *The Social Logic of Space* (Cambridge: Cambridge University Press, 1984).

There is no equivalent to the thematized homogeneous narrative spaces of *Death's Marathon* in the *Fantômas* films. Feuillade could not have accomplished by staging in depth what Griffith accomplishes by lateral exposition. David Bordwell has shown that Feuillade most certainly knew how to 'choreograph the shot'. In a scene set in the Crocodile nightclub, in Montmartre, in *Juve versus Fantômas*, a violin player strolls down the aisle to the centre left of the shot and serenades Joséphine, the female protagonist, who is seated at a table in the foreground. His fiddling directs our attention to this area of the shot; when he moves aside, his movement discloses the arrival in the room of the detective Juve and his sidekick Fandor. Juve and Fandor proceed down the aisle towards Joséphine. 'The violin player,' Bordwell concludes, 'an extra, has been a spatial pretext, a mere pointer marking a zone for the major characters to occupy.'[31] The telegram boy in *Death's Marathon*, is also an extra; he, too, could be considered a 'spatial pretext'. The difference is that the space for which he is the pretext is not *itself*, as it would be in the *Fantômas* films, a pretext for narrative event. It is text rather than pretext: always already thematized. In the restaurant scene in *Juve versus Fantômas*, by contrast, the aisle for which the violin-player is the pretext only holds our attention for as long as it will take Juve and Fandor to fill it. It does not exist as a space organized architecturally for social purposes. It is, in fact, a time rather than a space: the seconds which must elapse before Juve and Fandor can be brought convincingly into relation with Joséphine. It is no less of a zone (no less abstract) than the spaces through which the protagonists speed in one of Griffith's races to the rescue.

More often than not, Feuillade's staging in depth divides narrative space into a foreground, in which or towards which meaningful action occurs, and a decorative background. In *Juve versus Fantômas*, Juve and Fandor pose as potential purchasers in order to gain entrance to the deserted villa belonging to Lady Beltham, Fantômas's accomplice, mistress, and victim. The tour of inspection led by the custodian proves desultory in the extreme until the party reaches Lady Beltham's bedroom. Here, Juve advances towards the camera, while Fandor and the custodian retreat into the background. Juve notices an inkstand on the table at the foot of the bed. Narrative space has been divided into two areas, or planes: a foreground replete with narrative meaning, and a background of no interest whatsoever. Juve shows the pen to the other two, thus bringing them forward into significance. Used less than three days ago! The villa clearly remains a place of rendezvous. A medium close-up shows Juve scrutinizing the pen, framed by Fandor and the custodian. Although the episode at the villa has involved passage from the vulgar public street to deep space, it has done nothing at all to expound the social logic which renders urban space intelligible.

'Griffith,' as Bordwell quite rightly remarks, after an instructive survey of staging in depth in European cinema before the First World War, 'seems to have had little recourse to the fine-grained intrashot choreography developed by his contemporaries.'[32] It is not that Griffith did not conceive of staging in depth as the basis for such a choreography. The scene at the club in *Death's Marathon* demonstrates

31   Bordwell, *On the History of Film Style*, p. 190.
32   Ibid., p. 196.

a full awareness of the dramatic advantages it might yield. As Salt points out, the outdoor subjects he produced from 1909 onwards often have 'Red Indians' or fisher folk going about their colourful business in a 'space behind' that in which the main action unfolds.[33] But he seems also to have wanted to find out what advantage other methods might yield. There is choreography, of a kind, I would argue, in the lateral exposition of the Biograph films: a choreography of spaces rather than persons.

Gender and the Space Beside

It was by such 'choreography' that Griffith developed his critique of the patriarchal family. Sweet's marriage to Walthall runs rapidly into trouble. The brief scene of contented home-coming is followed immediately by a scene at the club, and an ominous intertitle: 'The self-centred husband bored with the monotony of married life.' A further scene, consisting of three shots, and played out across or between the sub-spaces which together compose the thematized narrative space of the family home, gives substance to Walthall's boredom, and the pain it causes Sweet. In the first of these shots, Walthall, in the inner or right-hand domestic space, and dressed to go out, pulls on his gloves. He has already, in effect, left home. A hand reaches out from off-screen right (that is, from the bedroom), to proffer his hat; and rests on his arm, detaining him.[34] Sweet enters. He glances down at the hand resting on his arm, and, in particular at the wedding-ring on one finger. In shaking her off, he seems also to have shaken off marriage itself. The next shot shows Walthall alone in the outer or left-hand domestic space, speaking and gesturing off-screen right, to Sweet, we assume, who has remained on the other side of the curtain; he puts his hat on his head, and leaves. Griffith then cuts back to Sweet, in the inner domestic space. She seats herself on a chair at frame right, stares into the mirror on a dressing-table at the back of the set, and bursts into tears. Gunning notes that this is the only occasion in the Biograph films on which Griffith used a mirror to reveal state of mind. Sweet's removal from the camera's direct gaze reinforces her isolation, 'the pushing of her to the right edge of the frame'.[35] Like the safe in the inner office, the mirror is a recess within a recess: the deepest space of all, where there is no hiding from the truth. Sweet looks into the mirror and sees that there is nothing to marriage, to Walthall as a husband. Miller will later look into the safe and see that there is nothing to partnership, to Walthall as a professional man.

This pattern of cuts from one side of the curtain dividing the main room of the house to the other is repeated in a later scene. 'Soon estranged from his wife', an intertitle announces. Walthall, in the inner domestic space, pulls on his gloves. Sweet appears from the left, dressed to go out for the night, gloves in hand. They quarrel. He almost strikes her, before storming out to in the direction of the outer domestic space. We see him there, speaking and gesturing off-screen right, as on the

33 Salt, *Film Style and Technology*, p. 104.
34 Gunning says that the hand appears from the left of the frame: '*Death's Marathon*', p. 62. In a scene like this, constituted by lateral exposition, it matters that the hand should in fact appear from the right, which in the family home is the direction of interiority.
35 Gunning, '*Death's Marathon*', p. 62.

previous occasion (it's hard to tell whether or not Griffith has simply used the same shot again). A final shot of a distraught Sweet in the inner domestic space completes the triptych. The repetition of the pattern of shots firmly identifies her with that space. Griffith thus stages Walthall's departure from home, and from marriage, across a gendered distinction between deep and shallow sub-spaces.

The thematization of the homogeneous narrative space of the family home does more to define Sweet's part in the climactic race to the rescue than any amount of cross-cutting. It defines her conduct, as she tries desperately to stay her husband's hand, as a transformation or emergence. She emerges from the paralysis brought on by her humiliating confinement to deep space. Crisis will oblige her to negotiate the exposure to what others know or sense about her, and to what they expect of her, which an occupation of shallow space always entails. As the crisis begins to unfold, Miller arrives at the family home by car, having failed to locate Walthall. Sweet is seated in the outer room, to the right of the frame. The maid announces Miller, who enters hat in hand. Griffith has thus gently re-thematized narrative space by reminding us of the connection between this semi-public interior and the public street. Walthall is soon on the phone, declaring suicide. 'The wife holds him on the wire until the friend can reach the office in town.' Sweet holds Walthall on the wire by putting on a performance of which we might well have thought she was not capable. She expresses the loving concern of a wife for her husband, of a mother for the father of her child. There is a rigour to the expression of these feelings which raises it above expression into performance. No more so than when, in a sequence of shots traversing inner and outer domestic spaces, the baby is brought to the phone. The baby's evident fascination with the apparatus itself, as Walthall continues to declare suicide, confirms that shallow space is indeed the realm of the inessential. Sweet has put herself at risk in that realm. In narrative terms, her intervention proves a failure. But the performance she puts on in failing (that excess of symbolism over function) has made her a new person.

Griffith's races to the rescue invariably involve three parties, each active in his or her own way: the assailant assailing, the victim staving off assault, and the rescuer racing to the rescue. In a suicide attempt, however, the victim is also the assailant. In *Death's Marathon*, Sweet takes the spare role, which is really that of narrative process itself, since it is her appalled reaction which first informs us that Walthall has taken his own life. Her response alone conveys the meaning of the event. The performance she puts on has made her a new person in a new film, a film which cannot do without her. The phone conversation is shot in relative close-up throughout. Sweet could be said to have stepped forward for the first time into that abstract space between screen and audience which mirrors the depth of the image. Her look, Joyce Jesionowski observes, 'directed out of the fragile frontal plane, creates a link with the image of her husband that reflects the fluctuation between the real and the imaginary in the film, between expectations and resolution, between anxiety and knowledge.' By thus developing the extreme foreground position Sweet occupies as the 'abstract limit of the frame', Griffith has brought forward into view not only her new strength of purpose, but film-making itself.[36]

36   Jesionowski, *Thinking in Pictures*, pp. 45–46.

Griffith, of course, was no feminist. When Miller comes courting again after it is all over, he finds Sweet in confident occupation of the outer domestic space; but now viewed in long shot. The solution to a bad marriage is a good marriage. It would take little short of a further marital cataclysm, we imagine, to bring her back to the frame's absolute limit — or get her out of the house. Even so, the film can be considered to have had its say about the ways in which a woman might come into her own within marriage: about the overcoming of patriarchally enforced distinctions. Griffith's lateral exposition has expounded a point of view as well as a narrative space.

If the telegram boy's incidental business with the cigarette might have been an opportunity for Robert Harron, then how much more of one might Blanche Sweet's far from incidental business with telephone and baby have been for her? In June 1913, the month in which *Death's Marathon* was first shown, Biograph, which had hitherto been slow to promote its players, released a striking head shot of Sweet in one of the first fan magazines.[37] The extreme foreground position into which she had stepped forward in the climax to *Death's Marathon* was that of stardom. She had become a star (if not the kind of star Griffith could be altogether sure he wanted to work with).

Thematization after Continuity

Lateral exposition was the road not taken either by Griffith, in his subsequent work, or by American film-makers in general. But it is worth considering, by way of brief, speculative conclusion, whether the idea which informs it — of a 'world' expounded, rather than edited or staged, into being — might not have continued to inform American film-making, in one way or another, long after the establishment of the classical continuity system. When Elsaesser and Barker consider the after-life of the distinctive 'spatial articulations' of Griffith's Biograph films, they make reference primarily to the 'counter-cinema' of the post-First World War European avant-gardes.[38] Jacques Aumont speaks, with Godard's *La Chinoise* in mind, of a '*return of Griffith* in certain modern films' which is 'in no way, of course, a return *to* Griffith.'[39] But there are other ways to conceive of that after-life. Scott Simmon, for example, has identified Griffith's Biograph domestic melodramas as the origin of the Hollywood 'woman's film'.[40] My suggestion here is that Howard Hawks, master of continuity editing, also found a use for thematized homogeneous narrative space.

I have in mind the openings of two films which exemplify the two basic types to which, in Peter Wollen's view, Hawks reduced the genres available to him: crazy comedy, and adventure drama.[41] *His Girl Friday* (1940) and *The Big Sleep* (1946) are

37   Gunning, 'Death's Marathon', p. 61.
38   Elsaesser and Barker, 'Introduction', pp. 312–13.
39   Jacques Aumont, 'Griffith: The Frame, the Figure', in *Early Cinema: Space, Frame, Narrative*, pp. 348–59 (p. 353). Emphasis in the original.
40   Scott Simmon, *The Films of D. W. Griffith* (Cambridge: Cambridge University Press, 1993), pp. 68–103.
41   Peter Wollen, *Signs and Meaning in Cinema*, 2nd edn (London: BFI Publishing, 1998), p. 53.

of course far from silent; and the techniques which fashion their openings bear little resemblance to the static camera, frontal staging, and room-to-room cuts of the Biograph melodramas. Those openings do none the less make supremely inventive use of the principle of emphatic contiguity. They ensure the homogeneity of narrative space by expounding a social logic comparable to that expounded in *Death's Marathon*.

In *His Girl Friday*, we are introduced to the newsroom of the *Morning Post* by a sequence of lateral tracking-shots which carries us across it from the vicinity of the editor's office to the vicinity of the foyer where visitors can be deposited until someone finds time to attend to them. Hawks's grand lateral thus comprises, from left to right, a foyer (in effect, an extension of the public street); an outer office, open-plan, and full of activity, marked off from the foyer by a barrier and a 'No Admittance' sign; and an hermetically enclosed inner office, where, we soon learn, power and desire renew themselves. The sequence of tracking-shots comes to rest on the figure of Hildy Johnson (Rosalind Russell), emerging from an elevator in the company of Bruce Baldwin (Ralph Bellamy), her insurance salesman suitor. Bruce, whose full panoply of rain-wear has brought the vulgar public street in with it, stays in the foyer; while a second sequence of tracking-shots conveys Hildy across the newsroom, through a relay of rapid-fire exchanges, to the editor's office, where Walter Burns (Cary Grant) is murkily engrossed in dealings with henchmen. Here, Walter receives the double stimulus, to desire and to power, of the news that Hildy is about to marry Bruce, and that Earl Williams is about to be executed for a crime he did not intend. A third and final sequence of tracking-shots then accompanies Walter and Hildy as they trade gallantries on the way back to the foyer, and a memorable encounter with the handle of Bruce's umbrella. A social logic informs this arrangement of narrative space; just as a social logic had informed the emphatic contiguity of the inner to the outer office, and the outer office to the public street, in *Death's Marathon*. The camera-movements which cross it from one side to the other *are* its lateral exposition.

Those movements answer, I think, to something in the sort of behaviour generally thought appropriate to areas of transit: behaviour emblematic of the virtues of performance rather than of revelation. Stanley Cavell has argued that in Hollywood remarriage comedies, which begin in (or from) separation, the attempt to escape from an ex-partner 'is forever transforming itself into (hence revealing itself as) a process of pursuit.' During that process, 'we are permanently in doubt who the hero is, that is, whether it is the male or the female, who is the active partner, which of them is in quest, who is following whom.'[42] During the scenes in the inner office and in the foyer, in *His Girl Friday*, the male is the hero, the active partner. Walter's authority as editor, supplemented by wit, and an ability to improvise, give him the edge. Once the camera has begun to move, however, on the way back across the outer office to the foyer, the balance of desire and power shifts. Hildy, after all, has already shown us, during the second sequence of tracking-shots, that she is master

---

42 Stanley Cavell, *Pursuits of Happiness: The Hollywood Comedy of Remarriage* (Cambridge, MA: Harvard University Press, 1981), pp. 113, 122.

(both as newspaperman and as embodiment of feminine elegance) of that domain. Getting ahead of Walter, but only in order to usher him eloquently through the next gate ('Allow *me*'), she enacts the comic transformation of flight into pursuit. Robin Wood has argued that the interest of Hawks's women lies in the fact that they are 'anomalous and threatening, but *there*'.[43] But there *where*? In the opening scenes of *His Girl Friday*, lateral exposition shows us exactly where.

It is no surprise that the opening of *The Big Sleep* should offer a comparable grand lateral because the novel by Raymond Chandler from which the film was adapted opens with an intricate exposition of the social logic of narrative space. Marlowe has dressed for his visit to General Sternwood's Bel-Air mansion with pedantic dandyism. He is staunchly in uniform, right down to the black wool socks with dark blue clocks on them. After all, he is calling on 'four million dollars'. He passes through the hall, where Carmen Sternwood flirts with him, and falls against him, round the lawn behind it, to the greenhouse where the General sits in absolute recession, at the heart of darkness. The greenhouse is the mansion's primary cell, a deep space adapted for its owner's exclusive use. To reach it from the street, Marlowe must negotiate a whole series of shallow areas of transit, with the butler Norris as guide. 'Here, in a space of hexagonal flags, an old red Turkish rug was laid down and on the rug was a wheel-chair, and in the wheel-chair an old and obviously dying man watched us come...' The syntax mimics Marlowe's deferentially circuitous approach to the source of power and desire. The source, however, is no longer a source. General Sternwood still has the capacity to renew his far-reaching authority. The four million dollars will see to that. But he has run out of desire.

> 'A nice state of affairs when a man has to indulge his vices by proxy,' he said dryly. 'You are looking at a very dull survival of a rather gaudy life, a cripple paralysed in both legs and with only half of his lower belly.'

Sweating heavily in the intense heat, Marlowe proceeds to drink and smoke on the General's behalf. Absorption into deep space has already cost him his dapperness. On the way back out, however, he encounters the General's other daughter, Vivian, the far from dull survival of a less than gaudy life, and starts to do some desiring on his own account. 'She was worth a stare,' we learn. 'She was trouble.'[44] Shallow space is where the action is, in Chandler's Los Angeles.

In adapting the novel, Hawks and his scriptwriters reproduced the structuring social logic of its inaugural scene for cinema. As in *His Girl Friday*, fluid camera-movements (this time in the form of pans rather than tracking) unlock the potential of shallow space: its subtle incitement to performance. The room in which Vivian

---

43   Robin Wood, 'Retrospect', in *Howard Hawks: American Artist*, ed. by Jim Hillier and Peter Wollen (London: BFI Publishing, 1996), pp. 163–73 (p. 169).

44   Raymond Chandler, *The Big Sleep* (Harmondsworth: Penguin Books, 1948), pp. 9, 13–14, 22. For a discussion of this scene at greater length, in the context of hard-boiled fiction, see David Trotter, 'Fascination and Nausea: Finding Out the Hard Way', in *The Art of Detective Fiction*, ed. by Warren Chernaik, Martin Swales, and Robert Vilain (Basingstoke: Macmillan, 2000), pp. 21–35. Reprinted as Chapter 11 in this book.

(Lauren Bacall) entertains Marlowe (Humphrey Bogart) on his way out of the house has been given a new location, so that it now opens (somewhat incongruously) off the hall, opposite the staircase down which Carmen (Martha Vickers) had dawdled to intercept him on his way in. It has also been equipped with a conspicuous double bed. In the film, as in the novel, Marlowe smokes and drinks on behalf of impotent male authority, resigned, it would seem, to an unpleasant if highly profitable subservience. In both, he rediscovers his effrontery, and a good deal else beside, while in transit back across the unpredictable hallway. On his way in, he still belongs to authority (to his own dapper subservience to authority): hence the ease with which he repels Carmen, and his patronizing remark that they ought to wean her. But his spell in the greenhouse prompts in him a new and countervailing urgency. On his way out, he looks to express desire rather than to comply. This time, he even cheeks the silver-haired butler. For Hawks, as for Chandler, shallow space is where the action is.

Folds in narrative space have opened up to reveal Carmen and Vivian, both anomalous, both threatening, both exactly *there*. Yet it would be hard not conceive of a revitalized Marlowe (a revitalized Bogart) as the force which opens up the fold concealing an expectant Vivian (an expectant Bacall). On the way in, an uninquisitive pan carries Marlowe, who has just disentangled himself from Carmen, across the hallway — the entrance to Vivian's bedroom briefly glimpsed — in the direction of the greenhouse. On the way back out, a two-shot of Marlowe and Norris frames the (now open) bedroom-door at some length, as the two men discuss financial terms and generally bristle at each other. Norris then leads the way to the open door. 'Go right in, sir, you're expected.' Hawks cuts to the interior of the bedroom. A further track and pan carries Marlowe across it — the double-bed conspicuous in the background — to where Vivian awaits him. The sight of Vivian's legs will launch him not so much on an enquiry as on a riotous serial exhibition of sexual magnetism. Generic and other determinants have ensured that in this case it is the male who gets to perform in shallow space.

My argument has been that what made it possible for Griffith and Hawks to explore as inventively as they did the idea of performance — performance as identity, performance as what an actor or actress does in order to become a star, performance as movie-making itself — was a certain understanding, which their audiences could be assumed more or less to share, of the social logic of urban narrative space. Griffith's abortive experiment in lateral exposition had demonstrated what could be done with that logic. The conclusions to be drawn from it would thereafter vary, from historical moment to historical moment, from director to director, from film to film.

CHAPTER 14

Come-Hither Looks:
The Hollywood Vamp and the
Function of Cinema

My topic is the vamp film, a hugely popular sub-genre which flourished briefly in the United States between 1915 and 1925, at a time when cinema was still in the process of establishing itself as primarily a narrative medium. By 1915, it is generally assumed, the transition from a 'cinema of attractions' to a 'cinema of narrative integration' was more or less complete.[1] It may be, however, that some doubts remained about the medium's exact function. The claim I will advance here is that the vamp film — a multi-media event staged as vividly in the fan magazines as on the screen — played a significant (if in the long run ineffectual) part in perpetuating those doubts. Film history has had little to say about vamp films.[2] On the whole, they have been categorized as a 'relatively conservative' sub-genre of the fallen woman film.[3] According to Miriam Hansen, the 'perverted female look' they activate was one of a number of 'allegories' deployed by the film industry in order at once to empower and to contain 'female desire in general'.[4] My feeling is that they deserve further and more detailed attention, on account not only of their popularity at the time, but of their fabulous indiscretion. I want to propose a particular scene in a selection of these films as an index to the degree of uncertainty that persisted, for a while, in attitudes to film as a medium.

Between 1915 and 1925, most if not all of the major Hollywood production companies turned out one or more melodramas featuring a female vamp. These films were one of the means by which Hollywood established itself as the globally dominant mass medium which we sometimes take to exemplify the 'American century'. A 'vamp' was a woman hell-bent on seducing the nearest available millionaire: a courtesan, then, but one who would not rest content until she had

1   For an authoritative account, see Charlie Keil, *Early American Cinema in Transition: Story, Style, and Filmmaking, 1907–1913* (Madison: University of Wisconsin Press. 2001).

2   Sumiko Higashi, *Virgins, Vamps, and Flappers: The American Silent Movie Heroine* (Montreal: Eden Press, 1978), pp. 55–78.

3   Lea Jacobs, *The Wages of Sin: Censorship and the Fallen Woman Film, 1928–1942* (Berkeley: University of California Press, 1997), p. 12.

4   Miriam Hansen, *Babel and Babylon: Spectatorship in American Silent Film* (Cambridge, MA: Harvard University Press, 1991), pp. 122–23.

stripped her victim of everything he possessed and of everything he was, of his very being. The figure of the vamp required a new kind of star: a mature actress of (allegedly) exotic origin. According to the Fox Film Company's publicity department, Theda Bara (1885–1955) — born Theodosia Goodman, in Cincinnati, Ohio — was the daughter of an Arabian princess and an Italian sculptor brought up in Egypt. Fox touted her (optimistically) as a combination of the biblical Delilah and Lucrezia Borgia.[5] Pola Negri (1897–1987) was at least Polish: her father had been arrested and sent to Siberia. As Diane Negra points out, the 'hypersexual cinematic vamp' of the 1910s and 1920s was in essence 'a thinly disguised incarnation of the threat of female immigrant sexuality'. These florid embodiments of 'resistant female ethnicity' crystallized anxieties concerning race, gender, and sexuality widespread in post-war America.[6] 'Women are my greatest fans,' Bara declared in an interview she gave in June 1917, 'because they see in my vampire the impersonal vengeance of all their unavenged wrongs [...] Even downtrodden wives write to me to this effect. And they give me the perfect compliment. "I know I should sympathize with the wife, but I do not." I am in effect a *feministe*.'[7]

Negra goes on to explain that the vamp's 'transgressive ownership of her own labour' was to prove especially problematic, because it enabled her to 'carry off a kind of masquerade — a false femininity'.[8] I want to suggest that the masquerade involved a particular kind of labour — the production of the 'come-hither look' — which, while no doubt threatening, also generates an unexpected reflexivity: these are moments at which film itself, as a medium, is also on show, in all of *its* masquerade. What is especially striking about the labour involved in the vamp's masquerade is that it involves an act of pure (and resolutely unfeminine) calculation. For she plans the entrapment of her victim like a military campaign, having carefully researched his circumstances and habits. Furthermore, the initial encounter usually occurs in a public or semi-public space, and thus requires an exchange of coded signals. This is in effect a relationship consummated at a distance, with no need for physical contact, or the expression of feeling. Essentially, all that will ever be exchanged is information. While the encounter between vamp and victim undoubtedly puts race, gender, and sexuality in dramatic play, its animating force would appear to be, as I hope to show, a thought about the process or mechanics of communication. The scene of the encounter involves looking and being looked at, but its provocations extend beyond the poetics and politics of vision. It does not entirely fit the paradigms of visual pleasure which have long constituted a vital tradition in film theory. I will suggest later that the vamp film began to conform to those paradigms only at the moment of its disappearance, in or around 1925.

5   Ronald Genini, *Theda Bara: A Biography of the Silent Screen Vamp, with a Filmography* (Jefferson, NC: McFarland & Co., 1996), p. 16.
6   Diane Negra, 'Immigrant Stardom in Imperial America: Pola Negri and the Problem of Typology', in *Off-White Hollywood: American Culture and Ethnic Female Stardom* (London: Routledge, 2001), pp. 55–83 (pp. 62, 56).
7   Quoted by Lary May, *Screening Out of the Past: The Birth of Mass Culture and the Motion Picture Industry* (Oxford: Oxford University Press, 1980), p. 106.
8   Negra, 'Immigrant Stardom', pp. 72, 77.

A familiar, dependable account of the development of a twentieth-century media system or ecology chronicles the gradual emergence of analogue storage technologies (sound recording, film) from the shadow of a digital communication technology (the telegraph), to be challenged, in turn, at the height of their ascendancy, by analogue communication technologies (broadcast radio, television); before digital computing, at once storage and (from the 1960s) communication technology, brought the whole process 'full circle'.[9] The computer defines our era, a 'universal media machine' capable of converting 'all cultural categories and concepts' into algorithm.[10] 'By the late twentieth century,' John Durham Peters remarks, 'all media melt (incompletely, I would add) into digits.'[11] Peters's caveat is a salutary reminder that such transformations do not happen overnight. We might think of the vamp film as a comparable incompleteness in an otherwise decisive shift of emphasis, capital, and prestige, within the media system, from telegraphy to cinema. In what follows I will test two hypotheses: first, that considerable uncertainty persisted, well into the 1920s, concerning the exact function of cinema as a medium; secondly, that the vamp films prominent immediately after the transition to a cinema of narrative integration exploited a residual uncertainty concerning the uses of the medium in such a way as to create a 'come-hither look' which is not primarily about looking and being looked at.

Film as (Telegraphic) Medium

By 1900, the electric telegraph was the pre-eminent global telecommunications medium. Thanks to Guglielmo Marconi's indefatigable promotion of wireless telegraphy, it remained so well into the twentieth century. From the outset, cinema felt pressure from technologies such as telegraphy and telephony which had succeeded in defining an alternative version of what a truly modern medium actually does: make a connection, instantaneously, at a distance. In 1899, some New York vaudeville theatres hired Vitagraph to show pictures of the America's Cup yacht races a few hours after their occurrence. By arrangement with Marconi, others used wireless messages to plot the positions of the boats on a map displayed in the intervals between acts. The competition for instantaneity was fierce. The *New York Clipper* even felt moved to declare that 'the secret of Moving Pictures consists in their TIMELINESS.'[12]

The years immediately before the outbreak of the First World War saw the development of film as a news-gathering medium to rival the newspaper. Its further, very successful use for information and propaganda purposes during the

9   Friedrich Kittler, "The City Is a Medium," in *The Truth of the Technological World: Essays on the Genealogy of Presence*, trans. by Erik Butler (Stanford, CA: Stanford University Press, 2013), pp. 138–51 (p. 145).

10   Lev Manovich, *The Language of New Media* (Cambridge, MA: MIT Press, 2001), 47.

11   John Durham Peters, 'Strange Sympathies: Horizons of Media Theory in America and Germany', in *American Studies as Media Studies*, ed. by Frank Kelleter and Daniel Stein (Heidelberg: Universitätverlag, 2008), pp. 3–23 (p. 15).

12   Charles Musser, *The Emergence of Cinema: The American Screen to 1907* (New York: Scribner's, 1990), pp. 274–75.

war gave that development a massive further boost. George Creel, who ran the Congressional Committee on Public Information, claimed that during the war 'the screen' had brought the 'story of America' to millions world-wide, 'flashing the power of our army and navy, showing our natural resources, our industrial processes, our war spirit, and our national life.'[13] It was not just that the newsreels had become a 'necessary part' of the cinema programme, rather than mere filler. It was that cinema had begun to imagine itself as a 'screenpaper': an apparatus of 'animated journals' and sensational extras 'flashing to surprised audiences the record of events that the newsboys are even then shouting in the streets outside.'[14] Mutual had already named its twice-weekly newsreel the Screen Telegram.[15] By 1919, it was possible to describe the films made by Picture News and Pathé Gazette as the products of a 'film news medium'.[16] For the first half of the 1920s, at least, most commentators continued to think of film as a channel of communication with a built-in range of functions, none of them exclusive. The term almost invariably used with reference to film was not 'medium', but 'medium of'. It could not (yet) just *be* a medium. It had still to present itself as *a medium of* some already defined activity: dramatic expression, entertainment, art, education, news, advertising. By the end of the 1920s, it was possible, in some quarters at least, to speak confidently of 'the film medium'. A path had been cleared to the medium-specific approach of Rudolf Arnheim's *Film as Art* (1932). What most concerns me here is the fact that it needed clearing.

The consolidation of the 'film news medium' provoked an epidemic of appeals to timeliness in the advertising of fiction films or serials in the trade papers from 1915 to 1920. 'NOW, as the RUSSIAN REVOLUTION is gripping the world's attention,' one such advertisement announced, '*Darkest Russia* is released by the WORLD FILM CORPORATION at the PSYCHOLOGICAL MOMENT.'[17] Similarly, a slew of newspaper headlines serves to reinforce the 'timeliness' of Fox's *Bride 13*, a film about a sunken submarine.[18] The question of timeliness (of the 'psychological moment') was not just one for distributors and exhibitors to ponder. It also had a bearing on the way films were made. The Hollywood script editor and agent Agnes Platt believed that the exercise of control over facial expression was the best way to achieve the conciseness film as a medium requires.

> A scene which would take a quarter of an hour to play upon a stage may pass in the course of a single minute on the film. An idea is conveyed, and the audience jumps to its significance. If suggestion plays a large part on the stage, it plays a still larger part on the films. A thought passes from the screen to the spectator with the condensed and instantaneous significance of a Marconi message.[19]

13 George Creel, *How We Advertised America* (New York: Harper and Brothers, 1920), p. 273.
14 Jerome Shorey, 'The Romance of the Newsreel', *Photoplay*, February 1919, 74–75 (p. 74).
15 'Screen Telegram Comes to New York', *Moving Picture World*, 20 July 1918, p. 379.
16 'High Court of Justice', *The Times*, 12 March 1919, p. 4.
17 Advertisement for *Darkest Russia* (World Film Corporation), *Motion Picture News*, 31 March 1917, p. 1982.
18 Advertisement for *Bride 13* (Fox Entertainments), *Motion Picture News*, 25 September 1920, p. 2370.
19 Agnes Platt, *Practical Hints on Acting for the Cinema* (London: Stanley Paul, 1921), p. 35.

Film actors act at a distance from the viewer in both space and time: at the far end of a process of shot-selection and editing over which they have little or no control. How, then, to get the message through? How to achieve a 'condensed and instantaneous significance'? By a kind of wireless telegraphy. Even when it did not function as news item or advertisement, film had somehow to perform like a connective or messaging medium, rather than one that forever re-presents that which has been created somewhere else at some other time.

One way to grasp the aspiration to condensed and instantaneous significance is by examining how the term 'flash', which had long since furnished telegraphy with the idea of the 'newsflash', found its way into film discourse. A 'flash' was a scene shown momentarily, for a fraction of a second. In Hollywood movies, the flash-scene is a kind of newsflash: a headline without a report. It messages without even the faintest pretence of representation in full. Flash-scenes achieved their prominence in film discourse thanks to censorship, which until 1930 remained the primary responsibility of municipal and state authorities. During the 1910s, trade journals such as *Motography* ran regular items listing the latest idiocies committed by the censorship boards. Censorship worked by requiring that scenes either be cut altogether, or reduced to a flash. The changes required by the Chicago Board of Censorship in August 1914 apparently included the reduction to flashes of scenes which involved gambling, excessive violent, 'girls in tights', love-making performed on a couch, and people of colour behaving in an unruly fashion.[20] The flash-scene is a newsflash, a message in code. It demonstrates to those who possess the code that sex is happening, or violence, or savagery, or poker. Censorship required film to behave telegraphically.

Within Hollywood, the flash soon came to be understood as a way to pre-empt censorship: to message, without showing. There is an excellent example in Charlie Chaplin's *A Woman of Paris* (1923). Chaplin has to reveal that the heroine is a kept woman. He manages this by having her maid open a drawer, thereby dislodging the collar of a man's dress shirt, to the evident consternation of her ex-fiancé, who has come to paint her portrait. Adolphe Menjou, who plays her worldly protector, remarked in his autobiography that 'little touches' like this gave the film 'a flavour that was new to picturemaking'. But what created the flavour? Not the demand for continuity in editing which we now take to have been the basis of the classical Hollywood style, and which the starkness of the shot of the collar on the floor at the maid's feet palpably exceeds. Menjou also said that an earlier scene in the film in which a heavily disguised Chaplin plays a porter hurling luggage around was cut to a 'brief flash' because, although popular with preview audiences, it got in the way of the plot.[21] Narrative requirements prevailed, in this case. But a signal had nonetheless been sent, a newsflash about the star's presence in his own film. The practice of the flash, shaped in large measure by censorship, did a good deal to shape cinema as telegraphic, as a connective or messaging medium; even, or especially, when it sought to represent.[22]

20   'Weird Stunts of Our Censor Board', *Motography*, 1 August 1914, pp. 151–53.
21   Adolphe Menjou, *It Took Nine Tailors* (London: Sampson, Low, Marston, 1950), pp. 112–13, 115.
22   I develop the distinction between representational and connective media more fully in *Literature*

Vamping

From around 1900, 'sex' could be taken to mean an activity or behaviour as well as a gender. The cognate term 'sex appeal' was originally used, from around the same time, of a play which took sexuality or sexual relations as its theme. 'The play which contains no sex appeal is described by professional critics as being "undramatic" or "not a play at all",' an article in *Current Literature* explained in July 1910.[23] To lack sex appeal was to fail to function as a medium. Only subsequently did the term come to refer to personal magnetism, sometimes in the form of a transitive verb. To 'sex-appeal' someone was to make oneself attractive to them. 'Vampirism' became the term of art for sexual predation, or the calculating, carefully targeted exploitation of sex-appeal, thanks to a painting by Philip Burne-Jones which prompted a best-selling poem by Rudyard Kipling. In 1910, the poem in turn gave rise to a short 'picture dramatization' starring Margarita Fischer (1886–1975). All three were entitled 'The Vampire'. But it was not until 1915, and the further development of the feature-length film as the Hollywood staple, that the vamping scene assumed its definitive shape: its shape, I will argue, as a thought about telecommunication. In the volume of the standard *History of American Cinema* covering the period from 1907 to 1915, Eileen Bowser devotes a single paragraph to vamp films. But the scene she chooses to exemplify the new patterns of analytic editing which were later to be consolidated into the classical continuity system is a scene in *Red and White Roses* (1913) in which a vamp sex-appeals her victim across a crowded restaurant.[24] The questions raised by this scene, and others like it, do not only have to do with the consolidation of the classical continuity system. For it rapidly becomes clear that this vamp, like her many successors, does not so much embody or express or perform sexuality as transmit it. Fischer was soon to be outbid in the vamping stakes. The opening line of Kipling's poem ('A fool there was ...') had sufficient force to generate a full-length play, and then, in 1915, a sensational feature film starring Theda Bara.

Fox's *A Fool There Was*, directed by Frank Powell, set a seal on the vamp film's iconic scene. Scanning the paper one day, the Vampire discovers that John Schuyler (Edward José), a wealthy lawyer, has been appointed U.S. government representative in London, and swiftly books herself a cabin on the ship taking him to Europe. As he boards the ship, Schuyler passes the corpse of the Vampire's previous victim going in the opposite direction (he has just shot himself on the sun-deck). Schuyler's family have already arrived to see him off. They chat unconcernedly as the come-hither look flashed by the Vampire, after due preparation with powder-compact and mirror, strikes home (**Figs 14.1 and 14.2**). What this iconic scene makes amply clear is that the vamp's readiness to be more than looked at is *immediate*: no delay required, no beating about the bush. The news has been flashed from temptress to victim — and from screen to spectator.

in the First Media Age: Britain between the Wars (Cambridge, MA: Harvard University Press, 2013).

23   Anon, 'The Greatest French Playwright since Molière', *Current Literature*, 49 (1910), 85–86 (p. 86).

24   Eileen Bowser, *The Transformation of Cinema, 1907–1915* (Berkeley: University of California Press, 1990), pp. 187–88, 262–65.

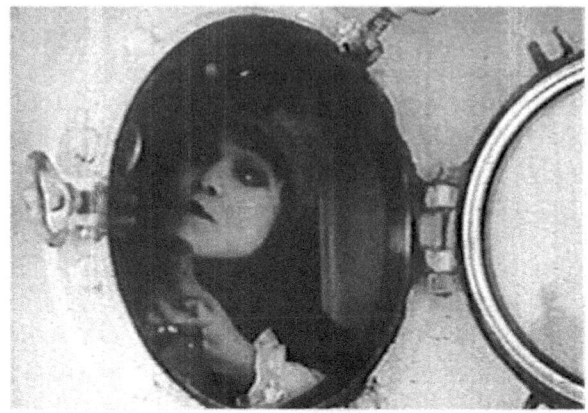

FIG. 14.1. The come-hither looks strikes home.
Frame grab from *A Fool There Was* (1915, Fox Film Corporation, dir. Frank Powell)

Bara went on to make many more such movies, including *Cleopatra* (1917) and *When a Woman Sins* (1918). Meanwhile, discussion of the significance of her signature role was intensifying in the trade journals and fan magazines. In a 1916 *Photoplay* article about Olga Petrova (1884–1977, born Muriel Harding) — a 'shadowland patrician' who can 'vamp quite a few' — Constance Severance noted that the term has several other senses, including an improvised accompaniment, and 'Something added to give an old thing a new appearance'. The vamp, Severance continued, is the 'unconventional, or improvised, accompaniment' to a man's life.[25] The senses she draws attention to might remind us of vamping's long association with telegraphy. To 'vamp' a telegram was to insert into it matter not in the original; that is, to hack it. In *A Fool There Was*, the Vampire's come-hither look is matter inserted into the message sent by the departing husband's embrace of his wife. Operating at a distance, by cyber-warfare, she has sucked the life out of a marriage. Does she at the same time suck the life out of a medium ostensibly dedicated to story-telling? For what we feel, at this moment, is the sheer force of a message sent.

25   Constance Severance, 'Our Lady of Troubles', *Photoplay*, October 1916, pp. 56–58.

Even when the vamp did get to close quarters, she remained in a way tele-communicative, as an April 1917 article by J. B. Waye in *Picture-Play Magazine* was to point out. The article describes a day in the working life of a young actress called Marie Wayne (1887–1949), which appears to have consisted of nine consecutive passionate embraces with nine separate men on nine separate sets; hence her designation as the 'kiss bandit'. But Waye clearly regards the kiss itself, the epitome of intimacy, as something communicated at a distance. 'When the lights went out and Marie started for home, the nine men who had used the receiver while she had used the mouthpiece were crowded about the entrance.'[26] The choice of metaphor is significant. By this account, the kiss is a message transmitted down the telephone wire from mouthpiece to receiver. Sex-appeal, it seems, had to do with getting a message through. Mae Busch (1891–1946), who starred in Erich von Stroheim's *The Devil's Pass Key* (1920) and *Foolish Wives* (1923), was soon to describe herself as the 'New Thought Vamp', telling an interviewer that 'I can do anything I choose if I project my thought toward an objective.'[27]

'In these piping days,' Severance had concluded her piece about Petrova, 'no moving picture corporation can maintain its self-respect unless it supports at least one vampire.'[28] *Film Fun* even built its own elaborate 'shrine' to the vamp.[29] Next off the production line was Pola Negri, who made her name in Ernst Lubitsch's *Madame Dubarry* (1919). The heroine's career involves two key transformations: from milliner to courtesan, and from courtesan to king's companion. In both cases, she is 'discovered' while running errands, seen (and seeing) at a distance in a public or semi-public space. In both cases, she makes up carefully before putting herself on display: the *toilette* is a signal in code. Paramount hired Lubitsch and Negri as a pair in 1922. Also prominent in *Film Fun*'s vamp shrine was Louise Glaum (1888–1970), who deserves mention, if only on account of her box-office smash of 1920, the unfussily titled *Sex* (**Fig. 14.3**). During a scene set in a night-club, the heroine transfers her affections from one rich idiot to another by means of a come-hither look rendered in close-up (**Fig. 14.4**). There is surely more 'hither' than 'look' in this expression reduced to a signal. The vampire business was still going strong, or quite strong, in 1925, with new contenders like Nita Naldi (1894–1961, born Mary Nonna Dooley) and Barbara la Marr (1896–1926, born Reatha Dale Watson) making an impact. Naldi and La Marr contributed side-by-side pieces on 'This Business of Being a Vampire' to *Motion Picture Magazine*. Naldi waxed lyrical about vamping Valentino in the toreador epic *Blood and Sand* (1922); and with some justice.[30]

In *Blood and Sand*, the scene of the come-hither look takes place at the bull-ring, as a triumphant Valentino acknowledges the crowd's applause (**Figs 14.5–6**). There is a difference, however: one which might suggest that the vamp film had begun to conform to the rules of a cinema which demanded the full representation of the

26   J. B. Waye, 'The Kiss Bandit: A Day on the Trail of the Rouged Lips', *Picture-Play Magazine*, April 1917, pp. 187–88 (p. 188).

27   Herbert Howe, 'The New Thought Vamp', *Motion Picture Magazine*, November 1921, pp. 40–41, 84 (p. 41).

28   Severance, 'Our Lady of Troubles', p. 57.

29   'The Shrine of the Vampire, *Film Fun*, January 1919, p. 2.

30   Nita Naldi, 'This Business of Being a Vampire', *Motion Picture Magazine*, March 1925, p. 42.

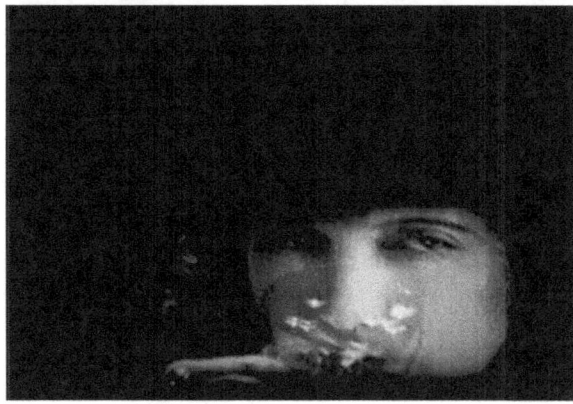

FIG. 14.3. 'H. A. Albright, manager of the American theatre, Butte, Mont., believes in keeping some single phrase consistently in the public eye. In this lobby display the title of the picture is used.' *Exhibitors Herald*, 29 May 1920, p. 57.

FIG. 14.4. The vamp transfers her affections. Frame grab from *Sex*
(1920, Pathé Exchange, dir. Fred Niblo).

male — and more particularly the female — body. Valentino's star-status may well have made the difference. For Naldi observes him, through a pair of opera glasses, before he observes her. There is, now, an explicit preoccupation with looking and being looked at, with the power of the gaze. According to Miriam Hansen, Valentino's films 'rehearse the classical choreography of the look almost to the point of parody, offering point-of-view constructions that affirm the cultural hierarchy of gender in the visual field.' Whenever Valentino lays eyes on a woman, Hansen adds, 'we can be sure that she will turn out to be the woman of his dreams, the legitimate partner in the romantic relationship.' Whenever a woman initiates the look, however, 'she is invariably marked as a vamp, to be condemned and defeated in the course of the narrative.'[31] Classical Hollywood cinema re-inscribed that cultural hierarchy over and over again upon the bodies of the vamp's many and

31   Hansen, *Babel and Babylon*, p. 269.

FIGS. 14.5 and 14.6. Vamped at the bull-ring. Frame grabs from *Blood and Sand* (1922, Paramount Pictures, dir. Fred Niblo).

various successors. In *Blood and Sand*, however, a thought about communication — about perverted, or vamped, communication — persists. After the show, Naldi manages to get Valentino's undivided attention. Knowing that he will not be able to resist her, Valentino asks a friend to send a reassuring telegram to his wife (the woman he had seen first, the woman of his dreams), which the film promptly vamps by superimposing upon it a question mark (**Fig. 14.7**). That extra-diegetic question mark passes from the screen to the spectator with the 'condensed and instantaneous significance', as Agnes Platt might have put it, of a Marconi message. The exploits of the ethnically hybrid vamp, and by implication of the ethnically hybrid star who plays the part, have marked cinema as a hybrid medium, at once representational and connective.

FIG. 14.7. An extra-diegetic message.
Frame grab from *Blood and Sand* (1922, Paramount Pictures, dir. Fred Niblo)

Cecil B. DeMille and the *toilette de Venus*

By the mid-1920s, there were a number of overlapping categories available to describe the New (or newly sexualized) Woman. Fox's *The Folly of Vanity* (1925), for example, included parts for a 'Siren' (Edna Gregory), a 'Russian Vamp' (Edna Mae Cooper), and a 'Blond Gold Digger' (Lotus Thompson). But the (older, wiser, darker) sirens and vamps were on the way out. The emphasis had shifted to a defiantly blonde or near-blonde gold-digging: the 'Cinderella story', in industry parlance.[32] There could be no objection to aggressive social mobility as long as it culminated in the expression of a 'naturally' feminine (and American) self. In 1925, Mary Pickford (1892–1979, born Gladys Louise Smith) invited readers of *Photoplay* to propose some possible screen roles, adding that she did not want to be in costume pictures, but only those dealing with the problems of the 'average American girl'. The role she eventually chose for herself was that of a shop assistant, in *My Best Girl* (1927). Maggie does not realize that her co-worker, Joe the stock-boy, is the owner's son. When Joe's father tells her that marriage to Joe will ruin his career, she attempts to sacrifice herself by pretending that she was only after his money. She smears on lipstick, smokes a cigarette, and dances to a recording of a song called 'Red Hot Mama'. Joe and his father, looking on, understand that it is only an act: her natural self shines through the masquerade. The gold-digging template was to prove immensely popular. Hollywood Cinderella stories include *Manhandled* (1924), *Orchids and Ermine* (1927), *Possessed* (1931), *Bed of Roses* (1933), and *Baby Face* (1933). *Baby Face*, in particular, is strong stuff. Even there, however, female sexual aggression is off-set by a powerful dose of natural (American) femininity. The same could be said of the celebrated flapper films of the 1920s. 'The flapper's sexuality was not perceived as overpowering men; she was soft and romantic, and although

---

32 Jacobs, *Wages of Sin*, pp. 11–13.

she viewed her paid work as a sign of her independence, she did not seek a career that would require her to forgo marriage.'[33] Such confidence in the power of self-expression — as opposed to tele-communicative technique — seems at once to produce and be produced by an understanding of cinema as a narrative mass-medium, or popular representational art.

The vamp, however, did not go quietly, even in films made by directors whose work was to set the pattern for classical Hollywood cinema. My final example of the tribe's power to unsettle a medium as well as a moral code is from Cecil B. DeMille's *Old Wives for New* (1918). The first in a divorce trilogy, *Old Wives for New* was to be followed (with a certain lack of imagination) by *Don't Change Your Husband* (1919) and *Why Change Your Wife?* (1920). These films look back to Griffith at his most sententious, and forward to the comedy of remarriage. They are cynical, and didactic. They sermonize; and they message mischievously.

DeMille came from a distinguished Broadway family. In December 1913, he abandoned a failing stage career and set off for California to take up the post of director-general of a new film studio, the Jesse L. Lasky Feature Play Company, before long to become Famous Players-Lasky. Lasky and DeMille presented themselves as purveyors of art rather than amusement. Reviews in the trade press began to put increasing emphasis on DeMille's ability to create pictorial effects, in particular through nuanced lighting. Rembrandt and Titian were among the names cheerfully taken in vain. DeMille certainly believed his own propaganda. In an interview he gave to *Moving Picture World* in July 1917, he spoke of the ways in which the audience might be made to 'feel' the background of a scene rather than 'see' it. 'We are beginning to pose our people in the settings as a painter would pose them, with consideration for the perfect balance of the scene.'[34] Those settings included a significant proportion of domestic interiors strewn with high-end consumer durables. An article in *Photoplay* described how the magazine's Home Furnishing Editor had been able to help a movie-struck bride to recreate the 'DeMille boudoir' from *The Golden Bed* (1925), complete with dressing-table.[35] Gloria Swanson (1899–1983), DeMille's favourite female lead, was said to regard that particular item of furniture as 'one of her chief assets' at work and at home.[36] The other star featured in the article was Negri: vamping could be understood as *toilette*'s dangerous telegraphic supplement.

There is, of course, a rich history of representations of *toilette* in high art. In paintings by Titian, Rubens, Velasquez, and many others since, the goddess Venus, or one of her mortal equivalents, fresh from the bath, and in varying degrees of *décolleté*, gazes into a mirror held by an amenable attendant.[37] Both Hollywood

33   Stephen Sharot, 'The "New Woman", Star Personas, and Cross-Class Romance Films in 1920s America', *Journal of Gender Studies*, 19 (2010), 73–86 (pp. 78, 75).
34   Cecil B. DeMille, 'Photodrama a New Art', *Moving Picture World*, 21 July 1917, p. 374.
35   Marguerite Henry, 'Use Picture Ideas to Beautify Your Home', *Photoplay*, April 1925, pp. 48–49.
36   William J. Moll, 'Have You a Dressing-Table? This Will Help You to Make One', *Photoplay*, April 1924, pp. 24–25.
37   David Trotter, 'Modernist *Toilette*: Degas, Woolf, Lawrence', in *The Uses of Phobia: Essays on Literature and Film* (Oxford: Wiley-Blackwell, 2010), pp. 77–96.

FIG. 14.8. A candid stare, followed by a wink.
Frame grab from *Old Wives for New* (1918, Paramount Pictures, dir. Cecil B. DeMille)

and the magazine discourse surrounding it enthusiastically re-worked the *toilette* pictorial tradition. Advertisements for the Tre-Jur compact show a 'Venus of Today' examining her make-up with its help, while a bust of the goddess looms behind her.[38] The compact is a palm tablet or code-book consulted prior to signalling. Similarly, lashes darkened by Winx Waterproof will convert an upward glance into a come-hither look.[39] These invocations of *toilette* recall the telegraphic triumphs of the vamp in order to normalize them.

No one did *toilette* quite like Cecil B. DeMille, in his pre-biblical epic days. Of special interest is his incorporation of vamp-like female sexuality into social dramas which evade mere advertisement by invoking high art, and mere high art, in turn, by the telegraphic connection they establish with the spectator. The opening shots of *Old Wives for New* introduce us to Charles Murdock (Elliott Dexter), an 'Oil King' who has fallen out of love with his wife, and to the five pairs of hands which are to weave the threads of his subsequent destiny. Each pair of hands merits a brief vignette. The most elaborate of these is the one which depicts the *toilette* undertaken by Viola, a demi-mondaine, or Painted Lady, played by Marcia Manon (1896–1973, born Marcia Elizabeth Harrison). The vignette's effect depends on a degree of familiarity with canonical Western art; in this case, with the variation on the *toilette* tradition exemplified by Titian's *Venus of Urbino* (1538) and its momentous modern consequence, Manet's *Olympia* (1863). The vignette shows the Painted Lady at her dressing-table, reflected in a triptych of mirrors. Like Olympia, she has a black maid whose gaze offers a reflection of and upon the success of her *toilette*. But the most startling effect is the Painted Lady's candid stare at the camera, accompanied by the faintest flicker of a wink, and a pout **(Fig. 14.8)**. The stare again suggests Manet, whose trademark effect was the gaze returned with interest: most immediately, perhaps, given the prominence of the powder-puff, the Manet of *Nana* (1877) rather

38   Advertisement for Tre-Jur compacts, *Motion Picture Magazine*, April 1925, p. 10.
39   Advertisement for Winx Waterproof, *Photoplay*, May 1925, p. 145.

than of *Olympia*. But it seems to me that, like the question mark in *Blood and Sand*, the wink supervenes on, or displaces, any great interest in looking and being looked at. The wink and the pout do what painting could never do. This meta-vamping could be said to break the picture-plane: to suspend narrative, at the very juncture when narrative was becoming what cinema as a medium is about.

I alluded at the outset of this essay to the fabulous indiscretion of the vamp films. I hope that my examination of these films as a media event which took place to equally vivid effect in the fan magazines and on the screen will by now have established that they were fabulously indiscreet with regard to the nature, scope, and function of cinema as a medium as well as of human sexual desire. How much more interesting, perhaps, to think of the come-hither look not as a representation, but as a message sent as if by some other medium altogether: a Marconigram, a newsflash, a phone-call, a Jazz Age emoticon. As cinema melts into digits, like everything else, it could do worse than recall some of the hybridities which flourished during a long-forgotten episode in its history.

CHAPTER 15

Representing Connection:
A Multimedia Approach to
Colonial Film, 1918–1939

The aim of this essay is to build on the premises established by Lee Grieveson in his illuminating account of the mutual reinforcement and mutual reconfiguration of the British film industry and the British imperial project between 1926 and 1933.[1] These premises are: a) that during the 1920s a new paradigm of empire took shape in Britain, with the emphasis on the gradual formation of a global economic bloc of self-governing nation-states, an emphasis enshrined as the British Commonwealth by the Statute of Westminster in 1931; b) that this new paradigm posed, for British capitalism, and for the (mostly Conservative or Conservative-led) British governments of the period, a problem of representation, or, if you prefer, propaganda; and c) that, from 1926, British cinema had an important part to play in solving this problem, under the auspices of the Empire Marketing Board (EMB) and other organizations, and underwent in the process a fundamental alteration, both formally, as a result of the emergence of documentary as a hallmark or signature genre, and institutionally, by means of the development of a range of non-theatrical distribution networks. I propose at once to narrow the focus of the argument, to images of Ceylon, a Crown Colony until 1948; and to broaden it, by approaching cinema as one of several media, some visual, some not, each to a significant degree given over, during the period between the World Wars, to promotion of the imperial project.

Grieveson describes British documentary cinema as an instrument of capitalist imperialism: that 'contradictory fusion', as David Harvey has put it, of two logics of power, one concerned primarily with command over and use of capital, the other primarily with command over and use of the human and natural resources specific to a territory or territories.[2] The main purpose of the EMB's extensive investment in film was to enable both domestic and colonial audiences to visualize the circulation of raw materials and manufactured goods which constituted the

1   Lee Grieveson, 'The Cinema and the (Common) Wealth of Nations', in *Empire and Film*, ed. by Colin MacCabe and Lee Grieveson (Basingstoke: Palgrave Macmillan, 2011), pp. 73–113.
2   David Harvey, *The New Imperialism* (Oxford: Oxford University Press, 2003), p. 26.

Commonwealth's common wealth. Grieveson takes as his main example *West Africa Calling* (1927), which demonstrates the capacity of British capital and technology to convert African swamp and desert into factory, hospital, and school. 'It is in these images,' he argues, 'and the connections made between them through editing, that the film effects a visual corollary to the pathways that connect imperial economics, to the hidden movements of capital that escape imagining but underpin so much of the colonial archive.' In EMB films, images of 'material connection, emphasized through the connective tissue of editing, are central to the visualization of the Conservative political economy that positions empire developments and markets as central to the sustenance of the wealth of the nation.'[3] Representing material connection was a task enthusiastically undertaken by the two films I will discuss here: Basil Wright's *Song of Ceylon*, and a British Pathé newsreel, *The Ceylon Tea Industry* (both 1934).

The connective pathways visualized in films like *West Africa Calling* and *The Ceylon Tea Industry* were the product of the 'round after round of time-space compression' which have by Harvey's account remorselessly driven the 'evolution of the geographical landscape of capitalist activity'.[4] The concept of time-space compression, originating in Marxism, indeed in Marx himself, but currently put to a variety of uses, can be taken to encompass the ways in which human societies have sought to convert distance into durations of shorter and shorter span with a view to the efficient and profitable exchange of goods and information. According to Barney Warf, time-space compression constitutes a 'mechanism' for the production of 'places' as 'nodes within increasingly wider networks of mobility and power'.[5] By 1930, there was a general understanding that the most recent round of time-space compression involved technological advances in aviation and in wireless telegraphy and telephony. Films about the global movement of raw materials by train, truck, and ship have to be seen in the context of the pre-eminence then attributed in fact and fantasy to air-routes and telecommunications networks. Telecommunication had already become, and still remains, capitalism's essential lubricant.[6] To put it another way, the media which substantially re-made empire in their own image during the period between the World Wars were the new media of wireless telegraphy and telephony, not the old medium of film. But radio signals do not 'have' an image. So efficient are they in making connections, by the compression

3   Grieveson, 'The Cinema and the (Common) Wealth of Nations', pp. 10–11.

4   Harvey, *New Imperialism*, p. 98. See also Harvey, *The Limits to Capital* (Oxford: Blackwell, 1982); and Harvey, *The Condition of Postmodernity* (Oxford: Blackwell, 1989).

5   Barney Warf, *Time-Space Compression: Historical Geographies* (London: Routledge, 2008), p. 9. Warf provides a lucid overview and critique of competing theories of time-space compression. I have tried to follow his example, if not exactly his method, in attending to the historical 'particularities' of the phenomenon in all of their 'messy complexity' (p. 39).

6   Gwen Urey, 'Telecommunications and Global Capitalism', in *Telecommunications Politics: Ownership and Control of the Information Highway in Developing Countries*, ed. by Bella Mody, Johannes M. Bauer, and Joseph D. Straubhaar (Mahwah, NJ: Lawrence Erlbaum Associates, 1995), pp. 53–83. For a comprehensive account of the history of these developments, see Peter J. Hugill, *Global Communications since 1844: Geopolitics and Technology* (Baltimore, MD: Johns Hopkins University Press, 1999).

of distance into instantaneity, that there is nothing left to represent, nothing that requires representation. We could not see the message moving even if we wished to. However, such almost absolute time-space compression did not render cinema redundant. The job of the representational media, including cinema, was to render palpable once again a connectivity which had become at once more necessary than ever before and more abstract.

Representing Connection: Newsprint and Other Media

Connection had long been understood as the key to that enhancement of the mere occupation of territory thought most likely to consolidate Great Britain's commercial and military power in an increasingly competitive world. The British government invested heavily in an 'all-red' global submarine cable network connecting the centre of empire to its most far-flung peripheries. By 1902, British capitalism controlled most of the world's major commercial cables, while the government had at its disposal a secure means of communication with all strategically significant colonial territories and naval bases.[7] That network played no small part in the defeat of Germany in the First World War. What really put the cat among the cable-laying pigeons, however, was the invention of radio.

Guglielmo Marconi's first experiments in the new medium, in the 1890s, had shown that radio waves follow the contours of the earth's surface below the horizon by diffraction, and that the distance they travel is proportional to their length and to the strength of the transmitter. During the period up to and beyond the First World War, the great powers and even greater corporations sought continually to outdo each other in the field of long-wave radio transmission. Before the War, the world's most powerful transmitter was located at Nauen, near Berlin; after it, at Sainte-Assise, near Paris. In the 1920s, the Post Office built a super-station at Rugby capable of reaching Australia or the entire Royal Navy at once, submarines included. It had twelve towers, each 250 metres high, supporting an antenna which covered ten square kilometres. Although radio was by now essential to shipping, it remained an adjunct to cable-borne telegraphy in long-distance communication. Cables, though more costly, were more reliable, and more secure. But the demand for communications grew so fast after the end of the war that both cable and wireless companies had as much business as they could handle.[8] The connections to be represented were those made possible by a new medium (wireless telegraphy) in competition with an old one (cable telegraphy); and by a surge of investment in a new mode of transport, the aeroplane, which could itself be conceived, as we shall see, as in some sense a medium.

On 3 February 1920, *The Times* reported that Major-General Sir F. H. Sykes, Controller General of Civil Aviation, had given a lecture on the topic of imperial

---

7   Daniel R. Headrick, *The Invisible Weapon: Telecommunications and International Politics, 1851–1945* (Oxford: Oxford University Press, 1991), pp. 93–98.

8   This paragraph relies heavily on Daniel R. Headrick, 'Shortwave Radio and Its Impact on International Telecommunications between the Wars', *History and Technology*, 11 (1994), 21–32

air routes at the Royal Geographical Society to an audience including the Prince of Wales and a generous selection of dignitaries. Sykes's theme was that the British Empire would henceforth be sustained by air rather than sea power, and by the development of telecommunication technologies. The Empire, he said, possessed a unique capacity to establish 'air depots, refuelling bases, and meteorological and wireless stations in every part of the world.' This network of depots and stations had already taken shape in his mind. 'Egypt,' he went on, 'for some time to come must be the "hub" or, as I have long called it, the Clapham Junction of the India, Australia, and Cape routes, and the heart of the whole system of their expansion.' Winston Churchill responded on behalf of the Air Ministry, arguing that the impulse given to aviation by war should be maintained during peace.[9] Sykes's lecture provided a template for the representation of empire as connectivity. But how was such a system to be established?

The Times took up the cause of time-space compression. Distance, a leading article announced,

> is the chief barrier between the scattered British peoples. But geographical distance should be measured not by the absolute standard of mileage on sea or land, but by mileage divided by the time taken to traverse it. Theoretically the time-mile is now a fraction of a second for telegraphy, less than a minute for aeroplanes, approximately a minute for airships and railway trains, under ninety seconds for light road-transport, and from two to ten minutes for various forms of sea transport.

The smooth and secure functioning of empire required 'the quickest transport and the most nearly instantaneous wireless and cable communication'.[10] The Times had for some time been doing rather more than merely report government initiatives to reinforce or recreate empire through connection. Its proprietor, Alfred Harmsworth, Lord Northcliffe, was at once a staunch imperialist and the chief exponent of the serialized photographic encyclopedia. The ambition of the Northcliffe press was, as Michael North has put it, 'to construct an empire of information at least as extensive as the British Empire itself.'[11] On 4 February 1920, the day after it had reported Sykes's speech about imperial air routes, The Times published the map of the route to be taken by an air-expedition it had itself funded to blaze a trail the length of Africa from Cairo to the Cape: landing grounds, emergency landing grounds, wireless stations.[12] The flight was undertaken by Alan Cobham, a First World War fighter-ace hitherto reduced to providing joy-rides at air-shows. The Times charted his progress from Cairo to the Cape assiduously. In 1921, Cobham joined the De Haviland Aircraft Company. He made the trail-blazing spectacular his business. Indeed, he made time-space compression his business. Speaking at a luncheon given

9   'Empire Air Routes', The Times, 3 February 1920, p. 6.
10   'Imperial Communications', The Times, 7 July 1921, p. 11.
11   Michael North, Reading 1922: A Return to the Scene of the Modern (New York: Oxford University Press, 1999), p. 126. For Northcliffe's personal reflections on the state of the Empire, see My Journey Round the World (16 July 1921 — 26 February 1922), ed. by Cecil and St John Harmsworth (Philadelphia, PA: J. B. Lippincott, 1923).
12   'From London to the Cape by Air', The Times, 4 February 1920, p. 9.

in his honour by the British Empire League in May 1925, he argued for more and better imperial air-routes. 'By aviation could be effected the quick passage of letters and individuals and acceleration of business. Life could only be judged in measures of time.'[13]

The maps accompanying and promoting the flights undertaken by Cobham and others represent empire as connection. By the 1920s, Michael Heffernan observes, news media were no longer content merely to describe or picture remote colonial territories. They also became engaged in 'actively constructing' the idea and reality of empire as 'an integrated space of flows, an abstract concept made real by the telegraph, radio, and aviation networks through which news items circulated between the imperial periphery and the metropolitan core'.[14] The newspaper map represents connection as contiguity: as a chain of depots, bases, and stations. The best way to conceive empire's 'integrated space of flows' — that 'abstract concept' — was to pin it to the earth's surface. Addressing the Imperial Conference in October 1926, Sir Samuel Hoare, Secretary of State for Air, announced that he and his wife were soon to attempt the new Cairo to Karachi route. The next step, he thought, should be an extension to Bombay and Calcutta. And how about Rangoon? 'If, in the not remote future, links can be inserted in some such way as I have suggested, a long chain of great tensile power will have been forged across the Empire's framework.'[15] Hoare's remarks indicate not just that political and economic connection could be imagined concretely, but that concreteness itself had taken on an important political and economic function. Empire's integrated space of flows would only ever be fully known as a paradigm of global integration if and when it became fully contiguous throughout that space, fully tensile: one link clasping, flexed against, the next.

Contiguity proved a tall order, but not an impossible one. Imperial Airways, established by multiple merger in 1924 with a working capital of £1 million, two government-appointed directors on a board of ten, and the promise of £1 million of subsidies over the next ten years, took on the task of developing the major empire routes. Regular passenger services from Croydon airport reached Delhi in 1929, Cape Town in 1932, Brisbane in 1934, and Hong Kong in 1936.[16] 'A single operating company, partly financed by the British government, has the job,' as the American magazine *Popular Mechanics* put it, 'of linking together an empire that compasses the globe and includes more than 350,000 people.' There was even the possibility of a 'globe-circling airway, 20,000 miles long,' operated in conjunction with Pan-American's Pacific line: English the only language spoken throughout.[17]

13 'Aviation and the Empire', *The Times*, 22 May 1925, p. 13.
14 Michael Heffernan, 'The Cartography of the Fourth Estate: Mapping the New Imperialism in British and French Newspapers, 1875–1925', in *The Imperial Map: Cartography and the Mastery of Empire*, ed. by James R. Akerman (Chicago, IL: University of Chicago Press, 2009), pp. 261–99 (p. 293).
15 'The Imperial Conference', *The Times*, 29 Oct 1926, p. 9.
16 Gordon Pirie, *Air Empire: British Imperial Civil Aviation, 1919–1939* (Manchester: Manchester University Press, 2009).
17 'Wings over the British Empire' *Popular Mechanics*, 64 (1935), 674–77 (pp. 674, 676–77).

Imperial Airways posters of the 1930s show an inverted Y with its base in London and its stem forking at Cairo: in one direction, the route stretches down through Entebbe, Nairobi, and Salisbury (Harari) to Johannesburg and Cape Town; in the other, across to Baghdad, Basra, Karachi, and Delhi, and then down to Rangoon, Bangkok, Singapore, and beyond. Cairo, Sykes's Clapham Junction, was regarded as the key link in the chain. Rather, the idea of Egypt, or of 'the Egyptian', overwhelmingly familiar in Britain since Howard Carter had re-opened King Tutankhamen's tomb on 29 November 1922, anchored a whole way of thinking about connection — about empire as an integrated space of flows. In one of the most evocative of all the Imperial Airways posters, an airliner approaches a pair of sharply-etched pyramids from the general direction of Karachi (snow-capped peaks) by way of Baghdad (minarets). These destinations had to be held within a single glance if the territories they occupied were to be understood as newly contiguous. Martin Stollery notes that the promotional films made by Strand for Imperial Airways in the late 1930s often include planes over pyramids: the ancient engineering feat now viewed afresh in all its grandeur courtesy of a modern one.[18]

Passengers alone did not establish contiguity. There were simply too few of them. From the outset, civil aviation had required significant subsidy. Postal services soon became instrumental in its growth, offering lucrative contracts to private carriers between selected cities. In Nevil Shute's *So Disdained* (1923), a veteran pilot recalls the early days of the London-Paris flights.

> They used to carry the much advertised Air Mails. That meant that the machines had to fly whether there were passengers to be carried or not. It was left to the discretion of the pilot whether or not the flight should be cancelled in bad weather; the pilots were dead keen and went on flying in the most impossible conditions.[19]

The Air Mail became at once agent and emblem of connectivity (**Fig. 15.1**). On one hand, it greatly reduced the amount of time monetary orders spent in the mails, thus accelerating capital's invisible flow;[20] on the other, it was easy to visualize as a series of linked physical actions (publicity material often features the transfer of a bulging mail-bag from van or launch to plane). A British Pathé newsreel of 1932 reports that the 38-seat liner inaugurating the weekly London to Cape Town service would accommodate no more than three passengers on this occasion in order to leave room for an 'enormous quantity of mail'.

Air Mail was a chain of events anyone could initiate simply by placing a letter in a letter-box. During the 1930s, Imperial Airways rebranded itself in spectacular fashion by securing a contract to carry *all* the British Empire's mail at a flat rate of a penny halfpenny per half ounce. The Empire Mail Scheme, launched on 29 June 1937, made use of a fleet of twenty-eight sveltely modern flying-boats which

18 Martin Stollery, *Alternative Empires: European Modernist Cinemas and Cultures of Imperialism* (Exeter: University of Exeter Press, 2000) pp. 167–68. Michael North describes Carter's exploits as 'the first truly modern media event': *Reading 1922*, p. 19.
19 Nevil Shute, *So Disdained* (London: Heinemann, 1951), p. 14.
20 Warf, *Time-Space Compression*, p. 148.

FIG. 15.1. Agent and emblem of connectivity. Frame grab from *Air Post*
(1934, GPO Film Unit, dir. Geoffrey Clarke)

became the company's best advertisement. To be sure, they carried more passengers in even greater luxury. But their *raison d'être* was to deliver packets of information rapidly and reliably. The Empire Mail Scheme did not merely represent connection. It converted a particular mode of transport into a telecommunications medium. That said, we should not necessarily assume that air travel created a 'discontinuous geography of collected rather than connected points'.[21] There was nothing at all impalpable about the links forming the Empire Mail chain. The British Pathé newsreel announcing the scheme's first return flight from Australia shows the boat's Captain not in the cockpit, but in a launch headed out into the harbour, mail-bag in hand.

Palpability was a quality not easy to associate with the new media of wireless telegraphy and telephony which set about compressing time-space during the 1920s, as a supplement to, or in competition with, cable. In 1921, *The Times* could still envisage a 'chain' or girdle of stations 'connecting the communities of the Empire by geographical steps of about 2,000 miles each'.[22] The long-wave station built at Rugby had physical presence enough and to spare. However, Marconi and his research engineers had been working with bandwidths under 200 metres. They knew that radio waves could be intensified by reflection; and that, because the reflector had to be proportional in size to the square of the wavelength, the method would only work for short-wave radio. Using a parabolic reflector made of

21   D. Simonsen, 'Accelerating Modernity: Time-Space Compression in the Wake of the Aeroplane', *Journal of Transport History*, 26 (2005), 98–117 (p. 100). For widely differing but equally informative accounts of the consequences of such acceleration for national sovereignty and national identity, see Gillian Beer, 'The Island and the Aeroplane: The Case of Virginia Woolf', in *Nation and Narration*, ed. by Homi Bhabha (London: Routledge, 1990), pp. 265–90; and David L. Butler, 'Technogeopolitics and the Struggle for Control of World Air Routes, 1910–1928', *Political Geography*, 20 (2001), 635–58.
22   'Empire Wireless Chain', *The Times*, 7 April 1921, p. 9.

wire, they were able to direct much of the transmitter's energy towards a receiver equipped with a parabolic antenna. In May 1924, Marconi announced that messages transmitted from Cornwall using his 'beam' system had been received by engineers in Australia, India, South Africa, and North and South America. Short-wave radio was a great deal cheaper than long-wave, and it transmitted at up to 200 words per minute, faster than long-wave, faster even than cable. The British Government signed a contract with Marconi to build short-wave stations in Canada, Australia, South Africa, and India. These stations were owned and operated by the Post Office. The BBC's Empire Service began broadcasting on short-wave on 19 December 1932.[23] 'The most striking development of all the electrical arts during the last quarter of a century,' declared Edward Appleton, Wheatstone Professor of Physics at London University,

> has undoubtedly been the advance in radio-communication. Such development has been much more than the registration of purely technical improvements, for wireless, by way of broadcasting, has introduced a new medium of cultural and political enlightenment in our social life and, by way of the overseas wireless telephone, has brought the parts of the Empire into closer and more intimate touch than ever before.

Progress in the development of high-definition television, Appleton continued, meant that the BBC would before too long be in a position to inaugurate a London service operating on ultra-short waves.[24]

For a variety of reasons, commercial, political, and technical, short-wave radio did not simply displace long-wave, any more than wireless transmission displaced transmission by submarine cable.[25] In fact, an Imperial Wireless and Cable Conference held in January 1927 recommended the merger of all British communications interests. The plan was approved by Parliament in August 1928. In April 1929, the new conglomerate, Imperial and International Communications, assumed control over 253 cable and radio stations, and more than half the world's cables. Each point on the network was now linked to all the others by at least two separate channels of communication. Cable and Wireless, as it was from 1934, had become as monumental a 'pillar' of Empire as Imperial Airways.[26]

Short waves do not curve around the earth's surface. Instead, they bounce off the upper layers of the atmosphere, reappearing far from their origin by means of a 'skip' effect. They make it hard to imagine contiguity as a principle of connection. This is one data-flow which cannot be mapped without interruption from point to point across a network. Short-wave radio exemplified the dilemma confronting

---

23   Headrick, 'Shortwave Radio', pp. 24–25. See also Hugill, *Global Communications*, ch. 5; and Aitor Anduaga, *Wireless and Empire: Geopolitics, Radio Industry, and Ionosphere in the British Empire, 1918–1939* (Oxford: Oxford University Press, 2009), pp. 63–72.
24   Edward Appleton, 'World-Wide Radio', *The Times*, 3 May 1935, p. 54.
25   For a detailed account, see Dwayne R. Winseck and Robert M. Pike, *Communication and Empire: Media, Markets, and Globalization, 1860–1930* (Durham, NC: Duke University Press, 2007), pp. 306–29.
26   Headrick, 'Shortwave Radio', p. 27. See also Hugill, *Global Communications since 1844*, pp. 118–19, 128–34.

representational media from the mid-1920s onwards. Representing connectivity had just got a lot harder. Maps of the period which display the imperial cable and wireless network tend to show radio beams curving delicately around the earth's surface to their remote destinations as though the transmitters were all long-wave. There could be continuity in fantasy — in representation — where there was now none in fact. It may be significant that Appleton's *Times* article on developments in short-wave radio, which has nothing at all to say about transport, should none the less include a large photograph of different kinds of aircraft on the tarmac at Croydon. Visualization there had still to be.

What of Ceylon, in all this? Ceylon became something of a representational crux for capitalist imperialism, because while the island was an important and venerable Crown Colony, and indeed one sometimes still held up as a model of annexation, it remained for much of the period on the periphery of the new imperial networks.[27] Speaking at Norwich in October 1925, Sir Samuel Hoare argued that for political, strategic, and commercial purposes 'flying lines' should be driven as rapidly and as extensively as possible across the Empire. All around the world there were British territories or spheres of influence 'which at almost regular intervals could be used as landing grounds or links in the great Empire air chain'. There was no technical reason, Hoare concluded, 'why Bombay should not be brought within four days of London instead of 14, why Calcutta and Colombo should not be reached in six or seven days instead of 16 or 17, why Singapore should not be reached in eight days rather than 24, and Melbourne in 13 instead of 32.'[28] It was to be some time, however, before Colombo could claim a status equal to those other cities. On 15 December 1927, *The Times* reported the imminent departure of two RAF officers who planned to undertake a 'propaganda flight and reconnaissance of air transport prospects' in India, Burma, and the Federated Malay States. Their intention was to fly on to Ceylon, though that would require the conversion of their machines into seaplanes at Calcutta.[29] The map of 'World Markets and Empire Trade' supplied with the *Graphic*'s British Industries Supplement on 19 November 1927 shows Ceylon as a crucial link in the network of shipping-routes; as does that which features in Elsie K. Cook's 1931 *A Geography of Ceylon*. 'The air-route to Australia,' Cook explains, 'does not touch Colombo, but goes via Karachi and Rangoon.'[30] By 1937, there were reports of 'the creation, stage by stage, of an organization which is throwing a chain of marine alighting, mooring, and re-fuelling points across India, equipped with all the latest devices available, and reinforced by an amplified service of wireless and meteorology.' Ceylon was at last to be 'brought regularly within the great Empire network of air-mail routes.'[31]

The story was the same with regard to telecommunications. Ceylon had long since been connected to the rest of the world by cable. An Eastern and Associated

27   Professor A. P. Newton, 'Forgotten Deeds of Empire', *Saturday Review*, 19 September 1936, p. 376.
28   'Air Defence', *The Times*, 21 October 1925, p. 11.
29   'Air Transport in the East', *The Times*, 15 December 1927, p. 13.
30   Elsie K. Cook, *A Geography of Ceylon* (Madras: Macmillan, 1931), p. 221.
31   'Air Route Developments', *Saturday Review*, 21 July 1937, pp. 73–77 (p. 73).

Telegraph Companies map of 1922 shows links in three directions: to Aden, Malaysia, and the African coast. But it was not until October 1935 that a reliable telecommunications route was finally established between London and Colombo: by radiotelephone to India and then onwards by land-line and cable.[32] In 1937, ten years after the inauguration of the world's first long-distance radiotelephone circuit, between Britain and the United States, Ralph Bown, a Bell Telephone Laboratories engineer, was able to report that connection had been established between 93% of the world's telephones. An accompanying map shows Ceylon connected firmly by indirect links to Britain in one direction and Australia in the other. London was at this point the only hub enjoying direct communication with every major world city.[33]

Ceylon, in short, became a representational crux during — and on account of — its belated integration into the empire transport and telecommunications chain in the early 1930s: shipping, but not yet aviation; cable, but not yet telephony. My hypothesis is that, as a result of this belatedness, films made about Ceylon in the early 1930s hesitate between the idea of empire as the occupation of territory and the idea of empire as connectivity.

Ceylon on Film

During the 1880s, tea cultivation, originally regarded as a last resort or makeshift, became Ceylon's 'staple industry'.[34] In 1883, 1,000,000 lbs of Ceylon tea had been imported into Britain; by 1888 the figure was 18,533,000 lbs.[35] Thereafter, despite some attempt at diversification, Ceylon *was* tea, with one or two other natural resources on the side; at least until the Japanese invasion of Malaya in December 1941 cut British industry off from its primary source of rubber. The identification of a particular colonial territory as the source of a particular commodity was a way to market the commodity in Britain; the commodity's marketing in turn further identified the territory as a British colony. The mechanism of that mutual reinforcement of status, as metropolis and periphery, was the relentless elaboration of some familiar distinctions: nature/culture, labour/capital, cultivation/technology, feminine/masculine. In James Joyce's *Ulysses* (1922), Leopold Bloom, halted before the window of the Belfast and Oriental Tea Company in Westland Row, regards the legend on the packets: 'choice blend, made of the finest Ceylon brands.' The name conjures the Far East. 'Lovely spot it must be,' Bloom muses: 'the garden of the world, big lazy leaves to float about on, cactuses, flowery meads, snaky lianas they call them. Wonder is it like that.'[36]

32   'Growing Use of Telephones', *The Times*, 25 October 1935, p. 11.
33   'Transoceanic Radiotelephone Development', *Proceedings of the Institute of Radio Engineers*, 25 (1937), 1124–35.
34   'The Tea Industry of India', *Gentleman's Magazine*, 270 (May 1891), 457–63 (p. 458).
35   Anandi Ramamurthy, 'Tea Advertising and Its Ideological Support for Vertical Control over Production', in *Imperial Persuaders: Images of Africa and Asia in British Advertising* (Manchester: Manchester University Press, 2003), pp. 93–130 (p. 96). See Denys Forrest, *A Hundred Years of Ceylon Tea, 1867–1967* (London: Chatto & Windus, 1967), pp. 170–71.
36   James Joyce, *Ulysses*, ed. by Jeri Johnson (Oxford: Oxford University Press, 1993), p. 68.

If anyone could claim responsibility for the contents of Bloom's daydreaming, it was probably Sir Thomas Lipton. Lipton began to advertise in the *Graphic* and other illustrated magazines in January 1892, two years after his company had acquired its first tea estates in Ceylon. These advertisements depict the tea estate as an oriental garden brought into being and thereafter ordered by European capital, scientific expertise, management skills, and access to transport. It was an idea stabilized throughout by the gendering of the relation between nature and culture, labour and capital. As Anandi Ramamurthy has shown, 'the otherness of South Asia could best be represented for Lipton's through the image of a Tamil woman tea picker.'[37] In the 1920s, at a time of intensifying class-conflict in Britain, such arrangements were sometimes taken to exemplify the benefits and benevolence of capitalist imperialism in general. In April 1926, Alfred Wigglesworth put forward as a model of mutually advantageous co-operation between capital and labour 'the expansion of the tea industry in Ceylon and Assam, rubber in Malaya, gold mining in South Africa, cocoa by natives in West Africa, jute in Bengal, wool in Australia and food stuffs in Canada, New Zealand and other sections of the Empire'. It was time, Wigglesworth concluded, 'to emulate such progress at home.'[38]

As Grieveson has demonstrated, the harvesting of products in colonial spaces and their subsequent transfer to and arrival at the metropolis became a 'dominant trope' in EMB films. For example, the portrayal of bodies and machines in *Cargo from Jamaica* (1933), directed by Basil Wright, 'marks acutely the standard contrast between an advanced technological modernity and its double, the "primitive" economy of colonized labour and agricultural produce.' The ubiquity of the large cargo ship in these films testifies at once to the idealization of transport and technology as instruments of control, and to the 'literal mobility', as Grieveson puts it, of British finance capitalism, its grip on global circulation.[39] Two representational regimes have been fused. The cargo ship stands in metaphorically for civilization as opposed to the primitive. Metonymically, it connects to machines, in the metropolis, and to bodies performing the work of machines, in the colonial space. The harvesting-and-transport trope amply informs *Gardens of the Orient*, a film about the cultivation of tea in India and Ceylon made by the GPO unit in 1936, and distributed by the very grandly named Empire Tea Market Expansion Bureau. In other Ceylon films, however, the representational regimes don't fuse quite so seamlessly.

The Ceylon Tea Industry, like *Cargo from Jamaica*, is a harvesting-and-transport film. It tells the story of the colonial production of tea, from cultivation through processing and quality control to export by cargo ship. Apart from a brief episode concerning recreation and religious ceremony, the narrative is straightforwardly sequential. Each scene connects metonymically to the next as one part of a coherent representation to another. Metonymy gains an additional edge once the tea has been packed into crates. We see the crates being transported by cart and railway from the estate to a central warehouse, and then by cart and elephant from the warehouse to

37   Ramamurthy, 'Tea Advertising', p. 119.
38   Alfred Wigglesworth, 'Britain's Purge', *Saturday Review*, 17 April 1926, p. 503.
39   Grieveson, 'The Cinema and the (Common) Wealth of Nations', p. 33.

the docks. Each crate is marked with a clearly visible LIPTON. The whole of which each image forms an interconnected part is not so much a territory as a corporation. This is capitalist imperialism in action.

The Ceylon Tea Industry, like Cargo from Jamaica, can also be read metaphorically. Like the Lipton's advertisements in the Graphic and other magazines, it further reinforces the opposition between labour and capital in the shape of technical expertise by gendering labour not just as female, but as exotically feminine. Indeed, when it came to exoticism, cinema's own technical expertise proved more than a match for mere magazine illustration. The camera pans across a hillside thronged with women picking tea. Cut to a medium shot of an individual picker: beautiful, bare-shouldered, wearing elaborate nose- and ear-rings. She breaks off the top of the plant and holds the leaves up to the camera, with level gaze. Cut to a close-up of her fingers holding the leaves. The sequence concludes with a medium shot of a group of women picking in unison. What these changes in shot scale have accomplished is both to connect the leaves the woman has picked metonymically to all the other leaves which will make up a consignment, and to isolate her metaphorically as an embodiment of otherness. The metaphoric micro-system becomes complete when, later in the film, we encounter white-coated European male tea-tasters at work in a laboratory, presumably on the same consignment. Thus far, the film's vertical axis (metaphor) could be said to predominate over its horizontal axis (metonymy).

But that's not the whole story. After the consignment of tea has been tested for quality, it makes its way by cart — and, rather less plausibly, by elephant — to the docks, where labourers load it into a lighter, and then, the Lipton trade-mark still very much in evidence, into the waiting cargo ship. The ship departs. That, we might suppose, is the end of it. Gardens of the Orient was to conclude in just such a fashion with the loading of crates of tea onto a liner, which departs majestically to a majestic final flourish of commentary. 'Thus the fragrant leaf begins its long journey over thousands of miles of land and sea to fill the world's tea-cups with the essence of perfection.' Alternatively, we might expect to follow our chosen consignment across the high seas to a British port equipped with British cranes and conveyor-belts. In fact, neither conclusion applies. What greets us instead is a shot of camels laden with Lipton tea passing a battered sphinx, in the direction of a distant pyramid. And then, aligning the company with empire itself: 'Lipton's — the organization on which the sun never sets.' There is no reason to believe that the company regarded Egypt as an especially important market. The only explanation for the presence of sphinx and pyramid in the Pathé film is the prominence Egypt had achieved since the mid-1920s, both in fact and in fantasy, as the Clapham Junction of imperial air networks. The film has in effect grafted a new piece of circuitry (aviation), for which there was as yet no material basis in Ceylon, onto an old one (shipping). Of course, the camels could be taken, along with the elephant and all the other beasts of burden, both animal and human, to symbolize the primitive condition of the colonial in general. But this is a film which wants to make its point by metonymy as well as by metaphor. Lipton's, after all, depended for its profitability on those long chains of 'great tensile power' enveloping the

'Empire's framework'. The more tensile the chain could be made to appear, by association with technological advance, the better.

Song of Ceylon, a four-part documentary commissioned from the GPO Film Unit by the Ceylon Tea Propaganda Bureau in 1933, was from the outset, and still remains, the focus of intense debate on account of its 'strange mixture of anthropological observation, travelogue, poetic rhapsody, and sound-image experimentation'.[40] Much recent commentary has been concerned with the film's 'authoring of otherness': its construction of yet another garden of the orient replete with unalienated labour and, in a departure from previous savourings of oriental femininity, a gentle homoeroticism. Stollery points out that in *Song*, as in the Imperial Airways films, modernity takes the form of speed, but here 'speaks with the hurried and intrusive "Voices of Commerce"': the montage of voice, sound, and electronic interference laid over images of labour in its third and most vividly experimental section.[41] Opinions still vary as to how successful Wright and his co-director Walter Leigh were in reconciling tradition with modernity through a poetics of cinema. What is not in doubt is that *Song* represents Ceylon metaphorically, as an Edenic 'virgin island' ripe for exploitation. I want to conclude by suggesting that the sound-montage of the 'Voices of Commerce' section, recorded in the GPO's Blackheath studio, also constitutes a metonymic representation of connectivity per se.

Walter Leigh firmly believed that the use of sound contrapuntally would produce a 'new and far more expressive form of film art'. Audiences, he wrote, had to learn to listen to sounds 'bound up with, and yet separate from, the picture': sounds whose primary value was allusive. 'The *sense* of the sounds is related to the *sense* of the picture, and a specific emotion results.' So far, so Soviet. Yet the allusion, in *Song*, was to the achievements of imperialist capitalism. 'Morse and radio announcers reciting market prices are heard over shots of tea-pickers,' Leigh explained, 'sounds of shipping over the gathering of coker-nuts.'[42] The opportunity, and perhaps the danger, lay in the divergence of the sense of the sounds from the sense of the picture. Charles Davy, reviewing *Song* for *Cinema Quarterly*, argued that the third section was its weakest part, 'for the voices are ghostly, and the influence of England on Ceylon is not at all ghostly; it is a forcibly transforming influence, leading to fever and conflict.'[43] It seems to me that these voices are indeed ghostly, but that their ghostliness has a purpose.

The theme of the 'The Voices of Commerce' is the harvesting of crops for export. 'New clearings,' the narrator intones, 'new roads, new buildings, new

40   Jamie Sexton, 'The Audio-Visual Rhythms of Modernity: *Song of Ceylon*, Sound, and Documentary Film-Making', <http://www.scope.nottingham.ac.uk/article.php?issue=may2004&id=249&section=article>, [accessed 31 January 2020]. I am grateful to Jonny Hoare for sharing with me a knowledge of the film far more detailed than my own.

41   Stollery, *Alternative Empires*, p. 196. See also William Guynn, 'The Art of National Projection: Basil Wright's *Song of Ceylon*', in *Documenting the Documentary*, ed. by Barry Keith Grant and Jeanette Sloniowski (Detroit, MI: Wayne State University Press, 1998), pp. 83–98.

42   Walter Leigh, 'The Musician and the Film', *Cinema Quarterly*, 3 (1935), 70–74 (pp. 73–74).

43   Charles Davy, 'The Song of Ceylon', *Cinema Quarterly*, 3 (1935), 109–10 (p. 110).

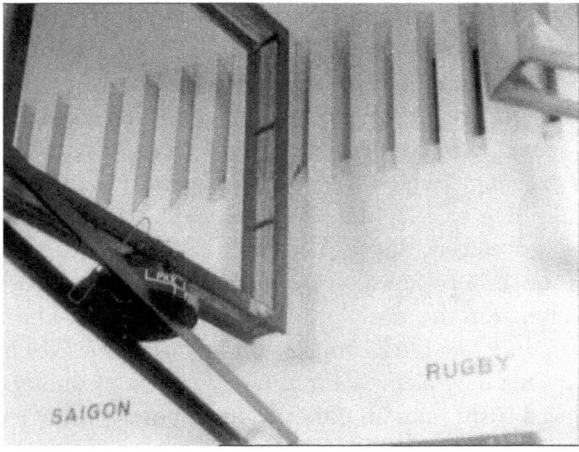

FIG. 15.2. From Saigon to Rugby. Frame grab from *Song of Ceylon*
(1934, GPO Film Unit, dir. Basil Wright)

communications, new developments of natural resources.' To put it more precisely, the sequence pays particular attention to the ways in which modern transport systems and communications technologies have already enhanced, and might yet further enhance, the incorporation of a hitherto relatively isolated local economy into the world market. The natural resources at issue are tea and copra. As in *The Ceylon Tea Industry* and *Gardens of the Orient*, we witness (again, with the help of women in close-up) the harvesting of the crop, its passage through the factory, and transfer to a cargo-ship. As Leigh himself noted, 'sounds of shipping' accompany the collection of nuts: 'for Australia,' a voice announces, 'calling Toulon, Naples, Port Said, Suez, Aden, Colombo.' Ceylon, we are to understand, has long been firmly embedded in the imperial network of sea-routes. But will that prove enough to keep the island economy competitive as time-space compression accelerates? Other voices dictate letters and recite market prices. Morse-code jabs and flickers along the sequence of images. Such methods of communication constitute further links in the empire chain: they facilitate and speed up commerce. Sound-track and image-track have been edited contrapuntally, so that the source of one is never the source of the other. But the mutual reinforcement of the rhythm of one by the rhythm of the other does strongly imply that the voices of commerce have been folded into the garden of the orient, and animate it throughout.

Doubts remain, however. One brief sequence appears to concern the reception of messages about the movements of steamers by wireless telegraphy and their onward transmission by broadcast radio (the voice and the pulses of code are heard simultaneously). But the broadcaster speaks French, and a kind of intertitle informs us that this particular wireless traffic, though it may well involve Colombo, has in fact passed between Saigon and Rugby (**Fig. 15.2**).

These thoroughly up-to-date communications technologies, replete with antennae and arrays of knobs and valves, seem to bear only an oblique relation to what we have been shown of Ceylon; though almost immediately telegraph-poles shadow the spindly trees in a scene set somewhere in the interior. The most up-to-date technology of all, wireless telephony, cannot be represented *in situ*, since in 1933 there was no direct communication by telephone between Britain and Ceylon. The sound-montage does however include a telephone conversation during which two British men, speaking in clipped professional tones, discuss the blueprints for a new factory. This exchange, which has no visual correlative, achieves a sonic clarity almost entirely unknown to telephone systems, then or now. 'New buildings,' the film's narrator had announced. But the eerily sound-proofed debate about blueprints takes place not so much between discrete physical locations in Britain, Ceylon, or indeed anywhere else, as in the abstract space of capital flows. The ghostliness of the voices of commerce, like that of the conclusion of *The Ceylon Tea Industry*, arises out of the attempt to graft a new piece of circuitry (wireless telephony), for which there was as yet no material basis, onto an old one (correspondence by letter or telegram).

Wright and Leigh evidently, and for good reason, found instantaneous connection of the kind made possible by wireless telegraphy and telephony hard to visualize. They did not try to conceal the fact. The Rugby-Saigon exchange, for example, requires a palpably laborious articulation of shots: a tilt up the transmitter's aerial, then a tilt down from the receiving antenna into the radio-hut; and then, as though that wasn't schematic enough, the intertitle identifying the signal's source and destination. Metonymy, the figure best able to represent the transport and telecommunications chains which had reconfigured Empire into Commonwealth, simply could not cope with short-wave radio's skip-effects. It is not just metonymy which has fallen short rhetorically, or 'the visual' in general. After all, the telephone conversation about blueprints remains a purely aural event: an event altogether too pure in its aurality to contribute to the 'sense' of a film about Ceylon, or indeed anywhere in particular beyond the studio in which it was staged. Representation fails, as a form of knowledge and power, when confronted by a connectivity that no longer has any need for it. The ghost heard wailing among the voices of commerce might be the ghost of cinema itself.

CHAPTER 16

The Woman in the Plastic Mackintosh: Sexuality, Material Substance, and Narrative Space in 1930s Film

The narrator of Jean Rhys's *Good Morning, Midnight* (1939) is picked up in a Paris bar by a gigolo. 'Is it true,' he asks, 'that Englishmen make love with all their clothes on, because they think it's more respectable that way?' Her reply is unequivocal. 'Yes, certainly. Fully dressed. They add, of course, a macintosh.'[1] That was amusingly unfair to men, and to Englishmen in particular. Anyone who spent a lot of time at the movies, in the 1930s, would have been struck by the fact that, at moments of crisis or opportunity, it is the women who add the raincoat; and that, although the English should by no means be disregarded, she is quite likely to be French. At the beginning of *Rich and Strange* (1931), a lesser-known early Hitchcock, the heavens open as the rather dim and sluggish hero leaves work, and he soon finds himself on an underground train next to an attractive blonde in a beret and a white raincoat who promptly hits on him: he ignores the pressure of her look, and she disappears from the narrative, taking with her the film's only hope of sexual magnetism. Rain, it should be stated at the outset, rarely has much to do with it. Keeping dry is not a priority for mackintosh-clad Greta Garbo, for example, in *Anna Christie* (1930), when she first encounters the man who will free her from her past as a prostitute (**Fig. 16.1**); or, indeed, for Bette Davis, in *Of Human Bondage* (1934), when she ruthlessly dumps diffident Leslie Howard for a more worldly rival.

There is an intriguing conjunction, here, between women, plastic mackintoshes, and sexual availability (either permanent, or suddenly renewed). In a pioneering essay on 'melodramatic realism' in 1930s French women's films, first published in *Screen* in 1989, Ginette Vincendeau remarks in passing that Michèle Morgan in *Quai des brumes* (1938) and Danielle Darrieux in *Abus de confiance* (1938) wear the black beret and plastic raincoat that were 'emblems' of the 'lost girl'.[2] Vincendeau might also have mentioned Nadia Sibirskaïa, in Jean Grémillon's *La Petite Lise* (1930), playing a prostitute as oddly inseparable from her tartan plastic mackintosh as she is

1   Jean Rhys, *Good Morning, Midnight* (Harmondsworth: Penguin Books, 1969), p. 132.
2   Ginette Vincendeau, 'Melodramatic Realism: On Some French Women's Films in the 1930s', *Screen*, 30 (1989), 51–65 (p. 53).

FIG. 16.1. Raingear. Frame grab from *Anna Christie* (1930, MGM, dir. Clarence Brown)

FIG. 16.2. A *femme* (almost) *fatale*. Frame grab from *The Stars Look Down* (1940, MGM, dir. Carol Reed)

FIG. 16.3. Approaching Manderley. Frame grab from *Rebecca* (1940, United Artists, dir. Alfred Hitchcock)

from her convict-father (indeed, she wears it even when amorously ensconced on his knee). And we could add some further mackintoshed Englishwomen, too. In Carol Reed's break-through film, *The Stars Look Down* (1939), the garment worn by *femme fatale* Jenny Sunley (Margaret Lockwood) crackles gratifyingly when touched — though Lockwood can scarcely be said to have worn it with as much conviction as Morgan, Darrieux, or Sibirskaïa (**Fig. 16.2**). And then, more ambiguously, there is far from *fatale* Joan Fontaine, sitting beside Laurence Olivier on the approach to Manderley, in Hitchcock's *Rebecca* (1940) (**Fig. 16.3**). But why should these mackintoshes be quite so ostentatiously *plastic*? The representations I will investigate in what follows are of a particular kind of raincoat, as worn by a particular kind of woman, in particular films made in Britain, France, and the United States in the 1930s (or for the most part in the 1930s).

Techno-Primitivism

One of the most powerful narrative paradigms in interwar literature and cinema concerns the displacement of feminine sentimentality by female sexuality. As readily discernible in D. H. Lawrence's *Lady Chatterley's Lover* (1928) as it is in a multitude of Hollywood melodramas, this paradigm reeks of primitivism.[3] It chronicles a 'regression' on the woman's part, fortunate or unfortunate, from culture to nature. The hypothesis I aim to develop here is that the primitivism which crossed and thereby constituted so many narratives of the displacement of feminine sentimentality by female sexuality was itself crossed (and thus re-constituted) by a further *techno*-primitivism operating within and upon technologically mediated experience by means of a strong awareness of synthetic or semi-synthetic *substance*.[4] That strong awareness of substance could itself be considered 'primitive', despite its preoccupation with a modern synthetic or semi-synthetic material such as plastic, in so far as it drew primarily on the evidence of senses which nineteenth-century psychophysiology had classified as primitive: touch, taste, and smell. The garments worn by sexually available women in the films I will discuss are there *as a substance*. We cannot taste or smell them, perhaps, but they look as though they are asking to be touched. Furthermore, we quite often *hear* them, as a random sonic flutter which is itself an affront to the hegemony of vision.

The answers I will give to my question about the filmic qualities of plastic rainwear are speculative, but not, I hope, wildly so. They arise out of the broad observation that from the mid-1920s on writers, artists, and film-makers felt an increasing responsibility to depict or figure the widespread technological mediation of individual and collective experience. 'Comfort isolates,' Walter Benjamin observed in 1937, in an essay on Baudelaire and urban shock: 'on the other hand,

---

3   On literary fiction, see John Marx, *The Modernist Novel and the Decline of Empire* (Cambridge: Cambridge University Press, 2005), pp. 122–66. On Hollywood, see Lea Jacobs, *The Wages of Sin: Censorship and the Fallen Woman Film, 1928–1942* (Berkeley: University of California Press, 1995), and *The Decline of Sentiment: American Film in the 1920s* (Berkeley: University of California Press, 2008).
4   David Trotter, *Literature in the First Media Age: Britain between the Wars* (Cambridge, MA: Harvard University Press, 2013), pp. 86–119.

it brings those enjoying it closer to mechanization.' The first example Benjamin gives of this enhanced closeness is a new kind of telephone apparatus 'where the lifting of a receiver has taken the place of the steady movement that used to be required to crank the older models.' The second is the still camera. 'Of the countless movements of switching, inserting, pressing, and the like,' he added, 'the "snapping" of the photographer has had the greatest consequences.' By mediating experience, technology had in fact rendered it all the more 'haptic'.[5] Our first contact, when someone calls us up, is (or used to be) with the mechanism itself: we 'answer the telephone', not the person. This new haptic immediacy — the felt pressure of hand on apparatus — now mediated mediation itself.

In the late 1920s, cinema had to adjust to the demands not only of sound, but of haptic immediacy. For example, a basic element of mise-en-scène in the emergent classical continuity system is the telephone which squats unnoticed in the depths of an establishing shot until, provoked into action, it draws human presence towards it, and so momentarily takes centre stage, as the exclusive medium of a critical speech-act, a narrative hinge-point, a life abruptly 'on the line'. Sometimes the device hovers at the edge of the frame, waiting to become an instrument of expression. Sometimes it remains silent, and to that extent overlooked, throughout a scene of intense confrontation, thus performing what the social anthropologist Daniel Miller has called the 'humility of things': their capacity to enable or constrain even when, *or especially when*, overlooked.[6] Cinema, to adapt the title of Norman Bryson's book on still-life painting, looks, or half-looks, at the overlooked.[7] In late silents and early talkies things sometimes remain overlooked to positively baroque effect, as during a fraught conversation between capitalists in Julien Duvivier's *Au bonheur des dames* (1930) (**Fig. 16.4**). In the 1931 *Maltese Falcon*, Sam Spade's offices are a telephonic cornucopia: Cairo's gun seems a lot less fearsome than the instruments which frame its wavering barrel (**Fig. 16.5**). By the mid-1930s, the humble things had sobered down somewhat, however fraught the circumstances. But that relative quiescence did not render them any the less immediate, to those with eyes for them, when they did come into view as elements in a technological still life.

In *Society and Solitude* (1870), Ralph Waldo Emerson defined modernity as the breeding of invention upon invention. 'No sooner is the electric telegraph devised,' Emerson wrote, 'than gutta-percha, the very material it requires, is found.'[8] Gutta-percha, a kind of rubber, proved an ideal insulating material for the submarine cables, first telegraphic and then telephonic, which made global communication possible. Emerson's formula soon acquired further applications. No sooner had the telephone apparatus become a permanent fixture in offices and homes around

5   Walter Benjamin, 'On Some Motifs in Baudelaire', in *Illuminations*, ed. by Hannah Arendt, trans. by Harry Zohn (London: Fontana, 1970), pp. 157–202 (pp. 176–77).

6   Daniel Miller, 'Materiality: An Introduction', in *Materiality*, ed. by Daniel Miller (Durham, NC: Duke University Press, 2005), pp. 1–50 (p. 5).

7   Norman Bryson, *Looking at the Overlooked: Four Essays on Still Life Painting* (London: Reaktion Books, 1990).

8   Ralph Waldo Emerson, *Society and Solitude*, in *Collected Works*, vol. VII, ed. by Douglas Emory Wilson and Ronald A. Bosco (Cambridge, MA: Belknap Press, 2007), p. 81.

FIG. 16.4. A fraught conversation between capitalists. Frame grab from
Au bonheur des dames (1930, Le Film d'Art, dir. Julien Duvivier)

FIG. 16.5. Telephone cornucopia: Cairo takes aim. Frame grab from *The Maltese Falcon*
(1931, Warner Bros., dir. Roy Del Ruth)

the world than it, too, found the material it required: phenol-formaldehyde, the
first wholly synthetic plastic, patented by Leo Baekeland in 1907, and thereafter
commonly known as Bakelite. Should we say that the overlooked telephone
performs the humility, not of things in general, or of a specific thing, but of Bakelite
as a synthetic substance? To be brought comfortably close to mechanization,
during the period between the world wars, was in significant measure to see, hear,
touch, taste, and smell plastic. Modern comfort was made out of many substances,
including the wholly natural (such as shellac, as in phonograph records), at one end
of the spectrum, and the wholly artificial (Bakelite), at the other. But it is probably
true to say that Western societies between the wars were societies transformed by,
and in the distinctive image of, the *semi*-synthetic: rubber, above all, and celluloid,

essential in the manufacture of photographic film, of course, and of more mundane equipment such as washable cuffs. An anatomy of modern comfort during the interwar period requires us to distinguish among the overlapping and mutually definitive appearances on the market and in social and cultural view of plastics of different origin and composition. How was the semi-synthetic imagined?

Rubber began as a natural plastic, but proved of little use industrially until, in or around 1839, someone (in fact, two people separately) figured out how to combine it with sulphur at a high temperature: a process known as vulcanization. Rubber's hybridity, the tension it encodes between the raw and the chemically cooked, becomes subtly manifest at crucial junctures in novels such as Radclyffe Hall's *The Well of Loneliness* (1928), H. D.'s *Bid Me to Live* (begun 1918, published 1960), and Lawrence's *Lady Chatterley's Lover*: all primitivist, in their different ways.[9] The manifestation did not have to be subtle. Rubber overcoats became notorious for their lack of ventilation: witness Doris Kilman, in Virginia Woolf's *Mrs Dalloway* (1925).[10] The hero of Elizabeth Bowen's *The House in Paris* (1935) wears one during a dirty weekend in Romney. 'The mackintosh, with its new rubbery smell, slid about during the drive out, showing its check lining and the chain inside the collar to hang it up by.' *Pace* Jean Rhys, the person wearing it is described as 'a French-English-Jewish man in a bank'.[11] But the garments worn by Morgan, Darrieux, and the others do not look as though they might smell of anything in particular. The techno-primitivism they evince has rather to do with the challenge they present to vision.

The second half of the 1920s saw the development of new resins in competition with celluloid and Bakelite. These advances seem to have been driven by an emphasis on improvements in transparency. For once plastic had matched glass for transparency, it would be possible to exploit its existing virtues, such as robustness and flexibility, more fully. The new thermo-plastics available by the end of the 1920s (cellulose acetate, cellophane) altered the terms of the interpositions glass had made possible by adjusting a material's properties as medium to its properties as barrier. They produced, in effect, a new relation between subject and object. What they had to offer, in short, was an *applied* transparency: one that, in surrounding or coating people and objects the better to protect them, or to show them off, took its shape from them. The sense of touch pre-dominates in the way cellulose acetate was marketed during the early 1930s. It was said to be indispensable, for example, in the manufacture of 'coverings for hand-rails' and 'transparent wrapping paper'.[12] Cellophane, too, was to prove exemplary as a form of flexible transparency used in the packaging of cigarettes and other commodities. It clung to that which it proofed. 'Say, I must be transparent' is Cary Grant's response, in the Paramount comedy *I'm No Angel* (1933), when Mae West tells him that she always knew he was mad about her. 'Honey,' she agrees, her hands all over him, 'you're just wrapped

9   Trotter, *Literature in the First Media Age*, pp. 102–15.
10 Virginia Woolf, *Mrs Dalloway* (Harmondsworth: Penguin Books, 1992), p. 12.
11 Elizabeth Bowen, *The House in Paris* (London: Vintage, 1998), pp. 149, 89.
12 H. V. Potter, 'New Plastic Materials', *The Times*, 1 November 1932, p. xxiv.

FIG. 16.6. A single shiny black carapace. Frame grab from
La Bête humaine (1938, Paris Film, dir. Jean Renoir)

in cellophane'. Cellophane informs and is informed by that which it adheres to. Vision had acquired the immediacy of touch. To see was to feel. No wonder Aldous Huxley was to describe cinema, rather than television, as the medium best adapted to 'primitive sensation'. In *Brave New World* (1932), cinema is 'the feelies'.[13]

That said, the garments worn by Garbo in *Anna Christie* and Bette Davis in *Of Human Bondage* do not so much absorb vision as repel it. The light glancing harshly off them reveals something impermeable, utterly opaque, a dense mass. Think of the climactic scene in Jean Renoir's sombre *La Bête humaine* (1938), in which the doomed lovers meet in a toolshed in the railyard, and let their rainwear do the love-making for them. The faces of Jean Gabin and Simone Simon tilt ethereally at the light: but the bodies beneath them have been swathed from neck to foot in a single shiny black carapace, before, during, and after (**Fig. 16.6**). In this instance, it has indeed been raining, hard. But these garments do not so much keep the lovers dry as encase them in technology. There is blackness in the plastic out of which they have been engineered, but it is an insect's blackness, at once dazzling, robust, and abject. Neither rigid exoskeleton, nor body-hugging sheath, the garments worn by Garbo, Davis, and Simon make the wearer over into a posture as hard to associate with femininity as it is with femaleness. There is a primitivism at work, here; but it is hard to fathom. The woman in the plastic mackintosh in 1930s films can easily be construed as a prostitute, or 'loose' woman. She is *already* 'primitive' to the extent that she might be thought to have become the creature of her own sexuality. The films ask if there is a way back into the modern for her other than through the renewal of feminine sentimentality. They do not give up on change (on the chances of change). That is where the rainwear comes in, as provocation to an awareness of new substances capable equally of absorptive transparency and of

13   Aldous Huxley, *Brave New World* (London: Flamingo, 1994), p. 115. See Laura Frost, 'Huxley's Feelies: The Cinema of Sensation in *Brave New World*', *Twentieth Century Literature*, 52 (2006), 443–73.

armoured intransigence: a techno-primitivism.

Narrative Space

We can trace the evolution of Hollywood's techno-primitivism by examining the mackintoshes in three successive versions of 'Rain', a ferociously primitivist Stevensonian short story by Somerset Maugham, each of which featured a notable female star: Gloria Swanson, in *Sadie Thompson* (1928); Joan Crawford, in *Rain* (1932); and Rita Hayworth, in *Miss Sadie Thompson* (1953). To do so is to bring into play a further consideration. In Hollywood, at least, what a garment means counts for less, on the whole, than what it does: or, to be more precise, where it is worn. We need to take account of the spaces in which, or by means of which, it manifests itself.

These films are rarely discussed, so a rapid plot-summary may be in order. 'Rain' (the short story) is set on the South Seas island of Pago-Pago, and concerns a group of travellers quarantined during an epidemic of measles: Dr and Mrs McPhail; the Davidsons; and a prostitute, Sadie Thompson. Alfred Davidson is a missionary and professional reformer whose aim is to inculcate a sense of sin into the happy-go-lucky islanders. Will Sadie be converted back from female sexuality into feminine sentimentality under Davidson's guidance, and so accept deportation, and the prison sentence which awaits her in San Francisco? The plot-twist is that at the very moment of her sincere conversion, Davidson himself lapses into bestiality, rapes her, and commits suicide (in the film versions, she will be offered the possibility of sexual-romantic fulfilment in the arms of Marine Sergeant Phil, or Tim, O'Hara). Most of the action takes place in and around two buildings in the island's main town: the Governor's residence, seat of civilized authority, and comfort, to which an as yet unrepentant Sadie must go to plead her case: and the ramshackle hotel run by a 'half-caste named Horn, with a native wife surrounded by little brown children,' as Maugham puts it, where the travellers stay.[14] We are also aware of a penumbra of native village surrounding the town, notable chiefly for sun-drenched fishery by day and orgiastic dances by night. In the 1928 and 1932 versions, the hotel has been sketchily sub-divided into the semi-public space of the lounge and veranda where the guests congregate, and the private space of the bedrooms to which they retire. From the lounge, a stairway leads to an upper floor, where the middle classes have been accommodated in relative seclusion. Sadie's room opens beside the stairway, its separateness subtly challenged in the 1928 version by the shadow of the bead-curtain falling on the rough stone wall which flanks the door. A veranda and front yard at once separate the interior of the building from the public street, and provide access to it. The 1953 version will sharpen the distinction between private, semi-public, and public spaces yet further.

For some years now, I have been nagging away at the proposition that the cavernous sound stages of the studio era became a laboratory for experiments in

---

14   W. Somerset Maugham, 'Rain', in *Selected Stories*, ed. by Anthony Curtis (London: Nonesuch Press, 1990), pp. 96–151 (p. 104).

narrative space which configure the relation between a building's interior and exterior in social (and even political) terms readily intelligible from our experience of the world outside the cinema. The studio-built space in question consists of three distinct areas: the public street, exterior to the building, and implicitly that against which it must be defended; the semi-public reception rooms in the interior, designed for production or display, and for the temporary, casual entertainment of visitors; and the private office or bedroom, at the centre or rear of the building, far removed from the public street. More often than not, these areas have been organized in relation to each other in such a way as to make intelligible the 'social logic' identified by architectural historians Bill Hillier and Julienne Hanson, according to which hierarchy has been built into architectural design.[15] That 'social logic' distinguishes between the exclusive deep space within a building attainable only by passage through other spaces, and thereby adapted for its owner's sole use, as sanctuary or shrine; and the shallow spaces (neutral, inclusive, open-ended) which convert the stranger entering from outside into a visitor or guest who may or may not be granted access to deep space, and who will in any case not be staying long. Some such logic informed the development of narrative technique in early cinema.[16]

For me, the paradigmatic shallow space in studio-era Hollywood is the hotel lobby as revealed by Cedric Gibbons's set for the MGM multi-star vehicle *Grand Hotel* (1932), a caper (or failed-caper) movie featuring a fading ballet star, an aristocrat turned jewel-thief, a devious industrialist, one of his employees, a terminally ill accountant, and a plucky stenographer.[17] The lobby features conspicuously in the film, early and often. One prominent item in it is the revolving door seen here as Joan Crawford enters *en route* to a typing assignment which might also be an assignation (**Fig. 16.7**). The revolving door defines shallow space: it separates the public from the semi-public, the vulgar anonymous street from the already selective lobby of an office block or hotel, fit for ceremony. It requires not only courtesy, among those who use it, but active collaboration: all the parties involved must push at the same time, in the same direction, and with the same amount of force. Its successful operation enacts the regard, civic, functional, kindly, and perhaps playful, which the occupants of shallow space are ideally required to display towards each other. In this film, they mostly do. On the upper floors, the wide balcony outside the bedrooms, in which lurk those creatures of deep space, the industrial magnate and the *ancien régime* ballet star dreaming of full houses and Russia under the Czar, is a neutral, inclusive, open-ended zone over which the stenographer and the renegade aristocrat establish squatters' rights: the wit of their exchanges is proto-screwball. When the terminally ill book-keeper joins them, the alliance is complete, much to

15   Bill Hillier and Julienne Hanson, *The Social Logic of Space* (Cambridge: Cambridge University Press, 1984).

16   David Trotter, 'The Space Beside: Lateral Exposition, Gender, and Urban Narrative Space in D. W. Griffith's Biograph Films', in *Cities in Transition: The Moving Image and the Modern Metropolis*, ed. by Andrew Webber and Emma Wilson (London and New York: Wallflower Press, 2008), pp. 40–55. Reprinted as Chapter 13 in this volume.

17   Trotter, *Literature in the First Media Age*, pp. 186–91.

FIG. 16.7. Revolving door. Frame grab from *Grand Hotel*
(1932, MGM, dir. Edmund Goulding)

the irritation of the magnate, who emerges from his room to recall the stenographer to her stenography. It is a space already densely plotted, then, already meaningful, that the ballet star will sweep across when she leaves the hotel: for her, it is no more than a troublesome or diverting hiatus between bedroom and theatre. *Grand Hotel* creates a petit-bourgeois, semi-public sphere out of the alliances the book-keeper, the stenographer, and the renegade aristocrat form through ceremonial encounters in shallow space. The film is on the side of the petit-bourgeois aspirants. It belongs to Crawford's stenographer, rather than to the ballet star (Garbo, inevitably). When in 1966 Manny Farber deplored the disappearance from Hollywood cinema of 'those tiny, mysterious interactions between the actor and the scene that make up the memorable moments in any good film,' moments of 'peripheral distraction, bemusement, fretfulness, mere flickering of skeptical interest,' he had Crawford in mind, and in particular Crawford in *Grand Hotel*.[18]

In *Rain*, released on 12 October 1932, a month after *Grand Hotel*, Crawford, now playing a fully-fledged prostitute rather than a susceptible stenographer, dons a plastic mackintosh. Much of the imaginative energy around in both the 1928 and the 1932 versions goes into the development of a shallow space in which, or by means of which, various lower-class renegades can gang up against the bad (moral reforming) middle classes, in tacit alliance with the good (technocratic) middle classes. In the 1928 version, Sadie converts her bedroom into a replica of shallow space by introducing into it a gramophone and some cheerful marines. Shallow space is her element: she first gets to know Sergeant O'Hara by means of a South Seas revolving door or turnstile which separates the hotel's front yard from the street. In the 1932 version, a complex tracking-shot meticulously delineates the downstairs area, and the gramophone to which Sadie and her followers dance, while

---

18   Manny Farber, *Negative Space: Manny Farber on the Movies* (New York: Da Capo Press, 1998), pp. 145, 152.

Mrs Davidson looks on disapprovingly from above, before descending to intervene. Like *Grand Hotel*, *Rain* is on the side of Crawford, the lower-class insurrectionary. In these films, and others of the period, such as Jean Renoir's *Le Crime de Monsieur Lange* (1936), the sociability of the behaviour encouraged by shallow space — easy-going, promiscuous, yet respectful, a performance rather than a self-revelation — acquires urgent political value.[19] It is a space in which a Popular Front against fascisms of one kind or another might yet be formed.

However, the films based on 'Rain' inherit from Maugham a primitivism at odds with the creation through ceremony of a petit-bourgeois semi-public sphere. For primitivism abhors a shallow space: the immediacy it seeks is only ever to be found in the seclusion of a remote and exclusive inner sanctuary. *Rain* discovers among its petit-bourgeois insurrectionaries a great deal of curiosity, kindliness, wit, and irreverence (Mr Horn the hotel-keeper is fond of quoting from *Thus Spake Zarathustra*). But not enough to stave off primitivism. At the conclusion, it is the beat of native drums pounding in his head which drives Davidson to rape. And there is no techno- to this film's primitivism: no modern immediacy in its technological mediations. In both the 1928 and the 1932 versions, the rainwear Sadie dons in order to make the short journey from the hotel to the Governor's residence, where she will plead her case, serves a narrative function only: it connects the outside of one building to the outside of another. The downpour explains it. The garment itself, whether a cape borrowed from O'Hara, or a coat of her own, is never fully there as a substance.

By 1953, and the Rita Hayworth *Miss Sadie Thompson*, all that had changed. The topography is the same, and there is still an ample supply of scenes of native life. The difference lies, first, in the hard-to-overlook nattiness of the garment, now see-through, a bang up-to-date example of the unique capacities of wholly synthetic material; and secondly, in a decisive further sharpening of the distinction between deep and shallow space. When Sadie arrives at the Governor's residence, she first enters an outer office presided over by his secretary, before being shown through to the inner office where he awaits her. There is an explicit symmetry to the mise-en-scène, the placement of furniture and doorway in one matching their placement in the other. That Sadie should wear her mackintosh throughout challenges the social logic informing the articulation of narrative space. She has brought the public street with her, across the shallow space constituted by the outer office and its ceremonies into the deep space in which power and desire renew themselves, and each other, or are finally found out. The raincoat, almost as transparent a filming of her body as Mae West's figurative cellophane, no longer serves a narrative function. It no longer depends on rain. For Sadie now asserts herself through techno-primitivism rather than through the occupancy of shallow space (which is all Crawford had, in *Grand Hotel* and again in *Rain*).

But will it be enough? When Sadie returns to the hotel, she finds Davidson paternalistically ensconced in the lounge, listening to some local children, and asks to speak with him. Davidson proposes that they retire to the veranda which runs

19   Trotter, *Literature in the First Media Age*, pp. 193–95.

along the side and back of the house. Although it runs along the outside of the building, this veranda can be made to count as an impromptu deep space, because you have to go through the lounge to get to it. The hotel's veranda and lounge stand in the same relation to each other as the inner and outer offices in the Governor's residence. Once again, Sadie keeps her mackintosh on throughout. The mackintosh defies that social logic: it will not allow the establishment by *fiat* of the seclusion which primitivism requires. The scene lasts two minutes and twenty-six seconds, and involves ten separate shots. Most of these fall into the shot/reverse-shot pattern which would have been customary in classical Hollywood films for a confrontation of this kind, in which two people bare their emotional teeth at each other. But it begins with a track and pan which follows their progress along one side of the house, and around the corner. As a result, the shot which finally takes us in closer, exactly as Davidson says 'You're being evasive, Miss Thompson', is all about her back, not her front, and all about her plastic mackintosh (**Fig. 16.8**). A comparable, though shorter, tracking-shot concludes the scene, underlining its separateness from what has gone before and what will come after. These shots, moulded to movement, to the interaction of actor and scene, fasten us haptically to Sadie, to the back she has turned: her falsehood is somehow touching. Sadie, however, cannot sustain her defiance: she capitulates, and, in capitulating, arouses the brute in Davidson. It may be significant that the scene in which he rapes her in the sanctuary of her bedroom begins with her picking the mackintosh up from a chair and ends with it still in her hand as he forces her down onto the bed (**Fig. 16.9**). The downward pull of Maugham's story has proved too hard to resist.

European Alternatives

That was not always the case, when it came to the displacement of feminine sentimentality by female sexuality, outside of Hollywood. I want to conclude by returning to two films made in France in 1938: the poetic realist *Quai des brumes*, and *Abus de confiance*, which is generally thought to incline rather to boulevard comedy. There may well have been a Parisian code or iconography associating the plastic raincoat with prostitution. Photographs by Brassaï indicate as much.[20] In cinema, however, if not on the streets of Paris, what these garments mean is on the whole less interesting than when and where they mean. In *Abus de confiance*, Darrieux's orphaned law-student, Lydia, penniless and at her wits' end after the sudden death of her grandmother, pretends to be the long-lost illegitimate daughter of a famous historian of pre-revolutionary France, Jacques Ferney (Charles Vanel). For the first hour of the film, during which she suffers sexual persecution by a series of predatory men, Lydia proves inseparable from her shiny black raincoat, despite the enduring absence of rain. At the prompting of a friend, she decides to visit Ferney in his Versailles mansion, and pass herself off as his daughter. The mansion turns out to be a complex, barricaded haute-bourgeois palace with an expansive front yard

---

20   Brassaï, *'No Ordinary Eyes'*, ed. by Alain Sayag and Annick Lionel-Marie (London: Thames & Hudson, 2000), pp. 78–79.

FIG. 16.8. All about the plastic mackintosh. Frame grab from *Miss Sadie Thompson* (1953, Columbia Pictures, dir. Curtis Bernhardt)

FIG. 16.9. Capitulation. Frame grab from *Miss Sadie Thompson* (1953, Columbia Pictures, dir. Curtis Bernhardt)

and a lobby patrolled by a butler. When Lydia enters the deep space of the library where Ferney works, we see her framed by its pretentiously marbled door, plastic against glass. The scene is haptic, not by camera-movement, but in and through the contrast of textures established by mise-en-scène: the harsh shapeless sheen of the street garment Lydia has brought with her into this bourgeois, paternalist (or grand-paternalist) sanctuary against the soft fabrics which adorn it. Lydia's Sadie Thompson moment occurs when, after she has shown Ferney the document which 'proves' she is his daughter, and he asks 'Who are you?', she gathers herself in quiet defiance into a fringed armchair. Lydia's raincoat resists an entire *ancien régime* (**Fig. 16.10**). However, this is by no means a radical film, politically, and it does ultimately re-convert Lydia from female sexuality back into feminine sentimentality. Ferney's wife, Hélène (Valentine Tessier), discovers the truth. Fortunately, Lydia has just

FIG. 16.10. Resisting an entire *ancien regime*. Frame grab from
Abus de confiance (1938, UDIF, dir. Henri Decoin)

triumphed in court, as defence counsel for a young woman in a similar position to herself. The Verneys adopt her. Brought back into a family, albeit a somewhat incestuous one, she abandons her plastic mackintosh for a demurely pious outfit in church, and a demurely professional one in court. But who could forget her sojourn in the fringed armchair?

Like *Miss Sadie Thompson*, *Quai des brumes* gives us two mirrored sites, each divided into deep and shallow spaces: Panama's bar, down by the docks, where army deserter Jean (Jean Gabin) repairs on his arrival in Le Havre; and the knick-knack shop in a more respectable street owned by Zabel (Michel Simon), godfather or 'guardian' of Nelly (Michèle Morgan), the woman with a past (though we don't know what sort). Early scenes quickly and clearly establish the shallow space of Panama's bar, first from one angle, as the painter Michel Krauss (Robert le Vigan) enters, then from another, as Jean admits that he's hungry, and Panama (Edouard Delmont) leads the way towards the kitchen behind the bar. We are already in the kitchen when Panama comes through the door, the glance he casts to his right indicating a gap in scenographic space soon to be filled. As he stoops to fetch bread and sausage from a cupboard, Jean enters, and he too glances to his right. And this time our curiosity is fulfilled, as a pan opens up both the dimensions of deep space, and the source of fascination residing within it. The subsequent cut in to a closer shot gives us not so much a face and a body, as a radiant, randomly reflective shapelessness (**Fig. 16.11**). Just as Decoin had set Lydia's black plastic raincoat against the fringed armchair, so Carné sets Nelly's semi-transparent but ultimately no less opaque version against a net curtain. Jean, we might note, assumes from the outset that she is a prostitute. It is in the kitchen, in deep space, that Jean and Nelly reveal their mutual attraction, and from its window that, after having spent the night together, they will contemplate the dawn of a new day, in one of the film's iconic images (**Fig. 16.12**).

Quai des brumes finds meaning and value in deep space, and there alone. It

FIG. 16.11. Black beret and plastic raincoat. Frame grab from
Quai des brumes (1938, Franco London Films, dir. Marcel Carné)

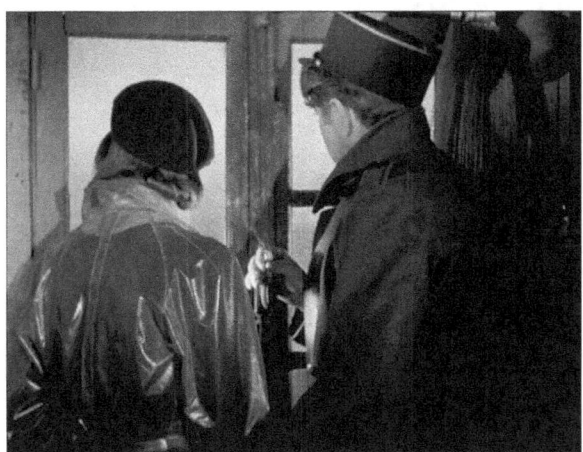

FIG. 16.12. Dawn of a new day. Frame grab from *Quai des brumes*
(1938, Franco London Films, dir. Marcel Carné)

constantly re-draws the boundary between deep and shallow space, as when Jean and Nelly leave Panama's the morning after, and Nelly inspects herself in the mirror hanging immediately outside the kitchen door, while (yet again) we inspect her back, and her raincoat (**Fig. 16.13**). Nelly, we might note, does not linger in shallow space, either at Panama's, or, on her return from the docks, in Zabel's shop. She passes rapidly through the shop itself, as Zabel awaits her at the entrance to the domestic quarters behind it. Resigned, it would appear, to her re-absorption into the deep domestic or quasi-domestic space presided over by her guardian, she removes her raincoat and hangs it up (this mirror-scene mirroring the earlier mirror-scene at Panama's) (**Fig. 16.14**). Here, it seems, is one deep space in which Nelly, unlike Sadie in *Miss Sadie Thompson*, will not be able to draw strength from the immediacy

FIG. 16.13. From the back, again. Frame grab from *Quai des brumes*
(1938, Franco London Films, dir. Marcel Carné)

FIG. 16.14. Return to domesticity. Frame grab from *Quai des brumes*
(1938, Franco London Films, dir. Marcel Carné)

of her own technological mediation. We are exactly halfway through the film: and at the moment at which Zabel declares ominously that Nelly is a girl no longer, but a woman. The jealous patriarch (or false patriarch, since he is her guardian, not her father) stands ready to re-impose his authority. Will she, too, like Lydia, in *Abus de confiance*, be reconverted back from female sexuality into feminine sentimentality? Well, no. For this deep space, unlike the kitchen at Panama's, like the bedroom in *Miss Sadie Thompson*, is a bad deep space, with a basement beneath it, in which Zabel's guilty secret is finally laid bare (out of jealousy, he has murdered Nelly's former boyfriend Maurice), and in which Jean, acting initially in self-defence, smashes his face to pulp with a brick. Jean had already described his adversary as a scolopendrid, a particularly revolting species of bug familiar to him from his military service in Vietnam. The brute will out, in the good man as well as the bad.

Conclusion

I have offered a sketchy and impressionistic account, from outside the history of cinema, strictly understood, of two developments which coincided in the appearance, in several films which we might still think worthy of attention, of the figure of the woman in the plastic raincoat. On one hand, the elaboration of production design on an industrial scale made it possible, though by no means necessary or sufficient, to inscribe in the arrangement of fictional worlds a social logic which notably enhanced their coherence. On the other, the aggressive marketing of new plastics encouraged in some film-makers a haptic treatment of Manny Farber's 'tiny, mysterious interactions between the actor and the scene'. That coincidence generated a productive tension. For the sensuous yet implacable garments these women wear are *too* modern, it seems, to please or to placate the man in attendance, whether as guardian, companion, or spiritual advisor. The 'primitive' violence they provoke is a renunciation of the modern: of the immediacy which now mediated mediation itself. The cinema of the period almost always ends up in a deep space whose rules require that such garments be left at the door. And yet whenever they are worn right up to or in breach of a boundary of some kind, in defiance of the social logic of narrative space, the image stays in the mind.

CHAPTER 17

Shakespeare in Tombstone:
Stanley Cavell Goes West

My topic is what I think of as Cavell's wager: the wager announced in the Introduction to *Pursuits of Happiness: The Hollywood Comedy of Remarriage* (1981). 'I am not insensible,' Cavell says there, 'whatever defences I may deploy, of an avenue of outrageousness in considering Hollywood films in the light, from time to time, of major works of thought.'[1] Not so much an *avenue* of outrageousness, one might think, with regard to the claims made on behalf of remarriage comedy, in that book, and on behalf of melodramas of the unknown woman, in *Contesting Tears* (1992), as a whole sunset boulevard.[2] I'm going to wager on Cavell's wager by addressing films which belong to genres he himself has done no more than allude to or touch upon: horror, and the Western.

Cavell takes Hollywood philosophically, of course, which I can't claim to do. But what I have to say will necessarily centre on the definitions his writings on film propose of scepticism, and of the overcoming of scepticism (or the endurance of scepticism), in and through an acknowledgement of ordinariness. What concerns me in particular is Cavell's understanding of scepticism as the product and expression of trauma. Or, historically, as the product and expression of an 'unhinging of our consciousness from the world' — as original sin, as a fall from grace.[3] The intricate thematic index to *Contesting Tears* directs us to treatments of scepticism with regard to the following conditions: astonishment, emptiness, excess, homosexual panic, madness, nihilism, panic, torture. Melodrama is the book's topic, so these associations are by no means inappropriate. But it does seem to me that Cavell consistently codes doubt as extraordinary, and the acknowledgement through which doubt might be overcome as an overcoming in and through ordinariness. My enquiry will turn out to be in effect an enquiry into ordinary doubt.

My starting-point is an intriguing moment in the chapter on *Adam's Rib* in *Pursuits of Happiness* when Cavell reflects on the need to supplement his own study

1   Stanley Cavell, *Pursuits of Happiness: The Hollywood Comedy of Remarriage* (Cambridge, MA: Harvard University Press, 1981), p. 8.
2   Cavell, *Contesting Tears: The Hollywood Melodrama of the Unknown Woman* (Chicago, IL: University of Chicago Press, 1996).
3   Cavell, *The World Viewed: Reflections on the Ontology of Film*, 2nd edn (Cambridge, MA: Harvard University Press, 1979), p. 22.

of a particular genre with comparable studies of the 'relation among genres', and of the *oeuvres* of the directors concerned. He finds himself compelled at this point to emphasize the 'abutment of films of remarriage with films of the creation of the woman (or the human) by other means'. Certain horror films, he goes on, could be thought to form a 'shadow genre' of the comedy of remarriage. 'I am speaking of horror here as I do in *The Claim of Reason*, as a perception of the instability of the fact of human existence, its neighbouring of the inhuman, the monstrous.' The horror film articulates a fundamental doubt concerning the fact of human existence. 'The comedy of remarriage,' Cavell goes on, 'is as much about separation from society, call it privacy, as the horror movie is; and as much about the establishing of civilization as the Western is.'[4]

Horror

The particular triangulation I want to explore first occurs at a crux in the argument of *Contesting Tears*, as Cavell seeks to establish a distinction between the 'male villainy' deployed by the male protagonist of the melodramas, in order to extinguish the female protagonist, and that deployed by the male protagonist of remarriage comedy, in order at once to re-seduce and to educate her. Feminist film theory, Cavell supposes, would maintain that in both cases the female protagonist has been equally subjected by the male gaze built into the classical Hollywood continuity system. 'Such an answer would, to my mind, take there to be no essential difference between, for example, the way Charles Boyer looks at Ingrid Bergman in *Gaslight*, or the way Spencer Tracy as Mr Hyde looks at Ingrid Bergman in *Dr Jekyll and Mr Hyde*; and the way Spencer Tracy looks at Katharine Hepburn in *Adam's Rib*.'[5] The triangulation is explicit: Spencer Tracy has a good look at Hepburn, in a remarriage film, and a bad look at Bergman, in a horror film; Bergman is looked at badly both in a horror film and in a melodrama of unknownness.

I want to suggest, to begin with, that Cavell is wrong about the horror film: that he has got it back to front. Spencer Tracy *as Dr Jekyll* looks at Ingrid Bergman in *Dr Jekyll and Mr Hyde*. Spencer Tracy as Mr Hyde instead looks *for* her, in such a way as to indicate that he is now incapable of looking at her. The bad gaze belongs to the good man, to the pursuit of happiness. The bad man, by contrast, has no gaze at all; that is, doubt has no gaze at all. The version of *Dr Jekyll and Mr Hyde* Cavell has in mind is that directed by Victor Fleming for MGM in 1941. Fleming is a director worth wagering on. He did not feature as an *auteur*, in the 1950s, and as a result his films have never received the attention they deserve. In 1941, however, he was hot property. Two years before, he had made (or at the very least seen through to completion) *The Wizard of Oz* and *Gone with the Wind*, a double whammy not matched until 1993, when Stephen Spielberg came up with *Jurassic Park* and *Schindler's List*. Tracy described Fleming as a Clark Gable among directors, and his tough-guy persona would seem to preclude any association with major works of thought.

4   Cavell, *Pursuits of Happiness*, pp. 222–23.
5   Cavell, *Contesting Tears*, p. 123.

Hollywood had long since fitted out Robert Louis Stevenson's homosocially inclined story with ample heterosexual love-interest. Harry Jekyll (Spencer Tracy), engaged to Beatrix Emery (Lana Turner), daughter of an eminent physician, first encounters Ivy Peterson (Ingrid Bergman), a barmaid who turns tricks, in a murky London street, where she has been the victim of an assault. She exaggerates the extent of her injuries, and he escorts her home in a cab. He carries her upstairs to her room (Bergman was a large woman, and Tracy rather ungallantly insisted on negotiating the scene with the help of a mechanical sling), and deposits her on the bed. A conversation ensues, about the transformation of solicitude (of curiosity) into desire. 'You'd better let down your blouse,' Jekyll tells Ivy, still very much the concerned physician (**Fig. 17.1**). 'Why?' she asks. 'You want me to have a look at you, don't you?' Indeed she does: she smiles, and moves her body so as to open it up to him: 'I don't know,' she says. Jekyll begins to get it. 'You're looking, ain't you?' Ivy says, settling back onto the bed (**Fig. 17.2**). He certainly is, and not, now, as a doctor. When she removes her blouse to reveal a slip, he catches himself out in an unabashed male gaze at her breasts. The pursuit, here, through conversation, through a conversation about looking, is a pursuit of happiness. Spencer Tracy, as Dr Jekyll, gets a very good look at Ingrid Bergman, as Ivy Peterson.

Still, this a horror film, and what drives it is not the pursuit of happiness, but the pursuit of knowledge: knowledge of humanity's neighbouring of the inhuman and the monstrous. Dr Jekyll converts himself into Mr Hyde in order to explore monstrosity. Jekyll's tragedy, like Lear's, as Cavell would have it, is the consequence not of too little knowledge, but of too much. As Jekyll, he relinquishes Ivy, desirously, having looked fully at her and seen her looking fully at him. As Hyde, he looks for her again, but will never look at her, as Jekyll had done, because his new knowledge is all doubt (about desire, about humanity).

He finds her, doubtfully, in the Palace of Frivolities, where she works as a barmaid. Fleming takes great care to establish with utmost clarity the shape and extent of the Palace of Frivolities as a narrative space. Hyde, seated at a table on a platform stretching along the right-hand wall, scans the spectacle laid out before him. His eyes dart eagerly around, as he looks for Ivy. And then he sees her, in the distance, behind the bar on the other side of the room. During that eager dart around, the camera pans from the dancers on stage down into and across the audience. Hyde himself is clearly the source of this survey of the scene. However, the tracking-shot which succeeds it, and which takes us right up to the bar, is distinctly ahead of him, and comes from a different direction and at a different height. Fleming cuts back from it to Hyde, who has not yet seen what we have seen. Once he has recognized Ivy, on the other side of the room, behind the bar, we see her again, in close-up, but at a distance from her which is clearly not his distance from her. We see her as he can no longer see her. The tracking-shot and subsequent close-up locate her in an unflustered happiness, in conversation, in an idea of community. The gaze by means of which she is now held is anonymous, but most likely gendered male: it cruises her. If it belongs to anyone, it was once Jekyll's.

The woman gazed at is of course Ingrid Bergman, as well as Ivy Peterson. There

Fig. 17.1. 'You'd better let down your blouse.' Frame grab from
Dr Jekyll and Mr Hyde (1941, MGM, dir. Victor Fleming)

Fig. 17.2. You're looking, ain't you?' Frame grab from *Dr Jekyll and Mr Hyde*
(1941, MGM, dir. Victor Fleming)

might be things to say, at this point, about stardom. Bergman, I think, as we see
her here, is not Cavell's idea of a star. What interests Cavell, in the 'great stars', in
Garbo, in Bette Davis, is 'their power of privacy, of a knowing unknownness'.[6] *Dr
Jekyll and Mr Hyde* was Bergman's fourth Hollywood film. *Intermezzo* (1939) made
her a star. But Selznick, who had brought her over from Sweden, and hoped to
exploit her naturalness, did not really know what to do with her. He loaned her
out to other studios. She was originally going to play the insipid Beatrix Emery, in

6   Cavell, 'Ugly Duckling, Funny Butterfly: Bette Davis and *Now Voyager*', *Critical Inquiry*, 16
(1990), 213–47 (p. 228).

Dr Jekyll and Mr Hyde, but managed to persuade Fleming, and Selznick, who was still coaching her from the sidelines, that bad girl Ivy Peterson was the right part for her. The rest is history: *Casablanca* and *For Whom the Bell Tolls*, in 1943, *Gaslight* (and her first Oscar) in 1944, *Spellbound*, in 1945. The gladness we gaze at, in the Palace of Frivolities, is Bergman's, as well as Ivy Peterson's.

Hyde sets Ivy up as his mistress, but he never looks at her as Jekyll had once looked at her, and she does her level best not to look at him at all. There is some sense that part of his new knowledge is a knowledge of what he has lost, of what he is no longer capable of. In one scene, he torments her by offering to take her out to the Albert Hall, and then deciding to stay in instead. They could play cards, he says, or she could read to him. 'Milton's *Paradise Lost* would be nice. But we haven't the book, have we?' *He* doesn't need the book. He is Satan, in Book IV of *Paradise Lost*, watching as Eve imparadises herself in Adam's arms, knowing desire, knowing too much desire, but not able to acknowledge it, by looking and being looked at (not able to educate himself further in desire, or to educate another). Cavell has spoken of *Gaslight* as Cukor's 'response' at once to *Dr Jekyll and Mr Hyde* and to Hitchcock's *Shadow of a Doubt* (1943).[7] Charles Boyer as Gregory Anton in *Gaslight* tortures Ingrid Bergman as his wife Paula rather as Spencer Tracy as Mr Hyde in *Dr Jekyll and Mr Hyde* tortures Ingrid Bergman as his mistress Ivy Peterson. We might note, in view of what I have said about Hyde's exclusion from paradise, that Cavell insists, shrewdly, I think, on Anton's impotence.[8]

However, the more disturbing parallel may be with *Adam's Rib*. Spencer Tracy as Adam Bonner in *Adam's Rib*, prosecuting a woman for the attempted murder of her husband, does on occasion look at Katharine Hepburn as his wife Amanda, counsel for the defendant, in the same way that Spencer Tracy as Dr Jekyll in *Dr Jekyll and Mr Hyde* looks at Ingrid Bergman. There is a further twist. He also looks *for* her, at certain moments, with a sudden intensity which suggests that he has forgotten how to look *at* her. At the climax of the trial, Amanda Bonner, viewed past the heads of members of the jury, just as Ivy Peterson had been viewed past the heads of customers at the bar at the Palace of Frivolities — and, similarly, on the other side of a wooden barrier — makes the case not so much for the accused woman, as for women in general. Adam Bonner, meanwhile, behind her, and at some distance, as Hyde had been in the Palace of Frivolities, grimaces (bares his teeth, rolls his eyes, touches his upper lip with his tongue). It seems to me that Tracy has carried an element of his performance as Mr Hyde over into his performance as Adam Bonner. The triangulation with horror has if anything made it harder to distinguish between a good and a bad male gaze (and thus, perhaps, between one genre and another). This scene, in which Amanda Bonner comes close to self-making, to self-education, to ecstasy, even, when her back is turned to her husband, who feels the exclusion acutely, repeats comparable domestic scenes earlier in the film.

It seems to me that this particular film of remarriage abuts on films of the creation of the woman (or the human) by other means to the extent of absorbing

---

7   Cavell, *Pursuits of Happiness*, p. 221.
8   Cavell, *Contesting Tears*, p. 56.

their worst fears (that is, their fear for the man, which might yet be a hope for the woman). *Adam's Rib* envisages the creation of the woman (or the human) through feminism, and through *aversion* (a-version: a turning away). To converse, in its root meaning, is to turn oneself about or to and fro in a given space in such a way as to inhabit it fully, to be at home in it. Fundamentally averse to her husband, turned away in order to educate herself, to enjoy herself, Amanda seems unlikely to enter into an enduring conversation with him. Either *Adam's Rib* is a good film, but not the kind of film Cavell thinks it is. Or it *is* the kind of film Cavell thinks it is, but not a good one.

The Western

In *Pursuits of Happiness*, Cavell describes Howard Hawks as an artist, as the possessor of a 'brilliant, educated, if brutal, mind'. 'Yet in the interviews Hawks submitted to upon his discovery by educated circles a decade or so ago, he presents himself as a cowboy.'[9] Hawks's tutor in presenting himself as a cowboy was undoubtedly Victor Fleming, whom he first met in 1916, and who by that time already had a formidable reputation as a mechanical genius and all-round daredevil. Does it take a cowboy to make a cowboy film?

We remember Cavell saying that remarriage comedy has as much to do with the establishment of modern civilization as the Western. And it's clear that for him modern civilization only ever established itself, in the Western, as elsewhere, in and through the overcoming of scepticism. The couple of illuminating pages in *The World Viewed* (1971) on John Ford's *The Man Who Shot Liberty Valance* (1962) take the film's topic to be the 'traumatic' birth of law in the new world. '*Liberty Valance* is the fullest expression of the knowledge of the cost of civilization to be found in this genre of film, and therefore it is the greatest instance of it.'[10] But it seems reasonable to ask whether or not the cost of establishing civilization in Connecticut might not be substantially different from the cost of establishing it in, say, Tombstone, Arizona, the setting of Ford's *My Darling Clementine* (1946). For a start, there doesn't seem to be all that much conversation out west: the very medium of remarriage, as Cavell conceives it, perhaps of the civilizing process itself. 'When a motion picture is at its best,' Ford remarked in an interview in *Cosmopolitan* in March 1964, 'it is long on action and short on dialogue.'[11]

One of American civilization's most durable costs, brooded on in a certain kind of Western, but of little concern to remarriage comedy, is racial hatred. Defending remarriage comedy's claim to educate, as well as entertain, on the grounds that it knows the moral and economic value of the work it does, Cavell invokes the pride Emerson and Thoreau took in writing, and Thoreau's confident reprimand of the feckless labourer John Field, in *Walden*, for 'not reckoning cost as he does'.[12] A cost

9   Cavell, *Pursuits of Happiness*, pp. 39–40.
10   Cavell, *The World Viewed*, p. 58.
11   Quoted by Sarah Kozloff, *Overhearing Film Dialogue* (Berkeley: University of California Press, 2000), p. 4.
12   Cavell, *Pursuits of Happiness*, p. 7.

Cavell himself has not reckoned, here, is Thoreau's racist reduction of Field and his family to the virtual status of beasts. 'But alas! The culture of an Irishman is an enterprise to be undertaken with a sort of moral bog hoe.'[13] That *The Man Who Shot Liberty Valance* plays down the question of race, without altogether ignoring it, might have consequences for its claim to be the 'greatest instance' of the genre. On the whole, Ford did not play down the question of race, and his own very deliberate Irishness may have had something to do with that.

My Darling Clementine is in some respects not at all un-Cavellian. It begins in darkness, in *film noir*, some have said, and proceeds towards the light, towards a new dawn in America.[14] Crucial to that process are the tragic self-transcendence of a doubter, drunken, tubercular, Dostoyevskyan Doc Holliday (Victor Mature), and the mutual education of Clementine Carter (Cathy Downs), Holliday's assistant and fiancée in his days as a Boston surgeon, who has followed him out West, and frontier marshal Wyatt Earp (Henry Fonda).

'Shakespeare? In Tombstone?' Doc Holliday exclaims, on hearing that a troupe of travelling players will stage *Hamlet*. The troupe's leading actor delivers Hamlet's most famous soliloquy in a saloon bar full of hoodlums. When he falters halfway through, Doc Holliday takes up the thread, only to be halted in his turn, by a fit of tubercular coughing, when he reaches the line 'Thus conscience does make cowards of us all' (III. 1. 83). Conscience, here, means the fact or faculty of knowing, as well as moral judgement's inner voice. When Doc Holliday is gunned down, in the shootout at the O.K. Corral, his white handkerchief flutters on some fencing. The camera has just signalled the moral direction of his departure by tilting to examine a cloud-flecked sky.

The film overcomes scepticism in and through conversation as well as gunfire. Its turning point is the moment when Clementine, realizing that there's no future for her with Doc Holliday, makes modest overtures to Wyatt Earp, who has already shown, tactfully, that he's strongly attracted to her. She invites him to accompany her to church. Wyatt's answer to Clementine's request is 'I'd admire to take you' (**Fig. 17.3**). In nineteenth-century American idiom, 'I'd admire to' meant 'I'd like to'. We already know that he admires her: the idiom expresses both his willingness to walk with her to church, and his liking for her. There is something here of what Cavell calls, in a different context, the 'appeal from ordinary language to itself': 'a rebuke of our lives by what we may know of them, if we will.'[15]

The root meaning of 'admire' is to wonder at: if you admire someone or something, you wonder at them; they seem to you a marvel. There is wonder in admiration, in desire, in civilization (that is, in the prospect of a brave new world). Since Shakespeare is already in Tombstone, Arizona, in this film, why not also invoke his 'American' play, *The Tempest*? I am thinking of the first encounter

13   Henry David Thoreau, *Walden*, ed. by Stephen Fender (Oxford: Oxford University Press, 1997), p. 185.

14   Scott Simmon, *The Invention of the Western Film: A Cultural History of the Genre's First Half-Century* (Cambridge: Cambridge University Press, 2003), p. 198.

15   Cavell, *The Senses of Walden: An Expanded Edition* (San Francisco, CA: North Point Press, 1981), p. 92.

between Ferdinand and Miranda, in Act I, Scene 2.

FERDINAND: [...] My prime request,
                    Which I do last pronounce, is, O you wonder!
                    If you be maid or no?
MIRANDA: No wonder, sir;
                    But certainly a maid.
                                         (*Tempest*, I. 2. 425–28)

Wyatt Earp and Clementine Carter are both a little too long in the tooth to be playing at Ferdinand and Miranda. But she is beyond doubt his 'Admir'd Miranda', his to-be-wondered-at, his to-be-admired (she is that which will finally allow him to know wonderment). Consider also the later exchange, in Act III, Scene I:

MIRANDA: You look wearily.
FERDINAND: No, noble mistress; 'tis fresh morning with me
                    When you are by at night.
                                         (III. I. 32–39)

Just as Ferdinand had not only wondered at Miranda, but been caught wondering whether she be maid or no, that is, maiden or not, so Wyatt has not only wondered at Clementine, but been caught wondering about what kind of woman she might be. When she first asks him to come with her, he doesn't know what she means. He wonders, for an instant, whether she has asked him to take her as his mistress. We have been set up for Fonda's double-take by an earlier scene in which Doc Holliday's mistress Chihuahua (Linda Darnell) asks him to take her with him when he leaves town. So, there is *ordinary* doubt, in this scene, of which something is to be made, but not too much. And then conversation: an appeal from ordinary language to itself. And then a tracking shot: the first in the film, and for Ford a rarity. Like Wyatt and Clementine, turning their corner, we are now *on the move*. What happens, when they reach the church, happens within the realm of the everyday rather than the realm of the sacred. The church itself is as yet no more than a wooden platform with a couple of American flags at one end and a makeshift bell-tower at the other. There is as yet no minister. Dancing ensues, rather than a service. There is festivity (a conversing, a pursuit of happiness) without festival (a ceremony, a solemn commemoration). Cavell might well find a great deal to admire and to be cheered by in this transition from tragedy to romance by way of doubt assuaged. But I am not convinced that he has the appropriate terms for the sheer ordinariness of the doubt which is the film's great subject. Doubt is everywhere in Tombstone, at once ineradicable and a matter of small concern.

When the Earp brothers first arrive in town, Wyatt solicits a shave. As he lies prone in the barber's chair, a bullet shatters the mirror above his head. 'What kind of a town *is* this?' he asks, understandably. The gunfire proceeds from Indian Charlie, who has drunkenly shot up a brothel on the other side of the street. With a minimum of fuss, Wyatt proceeds to disarm Indian Charlie and send him packing. '*What kind of* town is this,' he wants to know, 'that sells liquor to Indians?' 'What kind of a town?' and 'What kind of a person?' are the questions the film insistently poses. Wyatt's steady answer is a display of insouciance. For him, there is nothing more routine than a little ethnic cleansing.

FIG. 17.3. 'I'd admire to take you.' Frame grab from *My Darling Clementine* (1946, 20th Century Fox, dir. John Ford)

That racism is casual does not, of course, make it any less racist. Ford knew this perfectly well: *My Darling Clementine* was by no means his last word on race. Insouciance, however, is the film's signature. Wyatt is casually racist because he is casually everything. The scenes of ordinary doubt of which he is the focus remain closer to comedy than to tragedy. I am not sure that Cavell, steeped in Shakespearean tragedy, like Doc Holliday, can help us with the ordinariness of Wyatt's doubt.

My Darling Clementine conceives of ordinary doubt as the medium in which racial difference first makes itself felt: at least to a white man with the strength and authority to run any objectionable man or woman of colour out of town. This is not necessarily a racist thought. It is central, for example, to Frantz Fanon's description, in Chapter 5 of *Black Skin, White Masks*, of a casual encounter on the street between a black man and a white boy.

> 'Look, a Negro!' It was an external stimulus that flicked over me as I passed by. I made a tight smile.
> 'Look, a Negro!' It was true. It amused me.
> 'Look, a Negro!' The circle was drawing a bit tighter. I made no secret of my amusement.[16]

Of course, Fanon's amusement soured rapidly: this encounter was (or subsequently became) the provocation to his critique of colonialism. But for him, as for Wyatt Earp, in *My Darling Clementine*, the understanding of racial difference could be said to begin in ordinary doubt, comically. If remarriage comedy's abutment on horror brings out a provocative similarity, its abutment on the Western brings out an equally provocative difference.

---

16   Frantz Fanon, *Black Skin, White Masks*, trans. by Charles Lam Markmann (New York: Grove Weidenfeld, 1967), pp. 111–12.

CHAPTER 18

Hitchcock's Threshold Moments

review of:

PETER ACKROYD, *Alfred Hitchcock* (London: Chatto & Windus, 2015)

ALFRED HITCHCOCK, *Hitchcock on Hitchcock 2: Selected Writings and Interviews*, ed. by Sidney Gottlieb (Berkeley: University of California Press, 2015)

JAN OLSSON, *Hitchcock à la Carte* (Durham, NC: Duke University Press, 2015)

MICHAEL WOOD, *Alfred Hitchcock: The Man Who Knew Too Much* (Boston, MA: Houghton Mifflin Harcourt, 2015)

Hitchcock liked assembly lines. In the long, consistently revealing interview he gave to François Truffaut in the summer of 1962, he described a scene he had thought of including in *North by Northwest* (1959), but didn't. Roger O. Thornhill (Cary Grant) is on his way from New York to Chicago. Why not have him stop off at Detroit, then still in its Motor City heyday?

> I wanted to have a long dialogue scene between Cary Grant and one of the factory workers as they walk along the assembly line. They might, for instance, be talking about one of the foremen. Behind them a car is being assembled, piece by piece. Finally, the car they've seen being put together from a simple nut and bolt is complete, with gas and oil, and all ready to drive off the line. The two men look at it and say, 'Isn't it wonderful!' Then they open the door of the car and out drops a corpse!

The putative scene has the makings of a classic Hitchcock prank or hoax. 'Where has the body come from? Not from the car, obviously, since they've seen it start at zero! The corpse falls out of nowhere, you see!'[1] Hitchcock was just short of his sixty-third birthday when Truffaut interviewed him. He had remained staggeringly inventive throughout a long, prolific, and highly profitable career, and there were seven films yet to come, including *Psycho* (1960) and *The Birds* (1963). Two American television series — *Alfred Hitchcock Presents* (1955–62) and *The Alfred Hitchcock Hour* (1962–65) converted the 'master of suspense' into an international celebrity. Since his death in 1980, his reputation has continued to soar. He must by now be the most written-about film director of all time. In 2012, *Vertigo* (1958) displaced *Citizen Kane* at the top of *Sight and Sound*'s list of the best films ever made. But his art owed a great deal to its affinity with the assembly line.

---

1   François Truffaut, with Helen G. Scott, *Hitchcock*, rev. edn (New York: Simon & Schuster, 1984), p. 252.

Even the biographers, watching the life start at zero, have struggled to establish where the motivation for the inventiveness came from. The most popular hypothesis, not least because Hitchcock himself promoted it so vigorously, concerns timidity. 'The man who excels at filming fear is himself a very fearful person,' Truffaut observed, 'and I suspect that this trait of his personality has a direct bearing on his success.'[2] The most substantial biography to date, by Patrick McGilligan, includes plenty of anecdotes about fear, but supplies little by way of evidence of its ultimate cause, and draws no conclusions.[3] Peter Ackroyd, however, is firmly of the Truffaut school. His Hitchcock trembles from the very outset: 'fear fell upon him in early life.'[4] At the age of four (or eleven, or ...), his father had him locked up for a few minutes in a police cell, an episode which became, as Michael Wood puts it, the 'myth of origins' for his powerful distrust of authority. Ackroyd rummages dutifully for further evidence. Was young Alfred beaten at school by a 'black-robed Jesuit'? Or caught out in the open when the Zeppelins raided London in 1915? Did he read too much Edgar Allen Poe? It doesn't really add up to very much. And yet — or therefore — the strong conviction persists. Fear is the key; and not just to the life. Interview the films, he once told an inquisitive journalist. Those who have interviewed the films often conclude that like their creator, they, too, tremble. 'Hitchcock was a frightened man,' Wood writes, 'who got his fears to work for him on film.'[5]

For Wood, the question of fearfulness arises most pressingly when it comes to the tortures meted out to the women whose death or danger is such a dominant feature of almost all the movies. 'Is it sadism, as the dark view of Hitchcock proclaims, a pleasure in seeing beautiful women in harm's way? The solitary joy of the otherwise uxorious director? A revenge on the mother the child thought might leave him forever?' Wood doesn't believe that the motive was sadism. Nor does he think, like Hitchcock's first biographer, John Russell Taylor, that Hitchcock, far from enjoying the distress he was able to inflict on them, identified strongly with his victims. The women in the movies are, Wood proposes, 'whatever we most fear to lose'. This 'we' may be just a bit too comfortable. There presumably were and still are those even among Hitchcock's most ardent fans who feel that they could get by in life without a regular supply of blondeness. Still, it seems possible to agree that the women in harm's way represent whatever was most at risk, not just for Hitchcock, but for a culture heavily invested in blonde iconicity. At any rate, I find it difficult to disagree with Wood's further conclusion. The lingering over the heroine's demise could, he says, be masochism. 'But it could also be just an act of thinking the worst, an act of propitiation to the gods who take these treasures away.'[6] Hitchcock's films are at their most Hitchcockian, Wood proposes, when they think the very

2   Ibid., p. 11.
3   Patrick McGilligan, *Alfred Hitchcock: A Life in Darkness and Light* (Chichester: John Wiley, 2003), pp. 7–8, 448.
4   Peter Ackroyd, *Alfred Hitchcock* (London: Chatto & Windus, 2015), pp. 4, 8.
5   Michael Wood, *Alfred Hitchcock: The Man Who Knew Too Much* (Boston, MA: Houghton Mifflin Harcourt, 2015), p. 98.
6   Ibid., pp. 97–98.

worst. They are certainly lavish in their propitiations: it takes Marion Crane (Janet Leigh) 45 seconds to die, in *Psycho*, but the scene required 70 different camera set-ups. Ceremony enough, surely. Hitchcock, however, knew that the gods who took the treasures away were not the kind to be propitiated.

The best commentary on this aspect of Hitchcock's films may in fact be Philip Larkin's 'Aubade', a poem about the fear not so much of dying, as of the fact of dying, of mortality.[7] Waking at 4 a.m., the speaker understands, abruptly, and in anguish, that an event so long foreseen it barely registers is now a whole day closer. His mind 'blanks', not inwardly, in remorse or despair, but outwardly, at the prospect of extinction, of an eternity of emptiness. There is, he feels, something special in that anguish, something no trick of the mind will dispel. Hitchcock, I suspect, felt much the same.

The speaker of 'Aubade' begins by announcing that he works all day and gets half-drunk at night. That is pretty much what Hitchcock did for most of his life, except that as he grew older the drinking encroached increasingly on the work (champagne with lunch, vodka and orange in a flask on set). The justification for the briskness of Ackroyd's account (259 pages of text, when previous biographers have required twice as much, or more) is that Hitchcock, too, did not linger. He liked to think that he could complete one film in the studio, while starting another in his mind. The transitions between films became almost as swift and as seamless as the transitions within them. 'He already had another project in mind' is Ackroyd's constant refrain. By the same token, the rare periods of 'suspended animation' during the course of a long career, when there were 'no stories to consider, no treatments to contemplate, no stars to pursue,' became a 'form of torture'.[8] The final months of his life seem to have been truly harrowing for all concerned.

As far as I am aware, Hitchcock himself only ever approached the topic of our sure extinction obliquely, and in relation to his films. For example, he reassured Truffaut that staging violent death all day hadn't given him nightmares. He would go home afterwards and laugh about it.

> And that's something that bothers me because, at the same time, I can't help imagining how it would feel to be in the victim's place. We come back again to my eternal fear of the police. I've always felt a complete identification with the feelings of a person who's arrested, taken to the police station in a police van and who, through the bars of the moving vehicle, can see people going to the theatre, coming out of a bar, and enjoying the comforts of everyday living; I can even picture the driver joking with his police partner, and I feel terrible about it.

I think that the police are a red herring, here. All the vividness of the anecdote lies in the detail of the activities visible from the van, now conclusively beyond reach. Hitchcock identifies completely not so much with the suspected criminal as with the person (any person) whose number is up. The person taken out of circulation — it could be by a police van, or by an ambulance — sees, perhaps for the first

---

7   Philip Larkin, 'Aubade', in *Collected Poems*, ed. by Anthony Thwaite (New York: Farrar, Straus, and Giroux, 1988), pp. 208–09.
8   Ackroyd, *Alfred Hitchcock*, pp. 187, 137.

time, what the world will be like when she or he is no longer in it. Hitchcock had in fact already incorporated a version of the incident he so vividly pictures here into *The Wrong Man* (1956), a very good, if uncharacteristically neo-realist, film about a New York musician under arrest for a crime he did not commit. As he's driven away by the police, the musician (it's Henry Fonda) glimpses his wife, who doesn't yet know that he's been arrested, moving around in the kitchen. When describing this scene to Truffaut, Hitchcock dwelt on details that either weren't in the film to begin with, or got edited out.

> At the corner of the block is the bar he usually goes to, with some little girls playing in front of it. As they pass a parked car, he sees that the young woman inside is turning on the radio. Everything in the outside world is taking place normally, as if nothing out of the ordinary had happened, and yet he himself is a prisoner inside the car.[9]

Hitchcock's imaginary suspect has the same terrible feeling as the speaker of Larkin's 'Aubade', waking at 4 a.m. His mind, too, blanks, not in remorse, despair, or guilt, but at the prospect of an eternity emptied of normality, of the routines of everyday living. Hitchcock identifies with a fear of extinction rather than of imprisonment. What makes it worse is that normality seems unlikely to notice his passing.

The second film Hitchcock directed on his own was *The Pleasure Garden* (1925), a British–German co-production made in Munich. At its climax, an alcoholic husband gripped by *delirium tremens* is shot as he's about to stab his wife to death. 'When he is shot,' Wood notes, 'he comes to his senses, no longer drunk at all; he mildly says, "Oh, hello, Doctor," to the man who has interrupted his fury and dies.' The version of the film I have seen has no inter-title at this point, so I can't be sure of the exact words. But it's hard to mistake the jauntiness on the man's face. The German producer complained that the scene was impossible, and in any case too brutal to be shown. Hitchcock kept it (he may have sacrificed the clarifying inter-title by way of compromise). 'There is a sense, though,' Wood goes on, 'in which a casual, almost negligent registering of one's last moment is scarier — not brutal or incredible as the German producer thought, but too natural for art, as if the erratic truth of death's timing were more than we could bear in a story.'[10] I think that's dead right. Except of course that nature has little to do with the way people die in Hitchcock's films.

It took a very special kind of invention to get an awareness of the 'erratic truth of death's timing' into a medium of mass entertainment. In the course of a shrewd and properly demanding analysis of *Vertigo*, Wood draws attention to sequences of shots which occur during the first hour of the film, and which mark a narrative threshold: a step-change in its relation to its audience. During these moments, our eyes and ears are 'co-opted' for the 'sense of the world' somewhat precariously maintained by acrophobic private detective Scottie Ferguson (James Stewart), whose old acquaintance Gavin Elster wants him to trail his (apparent) wife, the luminous Madeleine (Kim Novak). We do not exactly see what Scottie sees, Wood argues.

9   Truffaut, *Hitchcock*, pp. 172–73, 200.
10   Wood, *Alfred Hitchcock*, pp. 7–8.

FIG. 18.1–4. To get closer just by wanting to. Frame grabs from *Vertigo*
(1958, Paramount Pictures, dir. Alfred Hitchcock)

Rather, we see what he would see if his eyes were a camera. If Scottie can establish
to his own satisfaction that Madeleine is prey to fugue states in which she assumes
the appearance and personality of an ancestress, Carlotta Valdes, who committed
suicide in 1857, he will feel justified in taking the job, and falling in love with her.
In the Legion of Honour museum in San Francisco, Madeleine sits absorbed in a
portrait of Carlotta, the bouquet on the bench beside her matching the one Carlotta
holds. Scottie watches from across the room. As his gaze narrows, the camera moves
in on the bouquet on the bench, and then by a swerve and sudden ascent, on its
equivalent in the portrait. Scottie subsequently tails Madeleine home. He peers at
her car, across the courtyard from him. Is that a bouquet on the dashboard? It's as
if he believes he could get closer just by wanting to. In the event, the camera does
it for him, not by moving in, but by a new set-up, from a different angle, halfway
across the courtyard. Yes, it is a bouquet (**Figs 18.1–4**). In Wood's view, the sheer
'extravagance' of these manoeuvres 'beautifully and scarily exploits the possibilities
of the medium,' making our dependence on such possibilities 'something like an
addiction'.[11] We become complicit with everything that has already happened, and
everything that will happen, to Scottie.

11   Ibid., pp. 90–91.

In fact, such moments had long been a feature of Hitchcock's film-making, as much of an authorial signature as the famous cameo appearances, if a lot less obtrusive; and a great deal more consequential than the various motifs, riddles, visual puns, and other traces he is sometimes said to have scattered throughout his films. The earliest I can think of occurs in *The Lodger* (1926), which he himself described as the 'first true "Hitchcock" movie'.[12] Quite distinct from the fluid, intricately choreographed camera movements which have generally been taken to exemplify his virtuosity (his 'art'), these five-to-ten-second tracks forward — or, alternatively, the abrupt transition to a new and noticeably discrepant camera set-up within the space originally defined by an establishing shot — are strictly functional.

In most cases, the dolly in or the discrepant angle follows a narrowing of the protagonist's gaze, as it does in *Vertigo*. In *Notorious* (1946), for example, Alicia Huberman (Ingrid Bergman), dining in Rio de Janeiro with the Nazi super-scientists among whom she has been planted, notices a commotion around the bottles of wine on the side-board. A dolly in on a label shows us what she would like to see, but can't quite from where she's sitting. Now she's truly hooked; and us with her. In *The Birds*, after the avian invaders have swept *en masse* down the chimney of the Brenner house and laid waste to the lounge, Melanie Daniels (Tippi Hedren) watches Lydia Brenner (Jessica Tandy), the mother of the man she's fallen in love with, picking up broken crockery and straightening a picture on the wall, while her son bickers with the sheriff, who's come to inspect the damage. After a couple of medium long shots of Lydia from Melanie's point of view, a third shot, now from a position she very evidently does not occupy, takes us in much closer. The change of distance and angle is an act of moral and emotional intelligence. While the men bicker, Melanie, noticing Lydia's distress, has understood something both about her, and about the scale of the catastrophe they all face (**Figs 18.5–8**). It's the sort of awakening conventional in melodrama. On this occasion, however, awakening has been out-sourced to a machine.

The changes of distance and angle sometimes arise out of the fiction's premise. The protagonist of *Rear Window* (1954), L. B. Jefferies (James Stewart), is a photographer who finds himself confined to a wheelchair by a broken leg; so it makes sense for him to put down the pair of binoculars through which he has been scrutinizing the suspicious goings-on in the apartment directly opposite, and pick up a telephoto lens instead. The closer view afforded by the telephoto lens reveals a man wrapping a saw and a butcher's knife in some newspaper. It doesn't in fact generate a great deal by way of additional detail; but we think it must do, because we've seen Jefferies swop the binoculars for a telephoto lens. Even more interesting, however, are those cases — *Blackmail* (1929), *Suspicion* (1941), or *The Wrong Man* — in which the camera's swift forward movement or re-positioning does not stem directly from the protagonist's immediate point of view, but nonetheless takes place as it were on her or his behalf. In *Shadow of a Doubt* (1943), for example, a dolly in on Uncle Charlie (Joseph Cotten), from a position other than that occupied by the person currently talking to him, his niece Charlie (Teresa Wright), confirms starkly

---

12   Truffaut, *Hitchcock*, p. 38.

FIG. 18.5–8. The change of distance and angle is an act of moral and emotional intelligence. Frame grab from *The Birds* (1963, Universal Pictures, dir. Alfred Hitchcock)

to us, but not to her, that he is indeed the killer we already know him to be. In such cases, an alliance has been created between audience and camera, an alliance in suspense: sympathetic to the protagonist, but apart from him or her.

These threshold moments are engrossingly human. They engage us fully in the protagonist's first full engagement with the world's meaningfulness. We, too, have been reanimated — thanks to the surrogacy of a machine's-eye view. The something too natural for art that Wood discerns in the death-scene in *The Pleasure Garden* has found a means other than jesting last words to embed itself in the narrative. Hitchcock, who never forgot what he'd learned as a director of silent films, understood that he didn't need words at all, jesting or otherwise. For all the light at their disposal, his threshold moments have something of the defining absence of sound that characterizes the 4 a.m. hiatus in Larkin's 'Aubade'. They all occur either without a word spoken, or deliberately against (or *over*) the distractions of speech. Their discrepant soundlessness puts us back inside the police van. The threshold moment could be our last glimpse of the 'comforts of everyday living': a world in which a bouquet is a bouquet, a bottle of wine a bottle of wine, a saw a saw, and a woman tidying a tidy woman. We know that the people on the streets are talking to each other, as people ordinarily do, but we can't catch a word of what they say. *Psycho* confirms the soundlessness of the 4 a.m. hiatus. We expect the threshold to announce itself during the scene in which Marion Crane (Janet Leigh), having just set foot in the Bates motel, fences warily with Norman (Anthony Perkins) in a room full of stuffed animals. But this is a heroine who will be dead before she's had a chance to notice anything truly suspicious. Hers is a post-mortem awakening. The camera starts on her lifeless face pressed against the bathroom floor, pans to take in the bedroom, and then speeds forward and up until it arrives at the newspaper on the bedside table which conceals the money she had stolen earlier in the day: the grim remnant of her all too human aspiration to a better life.

Of course, there are other kinds of Hitchcock film. He spoke sometimes of the need to adjust the 'dosage' of humour from one to the next, and the more humorous among them concern the special fear of dying only in so far as they resemble a trick used to quell it. In the films about nothing very much at all, we learn soon enough to stop worrying about what the villains have in store for the hero and heroine, and start worrying about what the hero and heroine have in store for each other. To demonstrate that romance, like danger, can keep us on tenterhooks, Hitchcock included in *Easy Virtue* (1927) a scene in which a switchboard operator eavesdrops on a marriage proposal. Pleasurable suspense, and its adroit resolution, took up a lot of space in his bag of cinematic tricks.

Hitchcock was an inveterate practical joker. Mercifully, the jokes themselves now seem too boring to merit much attention. But they certainly had a part to play in the publicity campaigns which transformed a film-director into a media brand. Jan Olsson has shown in great detail how Hitchcock consistently manipulated celebrity gossip in order to project the image of a creative genius who was as much 'prankster' as 'master craftsman'. The most substantial prank of all was his own body. Despite periodic bouts of binge-dieting, Hitchcock remained until the end of his life mountainously fat. In the mid-1930s, as his ambitions turned increasingly towards a career in Hollywood, he began to parlay his corpulence — and the appetites which had brought it about — into an instantly recognizable public persona. 'His film fame, food reputation, and fabulous physicality were supreme assets,' Olsson observes, 'when he signed up for *Alfred Hitchcock Presents* in 1955, on the cusp of Hollywood's television era.'[13] His Englishness, too, presumably: no more of a mere hoax than Larkin's, it had nonetheless to be kept in full working order, like the corpulence, by constant reiteration (the sober suit and tie worn to work every day, regardless of the weather). Not everyone would accept Olsson's linking of the food and the physicality to the films. Introducing the most recent of the two indispensable collections he has edited of articles, essays, and stories by Hitchcock, and interviews with him, Sidney Gottlieb notes that he has chosen to exclude material concerned primarily with food, weight, and family life, topics 'perhaps worth investigating' as an element in the construction of a public persona, but not as important as the comments on cinema.[14] Still, the cameo appearances did put

13   Jan Olsson, *Hitchcock à la Carte* (Durham, NC: Duke University Press, 2015), pp. 3–4.
14   Sidney Gottlieb, 'Introduction', in *Hitchcock on Hitchcock 2: Selected Writings and Interviews*, ed. by Sidney Gottlieb (Berkeley: University of California Press, 2015), pp. 1–18 (p. 2).

the corpulence on ample display in the films; while it's the confirmed pranksters, like Melanie Daniels in *The Birds*, who undergo the most rigorous examination by 4 a.m. hiatus. Even when he was at his most serious, in his commentary on cinema, Hitchcock had the air of a conjuror explaining his tricks.

He thought that montage was cinema at its most pure. In theory, his method involved a subordination to the capacities of the camera upheld with such completeness and consistency at each stage of the production process, from script and storyboards through principal photography to editing, that it became a kind of mastery. Before cinema, montage meant the action of assembling mechanical components. Interviewed about *Rear Window* in 1968, Hitchcock defined the technique as the 'juxtaposition' of 'pieces of film that went through a machine' in such a way as to create 'ideas on the screen'.[15] His own conjuring was by means of sleight of machine rather than of hand. In an article published in *Cassell's Magazine* in 1928, he set out to disillusion the movie-going public about one detail in particular.

> All the romance is in the story, not in the film making. The average applicant for a film test has no idea at all of the workaday, unromantic atmosphere of a studio. It is nothing more than an 'emotion' factory. Emotions of many varying sorts, shades, degrees and colours have to be *manufactured*, and all must be photographically clear.[16]

Montage used the machine against itself, creating out of its excess of indifference (the 70 set-ups for the shower scene) a spectacle guaranteed to wring the heart.

The best of the films about nothing very much at all end superbly, the fulfilment of the romantic fantasies they explore achieved by small miracles of montage. In his Hollywood memoir *Adventures in the Screen Trade*, the scriptwriter William Goldman offers an admiring analysis of the conclusion of *North by Northwest*. When we recall what happened at the end of the film, Goldman says, we suppose that it must have taken a narrative age to get from the moment at which Eve Marie Saint dangles helplessly from Cary Grant's hand on the face of Mount Rushmore — while America's implacable enemies stand poised to tip them both over the edge and make off with the state secrets they've been safeguarding — to the moment at which he pulls her up beside him into a bunk in an express train about to enter a tunnel. In fact, it takes a mere 43 seconds, so economical is Hitchcock's editing.[17] *North by Northwest* was modelled to some extent on *The 39 Steps* (1935), which permits itself three minutes to get from the climax of a national emergency involving the design of a new warplane to the blissful union of hero and heroine. Both films conclude at a lick: the pieces don't so much fall into place as cascade. There's a kind of heartlessness in that, too. Montage has become cinema's indispensable, delightful, futile prank. It's not just corpses that tumble out of the vehicles rolling off the Hitchcock assembly line, but pairs of newly-weds, in radiant, fully automated succession.

15   Alfred Hitchcock, '*Rear Window*', in *Hitchcock on Hitchcock 2*, pp. 95–101 (p. 96).
16   Hitchcock, 'An Autocrat of the Film Studio', in *Hitchcock on Hitchcock 2*, pp. 116–23 (p. 118). Emphasis in original.
17   William Goldman, *Adventures in the Screen Trade* (London: Macdonald, 1983), pp. 117–18.

PART III

Materialism Then and Now

CHAPTER 19

Modernism and Empire: Reading *The Waste Land*

In Chapter 5 of D. H. Lawrence's *Women in Love* (1920), Rupert Birkin and Gerald Crich travel up to London by train. Crich draws Birkin's attention to an essay alongside the leading articles in the *Daily Telegraph*, 'saying there must arise a man who will give new values to things, give us new truths, a new attitude to life, or else we shall be a crumbling nothingness in a few years, a country in ruin.' At first Birkin dismisses this as just another piece of 'newspaper cant'. But he has to recognize that it isn't all that far from what he himself believes.[1] Indeed, it isn't all that far from what Lawrence believed. The modernist apocalypse, that desire to regenerate a decadent society and a decadent literature, was formulated within hearing distance of a kind of 'newspaper cant' which we could identify with the militant imperialism of the time. Lawrence hints at a relation between the two versions of apocalypse which has not to my knowledge been fully explored. Should such a relation exist, it would have important consequences for our reading of a literature whose self-reference is usually thought to lodge it safely beyond politics.

In this essay, I will connect the apocalypse of *The Waste Land* to the sentiments pondered by Gerald Crich and Rupert Birkin: a country in ruin, a new attitude to life. Eliot, of course, did his best to discourage any such line of enquiry, describing the poem as 'rhythmical grumbling' rather than 'social criticism'. When Valerie Eliot enshrined this remark in her edition of the facsimile, it became (despite its less than Mosaic provenance) the key to interpretation.[2] Recent criticism of *The Waste Land* has concentrated almost exclusively on its achievement as confession or as literary revision.[3] I have myself emphasized the privacy of its rhetoric.[4] But it would be a mistake to lose sight altogether of the poem's criticism of the contemporary world. We should at least ask ourselves whether the very forms of its confession and its literary revision, the forms of its Modernism, might not have derived from that world.

1   D. H. Lawrence, *Women in Love* (Harmondsworth: Penguin Books, 1960), p. 59.
2   T. S. Eliot, *The Waste Land: A Facsimile and Transcript of the Original Drafts*, ed. by Valerie Eliot (London: Faber, 1971), p. 1.
3   Lyndall Gordon, *Eliot's Early Years* (Oxford: Oxford University Press, 1977); Ronald Bush, *T. S. Eliot: A Study in Character and Style* (Oxford: Oxford University Press, 1983); Peter Ackroyd, *T. S. Eliot* (London: Hamish Hamilton, 1984); Grover Smith, *The Waste Land* (London: Allen & Unwin, 1984).
4   David Trotter, *The Making of the Reader* (London: Macmillan, 1984), pp. 44–48.

Eliot tended to distance himself from imperialism by arguing that its lack of classical restraint and impersonality made it a poor basis for an aesthetic. Reviewing George Wyndham's *Essays in Romantic Literature*, he claimed that it was possible to discuss them 'only as the expression of this peculiar English type, the aristocrat, the Imperialist, the Romantic, riding to hounds across his prose, looking with wonder upon the world as upon a fairyland.' Wyndham — 'a man of character, a man of energy' — prompted political rather than literary speculation.

> It would be of interest to divagate from literature to politics and enquire to what extent Romanticism is incorporate in Imperialism; to enquire to what extent Romanticism has possessed the imagination of Imperialists, and to what extent it was made use of by Disraeli. But this is quite another matter: there may be a good deal to be said for Romanticism in life, there is no place for it in letters.[5]

This would indeed have been an interesting divagation. We can say that Eliot recognized the power of certain attitudes which he wanted to keep out of his art. In *The Waste Land*, he would not be riding to hounds across his allusions.

Still, many readers have felt that Eliot did not keep 'Romanticism' out of his art. Did he keep imperialism out? If we are to answer that question, we must first situate and define the sentiments pondered by Birkin and Crich: a country in ruin, a new attitude to life.

By the end of the nineteenth century, Empire had become the White Man's Burden, a dangerous project. 'At every turn,' the *Pall Mall Gazette* complained in 1885, 'we are confronted with the gunboats, the sea lairs, or the colonies of jealous and eager rivals [...] The world is filling up around us.'[6] The world was also filling up in economic and demographic terms. America and Germany were challenging the industrial and commercial supremacy of Britain, while the inexhaustible Russian and Chinese masses pressed in on her most valued possession, India. 'Now,' Lord Salisbury declared in a speech in May 1898 which alarmed and offended foreign governments, 'with the whole earth occupied and the movements of expansion continuing, she will have to fight to the death against successive rivals.'[7] The New Imperialism which emerged and gained strength during the 1890s was thus an act of reassertion rather than of assertion.

The New Imperialists promoted a spirit of defensive aggression which would, they hoped, stiffen the nation's resolve to meet internal and external threats. St Loe Strachey explained the cautionary value of a study of the Roman Empire: 'the way to prevent decay and to make sure of our foundations is for the citizens of the British Empire to be continually solicitous to her welfare, and anxious to cut out and eradicate the very first signs of dry rot.'[8] The New Imperialists were certainly solicitous. Their number included theorists (Seeley, Dilke, Froude), politicians

---

5   Eliot, 'A Romantic Patrician', *Athenaeum*, 2 May 1919, 265–67 (p. 266).

6   Quoted by Bernard Porter, *The Lion's Share: A Short History of British Imperialism, 1850–1970* (London: Longman, 1975), p. 117.

7   Ibid., p. 26.

8   St Loe Strachey, 'The Uses of History', *National Review*, 46 (1906), 877–93 (p. 891).

(Salisbury, Rosebery, Chamberlain), and Proconsuls (Rhodes, Milner, Cromer, Curzon).[9] It is true that the measures they advocated most strongly — tariff reform, national service, a government of national unity — were never implemented. But they had some success: Balfour's Committee of Imperial Defence, the growth of empire youth movements, the establishment of an 'Empire Day'. They led by example (Strachey set up his own Volunteer Company in Surrey in 1906); and they never ceased to warn the nation, often in apocalyptic terms, of the consequences of decline.[10] The Liberal triumph of 1905 seemed fatal to their hopes. The stroke suffered by Joseph Chamberlain in 1906 robbed them of their leader. 'I began to have an ugly fear,' John Buchan was to say of the period after 1905, 'that the Empire might decay at the heart.'[11]

Arthur Balfour surveyed the reasons usually given for the fall of the Roman Empire and concluded that the only plausible explanation was decay at the heart: 'when through an ancient and still powerful state there spreads a mood of deep discouragement, when the reaction against recurring ills grows feebler, and the ship rises less buoyantly to each succeeding wave, when learning languishes, enterprise slackens, and vigour ebbs away, then, as I think, there is present some process of social degeneration, which we must perforce recognize, and which, pending a satisfactory analysis, may conveniently be distinguished by the name of "decadence".'[12] What worried Balfour, and many other people, was evidence of the same processes of degeneration in the ancient and still powerful state of Britain.

An apocalyptic view of history insisted that empires decay from the heart outwards, unless they can be reinvigorated by contact with the colonial periphery, the frontier-zone where civilization meets barbarism. The centre of the British Empire had known civilization for so long that it had lost its originating vigour. It had become stagnant, clogged, decadent. Wealth, leisure, and propriety insulated its inhabitants against the energizing challenges of experience. At the periphery, on the other hand, those challenges could not be avoided. There society was still in the making, and its makers could not hide behind a screen of inherited wealth and inherited decorum; they had nothing to fall back on except their own reserves of energy and ability. Some, like J. A. Froude, felt that the vigour of the colonies could still be made to circulate through the dying heart of the system. Others did not. 'The centre of Imperialism, as Lord Rosebery is never tired of reiterating, rests in London. With a perpetual lowering of the vitality of the Imperial Race in the great cities of the kingdom through over-crowding in room and in area, no amount of hectic, feverish activity on the confines of the Empire will be able to arrest the inevitable decline.'[13]

9   For a concise account of these figures, see Richard Faber, *The Vision and the Need: Late-Victorian Imperialist Aims* (London: Faber and Faber, 1966), pp. 68–95.
10   Porter, 'The Edwardians and Their Empire', in *Edwardian England*, ed. by Donald Read (London: Croom Helm, 1982), pp. 128–44.
11   John Buchan, *Memory-Hold-the-Door* (London: Hodder and Stoughton, 1940), p. 126.
12   Arthur Balfour, *Decadence* (Cambridge: Cambridge University Press, 1908), p. 34.
13   Charles Masterman, 'Realities at Home', in *The Heart of Empire*, ed. by Charles Masterman (London: T. Fisher Unwin, 1901), p. 24.

The New Imperialists believed that the vitality of the race could be renewed by journeys to the frontier. Lord Curzon elaborated on this idea in his Romanes Lecture of 1907. He had travelled widely on the boundaries of the British Empire in Asia, and had recently served as Viceroy of India. His lecture consists largely of a discussion of frontier policy in recent history. But its tone changes towards the end, when he launches into some fervent remarks about the effect 'of Frontier expansion upon national character, as illustrated in the history of the Anglo-Saxon race.' American identity had been shaped by such an expansion. 'In the forests and on the trails of the Frontier, amid the savagery of conflict, the labour of reclamation, and the ardours of the chase, the American nation was born.' Might not the British nation be reborn on *its* frontiers? 'I am one of those,' Curzon said, 'who hold that in this larger atmosphere, on the outskirts of Empire, where the machine is relatively impotent and the individual is strong, is to be found an ennobling and invigorating stimulus for our youth, saving them alike from the corroding ease and the morbid excitements of Western civilisation.' Such was the Imperial rite of passage which promised to remove young men and women from a decadent society, and to bring out the best in them by giving them experience of life in the raw. 'The Frontiers of Empire continue to beckon.'[14]

They certainly continued to beckon in popular fiction. In 1900, John Buchan published *The Half-Hearted*. At the beginning of the novel, the hero is supercilious, cynical, lethargic, 'over-cultured', and 'enervated'. He is persuaded to use his knowledge of the Indian frontier to help foil a Russian invasion, and this new role unlocks hidden reserves of energy. He dies defending a pass against the entire Russian army, half-hearted no more.[15] The remedy for decadence is a journey to the frontier. It still was in 1916, when Maud Diver published the third in a series of novels about the Frontier Force, *Desmond's Daughter*. Again, the hero is initially half-hearted, but undertakes a journey to the frontier which he defines as a quest, and becomes a man — this time at the cost of a leg only.[16]

There were, of course, other frontiers. In Arthur Conan Doyle's *Tragedy of the Korosko* (1898), a group of tourists travel up the Nile by steamer, venture ashore, and are promptly kidnapped by dervishes. A middle-aged and half-hearted lawyer is just as promptly regenerated by the experience: 'he had begun to find himself — to understand that there really was a strong, reliable man behind all the tricks of custom which had built up an artificial nature.' The youth he had missed when young announces itself 'like some beautiful belated flower.'[17] Another candidate for regeneration — he reads Walter Pater on the boat — is not so lucky, being despatched by a Mad Mullah on page 140. Whatever the frontier, the rite of passage remains the same.

Eliot's poem resembles that fictions of empire in one respect only: it begins in

14   George Nathaniel Curzon, *Frontiers* (Oxford: Oxford University Press, 1907), pp. 3, 7, 55–58.

15   Buchan, *The Half-Hearted* (London: Isbister, 1900), p. 299.

16   Maud Diver, *Desmond's Daughter* (Edinburgh: William Blackwood, 1916).

17   Arthur Conan Doyle, *The Tragedy of the Korosko* (London: Smith, Elder, 1898), p. 170. This part of the world also saw the regeneration of the heroes of Rudyard Kipling's *The Light that Failed* (1891) and A. E. W. Mason's *The Four Feathers* (1902).

London, the dead heart of the system, and it ends on the frontier. It shows an 'Unreal City', a journey, a muted and perhaps empty promise of regeneration. Two models have been adduced for this skeletal narrative: spiritual autobiography and epic. 'From the close of "The Fire Sermon", the sordid city is blotted out by exemplary characters who escape contamination either by the practice of asceticism — like the Buddha or St Augustine — or by dreams of a voyage, a journey, a pilgrimage, the metaphoric clichés of spiritual autobiography.'[18] By this account, the poem is confessional, its landscape of city and waste land an attempt to dramatize spiritual conflict and its resolution. But allusions to the *Aeneid* suggest that Eliot might also have imagined an urban apocalypse: Troy burning, and a quester setting out to found Rome.[19]

In recent interpretations of *The Waste Land*, the first model has tended to overshadow the second. It can be substantiated more easily from Eliot's reading, and from his biography. Yet there are elements of the poem which it cannot explain. Why, for example, should 'What the Thunder Said' be built around such exotic allusions: Shackleton in South Georgia, Doughty's *Arabia Deserta*, Conrad's *Outcast of the Islands*? The landscape cannot be said to represent a *spiritual* danger, or to illuminate in any way the mind of the pilgrim. It is there in its own right, a dark expanse, alien and glamorous.

It is a frontier-zone traversed by pilgrims who are also explorers, as Shackleton and Doughty had been. Imperial mythology attributed great significance to exploration. For the explorer's testing was a supremely individual one, endured alone or virtually alone, in a hostile terrain, and often among hostile peoples, without easy recourse to European technology. And it yielded a kind of free-floating symbolism, a motive which could not be reduced to material gain. Shouldn't the system which inspired these men and women to endure extraordinary dangers and privations be admired for something more than its military and economic supremacy?

The intellectual community awarded them the gold medal of the Royal Geographic Society, the reading public devoured books and articles about them. Sir Harry Johnston laboured to compile a series of six volumes about *The Pioneers of Empire*. His publishers had asked him, he wrote, for stories 'in which the daring of white men (and sometimes of white women) stood out clearly against backgrounds of unfamiliar landscapes, peopled with strange nations, savage tribes, dangerous beasts, or wonderful birds.' A request thus framed, he wrote, was 'almost equivalent to asking me to write stories of those pioneers who founded the British Empire.' Some of these white men were, admittedly, foreigners. But had they lived to see the use made of their discoveries by the British, they would not be 'so sorry after all that we are reaping where they sowed.'[20]

Sir Henry Newbolt, writing after the mechanized devastation of the First World War, proposed that individual heroism was most likely to be met with in stories of

---

18   Gordon, *Early Years*, p. 111.
19   Frank Kermode, 'A Babylonish Dialect', in *T. S. Eliot: The Man and His Work*, ed. by Allen Tate (London: Chatto and Windus, 1967), pp. 225–37; Hugh Kenner, 'The Urban Apocalypse', in *Eliot in His Time*, ed. by A. Walton Litz (Princeton, NJ: Princeton University Press, 1973), pp. 23–49.
20   Sir Harry Johnston, *Pioneers of Empire*, 6 vols (London: Blackie, 1912–14), I, iii–iv.

exploration: 'the right stuff is there none the less, the stuff that we all want and can never do without.' These stories had other qualities, too, like interesting natives ('some among them even have names, and stand out as curious and delightful people'). Above all, they revealed that imperial adventure could be regenerative. Stanley's search for Livingstone 'was originally undertaken from no higher motive than that of journalistic enterprise and the love of adventure, but as it went on the journalist was transformed to an explorer, the young adventurer made himself into a great man.'[21]

'What the thunder said' takes place on some kind of frontier where 'hooded hordes' swarm over endless plains, while in the background the centres of spiritual and material empire crumble: Jerusalem, Athens, Alexandria, Vienna, London.[22] A footnote refers us to Herman Hesse's *Blick ins Chaos*, suggesting that it is the masses of Communist Russia which threaten to overwhelm these cities. But the idea of a deluging invasion by barbarian masses had accompanied imperialist anxieties about internal decay for a long time before 1917. As V. G. Kiernan points out, 'the word "horde" that had come into the European languages from the steppes of central Asia signified a mass of creatures on the move, less human than animal, a blind menace.'[23]

The menace had always hung over the frontiers of Empire, and it found many representatives: the Yellow Peril (after Japan's defeat of Russia in 1904–05), or Pan-Islamic revolt. Even Conan Doyle had paused in his administering of rites of passage to post a warning about Moslem fanaticism: 'Let a common wave pass over them, let a great soldier or organizer arise among them to use the grand material at his hand, and who shall say that this may not be the besom with which Providence may sweep the rotten, decadent, impossible, half-hearted south of Europe, as it did a thousand years ago, until it makes room for a sounder stock?'[24] The extinction of half-hearted Spaniards and Italians might be contemplated with equanimity, but what about British interests in Africa? What about 'a wave of Moslem fanaticism rolling in countless numbers across the African continent [...] one of the most irresistible forces the world will yet have seen'? As in all authentic paranoid fantasies, the lack of evidence was the best kind of evidence. 'When it will come no-one can tell, and this, to the thinking mind, is the greatest danger-signal about the whole business.'[25] Buchan was to make out of this lack of evidence the most thrilling moments of *Prester John* (1910), as young David Crawfurd, who has settled in South Africa after his father's death, awaits the outbreak of a more limited but equally irresistible Zulu revolt.[26]

For the prospect was, of course, exciting — a glimpse of Armageddon quite

21   Sir Henry Newbolt, *The Book of the Long Trail* (London: Longmans, Green, 1919), pp. vii, ix, 144–45.

22   Eliot, *Complete Poems and Plays* (London: Faber and Faber, 1969), p, 73.

23   V. G. Kiernan, *The Lords of Human Kind: European Attitudes towards the Outside World in the Imperial Age* (London: Weidenfeld and Nicolson, 1969), p. 172.

24   Conan Doyle, *Tragedy of the Korosko*, p. 158.

25   Captain H. A. Wilson, 'The Moslem Menace', *Nineteenth Century and After*, 62 (1907), 378–87 (pp. 387, 379).

26   Buchan, *Prester John* (London: Thomas Nelson, 1910).

compatible with the modernist apocalypse. In February 1916, as he was about to start work on *Women in Love*, Lawrence remarked in a letter that he had been reading a *History of the East*: 'And I cannot tell you the joy of ranging far back there seeing the hordes surge out of Arabia, or over the edge of the Iranian plateau [...] the world is very big, and the course of mankind is stupendous. What does a crashing down of nations and empires matter, here and there!'[27] A similar excitement informs Eliot's contemplation of hooded hordes swarming over endless plains, down onto the broken towers of Jerusalem, Athens, Alexandria, Vienna, London.

It is the frontier rather than the chapel which defines authenticity. What the Thunder says is that we have been most ourselves in the 'awful daring' of a momentary surrender, which an 'age of prudence' can never retract. No such evidence of self-possession is likely to be found in our obituaries, or the wills opened in the presence of a 'lean' solicitor.[28] Bourgeois routine cannot comprehend the daring aroused by hooded hordes and dead mountains (while the lean solicitor, appropriately enough, has been the least remarked of all the personages in the poem). How does such daring differ from that which allowed Charlie Marlow, in Joseph Conrad's *Heart of Darkness*, to turn on his comfortably somnolent listeners? 'This is the worst of trying to tell ... Here you all are, each moored with two good addresses, like a hulk with two anchors, a butcher round one corner, a policeman round another, excellent appetites, and temperature normal — you hear — normal from year's end to year's end. And you say "Absurd!".'[29] The epigraph that Eliot originally wanted to use — Kurtz's last words — might have clarified much. Eliot, too, tried to tell: about a possible end to half-heartedness, a possible regeneration. The narrative which shaped his anxieties, even if it could not resolve them, owed a certain amount to frontier-myth as well as to spiritual autobiography.

In defining that frontier-myth, I have allowed contexts to proliferate, and to proliferate away from the text. I believe that in this case the relation between text and context can best be understood in terms of the larger relation between imperial and modernist fantasies of apocalypse. Where the larger relation is concerned, it is only possible at the moment to outline the crucial issues, and to propose lines of enquiry. The New Imperialists constituted a distinct and identifiable pressure group. We need to know more about their presence in the clubs and the literary journals of the period. We need to know more about the activities of people like W. E. Henley and Andrew Lang. And we need to know more about the presence of modernists in clubs and journals, more about the pre-war London literary world remembered by Ezra Pound in the *Cantos*. Until that work has been done, we won't know what it was that Rupert Birkin and Gerald Crich saw in the essay in the *Daily Telegraph*.

As far as *The Waste Land* is concerned, I would claim no more than a certain compatibility. Attention to the mythology of Empire magnifies the traces of urban

27   Lawrence, *Letters*, vol. II, ed. James T. Boulton and George J. Zytaruk (Cambridge: Cambridge University Press, 1981), pp. 528–29. To Ottoline Morrell, 7 February 1916.
28   Eliot, *Complete Poems*, p. 74.
29   Joseph Conrad, *Heart of Darkness* (Harmondsworth: Penguin Books, 1973), p. 68.

and imperial apocalypse noted by Kenner and Kermode. It does not provide a coherent interpretation of the poem as a whole. But it does illuminate details and emphases which other interpretations have had to neglect in order to remain coherent.

Even if we cannot yet follow the progress of the New Imperialism through the clubs and journals, we do know something about its appearance in the guise of scientific discourse. For the anxieties it gave shape to became encoded into semi-autonomous disciplines such as anthropology or eugenics. If we can show that Eliot's criticism of the contemporary world was built upon categories derived from any of these disciplines, then we can propose a much closer alignment of text and context.

Here, I want to examine categories derived from theories of race, a major focus of Imperialist anxieties. 'An Empire such as ours,' Lord Rosebery told the readers of *The Times* in 1900, 'requires as its first condition an Imperial Race — a race vigorous and industrious and intrepid. Health of mind and body exalt a nation in the competition of the universe. The survival of the fittest is an absolute truth in the conditions of the modern world.'[30] Race was a unit of collective identity, established according to physical and moral and intellectual criteria, and located within a hierarchy. Only the fittest of races could acquire an empire, and then hold on to what it had acquired.

But was the British 'race' as vigorous and intrepid as it might be, as it had once been? During the Boer War a large proportion of recruits to the army turned out to be unfit for service, and many people took this as a sign of massive deterioration in the national 'stock'. Urban squalor and overcrowding were held to blame. Others talked of 'race-suicide', because the classes which produced the rulers of Empire were the ones to use birth control. As one observer put it, 'the families which tend to disappear are those with an honourable record, the reserve forces of manliness, ability, and old English courage. In the lowest depths children abound; as we go up the social ladder they become less numerous.' The race was flourishing at the bottom, but dying at the top, because late and sterile marriages had broken 'the strength of that proud order whose achievements made England free and gave it an empire in every Continent.'[31] This imbalance between the fertility of the upper and lower classes was a constant feature of Edwardian anxieties.

But even the most anxious felt that something could be done about it. For the Darwinian emphasis on natural selection was modified by a Lamarckian faith in the inheritance of acquired characteristics. Given a more favourable environment, the most debilitated of races might recover its strength, and pass this recovered strength on to succeeding generations. 'Is it possible,' enquired one writer, 'to improve the lowest classes, with no physical strength and no mental backbone?' He thought it was, because 'there is a physical standard which is the inheritance of the people as a whole, and although the baby's father and mother may have become puny and weak from poverty and unwholesome surroundings, the baby when born reverts to

---

30   Quoted by Porter, *Lion's Share*, p. 130.
31   William Barry, 'Forecasts of Tomorrow', *Quarterly Review*, 209 (1908), 1–27 (pp. 7–8).

the racial type, and if properly cared for after birth may possibly rival in strength and physique its far-away Viking ancestors.'[32] Indeed, the connection between Imperialism and social reform has long been recognized.[33]

The information supporting and directing reform was to be provided by eugenics, which Francis Galton defined as 'the study of agencies under social control that may improve or impair the racial qualities of future generations either physically or mentally.'[34] The Eugenics Education Society held its first General Meeting on 9 December 1907, and managed to attract members of considerable calibre and influence: Arthur Balfour, Havelock Ellis, William MacDougall, John Maynard Keynes. There can be no doubt that its deliberations encoded Imperialist anxieties about decay from within. 'Is it possible,' asked Galton's disciple Karl Pearson, who became Professor of Eugenics at University College London in 1911, 'to arouse a consciousness in the folk that the parentage of the next generation is not a personal but a national problem? — that a nation which has ceased to ensure that its better elements have a dominant fertility has destroyed itself far more effectually than its foes could ever hope to destroy it on the battlefield?'[35]

Eliot was certainly aware of these attempts to arouse a consciousness of race. In 1918, he surveyed 'recent British periodical literature in ethics' for the *International Journal of Ethics*. He selected two contributions as being of 'exceptional importance': a study of Plato's *Republic*, and a series of articles about depopulation and birth control by Professor John McBride, published in the *Eugenics Review*. 'Professor McBride,' Eliot wrote,

> draws two conclusions of social importance: 1. That in former times the struggle for existence was enough to keep down the defective element in the population; but under present conditions these people are protected and multiply. He advocates therefore segregation and sterilization for the benefit of society. 2. The transmissibility of acquired characters makes the problem of education of the highest importance: we must adopt such a system of education that 'the next generation may start at a very slightly higher level of capacity than their fathers'.[36]

This amounts to a summary of the theory of race, and of the relation between heredity and environment, which informed the New Imperialism. The 'defective element' in the population was multiplying too rapidly, and might have to be curbed by segregation or sterilization. The healthy and responsible element was not multiplying fast enough, partly due to birth control, partly due to a loss of will. It was an anxiety which persisted well into the 1920s, with Professor McBride

32   Lauder Brunton, 'National League for Physical Education and Improvement', *National Review*, 44 (1904), 489–98 (p. 498).
33   Bernard Semmel, *Imperialism and Social Reform: English Social-Imperial Thought, 1895–1914* (London: Allen & Unwin, 1960).
34   Francis Galton, *Essays in Eugenics* (London: Eugenics Education Society, 1909), p. 35. See G. R. Searle, *Eugenics and Politics in Britain, 1900–1914* (Leyden: Noordhoff International Publishing, 1976).
35   Karl Pearson, *National Life from the Standpoint of Science*, 2nd edn (London: Adam and Charles Black, 1905), pp. vii–ix.
36   Eliot, 'Recent British Periodical Literature in Ethics', *International Journal of Ethics*, 28 (1918), 270–77 (p. 274).

continually on hand to nourish it.[37] In his article, Eliot did not endorse eugenic theory; but the relative ease with which he extracted its implications for society from a long and highly technical argument indicates some familiarity, even sympathy. He was at home with the categories and the vocabulary of an intellectual discipline which consistently expressed anxiety about the degeneration of the Imperial Race.

When Eliot and Pound criticized contemporary society, they did so with the help of those categories. 'After the attempted revival of mysticism,' Pound wrote in 1912, 'we may be in for a new donation, a sort of eugenic paganism.' Eugenic paganism would strip away the layers of half-hearted Christianity, bestowing power and identity on those who could sustain it. The phrase was clearly meant to startle. But we should not suppose that Pound's interest in race was anything other than literal.[38] In a famous essay of 1913, 'The Serious Artist', he insisted that 'it is a crime rather worse than murder to beget children in a slum, to beget children for whom no fitting provision is made, either as touching their physical or economic wellbeing.'[39] 'The Garden', from *Lustra* (1916), describes an emotionally anaemic society woman — 'In her is the end of breeding' — surrounded by a 'rabble' of the dirty but robust children of the very poor.[40] The distinction is that articulated by eugenics, and it structures the poem.

Eliot, too, wrote a poem about breeding, 'Burbank with a Baedeker: Bleistein with a Cigar' (1919). Then, in 'A Game of Chess', in *The Waste Land*, he juxtaposed a sterile encounter between a neurotic upper-class couple with the conversation of two working-class women in a pub: one scene tortuously phrased and dense with literary allusion, the other naturalistic and purged of verbal ingenuity.[41] The edgy socialite and her boudoir replete with dizzying perfumes and pictures of rape are compounded of autobiographical and literary allusion. But she also has many analogues in the polemical and scientific literature of the New Imperialism: in her, too, is the end of breeding. Similarly, the reckless, scarred fertility of the women in the pub echoes the fear that the 'defective element' in the population was multiplying too rapidly, a fear which Eliot certainly recognized and perhaps shared. 'A Game of Chess', like 'The Garden', is structured by the distinction. In this instance, Eliot's urban apocalypse has exactly the same shape as the urban apocalypse of imperialism.

There is, then, at least one point at which a connection can be established between an element of New Imperialist mythology — its encoding into a specific vocabulary with which Eliot was familiar — and the structure of a section of *The Waste Land*. It is perhaps a more ordinary poem than we sometimes think, not quite so effectively insulated against commonplace public anxieties.

---

37   Trotter, *Making of the Reader*, pp. 42–44.
38   Pound, 'Patria Mia', *New Age*, 11 (1912), p. 466.
39   Pound, 'The Serious Artist', in *Literary Essays*, ed. by T. S. Eliot (London: Faber and Faber, 1960), p. 42.
40   Pound, 'Lustra', in *Collected Shorter Poems* (London: Faber and Faber, 1952), p. 93.
41   Donald Davie, *The Poet in the Imaginary Museum: Essays of Two Decades* (Manchester: Carcanet New Press, 1977), p. 101; Smith, *The Waste Land*, pp. 121–27; Trotter, *Making of the Reader*, p. 44.

CHAPTER 20

A Media Theory Approach to Representations of 'Nervous Illness' in the Long Nineteenth Century

The initial prompt for this essay was a historiographical shift of emphasis in the study of the diseases of modern life that took place during the 1990s, and that concerns the paradigmatic status of one of psychiatry's most celebrated patients, Daniel Paul Schreber. The event I have in mind was the hi-jacking of Schreber's *Memoirs of My Nervous Illness* by media theory.[1] In his influential *Discourse Networks 1800/1900*, first published in English translation in 1990, Friedrich Kittler argued that the *Memoirs* are the autobiography not so much of an individual patient as of the 'discourse network' of 1900: in particular, of those new analogue media, such as cinema and the gramophone, which had bypassed the filtering mechanisms of human intelligence through an exhaustive, direct transcription of the 'real'. Following Jacques Lacan, one of Schreber's most enthusiastic exegetes, Kittler maintained that the distinction between the imaginary and the real became impossible to sustain once symbolism — writing, the law, the father — had been deprived of its authority by technological advance. Psychotic hallucinations of the sort suffered by Schreber evoke — or could be said to theorize — the consequent universal collapse of the imaginary into the real.[2] From Freud onwards, psychiatrists and anti-psychiatrists alike have always shown a lively interest in Schreber's crazily disciplinarian father.[3]

1   Daniel Paul Schreber, *Memoirs of My Nervous Illness*, trans. by Ida Macalpine and Richard A. Hunter (New York: New York Review Books, 2000). First published as *Denkwürdigkeiten eines Nervenkranken* (Leipzig: O. Mutze, 1903).

2   Friedrich Kittler, *Discourse Networks 1800/1900*, trans. by Michael Metteer (Palo Alto, CA: Stanford University Press, 1990), pp. 293–304. For highly informative reflections on the shift of emphasis engineered by Kittler, see Jeffrey Sconce, 'On the Origins of the Origins of the Influencing Machine', in *Media Archaeology: Approaches, Applications, and Implications*, ed. by Erkki Huhtamo and Jussi Parikka (Berkeley, CA: University of California Press, 2011), pp. 70–94; and Steven Connor, 'Scilicet: Kittler, Media, and Madness', in *Kittler Now: Current Perspectives in Kittler Studies*, ed. by Stephen Sale and Laura Salisbury (Cambridge: Polity, 2015), pp. 115–31.

3   Morton Schatzman, *Soul Murder: Persecution in the Family* (London: Allen Lane, 1973); *The Schreber Case: Psychoanalytic Profile of a Paranoid Personality*, ed. by William G. Niederland (New York: Quadrangle, 1974); Zvi Lothane, *In Defense of Schreber: Soul Murder and Psychiatry* (Hillsdale, NJ: Analytic Press, 1992); Eric L. Santner, *My Own Private Germany: Daniel Paul Schreber's Secret History of Modernity* (Princeton, NJ: Princeton University Press, 1996).

Kittler laid the blame instead on his doctor, Professor Paul Flechsig, a pioneering neurologist who regarded the human mind as a data-storage device. According to Kittler, Flechsig's neurological account of the mind mediated to Schreber his understanding of himself as a machine programmed by alien software.[4]

Kittler's analysis of the *Memoirs* remains a brilliant provocation. But there is something rather too insistent about its anchoring of the genre of psychiatric memoir in the 'discourse network' of 1900, itself narrowly understood as an array of inscriptive technologies: gramophone, typewriter, film.

> Once the technological differentiation of optics, acoustics, and writing exploded Gutenberg's writing monopoly around 1880, the fabrication of so-called Man became possible. His essence escapes into apparatuses. Machines take over functions of the central nervous system, and no longer, as in times past, merely those of muscles.[5]

Communications technologies such as the telegraph and the telephone, which Schreber also invokes on occasion, do not fit this story.[6] Put simply, communications technologies presume, not a machine programmed by a machine, but 'thoughtful subjectivities' which 'transfer their thoughts to one another'.[7] We need to loosen the tourniquet knotted by Kittler's narrow understanding of what media were *c.* 1900 around an autobiographical form which had been taking shape in a variety of literatures since *c.* 1800: sometimes, as I shall show, by means of a broad understanding of what a medium is. Such a loosening will involve the historical investigation of psychiatric memoirs published before the advent of gramophone, typewriter, and film; and theoretical recourse to more recent speculations concerning the 'cultural techniques' we have become accustomed to describe as 'media'. It is an embarrassment for Kittler, as Steven Connor notes, that the first known example of a paranoid machine — 'the systematic fantasy of a mechanism that systematically controls the sufferer's own thoughts and powers of imagination' — was the 'Air Loom' so vividly endured by James Tilly Matthews, a product of the 'discourse network' of 1800, not that of 1900.[8] Matthews was put under arrest on 30 December 1796, after yelling 'Treason!' from the public gallery of the House of Commons, and admitted to Bethlem on 28 January 1797. 'The Air Loom's power was pneumatic, but its effects were accomplished by harnessing the mysterious magnetism which ran through all living things, a technique popularized in pre-Revolutionary France by the Viennese doctor Franz Anton Mesmer'.[9] The historical investigation conducted here will focus on two very remarkable, if less well known, asylum memoirs — one published in 1838, the other in 1840 — by

4   Kittler, *Discourse Networks*, pp. 297–99.
5   Kittler, *Gramophone, Film, Typewriter*, trans. by Geoffrey Winthrop-Young and Michael Wutz (Stanford, CA: Stanford University Press, 1999), p. 16.
6   Jay Clayton, *Charles Dickens in Cyberspace: The Afterlife of the Nineteenth Century in Postmodern Culture* (Oxford: Oxford University Press, 2003), pp. 65–70.
7   Jill Galvan, *The Sympathetic Medium: Feminine Channelling, the Occult, and Communication Technologies, 1859–1919* (Ithaca, NY: Cornell University Press, 2010), p. 15.
8   Connor, 'Scilicet', p. 128.
9   Mike Jay, *The Air-Loom Gang: The Strange and True Story of James Tilly Matthews* (London: Bantam Press, 2003), p. 11.

John Perceval, a self-proclaimed 'insane and nervous patient'.[10] In pursuing it, I will draw on the work of the always stimulating and informative post-Kittlerian media theorist, Bernhard Siegert.

Recent initiatives in the study of media have seen a fundamental re-examination of the idea of a medium: that's to say, of what it means to be *in the middle*. Generally speaking, it is still the case that 'media studies' involves research into the development of the major storage and transmission technologies which have over the last hundred and fifty years achieved institutional status as mass media: cinema, radio, telephony, television, the gramophone; more recently, of course, the many ramifications of the internet. The focus of that research has been on media understood as inherently powerful systems for the distribution of messages and meanings. But there have long been and still are all sorts of methods other than electromagnetic currents and waves by which messages and meanings are distributed. The variety of things which under different circumstances might take their place 'in the middle' is almost infinite. Mindful of that variety, media theory has begun to speak of a 'mediality' which includes, but is by no means restricted to, electromagnetism. Marshall McLuhan's once inflammatory insistence that all media are bodily 'extensions' now seems like the culmination of a 'rising sense', from the late eighteenth century onwards, of the absolute centrality of the 'medial' dimension of human life.[11] As Joseph Vogl puts it, the 'field of enquiry' claimed by media studies is a broad one,

> stretching from prehistoric registers of the tides and stars to the ubiquitous contemporary mass media, encompassing physical transmitters (such as air and light), as well as schemes of notation, whether hieroglyphic, phonetic, or alphanumeric. It includes technologies and artefacts like electrification, the telescope, or the gramophone alongside symbolic forms and spatial repre-sentations such as perspective, theatre, or literature as a whole.[12]

'To understand media,' John Durham Peters declares, 'we need to understand fire, aqueducts, power grids, seeds, sewage systems, DNA, mathematics, sex, music, daydreams, and insulation'. 'All complex societies,' Peters concludes, 'have media inasmuch as they use materials to manage time, space, and power'.[13] In a way, these lists *are* the method. The media concept has been ontologized, pluralized, and back-dated to the dawn of civilization. According to Sybille Krämer and Horst Bredekamp, media theory re-activates 'a conception of culture centring around techniques and rites, skills and practices that provide for the stability of lived-in space and the continuity of time, and have thus made our world into a human world by "cultivating" (or de-primitivizing) it'.[14]

10 John Perceval, *A Narrative of the treatment experienced by a gentleman, during a state of mental derangement; designed to explain the causes and the nature of insanity, and to expose the injudicious conduct pursued towards many unfortunate sufferers under that calamity* (London: Effingham Wilson, 1840), p. 113.

11 Marshall McLuhan, *Understanding Media: The Extensions of Man* (London: Routledge, 2001), p. 126; Dominic Boyer, *Understanding Media: A Popular Philosophy* (Chicago, IL: Prickly Paradigm Press, 2007), p. 25.

12 Joseph Vogl, 'Becoming-Media: Galileo's Telescope', trans. by Brian Hanrahan, *Grey Room*, 29 (2007), 14–25 (p. 15).

13 John Durham Peters, *The Marvelous Clouds: Toward a Philosophy of Elemental Media* (Chicago, IL: University of Chicago Press, 2015), pp. 29, 20.

14 Sybille Krämer and Horst Bredekamp, 'Culture, Technology, Cultural Technique: Moving

Some theorists now prefer to speak of 'cultural techniques' rather than of 'media'. As Siegert puts it, in a formulation which alludes to the work of Bruno Latour, cultural techniques comprise a 'more or less complex actor-network that includes technical objects and chains of operations (including gestures) in equal measure'.[15] In such networks lies the 'agency of media and things', as Cornelia Vismann has put it. That agency involves the 'execution of a particular act' in accordance with the scheme or manner of proceeding built into the network sustaining it. No wonder, then, that cultural techniques should seem to her to possess an 'almost algorithmic dimension'. Here is a little story culled from the theory of cultural techniques. Human beings decide to civilize themselves by building a city. They use a plough to draw the line in the ground which will mark out the city limits. That line generates the distinctions between inside and outside, culture and nature, 'us' and 'them', necessary to the creation of a new order. Everyone forgets about the plough. Or at least they had done so until media theory, which points out that 'the agricultural tool determines the political act; and the operation itself produces the subject, who will then claim mastery over both the tool and the action associated with it.'[16] What's admirable about the approach taken by Siegert, Vissmann, and others, I think, is that it so bloody-mindedly puts the cart before the horse. Indeed, it puts the cart before the animal that controls the animal that pulls the cart. Such bloody-mindedness may help us to understand what was eating John Perceval, whose two asylum memoirs devote subtle and prolonged attention to architecture as medium or cultural technique: if not to sewage systems or to insulation, then to doors, windows, staircases, ducts, and flues. I want to explore that attention to architecture as medium from the perspective established in Siegert's admirable essay on 'Door Logic, or, the Materiality of the Symbolic', from which I have just quoted. Appropriately for our purposes, the essay begins with an account of the design, construction, and use of doors as an exercise in cultural technique, and ends with an invocation of psychosis.

In *Minima Moralia: Reflections from Damaged Life*, which he began to write while living in America during the Second World War, Theodor Adorno complained that technology had made gestures 'precise and brutal, and with them men'.

> It expels from movements all hesitation, deliberation, civility [...] Thus the ability is lost, for example, to close a door quietly and discreetly, yet firmly. Those of cars and refrigerators have to be slammed, others have the tendency to snap shut by themselves.[17]

For Adorno, doors in effect constitute an analogue medium which when activated

beyond Text', *Theory, Culture & Society*, 30 (2013), 20–29 (p. 21). See also Bernard Stiegler, *Technics and Time, 1: The Fault of Epithemus*, trans. by Richard Beardsworth and George Collins (Stanford, CA: Stanford University Press, 1998).

15   Bernhard Siegert, 'Door Logic: Or, the Materiality of the Symbolic', in *Cultural Techniques: Grids, Filters, Doors, and Other Articulations of the Real*, trans. by Geoffrey Winthrop-Young (New York: Fordham University Press, 2015), pp. 192–205 (p. 193).

16   Cornelia Vismann, 'Cultural Techniques and Sovereignty', trans. by Ilinca Iurascu. *Theory, Culture & Society*, 30 (2013), 83–93 (pp. 83, 87, 84).

17   Theodor Adorno, *Minima Moralia: Reflections from Damaged Life*, trans. by E. F. N. Jephcott (London: Verso, 1984), p 40.

takes an impression of the moral and social being of the individual user; and then plays it back, by means of the location and density of the residue of physical contact. We learn from those who have been before us how to pass through a given aperture. In Adorno's view, the jerky movements modern machines had begun to demand of their users adumbrated a modern politics, namely, fascism. Siegert, by contrast, is an exponent of the original and enduring technicity of the human. Drawing on Georg Simmel, Franz Kafka, Carl Schmitt, and others, he argues that doors should be understood as architectural 'media' insofar as they at once operate and symbolize the 'primordial difference' between inside and outside upon the basis of which economic, social, political, and spiritual orders can be created. Walls are mute, Simmel maintained, while doors speak. Closure indicates the possibility of opening, opening of closure. Siegert's main interest (although he doesn't quite put it like this) lies in the traditional door as an analogue medium remediated by the analogue medium of early fifteenth-century Flemish painting. But his essay gravitates towards varieties of modern door which operate according to a different principle. According to him, the revolving door, a twentieth-century invention, for example, no longer marks a threshold. It no longer takes an impression of those who pass through it. It has instead become, Siegert says, a 'biopolitical device for managing humans in motion'.[18] This is debateable, since it requires as much hesitation and civility to negotiate a revolving door as it does to open and close the more traditional kind.[19] But Siegert is on stronger ground when he argues that a yet more modern device — 'cybernetic feedback loops of pairs of electronic doors, in which one door triggers the opening of another by its own closing, and vice versa' — has effectively withdrawn altogether from any conceivable symbolic function. The automated door does not depend upon human agency, or minister to meaning. The basic distinction such an architectural medium makes is not inside/outside, but on/off, or current/no current. It is a binary digital device. The result is not fascism, but madness: 'if the symbolic order is repudiated (as in the case of psychosis),' Siegert concludes, 'reality takes on hallucinatory features'.[20] Siegert's exemplary focus on architectural media enables us to understand how and why madness might have been regarded as a mistake in mediation long before patients began to endure torment by telegraph, telephone, or other 'influencing machine'. John Perceval certainly felt himself to be embedded in architectural media.

Perceval was born, on 14 February 1803, into a powerful sense of entitlement. He was the tenth of thirteen children of Spencer Perceval, the only British Prime Minister ever to have been assassinated (on 11 May 1812). After Harrow School, and a private tutor, he obtained a commission in the Grenadier Guards, serving in Portugal and Ireland. The army did not suit his earnestness. In 1830 sold his commission, and enrolled at Hertford College, Oxford. After visiting a radical evangelical sect at Row, near Glasgow, the members of which spoke in tongues,

---

18   Siegert, 'Door Logic', pp. 193–94, 201.
19   David Trotter, *Literature in the First Media Age: Britain between the Wars* (Cambridge, MA: Harvard University Press, 2013), pp. 189–90.
20   Siegert, 'Door Logic', p. 203–05.

he came to believe that he, too, was guided in his actions by the Holy Spirit. In December 1830, while he was visiting friends in Ireland, his behaviour became so bizarre that he was put under restraint, and eventually committed to Brislington House, a private asylum close to Bristol run by Dr Edward Long Fox. After a harrowing fourteen months he was transferred to Ticehurst Asylum, in Sussex, run by Dr Charles Newington. Here the treatment was more humane, and he was able to petition for his release. In 1834, he left Ticehurst, married, and went to live in Paris with his young family. There, he wrote a book about his treatment in Brislington House, which appeared anonymously in 1838.[21] In 1840, he published a second book, with the same title, but under his own name, about his campaign to obtain his release. It includes letters written from Brislington House to family and friends which had been omitted in 1838 at the publisher's request. In 1845, Perceval joined with other ex-inmates and their supporters to form the Alleged Lunatics' Friend Society, which over the next twenty years took up the cases of more than seventy patients, and exposed abuses in a number of asylums. On 11 July 1859, he testified before a parliamentary select committee on the care and treatment of lunatics, describing himself, with considerable pride, as 'the attorney general of all Her Majesty's madmen'.[22] Perceval died in Munster House Asylum, in Fulham, on 28 February 1876, at the age of seventy-three. He is now remembered primarily as a champion of patients' rights.[23]

The only modern edition of Perceval's writing is a synthesis of the two books edited in 1961 by the pioneering biologist, anthropologist, psychiatrist, cybernetic theorist, and natural philosopher, Gregory Bateson. I won't use this edition, because it matters to my argument that Perceval should have felt it necessary to explain himself on more than one occasion. But Bateson's interest in these forgotten nineteenth-century narratives is nonetheless itself of interest. Although his writing has exerted no discernible influence over recent media theory, it was in its time remarkable within the social sciences for its vivid embrace of the sort of mathematical enquiry into the nature of communication which has since become crucial to the work of leading media theorists.[24] In March 1946, Bateson was one

21   John Perceval, *A narrative of the treatment experienced by a gentleman, during a state of mental derangement; designed to explain the causes and the nature of insanity, and to expose the injudicious conduct pursued towards many unfortunate sufferers under that calamity* (London: Effingham Wilson, 1838).

22   Quoted by Andrew Scull, *The Most Solitary of Afflictions: Madness and Society in Britain, 1700–1900* (New Haven, CT: Yale University Press, 1993), p. 80. See Nicholas Hervey, 'Advocacy or Folly? The Alleged Lunatics' Friend Society, 1845–63', *Medical History*, 30.3 (1986), 245–75.

23   Richard Hunter and Ida Macalpine, 'John Thomas Perceval (1803–1876): Patient and Reformer', *Medical History*, 6.4 (1962), 391–95; Peter McCandless, 'Liberty and Lunacy: The Victorians and Wrongful Confinement', in *Madhouses, Mad-Doctors, and Madmen: The Social History of Psychiatry in the Victorian Era*, ed. by Andrew Scull (London: Athlone Press, 1981), pp. 339–62; Steven Connor, *The Matter of Air: Science and the Art of the Ethereal* (London: Reaktion Books, 2010), pp. 91–100; Helen Goodman, '"Madness and Masculinity": Male Patients in London Asylums and Victorian Culture', in *Insanity and the Lunatic Asylum in the Nineteenth Century*, ed. by Thomas Knowles and Serena Trowbridge (London: Routledge, 2015), pp. 149–66. See also E. M. Podvoll, 'Perceval's Courage', in *The Seduction of Madness: A Compassionate Approach to Recovery at Home* (London: Century, 1991), pp. 1–68; and Sarah Wise, *Inconvenient People: Lunacy, Liberty, and the Mad-Doctors in Victorian England* (London: Bodley Head, 2012), pp. 68–72.

24   Friedrich Kittler, 'Signal-to-Noise Ratio', in *The Truth of the Technological World: Essays on the*

of two anthropologists with extensive experience of field-work (the other being Margaret Mead) to attend the first of the celebrated Macy Conferences in New York. These Conferences brought together mathematicians, engineers, and social scientists keen to explore the application of new ideas emerging from wartime research into cybernetics, information theory, and digital computing.[25] There he met Norbert Wiener, the founder of cybernetics (from the classical Greek term for 'steersman'), who became his mentor in the assimilation of logical and mathematical concepts. Machines receive input (energy, data, commands) and produce output (behaviour). If and when that output can be converted into input — into information about performance thus far — the machine possesses a way to respond to the effects of its own behaviour. It has equipped itself with a purposeful 'mentality' which makes use of feedback in order to achieve a predetermined goal. For Bateson, the Macy Conferences, and in particular the exchanges with Wiener, proved a turning point. He became convinced that feedback — or, more broadly, a paradigm involving form, pattern, and circularity — was the key to human as well as machine 'mentalities'.[26]

Bateson began to apply information and cybernetic theory to the study of psychosis and alcoholism: pathologies not of the mind, he thought, but of the mind's relation to its environment, that is, of *communication*: of signs and signals, of interpretative dilemma, of steerage. With Jurgen Ruesch, he published a theoretical manifesto, *Communication: The Social Matrix of Psychiatry*, in 1951. The preface to the 1968 edition describes the Macy Conferences as the start of a 'new era'. Theoretical developments in the fields of cybernetics and communication engineering had provided a way to 'represent the person, the group and society all within one system'. In psychiatry, 'message' and 'circuit' would thenceforth become the 'units of study'.

> Notably in human systems the circuit which must be studied usually includes at least two persons. Indeed, the message must often be traced from its origin, as it passes from person to person through groups and machines, undergoing transformation, until it eventually reaches its intended destination, where its effects commonly act back upon the original source.[27]

Genealogy of Presence, trans. by Erik Butler (Stanford, CA : Stanford University Press, 2013), pp. 165–77; Siegert, 'Cacography or Communication? Cultural Techniques of Sign-Signal Distinction', in *Cultural Techniques*, pp. 19–32. See also N. Katherine Hayles, *How We Became Posthuman* (Chicago, IL: Chicago University Press, 1999), and Bernard Dionysius Geoghegan, 'From Information Theory to French Theory: Jakobson, Lévi-Strauss, and the Cybernetic Apparatus', *Critical Inquiry*, 38.1 (2011), 96–126.

25   Peter Galison, 'The Ontology of the Enemy: Norbert Weiner and the Cybernetic Vision', *Critical Inquiry*, 21.1 (1994), 228–66.

26   David Lipset, *Gregory Bateson: The Legacy of a Scientist* (Englewood Cliffs, NJ: Prentice-Hall, 1980), p. 182. See also Steve P. Heims,'Gregory Bateson and the Mathematicians: From Interdisciplinary Interaction to Societal Functions', *Journal of the History of the Behavorial Sciences*, 13.2 (1977), 141–59. For a shrewd and highly informative commentary on the generalization of cybernetic models and methods from the 1940s onwards, see Seb Franklin, *Control: Digitality as Cultural Logic* (Cambridge: MIT Press, 2015), pp. 39–81.

27   Jurgen Ruesch and Gregory Bateson, *Communication: The Social Matrix of Psychiatry* (New Brunswick, NJ: Transaction Publishers, 2008), pp. vii–viii.

This focus on messages passing around a circuit led Bateson to formulate the concept of the 'double bind'. He regarded 'Towards a Theory of Schizophrenia' (1956), a collaborative paper, as premature; but its core definitions were to provide a topic of debate for the next forty years or so. A 'double bind' involves a conflict between injunctions which cannot be resolved because one occurs at a more abstract level than the other. For example, an explicit verbal command might be accompanied by a gesture implicitly indicating that it is not to be taken seriously. The 'victim' does not know which level or type of injunction constitutes the appropriate reality. To acknowledge one is to fail to acknowledge the other.[28] Perceval's *Narrative* certainly played its part in these definitions. Introducing his edition, Bateson argued that the voices Perceval heard in his head had put him in a 'double bind', such that 'even if he does the right thing he is blamed for doing it for the wrong reasons.'[29] *Perceval's Narrative* featured in the bibliography of the paper he gave on the topic in August 1969.[30] The republication of these essays and others in the bestselling *Steps towards an Ecology of Mind*, in 1972, earned Bateson a measure of celebrity, not least among proponents of the 'counter-culture'.[31] Double bind theory, however, remained a theory; it was hard to demonstrate in practice. Furthermore, the 'situation' in which it was most likely to occur, according to Bateson, was that of the family. While Perceval certainly did not hold back from blaming his mother, in particular, for the predicament in which he found himself, the enduring interest of the story he had to tell lies in its recognition of the formative effects of institutional life. That said, Bateson's understanding of the human brain as in some significant respects comparable to an environmentally sensitive control mechanism can be triangulated with recent media theory to provide valuable insight into the phenomenology of incarceration. The schizophrenic, Bateson noted, does not know how to 'discuss the messages of others'. 'Without being able to do that, the human being is like any self-correcting system which has lost its governor; it spirals into never-ending, but always systematic, distortions.'[32] I will argue that Perceval discovered in the conventions of the asylum memoir — including the material affordances of the printed book as medium — a 'governor' or steersman of his own which would prevent, temporarily at least, a downward spiral into endless, systematic distortion. For him, those conventions were not merely expressive, but a system permitting self-correction; that is, self-cure.

Perceval's books are books of complaint. They are repetitive, snobbish, and embittered. But they include remarkable passages of commentary and description

---

28   Gregory Bateson, Don G. Jackson, Jay Haley, and John H. Weakland, 'Towards a Theory of Schizophrenia', in Gregory Bateson, *Steps to an Ecology of Mind: Collected Essays in Anthropology, Evolution and Epistemology* (St Albans: Paladin, 1973), pp. 173–98 (p. 178).

29   Bateson, 'Introduction', in *Perceval's Narrative: A Patient's Account of His Psychosis, 1830–1832*, ed. by Bateson (London: Hogarth Press, 1962), pp. v–xxii (p. x).

30   Bateson, 'Double Bind', in *Steps*, 242–49.

31   Fred Turner, *From Counterculture to Cyberculture: Stewart Brand, the Whole Earth Network, and the Rise of Digital Utopianism* (Chicago, IL: University of Chicago Press, 2006), pp. 121–25. The most formidably intelligent response to Bateson's ideas remains Anthony Wilden, *System and Structure: Essays in Communication and Exchange* (London: Tavistock Publications, 1972).

32   Bateson et al., 'Towards a Theory', p. 183.

which make it clear that for him insanity was a process, not a condition: a process which could be reversed. His account of the crucial stages in that process coincides with an enhanced attention to infrastructure as medium or cultural technique. Insanity was the medial life gone horribly wrong.

Perceval became embedded in madness, or the bad medial life, in two stages. The first was his original detention, in Dublin, in December 1830, to which I will return. The 'second ruin', as he put it in the 1838 *Narrative*, occurred shortly after his arrival at Brislington House. The 'voices' in his head persistently incited him to demonstrate his 'faith' and 'courage' by wrestling with the asylum attendants. 'Yet I wrestled with the keepers, and offered to do with others, and struck many hard blows; sometimes, as one informed me, making it difficult for three strong men to control me, yet whenever I did this, I was commanded to do so.'

> I could not help laughing now at the delusions which made me constantly choose that conduct which was most disagreeable and terrifying to my doctor and his keepers, as in the reality the most agreeable to them, if I were not overcome by a sense of the cruel state of abandonment and exposure to their malice and ignorance in which I was left.

How strange that the behaviour he thought would most please the Almighty, and therefore his fellow men, should turn out to be that which most offended both parties! But the paradox runs deeper. The double bind lies in the further recognition that this offensive behaviour did in fact please his fellow men, at least, if not the Almighty, because it confirmed to them his evident insanity: an insanity requiring incarceration. Before he came to Brislington House, Perceval did not know, he says, that he was mad. Being there made him so. 'I can no longer, after arriving at this period of my trials, call Dr F — 's house by any other name than that it deserves, *mad-house*, for to call that, or any like that, an *asylum*, is cruel mockery and revolting duplicity!'[33]

What is perhaps most striking about the development of this tale of incarceration is its immediate, and intricately detailed, focus on architecture. As a result of his determination to wrestle with the keepers, Perceval was put in a straitjacket, and manacled to his bed. The next morning, he was taken downstairs, not to the small room in which he had hitherto spent the day, but to a large saloon or parlour.

> There was a long table in the middle of the room, allowing space to pass round it, a fire on the left hand side, and a glass bow window and door at the further end. I was fastened in a niche on a painted wooden seat between the fire and the glass window, in the curve in the wall forming the bow at the end of the room; another niche opposite to me was occupied by a trembling grey headed old man; there were several other strange looking personages on the chairs about the room, and passing occasionally through the glass window door which looked out in the same direction as the windows of the room I had quitted, into a small yard. I think I hear the door jarring now, as they slammed it to and fro.[34]

Seven years after the event, Perceval stills hear the sound of the glass door jarring.

---

33   Perceval, *Narrative* (1838), pp. 91–93.
34   Ibid., p. 93.

He seems to have found himself caught up in some sort of nightmarish preview of Adorno's fascist modernity, in which refrigerator- and car-doors 'have to be slammed'. Kittler's Schreber was to endure analogue trauma: there is too much inscribed on his mind, too much that's utterly alike. He is all analogy, and nothing else. Perceval, by contrast, endures digital trauma. For the men passing through the glass door without either hesitation or civility have stripped it of its symbolic function by reducing it to a device which at any given moment is either on or off, open or shut, regardless of who passes through it, and how. They have laid bare its function as medium. The sound Perceval hears is the sound of Siegert's pairs of electronic doors.

But Schreber, too, heard the doors slam; as they often did, apparently, in nineteenth-century asylums.[35] The remarkable plans for the design of a new Bethlem which James Tilly Matthews submitted to the governors on 1 April 1811 included a proposal to extend the length of each bedroom by an inch or two. Matthews was himself an inmate at the time. One of the features of asylum life, as he had reason to know, was that a patient troublesome enough to be chained to his bed could manoeuvre himself so as to reach his door, and thus 'amuse himself by forcing the door to shut with violence sufficient to produce almost cannon report and spring back for him to repeat it, nearly forcing the door case out of the wall'.[36] Both Matthews and Perceval understood that the architecture of insanity had created its own mise-en-abyme: a door which in effect opens and shuts itself by means of the actions of a human servo-mechanism existing for that purpose only, since, resigned to incarceration, it no longer has any need or desire to cross the threshold in one direction or the other.

Perceval, however, was by no means consumed by trauma. Indeed, he may have something to teach media theory. He never lost faith in the human mind's capacity to act, even under great duress, as the 'mediator of mediations'.[37] The evidence for this faith lies in the uses to which he put not just generic convention, but the material affordances of the printed book. One example occurs in the 1840 *Narrative*. It concerns a letter Perceval wrote to one of his brothers from Brislington House, which was omitted, on the grounds of the distress it might cause, from the 1838 edition. In the letter, Perceval begs once again to be removed, but at the same time admits that he is not entirely 'dissatisfied' with the 'arrangements' made for him by Dr Fox. Attached to the first word of the relevant sentence is an immense footnote which straggles over two further pages. The footnote attempts to explain, in 1838, why he might conceivably have felt, in 1831, that, despite all appearances to the contrary, the Brislington House regime had something to be said for it. In the process, it develops an extraordinary and compelling comparison between the plight of the asylum inmate and that of Irish Roman Catholics. 'The Irish Roman Catholics,' Perceval declares, 'have been treated by the British Protestants much in

---

35   Schreber, *Memoirs*, pp. 135, 187, 237.
36   Mike Jay, *The Air-Loom Gang: The Strange and True Story of James Tilly Matthews* (London: Bantam Press, 2003), p. 220.
37   A phrase I borrow gratefully from Connor, 'Scilicet', p. 130.

the manner of lunatics; and Ireland was their prison.'

> Having, like other lunatics, or so called lunatics, no sense of their own deficiencies, and not acknowledging their loss of title to civil privileges, or the rights of those why tyrannized over them, they resisted and rebelled; and each rebellion, the consequence of oppression, was treated as in lunacy, as the evidence of new malignity and fresh evil principles, and a just cause for the chains of slavery being fastened on them more heavily.

Thus, by way of feedback loop, 'oppression begot oppression.' The madman's treatment as mad confirms to him his own madness. However, it is possible for the madman, like the victim of political persecution, to create an alternative feedback loop, a virtuous rather than a vicious spiral.

> But with each successive act of reason, with each successive exercise of self-respect, with each successive resolution to die rather than to miss the opportunity of asserting his rights, new light dawns on the mind, and with new light new desires and claims; and new hopes with each concession, because they are an evidence of power respected, and a source of power achieved.

So, Perceval says, the Irish Roman Catholics are quite right to keep making 'fresh demands' even, or especially, after repeatedly being granted precisely those concessions with which they have hitherto said that they would rest satisfied. What he himself had meant to praise in Dr Fox's otherwise brutal system was the evidence in it of concessions made to the desires and claims of the inmates.

> But I remember in one particular being very much smitten by the iron veranda blinds, or jalousies, which were attached to most of the windows, so as to give all the security of bars, without the recollection of them; except, to those who knew how heavy, dull, and everlasting they appeared to be.[38]

On one level, the blinds are bars. On another, they are evidence that the asylum managers do not want to treat the people behind those bars like animals in a cage. Perceval understands that the blinds, like various other features of the building, are a concession: a mark of respect, and thus a source of power.[39]

Fox was a Quaker, and it's worth noting that the model Quaker asylum, the York Retreat, had been designed to resemble a home rather than a prison. The keynote was cheerfulness and consideration.

> A great deal of delicacy appears in the attentions paid to the smaller feelings of the patients. The iron bars, which guarded the windows, have been withdrawn, and neat iron sashes, having all the appearance of wooden ones, have been substituted in their place; and, when I visited them, the managers were occupied in contriving how to get rid of the bolts with which the patients are shut up at night, on account of their harsh ungrateful sound, and of their communicating to the asylum somewhat of the air and character of a prison.[40]

In general, Fox's asylum does not appear to have met such high standards.

---

38   Perceval, *Narrative* (1840), pp. 41–43.
39   Schreber couldn't bring himself to view them in the same light: *Memoirs*, pp. 160–61, 181–84.
40   William Stark, *Remarks on the Construction of Public Hospitals for the Cure of Mental Derangement* (Glasgow: James Hedderwick, 1810), p. 12.

Furthermore, doubts have long been raised concerning the advances made in psychiatric care by means of the so-called 'moral treatment'.[41] My point is simply that Perceval's awareness of the design features of Fox's asylum created the prospect of a positive feedback loop, a virtuous spiral. At least, it did so autobiographically, in the 1840 version of his *Narrative*, by means of scholarship's very own positive feedback loop: the footnote. As Anthony Grafton has demonstrated, the footnote is 'bound up, in modern life, with the ideology and the technical practices of a profession.' It locates the production of the work in question 'in time and space, emphasizing the limited horizons and opportunities of its author, rather than those of its reader.'[42] Perceval's footnote performs the professional identity he was hoping to reclaim from madness by means of autobiography. The performance creates a feedback loop. Having read it through, we must turn back two pages to find our place again in the middle of the sentence to which it is attached. We resume the sentence in a different mood, otherwise informed.

The emphasis throughout this essay has been on Perceval's understanding of the mediation of madness by bricks and mortar (or glass and iron). Equally significant to that understanding, it could be argued, and of equal implication for the history of psychiatry, was the role of the asylum attendant. As it happens, 1961, the year of Bateson's edition of *Perceval's Narrative*, also saw the publication of a key anti-psychiatry text, Erving Goffman's *Asylums*. As far as I am aware, Goffman took no interest in cybernetics or information theory. But he does draw on Bateson to support his claim that in a 'total institution' such as an asylum the 'lowest level of staff' perform a crucial mediating function. It is the nurses and attendants who train the inmates in a deference which the upper level of staff receives as though it were entirely 'uncoerced'.[43] In a three-way system of communication, Bateson had written in an essay first published in 1953, the second or 'middle' member of the institutional triad instructs and disciplines the third in the 'forms of behaviour' she or he should adopt towards the first. Thus, for example, the N.C.O. teaches the private soldier how to behave towards an officer.[44] There might be further scope, here, for a triangulation of post-war anti-psychiatry with recent media theory, which has sought to establish structural affinities between human and electronic 'servers': search engines, mail delivery systems, web-crawlers, bots.[45] 'By continuously embracing technologies,' McLuhan observed in *Understanding Media* (1964), 'we relate ourselves to them as servo-mechanisms.'[46] Building on McLuhan's

41   Andrew Scull, 'Moral Treatment Reconsidered: Some Sociological Comments on an Episode in the History of British Psychiatry', *Psychological Medicine*, 9 (1979), 421–28.

42   Anthony Grafton, *The Footnote: A Curious History* (London: Faber and Faber, 1997), pp. 5, 32.

43   Erving Goffman, *Asylums: Essays on the Social Situation of Mental Patients and Other Inmates* (New Brunswick, NJ: Aldine Transaction, 2007), p. 116.

44   Bateson, 'Formulation of End Linkage', in *The Study of Culture at a Distance*, ed. by Margaret Mead and Rhoda Métraux (New York: Berghahn Books, 2000), pp. 409–20 (p. 414). Goffman misattributes the quotation to another essay by Bateson in the same volume, 'An Analysis of the Nazi Film *Hitlerjunge Quex*'.

45   Marcus Krajewski, 'Ask Jeeves: Servants as Search Engines', trans. by Charles Marcrum, *Grey Room*, 38 (2010), 6–19.

46   McLuhan, *Understanding Media*, p. 51.

insight, Marcus Krajewski has demonstrated how service functions as a medium or cultural technique in a wide variety of circumstances.

> Just as the clerk is an underling to his clock, and the Native American to his canoe, according to McLuhan, the servant appears literally as the service mechanism of his respective technique, which manifests itself in the form of the dinner tray, the door to be attended, the message to be relayed.

Krajewski insists on the 'agency' of service. Servants tend to be positioned strategically at the 'hubs of action': in doorways, for example, to which they control access; or in the background, waiting with a tray, while policy is made over brandy and cigars. Through his or her actions and small gestures, 'the subaltern exercises a specific power, even if this power may seem marginal to outsiders.'[47] Before concluding, I want briefly to describe Perceval's response to the specific — and to him utterly maddening — power exercised over him by his social inferiors.

Perceval insists over and over again on the utter humiliation he felt at the degree of control exerted over him by the asylum attendants, so evidently his social inferiors. There had been a servant present at the scene of his original detention, in Dublin, in December 1830. His Dublin friend Captain H — left him in a hotel room while he went to consult a Dr Piel. Thinking that he needed a new hat for his journey to England the next day, he opened the door of his room to find 'a stout man servant on the landing, who told me that he was placed there to forbid my going out.' Informing the man that he was a 'prophet of the Lord', Perceval tried to force his way past. The 1838 *Narrative* then describes how, finding himself thwarted, he had seized the man's arm, 'desiring it to wither'.[48] The 1840 *Narrative* omits any mention of physical violence, and adds instead a footnote explaining how the man's 'presence' had 'operated' on him. He had felt himself required for his own salvation to act towards him in ways he no longer considered appropriate.[49] Thereafter, the presence of servants continued to operate on him on occasions too numerous to record. One could say that for Perceval the medium was indeed the message. The degree of control exercised over him by his social inferiors became a training in madness. After his arrival at Brislington House, he got into the habit of throwing himself off his bed, in obedience to his 'monitors': 'the command was usually given about the time the keeper came into the room either to look after me, or to sleep'.[50] The external monitor's approach has clearly provoked an internal monitor into actions: the voices telling him to throw himself off his bed. So sensitive did he prove to human mediation that he came vastly to prefer that of bricks and mortar, glass and iron. This preference accompanied him from asylum to asylum. The 1840 *Narrative* includes a letter complaining bitterly about the surveillance maintained upon him after his transfer to Newington's Ticehurst Asylum.

> I mean, that I have a bolt to my door outside, which might be fastened, and

---

47   Krajewski, 'The Power of Small Gestures: On the Cultural Technique of Service', *Theory, Culture & Society*, 30.6 (2013), 94–109 (pp. 95, 104).
48   Perceval, *Narrative* (1838), pp. 43–44.
49   Perceval, *Narrative* (1840), p. 9.
50   Perceval, *Narrative* (1838), p. 129.

bars to my windows, which I have no means of breaking through; besides a slide-hole in the door, through which I could be occasionally observed from without, without having my privacy destroyed, and myself annoyed by the presence of the attendants, who, you must have observed, are not fit company for me, nor ought to sit with any gentleman who feels that he has any command over himself.[51]

In this as in other respects, Perceval's sense of entitlement was no doubt a great deal more acute than that of the majority of asylum inmates. But the vigour and exactitude of his commentaries might nonetheless serve to alert us to the variety of mediations by means of which those inmates were subdued to their condition, or, in some cases, found a way to make sense of it, and to resist. Perceval was, in his own way, like Schreber, a media theorist of psychiatric practice.

51   Perceval, *Narrative* (1840), pp. 385–86.

CHAPTER 21

Posthuman?
Animal Corpses, Aeroplanes, and Very High Frequencies in the Work of Valentine Ackland and Sylvia Townsend Warner

The aim of this essay is to establish the critical significance and value of the work which was the product of the unique creative partnership developed by Valentine Ackland and Sylvia Townsend Warner during the 1930s. This was for both partners a period of a rich engagement not only with each other — and shared domestic circumstance in rural Dorset and Norfolk — but with the looming import of national and international crisis. During that period, I argue, they imagined more variously and more incisively together, through mutual awareness and acceptance, than they would in all likelihood have done had they never met and fallen in love. An understanding of the sharp differences in temperament, outlook, and reputation which precluded full-scale collaboration freed each of them, in turn, to pursue contrasting aspects of concerns held in common. So adventurous was that pursuit, at times, that it merits comparison with recent investigations of the idea of the 'posthuman'. Since Warner was by far the more prolific author, I have tried to balance my account of her partnership with Ackland by drawing extensively not only on published fiction and poetry, but also on diaries and letters, and on a variety of other kinds of material from the archive.

Their first (and only) formal declaration of creative partnership was *Whether a Dove or Seagull*, a collection of poems written between 1927 and 1933, fifty-four by Warner, fifty-five by Ackland, published in the United States in 1933 and in Britain in 1934. An opening statement made it plain that the volume was not 'collaborative', but rather 'both an experiment in the presentation of poetry and a protest against the frame of mind, too common, which judges the poem by the poet, rather than the poet by the poem.'[1] The experiment was not enough of a success to merit

---

1   Valentine Ackland and Sylvia Townsend Warner, 'Note to the Reader', in Valentine Ackland, *Journey from Winter: Selected Poems*, ed. by Frances Bingham (Manchester: Carcanet, 2008), pp. 204–05 (p. 205).

resumption. However, by evolving further in different guises, the partnership continued to shape the kinds of imaginative enquiry each undertook individually. The most decisive of those guises was membership, from the beginning of 1935, of the Communist Party of Great Britain (CPGB). As Wendy Mulford has shown, Ackland and Warner became 'writers in arms' against Fascism and in support of Republican Spain.[2] Glyn Salton-Cox, mindful of their devotion to Lenin, describes them as exponents of a 'queer vanguardism'. 'Equally active in the Communist movement, they worked together on local, national, and international campaigns, repeatedly and explicitly conceptualizing their relationship as a shared political engagement.'[3] My focus here will be on their writing, published and unpublished, before, during, and immediately after that period of shared political engagement.

A preliminary reading of much of this material suggested that the customary approaches to the literature of the 1930s, although entirely justifiable in their own terms, will not do justice to its adventurousness. I have accordingly chosen to invoke instead current debates about the 'posthuman'. According to Rosi Braidotti, the concept of the 'posthuman' amounts to an hypothesis about the 'kind of subjects we are becoming' — for better and worse — in the current conjunction of runaway capitalism, digital revolution, and climate emergency: a topic likely to prove of especial (although by no means exclusive) interest to a branch of study designated the 'humanities'.[4] The theories informing that hypothesis are too various (and in some cases too intricate) to be summarized readily. But it is safe to say that they are likely to involve some account of the human relation either to technology, or to animals, or more likely to both.[5] The adventures undertaken by Ackland and Warner in the 1930s often had to do with technology, or animals, or both.

In 1985, Donna Haraway's 'Cyborg Manifesto' drew vivid and decisive attention to the breakdown of boundaries not only between 'organism' and 'machine', but between 'human' and 'animal'.[6] Although the figure of the cyborg has lost some of its polemical force in an age of networked, programmable media, as Katherine Hayles points out, it is not quite due for the scrapheap yet.[7] Haraway's equally compelling *Companion Species Manifesto* followed in 2003.[8] She has continued to insist that human–animal encounters can generate 'material-semiotic nodes or knots' out of which arise creatures at once of 'imagined possibility' and 'fierce and

---

2   Wendy Mulford, *This Narrow Place: Sylvia Townsend Warner and Valentine Ackland: Life, Letters and Politics, 1930–1951* (London: Pandora, 1988), pp. 70–103.

3   Glyn Salton-Cox, *Queer Communism and the Ministry of Love: Sexual Revolution in British Writing of the 1930s* (Edinburgh: Edinburgh University Press, 2018), p. 78.

4   Rosi Braidotti, *Posthuman Knowledge* (Cambridge: Polity, 2019), p. 2.

5   Human beings are, of course, animals. In this essay, I follow custom in using the term 'animal' to refer to species other than *Homo sapiens*.

6   Donna Haraway, 'The Cyborg Manifesto', in *Simians, Cyborgs, and Women: The Reinvention of Nature* (London: Free Associations Books, 1991), pp. 149–81 (pp. 151–52).

7   N. Katherine Hayles, 'Unfinished Work: From Cyborg to Cognisphere', *Theory, Culture & Society*, 23.7–8 (2006), 159–66 (pp. 159–60).

8   Haraway, *The Companion Species Manifesto: Dogs, People, and Significant Otherness* (Chicago, IL: Prickly Paradigm Press, 2003).

ordinary reality'.[9] Like Haraway, Cary Wolfe, also writing in 2003, was able to draw on new developments in cognitive ethology — the comparative, evolutionary, and ecological study of animal minds — when he argued that 'the humanist habit of making even the *possibility* of subjectivity coterminous with the species barrier is deeply problematic.' Cognitive ethology had shown that the capacities traditionally attributed to humankind (possession of a soul, or reason, then language, then tool use, then tool making, and so on) 'flourish quite reliably,' as Wolfe puts it, 'beyond the species barrier.'[10] What seems to me open to dispute about the concept of the posthuman is the built-in assumption that at some moment in (fairly recent) history one understanding of what it means to be human abruptly gave way to another. If so, the news has not yet reached most of us. According to a 'well-known genealogy' informing many approaches to the posthuman, the moment of rupture occurred during or by means of the Macy Conferences on cybernetics and information theory held in New York from 1946 to 1953.[11] These new sciences reconfigured human consciousness from the 'seat of identity' to an 'informational pattern' which just happens to be 'instantiated in a biological substrate'. They also envisaged the penetration of 'computational process' into every aspect of human experience, including the 'construction of reality itself'.[12] But it may be that there never was a moment at which we became posthuman. Cyborgs (or quasi-cyborgs) have been around for a while; as have networked (although strictly speaking not programmable) media.[13] My aim is to show how Ackland and Warner first got wind, a couple of decades before the Macy Conferences, of the proposition that 'humans are no longer the most important things in the universe.'[14]

The key to the strength of their partnership lay, I believe, in the awareness each partner was able to develop of the imaginative possibilities of the roles enabled by it. 'Yesterday I found a book on Bisexuality,' Ackland wrote to Warner on 2 January 1931. 'After reading it carefully I discover that you and I are admirably suited to each other.'[15] There is good reason to think that the book was *Bisexuality: An Essay on Extraversion and Introversion*, by Theodore J. Faithfull, published in London in 1927.[16]

9   Haraway, *When Species Meet* (Minneapolis: University of Minnesota Press, 2008), p. 4.
10   Cary Wolfe, *Animal Rites: American Culture, the Discourse of Species, and Posthumanist Theory* (Chicago, IL: University of Chicago Press, 2003), pp. 1–2.
11   Wolfe, *What Is Posthumanism?* (Minneapolis: University of Minnesota Press, 2010), p. xii.
12   Hayles, 'Unfinished Work', pp. 160–61. Hayles has done much both to expound and to challenge the terms in which this reconfiguration was conceived: see, in particular, *How We Became Posthuman: Virtual Bodies in Cybernetics, Literature, and Informatics* (Chicago, IL: University of Chicago Press, 1999), pp. 50–70.
13   David Trotter, *The Literature of Connection: Signal, Medium, Interface, 1850–1950* (Oxford: Oxford University Press, 2020).
14   Robert Pepperell, *The Posthuman Condition: Consciousness beyond the Brain* (Bristol: Intellect, 2003), p. 177.
15   *I'll Stand by You: Selected Letters of Sylvia Townsend Warner and Valentine Ackland*, ed. by Susanna Pinney (London: Pimlico, 1998), p. 40.
16   Theodore J. Faithfull, *Bisexuality: An Essay on Extraversion and Introversion* (London: John Bale, Sons, & Daniellson, 1927). The only downside to Faithfull's promotion of the idea of bisexuality, Ackland joked, was that it seemed to involve membership of the Order of Woodcraft Chivalry, a movement popular for a while during the 1920s as a less gung-ho version of the Boy Scouts, with

Faithfull is described on the title page as Principal of the Priory Gate School; he had evidently read a good deal of Freud. 'How nice that we are bi-sexual,' Warner responded.[17] By bisexuality, Faithfull meant the bipolar presence in each individual of the 'psychological attributes, instincts and desires generally attributed to males and females respectively.'[18] Warner imagined a kind of physiological oscillation. 'Do we do it in alternate spasms, do you think, like synchronised oysters [...] or is one both at once?' One is psychologically bisexual, Ackland explained, not physiologically, 'which would be dreadful.' She was thinking in the longer term. 'Darling — do you want to have children? [...] Think it over seriously. Perhaps you had better read all about extroverts, which is me, and introverts, which is you, before you develop any new desires.'[19] In Faithfull's unorthodox use of the terms, an extravert was a person whose 'psychological sexual balance is in favour of the discharge of libido'; an introvert, by contrast, prefers to 'retain' and 'receive' it.[20] The exchange demonstrates that from the very beginning of their relationship Ackland and Warner were investigating the kinds of performance uniquely available to the lesbian couple.

Ackland had always worn the trousers. She was a serial seducer, 'so skilled in love,' as Warner put it, 'that I never expected her to forego love-adventures.'[21] As Salton-Cox emphasizes, Ackland regarded her 'female masculinity' — trousers and all — as an asset in her Communist organizing.[22] Warner stayed at home, remaining steadfastly faithful through all the affairs, at least one of which caused lasting mutual unhappiness. She noted that 'Tib' and 'Tibby' were names for the 'domestic side' of her character.[23] She was, from the outset, the dove to Ackland's seagull. An engagingly ribald Valentine's Day poem by Ackland describes a Bishop motoring in the 'lost locality' of East Dorset, in the company of his chaplain and 'plenty | Of chicken sandwiches'. The chaplain spots something amiss.

> 'A seagull and a dove. How odd
> A pair!' The Bishop shouted, 'God
> Forbid such incongruity!'

The Bishop sets off in angry pursuit of the odd couple, only to tumble into a ditch. At this point, St Valentine materializes, to confirm that the marriage, however unorthodox, is a happy one. 'This seagull, and this dove, called Tib, | Are patterns of felicity.' The Bishop, alas, sinks ever deeper into the mud. 'Meanwhile an eel, by

---

mildly neo-pagan overtones (*I'll Stand by You*, p. 40). The book's Preface announces that sunlight, 'both real and artificial, will be used to bathe our bodies.' It concludes with an invitation to readers to visualize 'two boys in early adolescence, disporting themselves in gaily coloured Greek costumes in a setting of green grass, sunlight, and rose bushes. Or busy at artistic crafts or at cooking, washing, and ironing, domestic activities generally associated with a conception of women' (pp. 11, 15).

17   *I'll Stand by You*, p. 41.
18   Faithfull, *Bisexuality*, p. 95.
19   *I'll Stand by You*, pp. 41, 43.
20   Faithfull, *Bisexuality*, p. 95.
21   *I'll Stand by You*, p. 163.
22   Salton-Cox, *Queer Communism*, p. 94.
23   *I'll Stand by You*, p. 106.

way of Finis, | Nibbled away his balls and penis.'[24] My concern here is not with the marriage itself. It is, rather, with the readiness built into it to think and speak openly about diverse gender roles. That readiness enabled each partner to imagine, as Donna Haraway was to do fifty years later, creatures at once of 'imagined possibility' and 'fierce and ordinary reality'.

Aeroplanes

Ackland's performance of the role of seagull-like 'extravert' acquired an enduring technological edge. Guns mediated her adjustment to country life. It was she who set about the rats in the barn at Frankfort Manor, in Norfolk, which they rented for just over a year from July 1933. 'She has only one request,' Warner reported: 'for more rats to shoot with her rifle. I could almost wish for more rats too, since today, failing other targets, she must needs put three bullets through a fine sleek swelling jargonelle pear, hanging harmlessly on the south wall.'[25] Salton-Cox argues persuasively that Ackland's marksmanship contributed to her view of herself as a 'shape-shifting insider-outsider to the rural ruling classes'. He quotes diary entries from May 1935 which mingle comments on election results in France with reference to the study of *Left Review* poets and figures for the number of rabbits she has shot that day.[26] But some, at least, of the rabbit-related entries assume a rather different tone. 'Shot 4 rabbits — one shot each — & one at a good 50 yards off — clean through the head' (15 May 1935). What is at issue here is expertise: the relation between technique and technology. For the totting-up proved relentless. By 21 October, Ackland had amassed a total of 100 rabbits shot in the year. She even drew a box around the figure, to indicate a target achieved: proof, indeed, of expertise. And there was further cause for satisfaction. It looks to me as though she was using her concentration on marksmanship as a way to measure progress made in her long-drawn-out struggle against alcoholism. Each alcohol-free day is marked 'D. D.', for devoid of drink. In October 1935, she reached a century of abstentions, on very nearly the same day as she reached her century of rabbits. Technical expertise appears to have been enlisted as a form of moral self-discipline. Wildlife in general had, however, no reason to relax. On 2 November, she killed a partridge. 'One shot — at *running* bird — hit him through breast.'[27]

On 23 September 1930, Ackland drove Warner and a cargo of furniture down from London to East Dorset, where they shared a cottage in the remote village of Chaldon Herring. Warner could not help 'abandoning' herself to 'a suavity of driving which was like the bowing of a master-violinist'.[28] In July 1931, she rewarded that suavity by purchasing a second-hand Triumph two-seater at a cost greater than that of the cottage in which they were then living.[29] On one occasion, an unwary

24 Ackland, 'A Valentine for Sylvia 14.2.35': Sylvia Townsend Warner Papers, Dorset County Museum, STW: H(R)/5/3.
25 Warner, *Letters*, ed. by William Maxwell (London: Chatto & Windus, 1982), p. 25.
26 Salton-Cox, *Queer Communism*, pp. 94–95.
27 Ackland, diary for 1935, STW: T(LL)/11.
28 *I'll Stand by You*, p. 11.
29 Claire Harman, *Sylvia Townsend Warner: A Biography* (London: Chatto & Windus, 1989), pp. 119–20.

garage mechanic took the Triumph out for a spin. Ackland became incensed. 'I said I knew the noise of the engine, and that it must remain pure and unsoiled.'[30] It was this (mildly fanatical) degree of attunement to the proper functioning of a still relatively new technology that ensured an exercise of technique as smooth as that of a master-violinist. Media theorists have always delighted in the study of the many and various collaborations between 'life' and 'programming' that together define the 'essential technicity' of human being.[31] Programming a machine, Ackland was herself programmed by it. As the boundary breaks down, Haraway observes, 'our sense of connection to our tools is heightened.'[32] Warner once spoke of longing to see Ackland's body 'limpeted to the car by trousers'.[33] A cyborg, indeed. Ackland was subsequently to answer a CPGB call for volunteers by offering a lift to Spain to anyone willing to share her 'small fast 2-seater' (an MG Midget had by this time replaced the faithful Triumph).[34] According to the AA's *Continental Road Map*, she reassured Warner, the distance was only 850 miles. 'That is very small indeed.'[35] Fast cars, however, were by no means the only show in town — or even in rural Dorset.

On 19 July 1932, Warner noted an unusual event which had taken place during the previous day. 'Aeroplanes were flying over the house. The last went over with a fierce metallic clang, like a dragon.'[36] There was nothing odd about aeroplanes, of course. Warner's close friend David Garnett obtained his pilot's licence on 24 September 1931, and by May 1932 was the proud co-owner (with Hamish Hamilton) of a plane. He had even got a couple of books out of it, *The Grasshoppers Come* (1931) and *A Rabbit in the Air* (1932). *The Countryman*, to which she contributed articles and poems, boasted a regular column on 'The Country House Aeroplane', which was mostly about how to land on the lawns of stately homes owned by one's friends. The increase in air travel might inconvenience or even distress the 'countryman', the journal remarked, but he (and she) would just have to put up with it in the national interest.[37] What Warner witnessed, however, was an event of a different order. The planes she heard were flying in formation.

Royal Air Force exercises began at 6 pm on Monday 18 July, and lasted twelve hours. Their purpose was to establish how effective fighter command would be in intercepting squadrons of bombers crossing the south coast of England at points between Selsey Bill and Lulworth, and heading for targets in the Midlands: 'the scheme is intended principally to afford combined tactical training for units of the Royal Air Force and (to a limited extent) to exercise the members of the Observers' Corps.'[38] Chaldon Herring is slightly to the west of Lulworth. My guess is that Warner had witnessed one of these squadrons passing overhead, having drifted

---

30   *I'll Stand by You*, p. 73.
31   John Durham Peters, *The Marvelous Clouds: Towards a Philosophy of Elemental Media* (Chicago, LL: University of Chicago Press, 2015), p. 16.
32   Haraway, 'Cyborg Manifesto', p. 178.
33   *I'll Stand by You*, p. 131.
34   Mulford, *Journey from Winter*, p. 88.
35   *I'll Stand by You*, p. 148.
36   Warner, *Diaries*, ed. by Claire Harman (London: Chatto & Windus, 1994), p. 91.
37   N. N., 'The Future of Air Travel', *Countryman*, 9, October 1934, 23.
38   'The Air Exercises', *Flight*, 22 July 1932, pp. 697–98.

slightly off course on its way north, on the evening of the 18th. It is hard to know what caused the 'fierce metallic clang' she heard as the last plane flew over. But there could be no mistaking the seriousness of the occasion. On 10 November 1932, Stanley Baldwin, speaking in the House of Commons on the eve of his departure for a disarmament conference in Geneva, popularized the axiom that 'The bomber will always get through'.[39] 'By the mid-1930s,' Brett Holman notes, 'many people in Britain had come to fear what was sometimes referred to as *the knock-out blow from the air*: a sudden, rapid and overwhelming aerial bombardment of its cities, as impossible to predict as it was to resist.'[40]

These long-forgotten air exercises became an intermittent but unignorable feature of life in the house in nearby West Chaldon which Warner and Ackland rented from November 1934 to August 1937: a counterpoint to all the organizing. On 30 July 1935, Ackland wrote to Warner: 'My darling Dear, I m a bloody bad Communist — I should be doing the N-B [News Bulletin], but somehow I can't make it go on.' 'The air,' she went on, 'is busy with aeroplanes, and the valley full of voices.'[41] On this occasion, the exercise involved an attack on London from west and east.[42] The noise the planes made, blending with the voices in the valley, seemed to Ackland a welcome stir of activity, rather than a threat. Her pronounced interest in technology ensured a more subtle — or more ambiguous — response to these intimations of future warfare than Warner's recourse to the figure of the dragon. In the pithy 'Weymouth Manoeuvres, 1936', she seems instinctively to grasp the force latent in defensive as well as offensive measures.

> Where, on the night, a stain of light
> Runs over, there shudders the fear we dread;
> The beam that lightly runs over the sky
> Is death — is a searchlight overhead.[43]

The initial dislocating enjambment, so characteristic of Ackland's poetic technique, leaves us not quite knowing where to look for evidence that the threat we anticipate has in fact taken shape. But the next two lines straighten out the idea of a light that 'runs over' by rendering it uncomplicatedly transitive. A light that runs over the sky is a light directed, a beam. This light runs 'lightly' over, I think, because Ackland is warming to the technical skills required to direct it. There will be further occasion for marksmanship. Few activities are more cyborgian that the direction of anti-aircraft fire. A semi-automated anti-aircraft gun is already a kind of analogue computer. In the Second World War, both Claude Shannon, the founder of information theory, and Norbert Wiener, the founder of cybernetics, worked on the design of such systems.[44] Ackland, as we shall see, had long been attuned to the delights of the feedback loop.

39   'Mr Baldwin on Aerial Warfare', *The Times*, 11 November 1932, p. 8.
40   Brett Holman, *The Next War in the Air: Britain's Fear of the Bomber, 1908–1941* (Farnham: Ashgate, 2014), p. 3.
41   Ackland, 'Weymouth Manoeuvres, 1936', in buff folder inscribed '1936–37', STW: J(FR)/11.
42   *I'll Stand by You*, pp. 134–35.
43   'The Air Exercises', *Flight*, 25 July 1935, pp. 97–98 (p. 98).
44   James Gleick, *The Information* (London: Fourth Estate, 2011), pp. 187–88, 236–37.

Very High Frequencies

The air above and around Ackland was 'busy', of course, not only with the sound of aeroplanes and voices, but with electrical and magnetic fields travelling through space at the speed of light in the form of imperceptible waves. The discovery and measurement in the 1880s of what Friedrich Kittler terms the 'Olympian frequency domain', and its subsequent rapid exploitation at the beginning of the twentieth century, did almost as much to unsettle traditional understandings of consciousness as the seat of identity as the proliferation of networked, programmable media has done at the beginning of the twenty-first.[45] In the light of such knowledge, all life became, as Gillian Beer has put it, 'a medium, a discharge, a pathway'.[46] During the twentieth century, public awareness of electromagnetism was to be extended yet further in various directions, before finally reaching the end of the spectrum with the detonation of an atomic bomb in 1945.

The lively interest Warner took in the still relatively new science of astrophysics brought her into touch with theoretical enquiry into the frequency domain at its most Olympian. 'Rigel — a star infinitely brighter than the sun, and *blue*,' she noted in her diary on 11 May 1929. 'I should like to see it.' The next evening, Warner had a date with her then lover, Percy Carter Buck ('Teague'), director of music at Harrow School. 'Teague came to dinner and listened with admirable meekness to my attempts to expound Mr Eddington's views on limited space.' Teague proved amenable to the star-gazing, as well. 'Rigel came in most conveniently, for there is never any privacy about my intellectual amours.'[47] Arthur Eddington, a leading astrophysicist and staunch advocate of the new physics of relativity and quantum mechanics, was 'also, par excellence, the scientist whose writing attracted philosophers and the general public alike.'[48] Warner may have been trying to expound to Teague Eddington's claim that space is 'finite but unbounded'.[49] The astrophysics she seems to have taken in her stride, to judge by a poem which admires the 'not believable blue' of a distant star: Rigel, presumably.[50]

Eddington did not believe in Rigel's blue, either. For him, colour was a subjective event. Science aimed to describe its counterpart, 'electromagnetic wave-length'. 'The wave is the reality — or the nearest we can get to a description of reality; the colour is mere mind-spinning.'[51] That reality took many forms, from the 'Hertzian waves' of early wireless transmission at one end of the spectrum through visible

45   Friedrich Kittler, 'Lightning and Series: Event and Thunder', trans. by Geoffrey Winthrop-Young, *Theory, Culture & Society*, 23.7–8 (2006), 63–74 (p. 69).
46   Gillian Beer, '"Authentic Tidings of Invisible Things": Vision and the Invisible in the Later Nineteenth Century', in *Vision in Context: Historical and Contemporary Perspectives on Sight*, ed. by Teresa Brennan and Martin Jay (London: Routledge, 1996), pp. 84–98 (p. 88).
47   Warner, *Diaries*, pp. 35–36.
48   Gillian Beer, 'Eddington and the Idiom of Modernism', in *Science, Reason, and Rhetoric*, ed. by Henry Krips et al. (Pittsburgh: University of Pennsylvania Press, 1995), pp. 295–315 (p. 295).
49   A. S. Eddington, *The Nature of the Physical World* (Cambridge: Cambridge University Press, 1929), p. 80.
50   Warner, 'Astro-Physics', in *Collected Poems*, ed. by Claire Harman (Manchester: Carcanet, 1982), pp. 71–72 (p. 71).
51   Eddington, *Nature of the Physical World*, p. 94.

light to ultra-violet, X- and Gamma rays, at the other.[52] By October, Warner was immersed in the latest book by Eddington's great rival Sir James Jeans, *The Universe Around Us* (1929).[53] He, too, had a great deal to say about the incommensurability of the frequency domain. 'When a speaker broadcasts from London his voice takes longer to travel 3 feet from his mouth to the microphone as a sound wave, than it does to travel a further 500 miles to the north of Scotland as an electric wave.'[54] Warner felt that she was lucky to 'get in on the ground floor' of the new science, before its hypotheses had hardened into assumptions.[55]

'Radio, or more strictly because more broadly, wireless signalling,' Steven Connor observes, 'unleashed a dream of absolute communication and universal contact.'[56] The early 1930s was a period of radical experimentation in the use of the Very High Frequency range of radio waves (30 to 300 MHz) in particular, for broadcasting, but also, less familiarly, as we shall see, for air navigation. Broadcasting has long been acknowledged as a context for the literature of the period.[57] For Warner and Ackland, however, the medium's interest lay in its form rather than its content. What they both wanted and were afraid to hear was noise, not sound: the 500 miles between London and the north of Scotland rather than the three feet between mouth to microphone. Louise Morgan, interviewing Warner for a book on *Writers at Work* (1931), asked her about her love of music. Did she approve of reproductive technologies such as gramophone and radio? Warner preferred the gramophone. 'It is more honest about its limitations ... a useful little instrument like a potato-peeler. Wireless is so damned God-like, and cheats all the time.'[58] Olympian in its powers, radio returns to the listener rather more than mere human input by way of bulletin and performance: the sound of the medium itself, of the frequency domain's overlapping oscillations. Ackland's '8th November 1936' imagines a warm room, with paper and ink to hand: 'only, as matching the threat of storm, | radio speaks to ear.'[59] As a medium, radio belongs with the storm's atmospheric disturbance rather than the merely human intention to communicate by letter. Officialdom's attempts to naturalize broadcasting by means of a (male, middle-class) standard of delivery only incite attention to the disturbances thus suppressed. 'June 1937' speaks of familiar messages 'from the air' — a weather forecast, a report on the horrors of

52 Eddington, *Stars and Atoms* (Oxford: Clarendon Press, 1927), p. 15.
53 Warner, *Diaries*, pp. 45, 47–48. See Matthew Stanley, 'So Simple a Thing as a Star: The Eddington–Jeans Debate over Astrophysical Phenomenology', *British Journal of the History of Science*, 40.1 (2007), 53–82.
54 Sir James Jeans, *The Universe Around Us*, 4th edn (Cambridge: Cambridge University Press, 1944), p. 32.
55 Warner, *Diaries*, p. 45.
56 Steven Connor, *The Matter of Air: Science and the Art of the Ethereal* (London: Reaktion Books, 2010), p. 195.
57 *Broadcasting Modernism*, ed. by Debra Rae Cohen, Michael Coyle, and Jane Lewty, (Gainesville: University Press of Florida, 2009).
58 Warner, 'Writers at Work', in *With the Hunted: Selected Writings*, ed. by Peter Tolhurst (Norwich: Black Dog Books, 2012), 393–99, p. 395.
59 Ackland, '8th November, 1936', in a booklet headed 'Brought back from Spain for Sylvia 1936', STW: H(R)/5/8.

war — which are superseded by something altogether more menacing: 'But what is this, untraceable messenger of woe?'[60] A diary entry of 14 June 1940 makes it clear that Warner understood the larger implications of all this untraceable messaging. 'But also, I think, the giving of news by wireless, which is *non-geographical*, has tended to give the war-news something of the quality of news of a pestilence. It has made it, in a fashion, an atmospheric rather than a territorial phenomenon.'[61] The dragon-bombers over Chaldon Herring had already been, in their way, the news of a pestilence. Radio constituted a further (and imminently posthuman) conversion of territorial into atmospheric phenomena.

Warner's fiction has often and rightly been celebrated for its creation of atmosphere. It might be more accurate to say that she was the writer of the moment in history when the idea of atmosphere became unthinkable without the idea of atmospherics. Atmosphere, according to a version of posthuman theory to which she might not have been altogether unsympathetic, 'seems to be awkwardly "there" in a space that is neither wholly within the environment, nor exactly within the person.' It precedes 'any clear distinction between subject and object'.[62] 'The Salutation', the title story of a collection published in 1932, is one of Warner's most purely atmospheric, and a favourite of Ackland's.[63] It opens at sunset, on the Argentinian pampas.

> But it was still the hour of the siesta, for a while yet nothing would move but the sun and the shadows. All round the house, for miles and miles, though there was no ear to hear it, a continuous small sound existed — the crackle of the ripened sunflower seeds breaking from their envelopes.[64]

Warner has transposed to the pampas the moment in Thomas Hardy's *The Return of the Native* (1878) when Eustacia Vye, wandering in the dark on Egdon Heath, hears the 'worn whisper, dry and papery,' made by the 'mummied heath-bells' of the past summer.[65] But her 'crackle', unheard by human ear, is a product of atmospherics, an event in the frequency domain. The inhabitants of the nearby grand house, re-awakening into human identity after the siesta, can know themselves only as one kind of creature among several of this all-encompassing atmosphere ('finite but unbounded'). 'A snake lay asleep on a stone, relaxed, its life narrowed into the pin-points of its eyes, and a bucket lay on its side, sleeping too.'[66]

Ackland did not really do atmosphere. Her feeling about the frequency domain's untraceable messengers was that they should be harnessed and put to work. 'The eyes of body, being blindfold by night', a sonnet of 1932 which was included in *Whether a Dove or Seagull*, is as irregular in theme, by the standards of the time, as

60   Ackland, 'June 1937', STW: J(FR)12 a-d.
61   Warner, *Diaries*, p. 104.
62   Steven D. Brown et al., 'Affect Theory and the Concept of Atmosphere', *Distinktion: Journal of Social Theory*, 20.1 (2019), 5–24 (pp. 8–9).
63   Ackland, 'Tinhead diary', entry for 28 September 1932, STW: T(LL)/6.
64   Warner, 'The Salutation', in *The Salutation* (London: Chatto & Windus, 1932), pp. 19–115 (p.19).
65   Thomas Hardy, *The Return of the Native*, ed. by Simon Gattrell (Oxford: Oxford University Press, 2008), pp. 55–56.
66   Warner, 'The Salutation', p. 20.

it is regular in form.[67] The poem is spoken by a cyborg lesbian lover whose brain has dispatched a hand to pass — without hesitation, and by 'strictly ordered ways' — between her partner's thighs. A startling neo-Metaphysical conceit compares the unerring hand to a 'ray-directed' aeroplane.[68]

The conceit has a precise historical context. The planes that flew over Chalton Herring in June 1932 were not guided to their targets by a directional radio beam. But the technology was available. In Germany in the early 1930s, the Lorenz Company developed a system which made use of twin beacons, one transmitting Morse dots, the other Morse dashes, on frequencies between 66 and 75 MHz. Where the beams overlapped, the pilot heard a steady note. Aircraft flew down the steady-note zone until they arrived at the airfield.[69] A similar system was installed at Croydon Airport, the first of several.[70] Aircraft equipped with the appropriate receivers could as easily fly away from as towards a wireless beacon. On 3 July 1931, the *Daily Herald* reported that an Italian inventor, Mr R. C. Galleti, had been able to follow a 'secret beam' south from Manchester as far as Upper Heyford, near Oxford, by means of a receiver connected to a dial held on his knee.[71] In such systems, the output generated by the plane's forward movement is fed back to the pilot as input (data concerning its position) via the dial held on his knee. Similarly, in the poem, the lover's hand follows a secret beam or ray transmitted at her brain's command.

Haraway's 'Cyborg Manifesto' puts a particular emphasis on the challenge posed by 'high-tech culture' to the distinction between human and machine. 'It is not clear what is mind and what is body in machines that resolve into coding practices.'[72] In Ackland's poem, the lover programmes her hand to navigate a biological substrate understood as an informational pattern — as map or maze — thus demonstrating the essential technicity of human behaviour even (or especially) at its most instinctual. Love-making is not the only technique at issue. Ackland was at this time greatly exercised by her desire to be a poet. Here, she deliberately boxes herself in by adopting a sonnet form laced yet more tightly into shape through the repetition of rhyme-words and phrases. The 'strictly ordered ways' are both those of the steady-note zone down which the lover's hand must pass and those of the poem's restriction by metre and rhyme: only the most rigorous, self-correcting observance of informational pattern by the adjustment of line-length will deliver its high-toned, celebratory conclusion. There is a technique to passion, and passion in technique.

Like Warner, Ackland had always suspected that the frequency domain's untraceable messengers would bring news of pestilence. In the autumn of 1940, the Luftwaffe shifted the burden of its night attacks away from London to the great

67 A list of poems to be included in the volume assigns it that date: STW: R(FR)/20/27.
68 Ackland, 'The eyes of body, being blindfold by night', in *Journey from Winter*, p. 46.
69 Alfred Price, *Instruments of Darkness: The History of Electronic Warfare, 1939–1945* (Barnsley: Frontline Books, 2017), pp. 22–23.
70 'New Wireless Beacon for Croydon', *Flight*, 27 November 1931, p. 1177; 'Guidance of Aircraft', *The Times*, 17 January 1934, p. 17.
71 'Radio "Roadway" for Fliers', *Daily Herald*, 3 July 1931, p. 2.
72 Haraway, 'Cyborg Manifesto', p. 177.

Midlands industrial centres. On 14 November, a bomber force crossed the southern coast of Britain at Christchurch, which lies just to the west of the Isle of Wight, and well within the area demarcated by the 1931 exercise, on its way to attack Coventry. It was following the route laid down by an approach-beam transmitted from a station on the Cherbourg peninsula.[73] These aeroplanes were ray-directed with a vengeance. One of Ackland's most vivid war-poems, 'Plane and Bugle-Call at Night', set on a 'warm May night' in the early 1940s, associates the directedness of the bombers with that of bats.

> High in the air, chequered with lines of flight
> Black, of the bats new wakened into spring,
> The frail noise of the engines sounds, retreating
> Over the sleeping hills.[74]

Bat sonar operates at Very High Frequencies inaudible to the human ear; as did the early radar systems developed in the mid-1930s. In an article published in *Science* in December 1944, Donald Griffin, a pioneer of cognitive ethology, put forward 'echolocation' as the term best describing the feedback systems that some human beings, some animals, and some machines use to convert energy transmitted as a pulse into the data necessary to plot a position or trajectory.[75] An understanding of the essential technicity of human being had begun to feed into an understanding of the essential technicity of animal being.

Animal Corpses

Animals were ever-present in the lives Ackland and Warner led both separately and together. One of the most poignant items in the archive is a Valentine's Day booklet Ackland hand-made for Warner in 1948. The booklet's miniature pages, bound with brass fasteners, contain poems on the theme of St Valentine as well as photographs of cats and dogs, some in Warner's company, some not (**Figs 21.1 and 21.2**).[76] Many more such photographs survive. William, a black chow, played as important a role in her life as Cayenne Pepper, an Australian Shepherd, was to in Donna Haraway's. Animal companions are more or less ever-present in the fiction, too.[77] But it is the corpses of dead animals, I will argue, that provoked her to radical reflection.

For the interest Warner took in companion species was compatible with the most advanced contemporary thinking about animal intelligence. The July 1934 issue of *The Countryman* included, as well as Warner's poem 'Delectable Mountains', a brief review of a recent book by the eminent biologist E. S. Russell, *The Behaviour*

---

73   Price, *Instruments of Darkness*, pp. 43–44.

74   Ackland, 'Plane and Bugle-Call at Night', STW: R(FR)/20/16. Warner, too, was fond of bats. On 13 December 1934, she sent Llewelyn Powys the latest number of *The Countryman*, for the photographs of birds and bats, 'and the bat story': *Letters*, p. 33.

75   Griffin, 'Echolocation by Blind Men, Bats, and Radar', *Science*, 29 December 1944, pp. 589–90.

76   Ackland, 'A Valentine 1948', STW: H(R)/5/30.

77   Mary Sanders Pollock, 'Animal Companions in Sylvia Townsend Warner's More-than-Marxist World', *Mosaic* 48.1 (2015), 65–81.

FIG. 21.1. Warner and cats. Pages from St Valentine's Day booklet hand-made by Valentine Ackland for Sylvia Townsend Warner, 14 February 1948. Reproduced with permission from the Sylvia Townsend Warner archive at Dorset History Centre: STW: H(R)/5/30; in box D/TWA/A09.

FIG. 21.2. Warner and cats. Pages from St Valentine's Day booklet hand-made by Valentine Ackland for Sylvia Townsend Warner, 14 February 1948. Reproduced with permission from the Sylvia Townsend Warner archive at Dorset History Centre: STW: H(R)/5/30; in box D/TWA/A09.

of Animals: An Introduction to Its Study.[78] Russell set out to refute Descartes's enduringly influential 'mechanistic' interpretation of animal behaviour as under all circumstances directly determined by immediate physical and chemical stimuli. On the contrary, Russell maintained, animal behaviour is 'directive' and 'spontaneous': 'an active *seeking* of means or ends, a going out to look for food, or a plaything or a mate.' Furthermore, there should be 'no great difficulty in thinking of animals as perceiving their surroundings, just as we ourselves live in worlds of our own perception.'[79] Russell's approach was functionalist. He wanted to know how an animal perceives its environment, and what that perception might enable it to accomplish. Cognitive ethology today places a much greater stress on emotion and social behaviour.[80]

Russell added to the second (1938) and subsequent editions of *The Behaviour of Animals* a chapter which adduces further evidence for the argument that animals take a very different view from ours of the environments they share with us. This, he wrote in conclusion, was a position also adopted by 'J. von Uexküll and his school in their "Umwelt" theory'.[81] The Estonian-German biologist Jacob von Uexküll had long maintained that all organisms experience life in terms of a species-specific, subjective, spatio-temporal frame of reference uniquely adapted to the environments they inhabit. That frame of reference he termed an *Umwelt*, or surrounding 'world'. *Umwelt* theory made it possible to understand animals 'not merely as objects but also as subjects, whose essential activities consist in perception and [the] production of effects.'[82] Uexküll's value to posthumanism lies in the challenge his work posed to assumptions concerning the uniformity of experience. 'Too often, he affirms, we imagine that the relations a certain animal subject has to the things in its environment take place in the same space and in the same time as those which bind us to the objects in our human world.'[83]

There is no evidence to suggest that Warner ever read Russell, let alone Uexküll. But her fiction of the 1930s certainly does attempt to imagine the other-than-human space and time in which an 'animal subject' sets about establishing a relation to the things in its environment. 'The Best Bed', for example, a treat tucked away at the back of *The Salutation*, maps the singular space and time in which a starving stray cat seeks shelter among things arranged for the convenience of human beings. This is not at all a philosophical creature, like the canine protagonists of Virginia Woolf's *Flush: A Biography* (1933) and Paul Auster's *Timbuktu* (1999). Warner remains

---

78   Review of E. S. Russell, *The Behaviour of Animals: An Introduction to Its Study*, *Countryman*, 9 (1934), p. 465. 'Delectable Mountains' is on pp. 413–14.

79   E. S. Russell, *The Behaviour of Animals: An Introduction to Its Study* (London: Edward Arnold, 1938), pp. 9, 5–6.

80   Marc Bekoff, *The Emotional Lives of Animals* (Novato, CA: New World Library, 2007); Frans de Waal, *Mama's Last Hug: Animal Emotions and What They Teach Us about Ourselves* (London: Granta, 2019).

81   Russell, *Behaviour of Animals*, p. 190.

82   Jacob von Uexküll, *A Foray into the Worlds of Animals and Humans*, trans. by Joseph D. O'Neill (Minneapolis: University of Minnesota Press, 2010), p. 42: first published in 1934 as *Streifzüge durch die Umwelten von Tieren und Menschen*.

83   Giorgio Agamben, *The Open: Man and Animal*, trans. by Kevin Attell (Stanford, CA: Stanford University Press, 2004), p. 40.

outside him, closely observing his behaviour. Yet it would be hard to deny him subjectivity, as delight taken in his own prowess gives way to a seeking which, while no longer unreservedly active, remains more than mere instinct. 'Though an accumulated fatigue smouldered in every nerve, the obdurate limbs carried him on, and would carry him on still, a captive to himself, meekly trotting to the place of his death.'[84] The place he finds, which may not yet be that of his death, is a Christmas crib in a church. The story cuts through to the outside of humankind's collective self-preoccupation. It turns the meaning presumed by ritual inside out to expose the contingency it strives perpetually to conceal.

For Warner, remarkably, staunch Leninist though she was, propaganda did not preclude the mapping of animal *Umwelten*. 'The Drought Breaks', first published in *Life and Letters* in the summer of 1937, is a Spanish Civil War story told from point of view of Rafaela Perez, whose husband was summarily shot, and her children taken into care, when Nationalist troops captured the town in which she lives. Before we learn any of this, we have been introduced to a cat — another half-starved scavenger — 'nosing in the gutters' for something to drink. 'Curious to think at all about a cat, curious to be so attentive to a grey cat slinking through the grey dusk.' Rafaela's thoughts understandably turn away from the cat to the fate of her husband and children. The next time she looks, it has gone.[85] No sustained narrative meaning attaches to the animal. The 'drought' of the story's title is a grand metaphorical affair which eventually 'breaks' when Republican bombers arrive overhead, bringing hope at the same time as death. What could be more humanly preoccupying than the bitter paradoxes of civil war? And yet the grey cat, taking its chances amid the symbolism human beings build obsessively into their world, has been attended to, in all its mere contingency. If there were ever to be a properly 'posthuman' war writing, this is what it might begin to look like.

In 1945, Warner published an essay in *Good Housekeeping* on the ghosts that haunt memoirs, diaries, and collected letters: 'minor characters' such as Gilbert White's gardener or Lord Byron's charwoman who 'appear but once, exist only in half a dozen lines — but for all that, exist.' The essay concludes with a reflection on the linnet bought by Jonathan Swift's Irish manservant, Patrick, as a present for Stella's companion, Mrs Dingley, which Swift discovers hidden in the closet. 'I believe he does not know he is a bird; where you put him, there he stands, and seems to know neither hope nor fears. I suppose in a week he will die of the spleen.'[86] Delighted to have some news to share with Stella, Swift shuts the cupboard door. So much for the linnet, dead or alive. For all that, it exists — at least for those who, like Warner, have not been beguiled by Swift's philosophizing about its lack of philosophy. The linnet, too, shows us the outside of humankind's collective self-preoccupation.

Warner and Ackland knew that there is an emotional cost to companionship with animals. In March 1934, while they were living at Frankfort Manor, in Norfolk, a 'murrain' or epidemic of pestilence carried off several of the cats with which they

84   Warner, 'The Best Bed', in *The Salutation*, pp. 287–92 (p. 289).
85   Warner, 'The Drought Breaks', in *With the Hunted*, pp. 153–57 (pp. 153, 155).
86   Warner, 'Soldiers, Weeding-Women and Linnets', in *With the Hunted*, pp. 264–68 (pp. 265, 268).

shared the house and grounds, including two kittens.[87] The distress this episode caused them had to do, I think, with its selectiveness. They did not succumb to pestilence, of course; nor, less obligingly, did the rats in the barn. Warner made out of her distress a companion species manifesto to rival Haraway's: the 'Introduction' to The Cat's Cradle-Book, a collection of fables told by mother-cats to their offspring which was published in America in 1940, and in Britain in 1960. The fables are funny and instructive, in Aesopian fashion, in their cool dissection of the essential narcissism of human beings. But the 'Introduction', three times as long as any of them, is a different matter altogether. Part memoir, part romance, part polemic, it opens with the unnamed narrator's arrival at a place very much like Frankfort Manor, to find a handsome young man and a tribe of cats in joint possession. The handsome young man quite closely resembles Valentine Ackland, and eventually makes love to the narrator on the lawn. By that time he has revealed himself as a student of the 'culture of cats'. He believes that cat-culture is universal and age-old, owing little to human intervention, and promptly enlists the narrator in the project of assembling and curating narrative material drawn from a wide range of feline sources. A wonderfully Haraway-esque passage leaves it unclear as to whether he had once fallen in love with a diplomat's wife or her Siamese cat (the latter, of course). Warner's functionalism would have acknowledged that animals communicate effectively, but drawn the line at the idea that they possess a 'culture'. Then the murrain strikes, killing most of the young man's informants; he abandons the project, and dies. This apocalypse effectively severs the stories which follow from any explanation of their origin. The severance is the point. Human beings might want to believe that 'The proper study of catkind is man', but the relevant expert testimony has just been killed by a disease to which human beings are immune.[88] Each species endures its own fatality, its own helplessness in the face of accident. That is how we know that each must forever occupy an *Umwelt* of its own devising.

Martin Heidegger, a careful reader of Uexküll's early work, differed from him in supposing that animals, unlike humans, cannot transcend their 'captivation' by the *Umwelten* they inhabit; and therefore cannot know death 'as such'.[89] The fairly obvious implication of such a view is that animals can be 'light-heartedly killed' because, after all, they 'merely perish'.[90] Warner would have been on Uexküll's side. For her, it is not death that distinguishes human from animal, but fatality. If death is the greatest leveller, then accident, from which no species is immune, cannot be far behind. Animals, however, have a whole other level of accident to confront: that imposed upon them by a species which kills not only for need and profit, but for the hell of it. Warner's abiding concern with that fundamental difference in fatalities led her inexorably to the topic of animal death.

---

87   Warner, *Letters*, p. 30.
88   Warner, 'Introduction', in *The Cat's Cradle-Book* (New York: Viking Press, 1940), pp. 9–40 (pp. 16, 28).
89   Martin Heidegger, *The Fundamental Concepts of Metaphysics: World, Finitude, Solitude*, trans. by William McNeill and Nicholas Walker (Bloomington: Indiana University Press, 1995), p. 267.
90   Paola Cavalieri, *The Death of the Animal* (New York: Columbia University Press, 2009), p. 11.

While Ackland shot rats and rabbits, Warner was piling up animal corpses in her fiction with equally cheerful abandon. On 4 August 1926, she had written to David Garnett to report that in *Mr Fortune's Maggot* she meant to kill a parrot during the course of an earthquake, and dislodge a hive of bees. 'But does one say hive for the wild bees, or is there a wilder word?' In 1932, she was still at it in 'The Salutation'. 'I have killed a rhea for local colouring,' she told Garnett, 'and put in some hens.'[91] Whatever their cause, these deaths mark, for the reader, if not for the protagonists, the limits of atmosphere: the moment at which the *Umwelt* generated by Mr Fortune's desire, in the novel, and his sorrow, in 'The Salutation', can no longer sustain itself. The Frankfort Manor pestilence undoubtedly darkened Warner's mood. Some of her most compelling late stories, such as 'Total Loss', from *A Stranger with a Bag* (1961), and 'But at the Stroke of Midnight', from *The Innocent and the Guilty* (1971), turn on the tragic significance of animal corpses.[92] But Warner was at her most radically 'posthuman', I would argue, when slipping animal fatality into *After the Death of Don Juan* (1938): a novel set in eighteenth-century Spain, and intended to serve as an 'allegory' of the rise of Fascism.[93] This particular dead or dying animal matters, like Patrick's linnet, by eluding significance altogether.

I want to build on Maud Ellmann's argument that in *After the Death of Don Juan* the 'closest thing to subjectivity' resides in the Spanish landscape, 'where human beings figure mainly as *staffage*, or emanations of its parched eviscerate soil.' Much the same could be said of the Argentinian landscape of 'The Salutation'. In this case, however, the central issue is not an individual's atonement through *Umwelt*, but the struggle for control over the means of production between ruling class and proletariat, a struggle as bitter in the 1930s as it had been in the 1760s. The plot concerns the pilgrimage to the remote region of Tenorio Viejo undertaken by Doña Ana and her husband Don Ottavio in order to inform Don Juan's father, Don Saturno, that his son, who has killed *her* father in a duel, has been dragged down into hell by a crew of demons; or so the Don's valet, Leporello, maintains. The novel begins as a comedy of manners sparked by feuding among the landed gentry and their variously resentful retainers, and ends on the verge of tragedy, as the villagers arm themselves to storm Don Saturno's castle, where Don Juan, the Fascist revenant, has taken charge. During these later stages, Ellmann observes, a stichomythic interplay of voices renders the 'chorus of the common people in their harsh surroundings'.[94]

The final act (as it were) of the comedy of manners takes place in the church in Tenorio Viejo, where Doña Ana has elected to conduct an all-night vigil in the company of her duenna, Doña Pilar: ostensibly in her father's honour, but in fact to sharpen yet further her desire for Juan, whom she cannot believe dead. As dawn breaks Pilar hears a cat begin to wail outside. 'Passionately, slavishly, the

91   Warner, *Letters*, pp. 16, 21.
92   Both are included in Warner, *Selected Stories*, ed. by William Maxwell and Susan Pinney (London: Virago, 2002), pp. 140–67 and 237–45.
93   Warner, *Letters*, p. 51.
94   Maud Ellmann, 'After the Death of Don Juan: Sylvia Townsend Warner's Spanish Novel', *Journal of the Sylvia Townsend Warner Society*, 17 (2017), 1–26 (p. 4).

cat yowled and yowled, venting its shameless desolate sexual cry.' This animal, expressing on Ana's behalf an erotomania she refuses to acknowledge, has been incorporated — thoughtlessly — into an atmosphere created by individual human self-preoccupation. Significance, however, is a luxury animals cannot afford. Daylight reveals the sentries who have guarded the church at their breakfast. 'They were sitting in the sun eating bread and sausage and flipping pebbles at a piece of dusty grey fur that lay in the road, stirring slightly every now and then as though a wind waggled it.' Ana emerges from the building and walks towards her coach. Looking down at her feet, 'she saw something lying — a dead cat, or almost dead, for its tongue was stretched out and draggled in the dust. She gathered up her skirts and stepped into the coach.'[95] How many of the novel's readers have spared another thought for this latest victim of humankind's propensity for gratuitous slaughter? The protagonists most certainly do not. The animal corpse marks a narrative watershed: the point at which collective (or class) self-preoccupation supersedes individual as the primary motivating force. And yet it belongs to neither. If we attend to it, as Warner attended to the linnet Swift shut in the closet, as Rafaela Perez attends to the grey cat slinking through the grey dusk, we will have reached the outside of humankind's self-preoccupation as a species. There, a different fatality obtains to that which will dispose of the novel's human *staffage*, those other emanations of a parched eviscerate soil.

In this essay, I have tried to illuminate, with help from the archive, the creative partnership in which Valentine Ackland and Sylvia Townsend Warner were equally involved during the 1930s. I would not myself describe theirs as a queer *posthuman* vanguardism. However, I do think that the role each adopted within that partnership was instrumental in permitting the exploration of a particular aspect of the breakdown of boundaries between the human and the non-human which has come to seem characteristic of the age we now live in. The attention they paid to the figures of cyborg and companion species is a reproof to the digital exceptionalism built into most accounts of the posthuman condition. To approach their writing in the 1930s from the angle created by that attention is to begin to see it, conversely, in a different light.

---

95   Warner, *After the Death of Don Juan* (London: Virago, 1989), pp. 81, 83, 88.

LIST OF PUBLICATIONS

1. Books

The Poetry of Abraham Cowley (London: Macmillan, 1979)

The Making of the Reader: Language and Subjectivity in Modern American, English and Irish Poetry (London: Macmillan, 1984; paperback edn, 1985)

Circulation: Defoe, Dickens and the Economies of the Novel (London: Macmillan, 1988)

The English Novel in History, 1895–1920 (London: Routledge, 1994)

Edwardian Fiction: An Oxford Companion (Oxford: Oxford University Press, 1997). With Sandra Kemp and Charlotte Mitchell.

Cooking with Mud: The Idea of Mess in Nineteenth-Century Art and Fiction (Oxford: Oxford University Press, 2000)

Paranoid Modernism: Literary Experiment, Psychosis, and the Professionalization of English Society (Oxford: Oxford University Press, 2001)

Cinema and Modernism (Oxford: Blackwell, 2007)

The Uses of Phobia: Essays on Literature and Film (Oxford: Blackwell, 2010)

Literature in the First Media Age: British between the Wars (Cambridge, MA: Harvard University Press, 2013)

Writing, Medium, Machine: Modern Technographies, co-edited with Sean Pryor (London: Open Humanities Press, 2016)

The Yellow Mackintosh: Sights, Sounds, and Smells in the Fiction of Katherine Mansfield (Bath: Katherine Mansfield Society Publications, 2017)

2. Chapters in Books

'Rochester's Wanton Expressions', in *The Spirit of Wit*, ed. by Jeremy Treglown (Oxford: Blackwell, 1982), pp. 111–32

'Circulation, Interchange, Stoppage: Dickens and Social Process', in *The Changing World of Charles Dickens*, ed. by Bob Giddings (London: Vision Press, 1983), pp. 163–79

'Modernism and Empire: Reading *The Waste Land*', in *Futures for English*, ed. by Colin MacCabe (Manchester: Manchester University Press, 1988), pp. 143–53

'Kipling's England: The Edwardian Years', in *Kipling Considered*, ed. by Phillip Mallett (London: Macmillan, 1989), pp. 56–70

'The Politics of Adventure in Early British Spy Fiction', in *Spy Fiction, Spy Films and Real Intelligence*, ed. by Wesley K. Wark (London: Frank Cass, 1991), pp. 30–54

'A Horse is Being Beaten: Modernism and Popular Fiction', in *Rereading the New*, ed. by Kevin Dettmar (Ann Arbor: University of Michigan Press, 1992), pp. 191–219

'The Avoidance of Naturalism: Gissing, Moore, Grand, Bennett and Others', in *The Columbia History of the British Novel*, ed. by John Richetti (New York: Columbia University Press, 1994), pp. 608–30

'Dickens's Idle Men', in *Dickens Refigured: Bodies, Desires and Other Histories*, ed. by John Schad (Manchester: Manchester University Press, 1996), pp. 200–17

'Lesbians before Lesbianism: Sexual Identity in Early Twentieth-Century British Fiction', in *Borderlines: Genders and Identities in War and Peace, 1870–1930*, ed. by Billie Melman (London: Routledge, 1998), pp. 193–211

'The Modernist Novel', in *The Cambridge Companion to Modernism*, ed. by Michael Levenson (Cambridge: Cambridge University Press, 1999), pp. 70–99

'Fascination and Nausea: Finding Out the Hard Way', in *The Art of Detective Fiction*, ed. by Warren Chernaik, Martin Swales, and Robert Vilain (Basingstoke: Macmillan, 2000), pp. 21–35

'Modernism, Mimesis, and the Professionalization of English Society', in *Rethinking Modernism*, ed. by Marianne Thormählen (Basingstoke: Palgrave Macmillan, 2003), pp. 24–39

'The British Novel and the War', in *The Cambridge Companion to the Literature of the First World War*, ed. by Vincent Sherry (Cambridge: Cambridge University Press, 2005), pp. 34–56

'Space, Movement, and Sexual Feeling in *Middlemarch*', in *Middlemarch in the Twenty-First Century*, ed. by Karen Chase (Oxford: Oxford University Press, 2006), pp. 37–63

'Dickens and Frith', in *William Powell Frith: Painting the Victorian Age*, ed. by Mark Bills and Vivien Knight (New Haven, CT: Yale University Press, 2006), pp. 29–39

'The Space Beside: Lateral Exposition, Gender, and Urban Narrative Space in D. W. Griffith's Biograph Films', in *Cities in Transition: The Moving Image and the Modern Metropolis*, ed. by Andrew Webber and Emma Wilson (London: Wallflower Press, 2008), pp. 40–55

'Ford against Joyce and Lewis', in *Ford Madox Ford: Literary Networks and Cultural Transformations*, ed. by Andrzej Gasiorek and Daniel Moore (Amsterdam: Rodopi, 2008), pp. 131–50

'Phoning', in *Restless Cities*, ed. by Gregory Dart and Matthew Beaumont (London: Verso, 2010), pp. 193–211

With Chris O'Rourke. 'Cinema Re-Mystified: R. S. Appelbee's Technological Ghost Story', in *Reading the Cinematograph*, ed. by Andrew Shail (Exeter: University of Exeter Press, 2010), pp. 37–57

'Representing Connection: A Multimedia Approach to Colonial Film, 1918–1939', in *Empire and Film*, ed. by Lee Grieveson and Colin MacCabe (Basingstoke: Palgrave, 2011), pp. 151–66

With Andrew Shail. 'Cinema and the Novel', in *The Oxford History of the Novel in English*, vol. IV: *The Reinvention of the British and Irish Novel*, ed. by Patrick Parrinder and Andrzej Gasiorek (Oxford: Oxford University Press, 2011), pp. 370–86

'Modernism's Material Futures: Glass, and Several Kinds of Plastic', in *Utopian Space of Modernism*, ed. by Rosalyn Gregory and Benjamin Kohlmann (Basingstoke: Palgrave, 2012), pp. 52–70

'On the Nail: Functional Objects in Thomas Hardy's *The Woodlanders*', in *Literary Bric-à-Brac and the Victorians: From Commodities to Oddities*, ed. by Jonathon Shears and Jen Harrison (Farnham: Ashgate, 2013), pp. 115–27

'Eliot and the Idea of "Media"', in *The Edinburgh Companion to T. S. Eliot and the Arts*, ed. by Frances Dickey and John D. Morgenstern (Edinburgh: Edinburgh University Press, 2016), pp. 248–61

'Literature between Media', in *The Cambridge History of Modernism*, ed. by Vincent Sherry (Cambridge: Cambridge University Press, 2016), pp. 386–403

3. Articles

'Hidden Ground Within: Matthew Arnold's Lyric and Elegiac Poetry', *ELH*, 44.3 (1977), 526–55

'Practic Resurrection: The Sermons of John Hales', *Yearbook of English Studies*, 9 (1979), 236–45

'Gold Standards: Money in Edwardian Fiction', *Critical Quarterly*, 30.1 (1988), 22–35

'Edwardian Sex Novels,' *Critical Quarterly*, 31.1 (1989), 92–106

'Auden's Immaturity', *Scripsi*, 5 (1989), 85–93

'Colonial Subjects', *Critical Quarterly*, 32.3 (1990), 3–20

'Hueffer's Englishness', *Agenda*, 27.4/28.1 (1989–90), 148–55

'Theory and Detective Fiction', *Critical Quarterly*, 33.2 (1991), 66–77

'Analysing Literary Prose: The Relevance of Relevance Theory', *Lingua*, 87.1–2 (1992), 11–27

'Fanon's Nausea', *Parallax*, 11 (1999), 32–50

'The New Historicism and the Psychopathology of Everyday Modern Life', *Critical Quarterly*, 42.1 (2000), 36–58

'Some Brothels: Nineteenth-Century Philanthropy and the Poetics of Space', *Critical Quarterly*, 44.1 (2002), 25–32

'The Invention of Agoraphobia', *Victorian Literature and Culture*, 32.2 (2004), 463–74

'Actual James Joyce', *James Joyce Broadsheet*, 72 (2005), 1–2

'Virginia Woolf and Cinema', *Film Studies*, 6 (2005), 13–26

'T. S. Eliot and Cinema', *Modernism/Modernity*, 13.2 (2006), 237–65

'Household Clearances in Victorian Fiction', *19: Interdisciplinary Studies in the Long Nineteenth Century*, 6 (April 2008) (on-line journal)

'Lynne Ramsay's *Ratcatcher*: Towards a Theory of Haptic Narrative', *Paragraph: A Journal of Modern Critical Theory*, 31.2 (2008), 138–58

'e-Modernism: Telephony in British Fiction 1925–1940', *Critical Quarterly*, 51.1 (2009), 1–32

'Naturalism's Phobic Picturesque', *Critical Quarterly*, 51.1 (2009), 33–58

'Hitchcock's Modernism', *Modernist Cultures*, 5.1 (2010), 106–26

'Dis-Enablement: Subject and Method in the Modernist Short Story', *Critical Quarterly*, 52.2 (2010), 4–13

With Vanessa Hodgkinson. 'Techno-Primitivism', *The White Review*, 8 (2013) (on-line journal)

'Modernism Reloaded: The Fiction of Katherine Mansfield', *Affirmations: of the modern*, 1.1 (2013), 21–43

'Mobility, Network, Message: Spy Fiction and Film in the Long 1930s', *Critical Quarterly*, 57.3 (2015), 10–21

'Modernism's Media Theory', *Critical Quarterly*, 58.3 (2016), 5–26

'Thomas Hardy', *Critical Quarterly*, 59.2 (2017), 126–30

'Claude McKay's Conjure Tale', *Critical Quarterly*, 60.3 (2018), 122–30

'A Media Theory Approach to Representations of 'Nervous Illness' in the Long Nineteenth Century', *Journal of Victorian Culture*, 24.2 (2019), 146–58

'Come-Hither Looks: The Hollywood Vamp and the Function of Cinema', *Critical Quarterly*, 62.2 (2020, forthcoming)

'Posthuman? Animal Corpses, Aeroplanes, and Very High Frequencies in the Work of Valentine Ackland and Sylvia Townsend Warner', *Sylvia Townsend Warner Society Journal*, 2020.1 (2020, forthcoming)

4. Public Scholarship

Essays and review-essays contributed to the *London Review of Books*:

'Kipling the Reliable', 6 March 1986
'English Butter', 9 October 1986
'Buffers', 4 February 1988
'Transcendental Criticism', 3 March 1988
'Troubles', 23 June 1988
'Apocalypse', 14 September 1989
'Six Hands at an Open Door', 21 March 1991
'Words Washed Clean', 5 December 1991
'Gesture as Language', 30 January 1992
'Costume Codes', 12 January 1995
'Saved for Jazz', 5 October 1995
'Bodily Waste', 2 November 1995
'Internal Combustion', 6 June 1996
'Modernism plc', 13 May 1999
'The Sorrows of Young Ford', 1 June 2000
'Wyndham Lewis', 25 January 2001
'Agoraphobia', 24 July 2003
'Good Fetishism', 20 November 2003
'Kafka at the Pictures', 4 March 2004
'Pound's Martyrology', 7 July 2005
'The Novel', 22 March 2007
'Phone Bootha', 28 January 2010
'The Tube', 21 October 2010
'Lady Chatterley's Sneakers', 30 August 2012
'Lifts', 2 July 2014
'Air Raid Panic', 8 October 2014
'Fu Manchu', 5 March 2015
'What Scared Hitchcock?', 4 June 2015
'Orwell's Nose and Prose', 16 February 2017
'Eisenstein', 2 August 2018
'Pushing Buttons', 22 November 2018
'Diary: Bearness', 7 November 2019
'Corridors', 19 December 2019

INDEX

www.ingramcontent.com/pod-product-compliance
Lightning Source LLC
Chambersburg PA
CBHW080719020726
47502CB00009B/2470